Art in Pursuit of Common Cause

Art in Pursuit of Common Cause

Edited by
Abigail Winograd and Jill Sterrett

The *Toward Common Cause* Legacy Project

In association with The Richard and Mary L. Gray Center for Arts and Inquiry, The University of Chicago

With the support of The John D. and Catherine T. MacArthur Foundation

Distributed by DelMonico Books • D.A.P.

We would like to thank our families for their forbearance and their encouragement. We hope that our project and projects like it will build a better world for our children, who are our inspiration in all things.

Contents

Sponsor Statement
John Palfrey

President, The John D. and Catherine T. MacArthur Foundation

I had the honor of becoming the sixth president of the John D. and Catherine T. MacArthur Foundation in 2019, at a moment in history marked by a pronounced sense that our country and the world are at a great crossroads. Wildfires and warming oceans, widening disparities in wealth and opportunity—still so often cutting along racial and ethnic lines—the implications of new technologies for democratic institutions, all these realities demand urgent action and informed response.

The MacArthur Foundation, headquartered in Chicago, is committed to building a more just, verdant, and peaceful world. We also strive toward transformative change in areas of profound concern, including climate change, criminal justice reform in the U.S., and corruption in Nigeria. The foundation also supports the fields of Impact Investing, Technology in the Public Interest, and Philanthropy. In addition to these grantmaking areas, the foundation runs the *100&Change* competition for a single $100 million grant to address a critical problem of our time, and the MacArthur Fellows Program, which recognizes exceptionally creative individuals working in an array of fields, providing them with five years of no-strings-attached support. The foundation's grantmaking is guided by our values: Creativity; Diversity, Equity, and Inclusion; Empathy; Integrity; and Learning.

To celebrate its fortieth anniversary, the MacArthur Fellows Program had the ingenious idea (pun intended!) of sharing the art of MacArthur Fellows with the people of Chicago in a public-facing, multivenue exhibition. I cannot think of a better way to celebrate a milestone anniversary than with an initiative as ambitious and inclusive as *Toward Common Cause* was. To witness this exhibition bring people together in thought and experience was to see the power of art in action, and the exhibition's overarching theme of access to resources speaks to the power of art's prescience.

As president of MacArthur, a major part of my charge is to ensure the foundation lives our values in all aspects of our work, from the organizations we support, to our staff and board, to our contractors and vendors. *Toward Common Cause* provides a model for living MacArthur's values. The exhibition prioritized trust and respect in its engagement with people and communities and through its sharing of vision and responsibility among numerous organizations. Like the MacArthur Fellows Program, the exhibition reveals new potentials and possibilities for trust-based philanthropy.

I want to acknowledge and applaud the foresight and support of my predecessor at the MacArthur Foundation, Julia Stasch, who gave this project the green light when it was first conceived in 2017 and who encouraged the MacArthur Fellows Program to "think big" once planning commenced. I'd also like to acknowledge Marlies Carruth, director of the MacArthur Fellows Program, and the entire MacArthur Fellows Program team, who took that encouragement so beautifully to heart.

My deep gratitude is due as well to the twenty-nine participating MacArthur Fellows who brought their art to Chicago; to the Smart Museum of Art at the University of Chicago for leveraging MacArthur's grant award to such extraordinary ends; to the Gray Center for Arts and Inquiry, also at the University of Chicago, for its creativity in conceiving this book project; and to the more than three dozen local organizations that brought *Toward Common Cause* to life.

Lastly, I wish to call attention to the flaps of this volume, which list the hundreds of individuals who contributed to *Toward Common Cause*. Their collective investments of time and care nourished this participatory endeavor every step of the way.

Introduction
Marlies Carruth

Director, MacArthur Fellows Program, The John D. and Catherine T. MacArthur Foundation

How *Toward Common Cause* came to be is a story worth sharing. It's a story about Chicago, about access to resources, and about the efficacy of art to make a real difference in the lives of everyday people. It's a story about creativity and adaptability in philanthropy. And it's a story about trust and the time and care it takes to achieve it.

Of course, *Toward Common Cause* is also about the twenty-nine artists, all MacArthur Fellows, who came together to realize this extraordinary experiment in exhibition-making. And it's about all the organizations and institutions that shared their expertise and resources to fulfill the exhibition's ambitious goal of extending its reach across Chicago to bring art by renowned artists to communities around the city. There was a particular emphasis on places that don't typically host art equally at home on the international biennial circuit—even though so much of that art (especially over the past several decades) addresses itself to the social conditions that perpetuate inequity.

The idea to create an exhibition featuring art by MacArthur Fellows dates to 2017 and emerged in the course of brainstorming ways to celebrate the fortieth anniversary of the MacArthur Fellows Program in 2021. My colleagues and I coalesced around the exciting prospect of marking the milestone with a public exhibition rather than a gala-type event. That way, we could invite all residents of Chicago and share the work of MacArthur Fellows with a broad and hopefully new audience over an extended period of time, not just for a single day.

Then history intervened. The world beyond the MacArthur Fellows Program—the global pandemic, extreme weather events, a reckoning with race in the United States—was demanding forms of urgent action at accelerated rates. The notion of an anniversary celebration fundamentally shifted and was reimagined as an opportunity to respond to pressing cultural and societal needs. The project of exhibition-making evolved into a question: How could we leverage the art of MacArthur Fellows to make a meaningful difference in the lives of Chicagoans facing such challenging current events?

The Smart Museum of Art at the University of Chicago answered that question by developing an exhibition—guided by the vision of curator Abigail Winograd—that was participatory by design.

This framework involved ceding control to an unusual degree for both the Smart Museum and the MacArthur Foundation. For the Smart, major curatorial decisions were made by the participating artists, the organizations with which they worked, and members of the communities those organizations served. As for MacArthur, as the Smart's vision for the project took definitive and inspiring shape, we became comfortable letting go of our preconceived ideas of what the exhibition might be. This is because over the years of collaboration and planning, my colleagues and leadership at the foundation, the team at the Smart, and our collaborators at the participating organizations, who brought the exhibition to the ground, all learned to be better listeners. As priorities shifted among the artists, we all listened closely, and through that listening and subsequent responsiveness to what we heard, a sense of trust beyond what I could have anticipated emerged and solidified.

Trust underwrites this project in a very fundamental way. Trust is at the heart of the MacArthur Fellows Program. Trust is implied, perhaps taken for granted, in the program's no-strings-attached funding. We trust that MacArthur Fellows—who have demonstrated records of achievement and promise—know better than we do how best to use the funds we award them.

At another level, one not usually discussed in publications accompanying art exhibitions, the trust of the MacArthur Foundation's Board of Directors—trust in both the model of the Fellows Program and in the promise of *Toward*

Common Cause—made this project possible in the first place. Trust is grounded in respect, and as this exhibition and the Fellows Program demonstrate, trust is also a condition for creativity to flourish, for imagination to thrive.

Our city is full of value, assets, and potential. I am so proud to call Chicago my home, and so full of hope for its future as a place where all people have the opportunity to share in its wealth of cultural and economic resources. But Chicago is also a city where great sources of potential are untapped, and where many anchoring institutions and vital resources have for generations been out of reach for many.

And yet, Chicago is also ground zero for highly engaged communities and highly resilient residents. Speaking to the power of art, *Toward Common Cause* sought to make the beauty, energy, and inspiration to which art gives rise widely available. *Toward Common Cause* reminds us that institutionally supported art and artmaking should be in as many places as possible in this city.

In the end, *Toward Common Cause* represents but a step in this journey of bringing resources to the places where they are most needed, and of making the space for patient collaboration and the building of trust.

I am so grateful to all the MacArthur Fellows who contributed their singular visions to *Toward Common Cause*, and to all the participating organizations that built out the infrastructure to realize this project's greatest ambitions. Without their vision and perseverance, this project would not have come to fruition. As I reflect on the exhibition and all the planning, coordination, and care that went into it, I understand now how this collaboration established much needed community as we diligently worked together, and focused our attention and energies on imagining productive paths forward at a time when the world was under lockdown, on fire, flooding, reckoning with race and political polarization, and generally threatening to fall apart. It was an early act of defiant rebuilding. We are stronger and more hopeful because of the risks we took in this project.

Toward Common Cause—an exhibition that reimagined the "city as gallery"—is the result of a unique journey of trust and hope. We are pleased to share it with you here.

Curator's Preface: A Common Place
Abigail Winograd

At least once a week for nearly two years, I went to see Njideka Akunyili Crosby's installations on the facade of the Minnie Riperton Apartments on Chicago's South Side in Fuller Park. Traveling north on the Dan Ryan Expressway, *I Still Face You* (2015) came into view as I approached the West 47th Street exit. Enlarged several times from its original modest dimensions, the image was over 36 feet tall, an imposing sight hanging 100 feet in the air. On rainy and overcast days, the affectionate gathering of six beckoned warmly from above. On sunny days, the figures glowed as light reflected off the vinyl. On trips south, its corollary, *Home: Say It Loud* (2017), popped up just past US Cellular Field. The still-life interior evoked the intimacies and comforts of home hidden behind the walls of the fourteen-story senior housing facility. From either direction, and no matter how many times I saw these murals, I marveled at what it took to get them there.

Our conversations with the Chicago Housing Authority started in the summer of 2019. The following summer, a group of young people in the Smart Teen Program began a yearlong dialogue with the artist, during which they designed a community engagement proposal, identified potential sites, and coordinated visits to determine feasibility, all the while adapting to the vagaries and restrictions of a seemingly endless global pandemic. We had overcome the concerns of architects and structural engineers, navigated supply-chain delays, tracked down the owners of potentially radiating cell-phone towers, debated the relative reliability of 1/2-inch or 3/8-inch screws, and struggled with the unpredictability of Chicago weather. *Toward Common Cause: Art, Social Change, and the MacArthur Fellows at 40* was four years in the making, and this was one of our last hurdles. Like almost every aspect of the exhibition project, getting to the point of completion involved endless negotiation, rebuttals, and frequently brutal defeats lightly peppered with moments of joy and grace. These stories—of negotiation, conciliation, and compromise; of setbacks and celebration—are the stories we will share here. They are the stories curators are not supposed to tell. We do not publicly discuss budgets, philanthropy, disasters, delays, or any of the attendant messiness of exhibition-making. In hiding our difficulties, we lose the opportunity to share the moments from which we learn the most.

Toward Common Cause was an experiment—a vehicle through which to explore the agency of art and its ability to respond in moments of social, political, economic, and ecological crisis. We wanted to ask questions about the role of the museum and its relationship to audiences, communities, and artists. We wanted to test the flexibility of the structures that are in place and push the boundaries of accepted practice. This was only possible because of the unwavering support of a funding organization that was willing to entertain even our most outrageous propositions. The pandemic forced us to abandon a single opening date and, as a result, *Toward Common Cause* sprawled across the city throughout 2021 and into 2022. In the end, the project included the work of twenty-nine MacArthur

Fellows presented in collaboration with more than three dozen partners. Accordingly, *Art in Pursuit of Common Cause* is a reader (of sorts), rather than an exhibition catalogue proper, one that attempts to convey the spirit of our project and share some of its lessons.

Through essays, interviews, quotes, and case studies, *Art in Pursuit of Common Cause* introduces the artists and partners who participated in the realization of *Toward Common Cause* and the artworks and venues that gave it form. Each chapter is named after an issue we encountered or one of the values we centered over the course of three years of exhibition-making.

Uncertainty addresses the incertitude and disruptions of the global pandemic, racial uprisings, economic catastrophe, and political convulsions that unfolded during the planning of *Toward Common Cause*. By necessity, confronting and embracing uncertainty as a generative force became a guiding principle of our work. The project was formed around questions of artistic and institutional agency, and identifying ways to tap art's potential in moments of social, political, and economic Urgency. In its support of extraordinarily creative individuals, Experimentation has guided the work of the MacArthur Fellows Program for forty years. Applying their values to the exhibition planning required us to embrace risk, acknowledge the potential for failure, and welcome open-ended engagement and adaptation. *Toward Common Cause* was a biennial-style exhibition but, with Reciprocity as a central tenet of our work, we sought a nonextractive, collaborative, and mutually beneficial form of exhibition-making that demanded particular attention be paid to the relationships we built with partners and space be made for discussions of artistic and institutional agency. As we worked, political divisions in the country deepened, reopening the fissures of the culture wars of the 1990s. During such moments, Complexity tends to be flattened in favor of either/or propositions. We hoped to foster debate that retained the knottiness and intricacies of real life, that compelled more questions. Along the way, we were frequently confronted by stakeholders who challenged our premise, questioned our motives, or exhorted us to do better. We heeded these difficult conversations and allowed our feelings of Discomfort to drive our individual and collective reckoning. Finally, does the importance of art in such times rest in its ability to prompt discussion? If so, it was crucial for us to understand, in dialogue with our partners, the Value of art beyond considerations of the market.

On days that I drove by the Minnie Riperton Apartments, I could almost forget that *Toward Common Cause* had ended. I can still visit Akunyili Crosby's vinyl banners at their second home on the facade of the city's soon-to-open National Public Housing Museum. There are other echoes of the project around town, including the installations that continue to evolve at Sweet Water Foundation. The Better Boys Foundation in North Lawndale has become the Building Brighter Futures Center for the Arts, a shift inspired by their work with Kerry James Marshall. The young people who worked with Wendy Ewald have opened Centro Romero's Pueblo Unido Gallery, a student-run arts space dedicated to elevating stories of immigration. *Black Wall Street Journey*, Rick Lowe's ongoing social experiment, continues its investigations into issues of African American economics in collaboration with local partners. I can still listen to Guillermo Gómez-Peña's *Mex Files: Audio Art & Strange Poetry from the US/Mexico Border* broadcast on Public Media Institute's Lumpen Radio, 105.5 FM.

Art in Pursuit of Common Cause lays bare the process by which we arrived here, shares what we discovered along the way, and presents the work of exhibition-making in all its untidiness. It is a retrospective reflection on what *Toward Common Cause* did and did not accomplish. And it is an offering toward how we and others might build for the future based on lessons learned.

Scenes from *Toward Common Cause: Art, Social Change, and the MacArthur Fellows Program at 40*

For more than two years, visitors came to *Toward Common Cause*, some as pilgrims enticed by reviews in the Chicago press or the *New York Times*, others to take part in some of the hundreds of programs or events offered through partnerships with artists and organizations across the city. Many were accidental participants, glimpsing a storefront installation or a mural on a building facade during their morning commutes. The exhibition's nineteen venues in neighborhoods throughout Chicago welcomed young people and families, students and lifelong learners, artists and art lovers, and plenty of first-time museum-goers. What all of them experienced was the culmination of the efforts of thousands of individuals—artists, culture workers, and community members—whose ideas, time, energy, and talents are necessary to make such events happen.

The exhibition gave Chicagoans—some of them venturing out after months of COVID lockdown—a reason to return to their favorite museums, to gather again with family and friends, and to encounter powerful artworks in person. Many others from Chicago and beyond were unable to attend because of travel- or health-related restrictions. For them, this sixteen-page portfolio provides a small sampling of the myriad spaces and extraordinarily diverse works that were a part of the *Toward Common Cause* experiment.

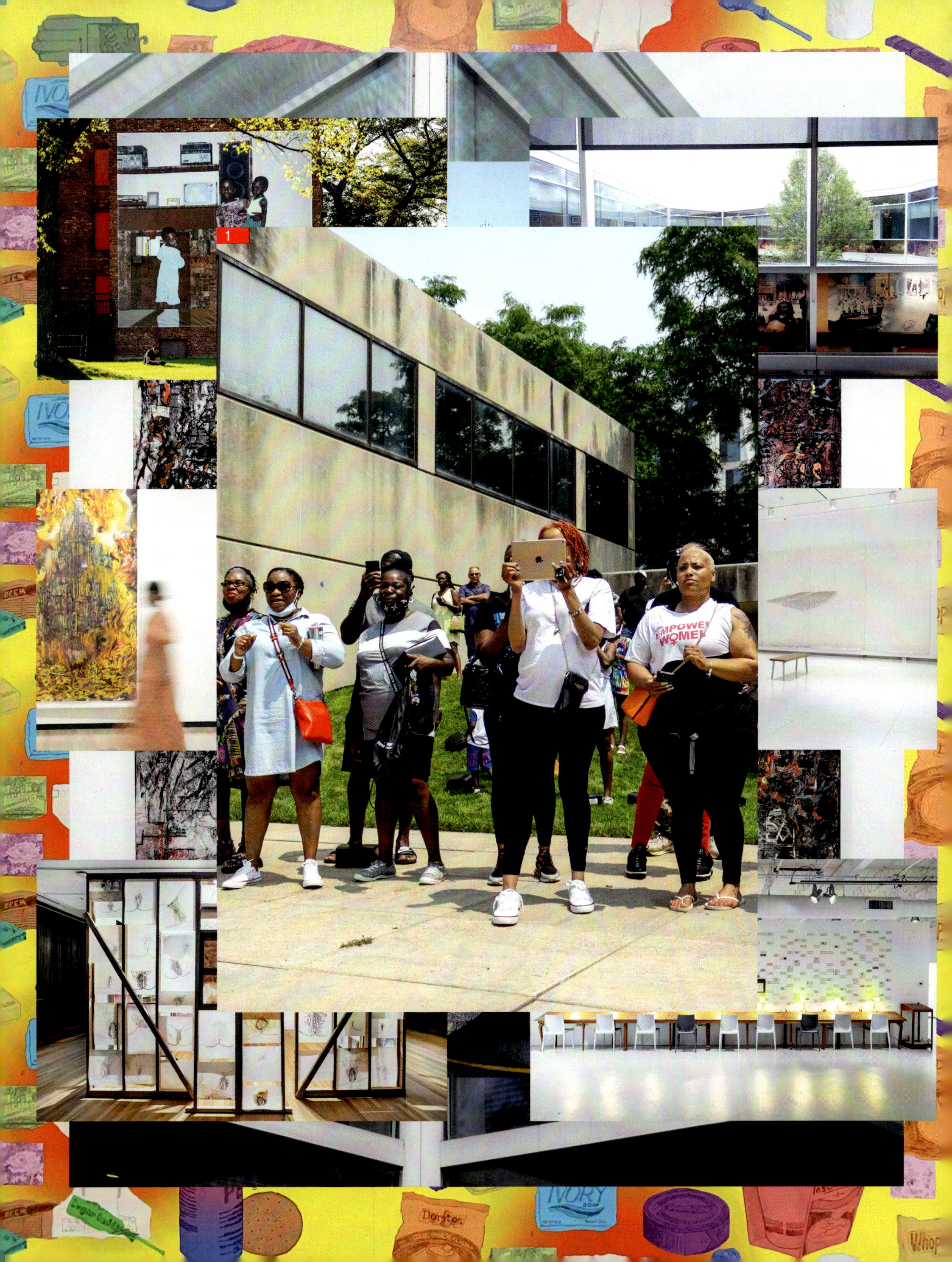
1
IVORY
SOAP
Doritos

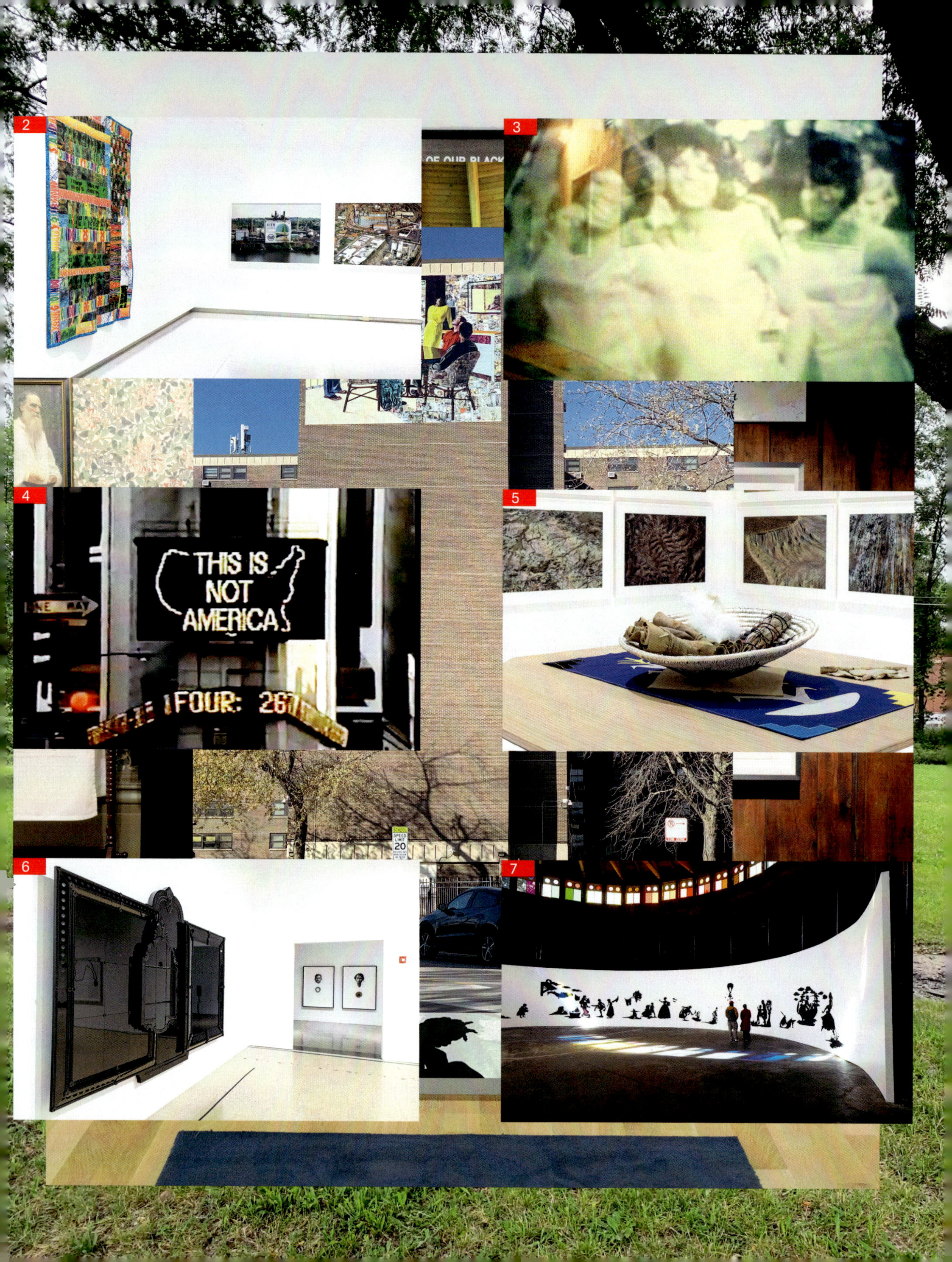
2
3
4
THIS IS
NOT
AMERICA
5
6
7

8

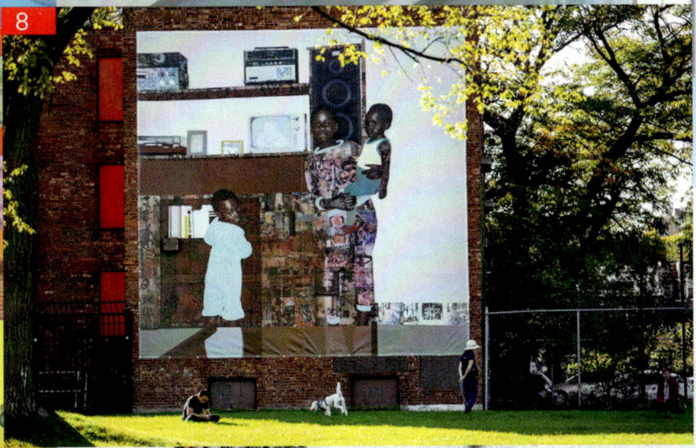

9

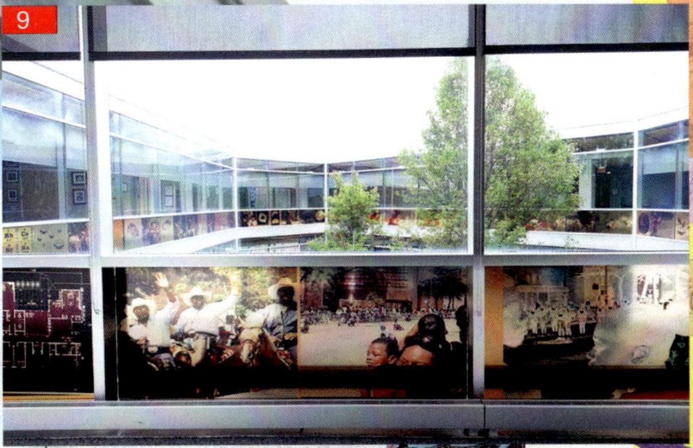

10

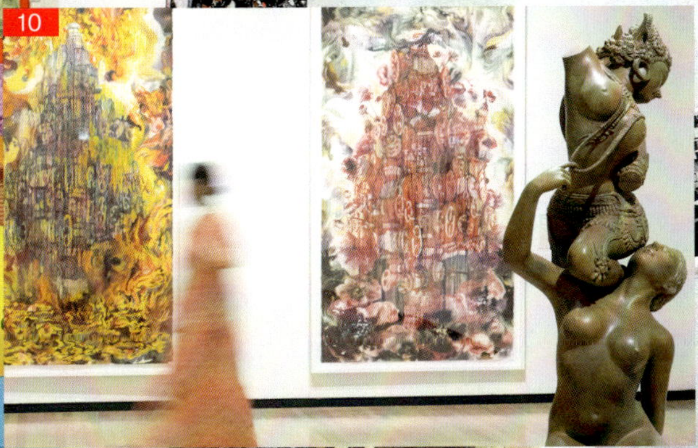

11

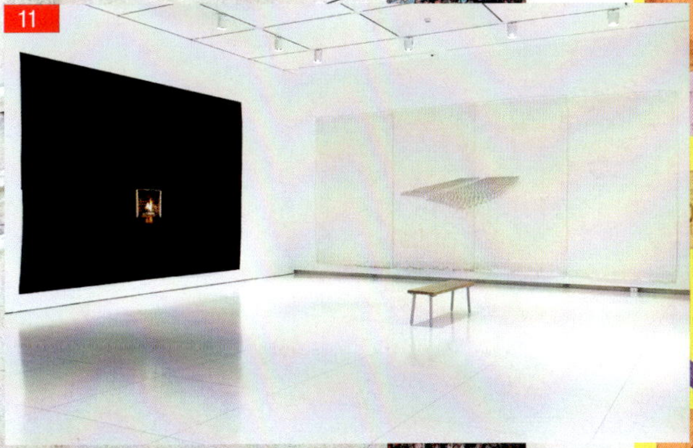

12

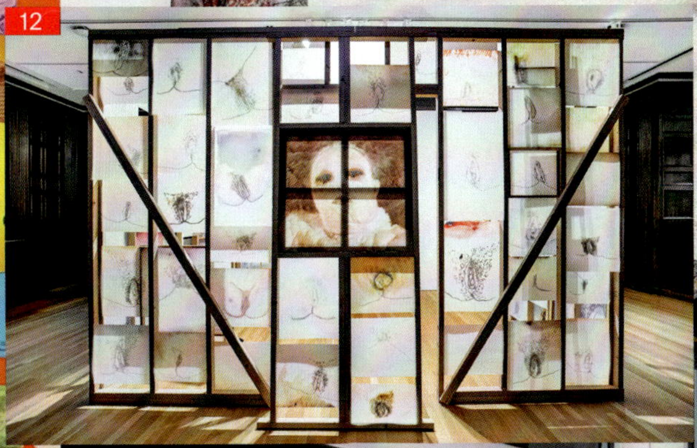

13

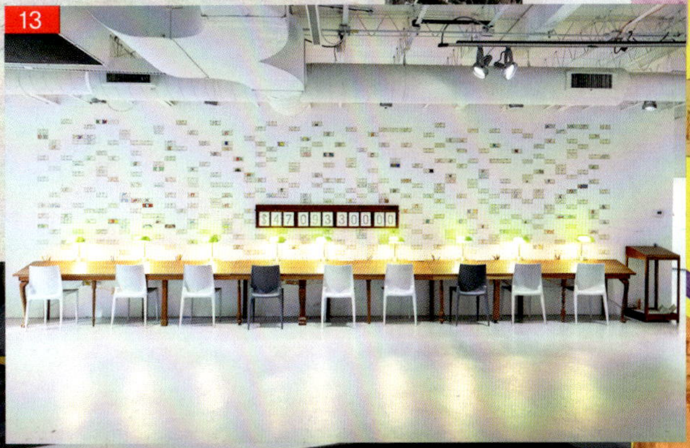

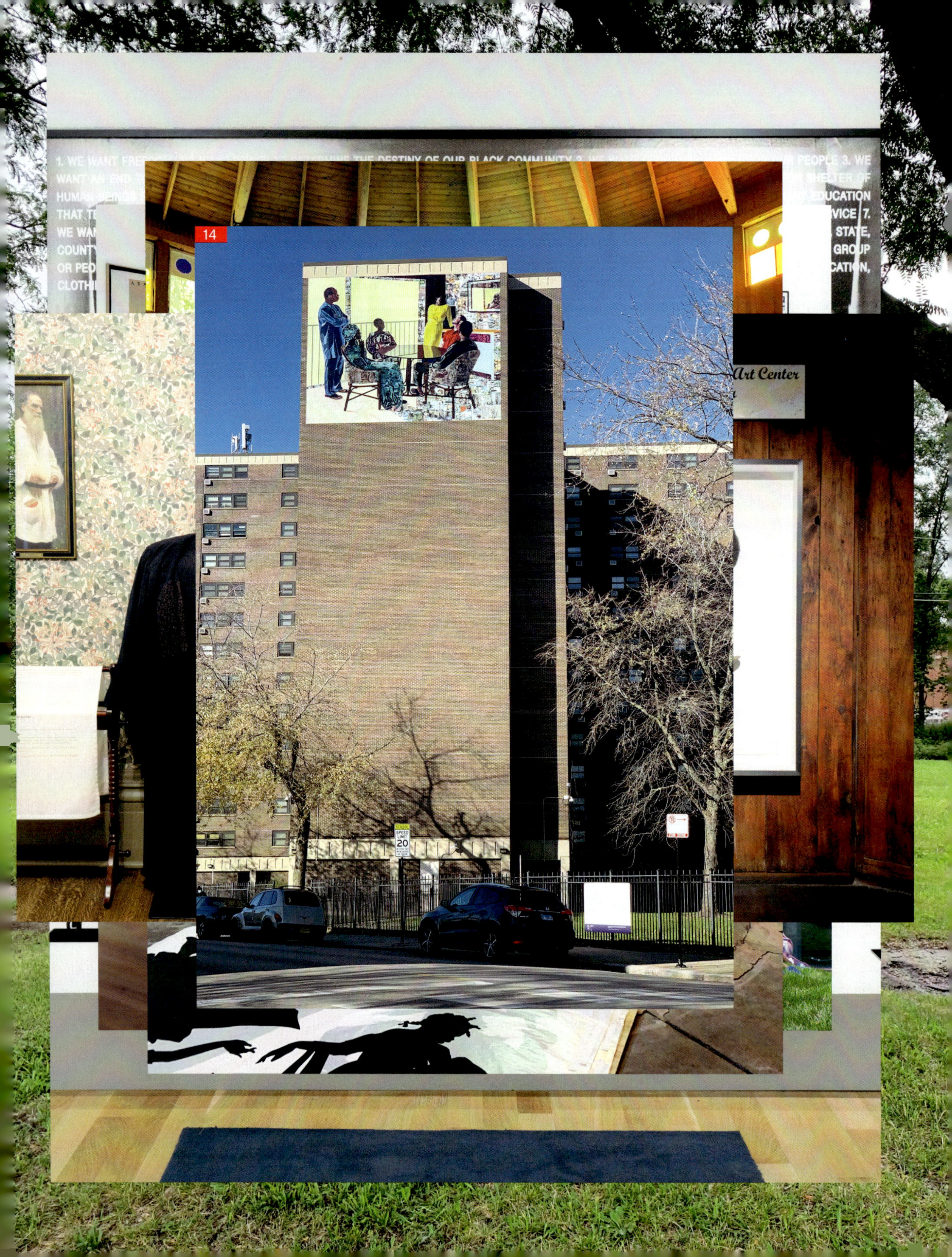
14
Art Center

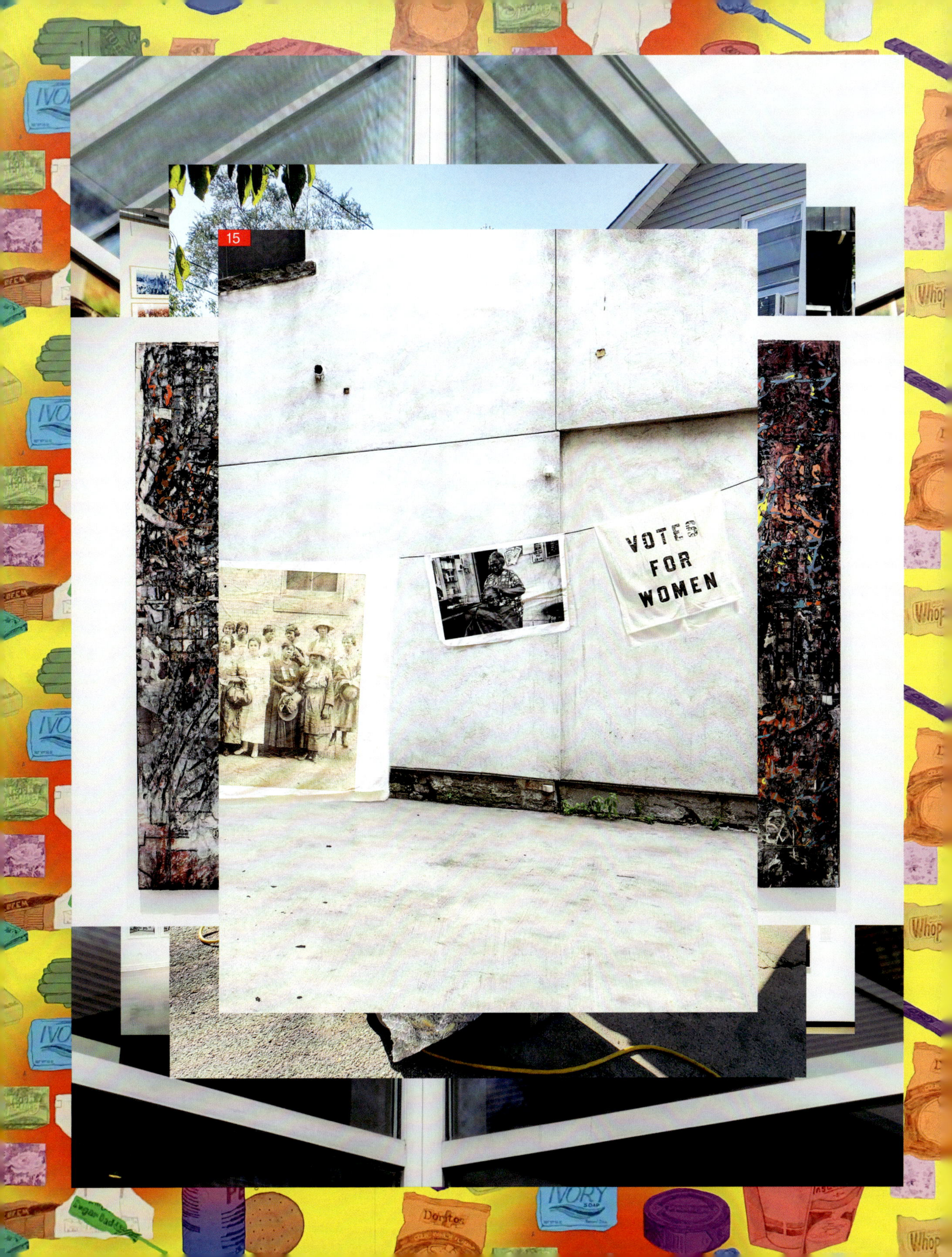
15
VOTES
FOR
WOMEN
IVORY
SOAP
Doritos
Sugar Daddy

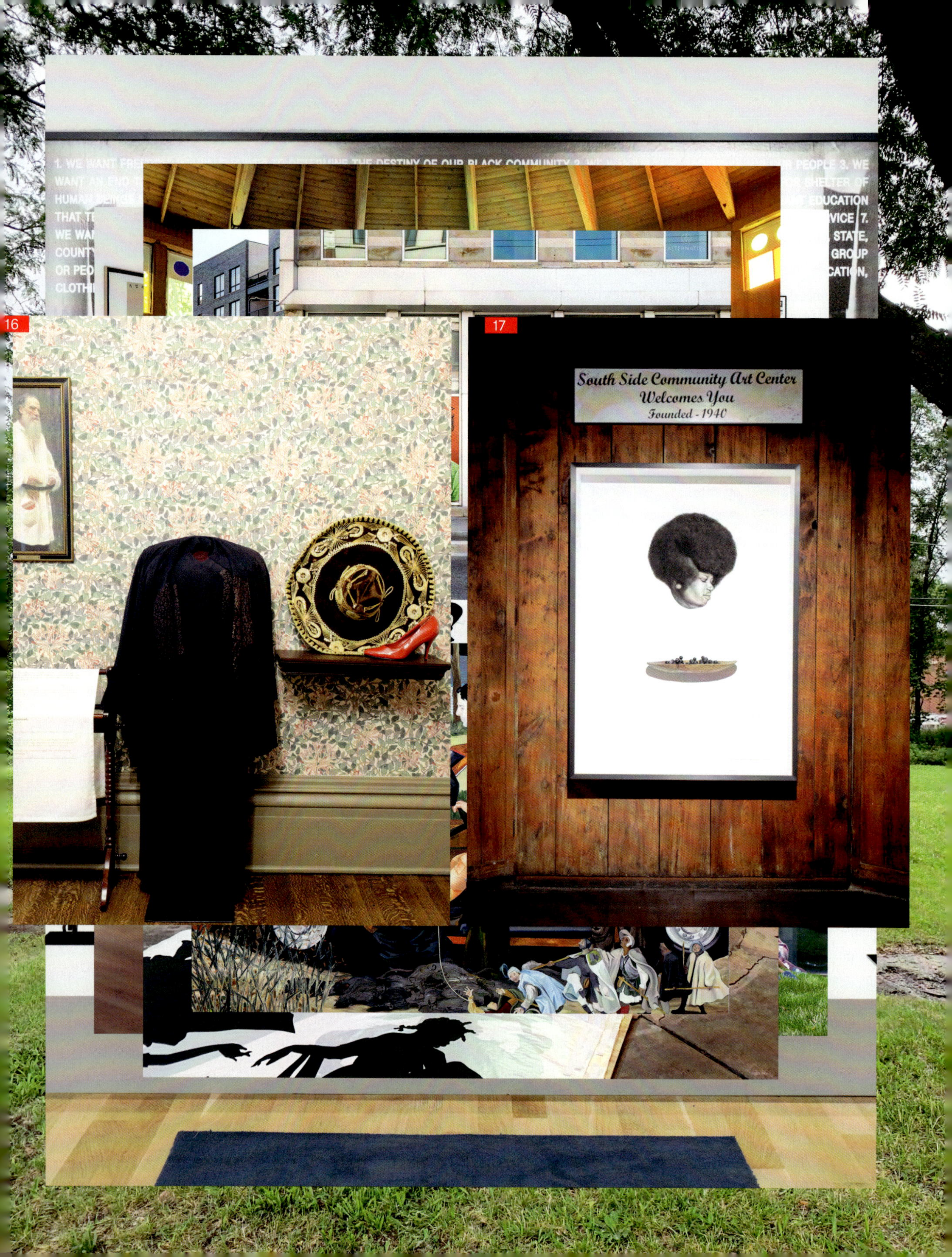
16
17
South Side Community Art Center
Welcomes You
Founded - 1940

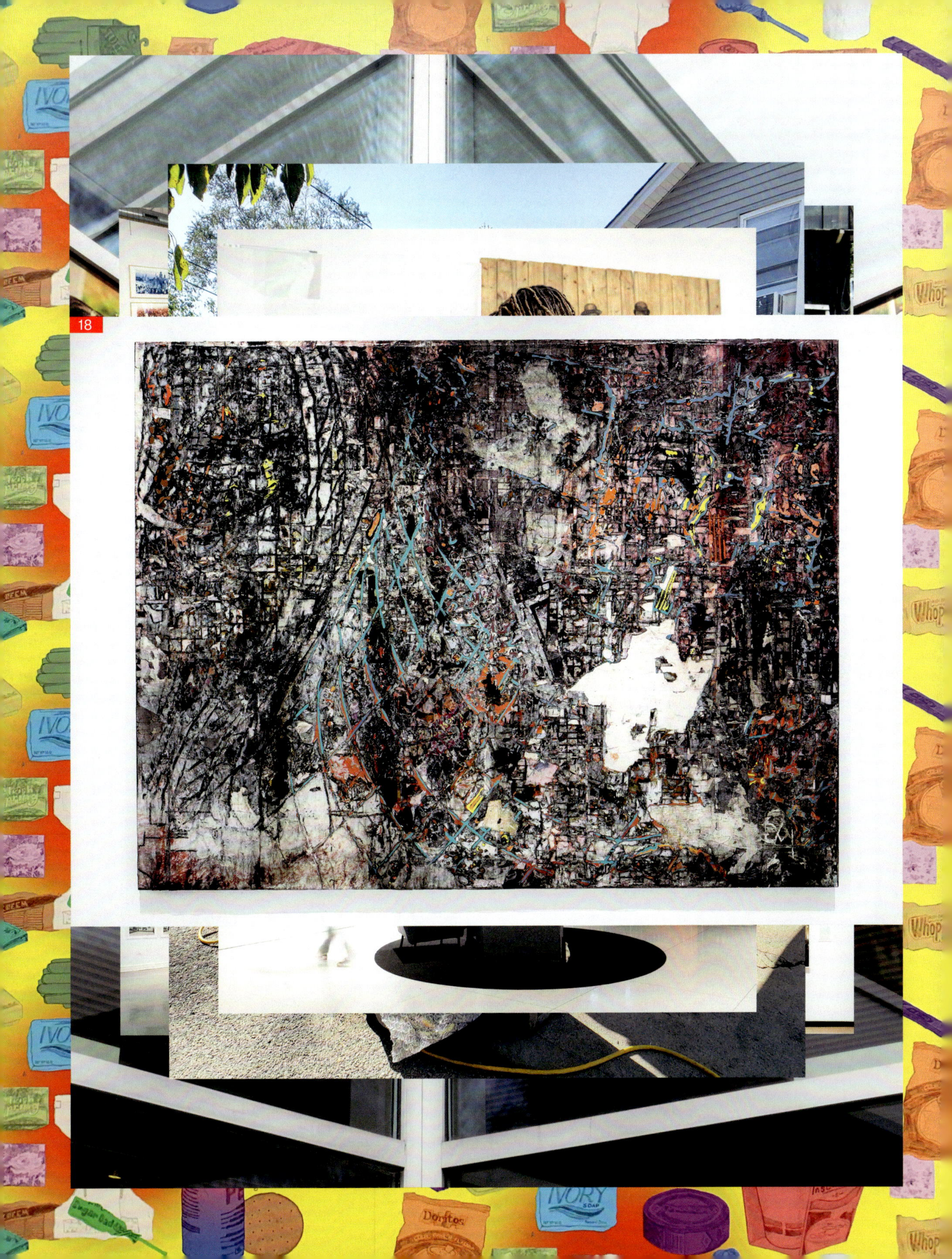
18
IVORY
Doritos
Whop

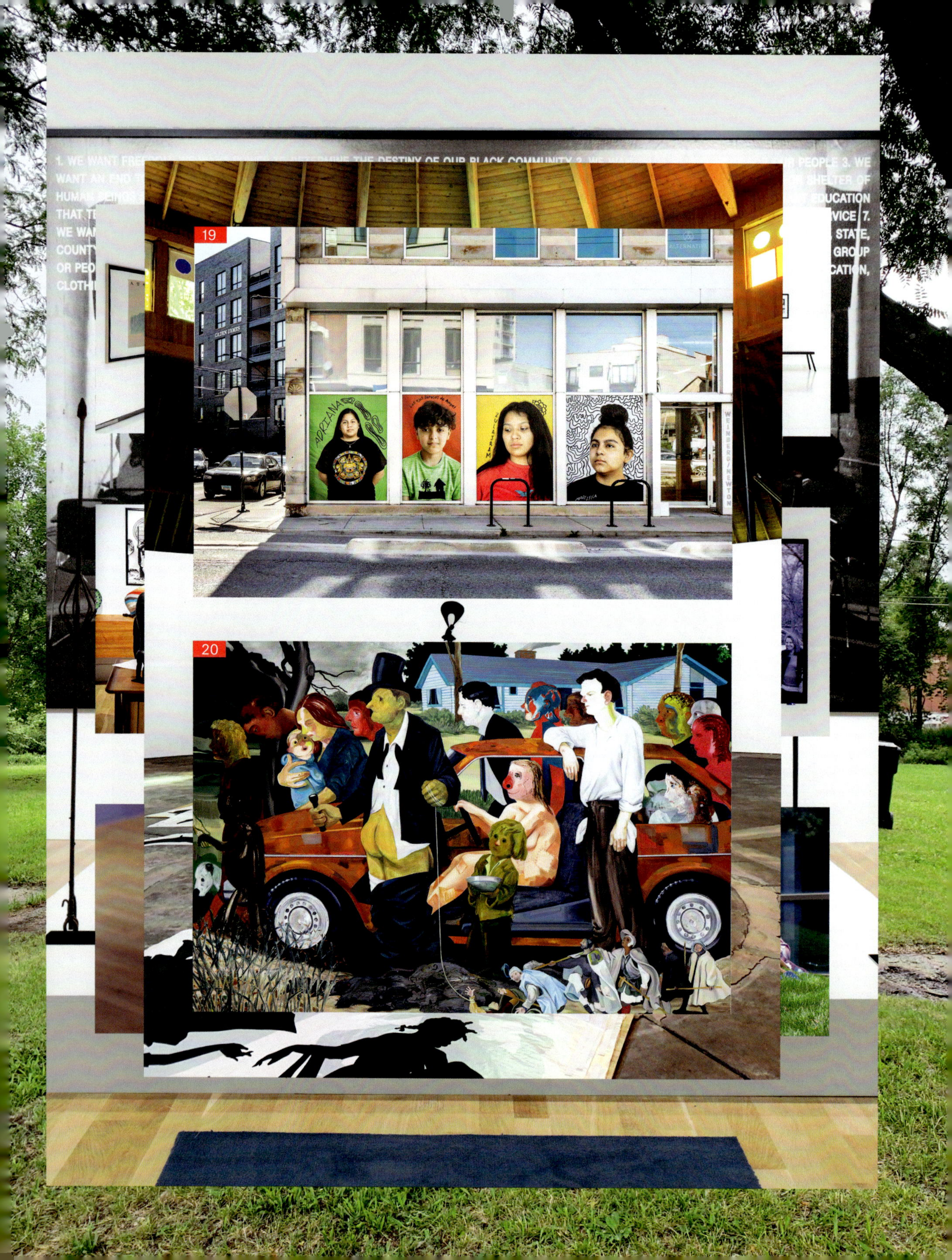
19
20
ADRIANA

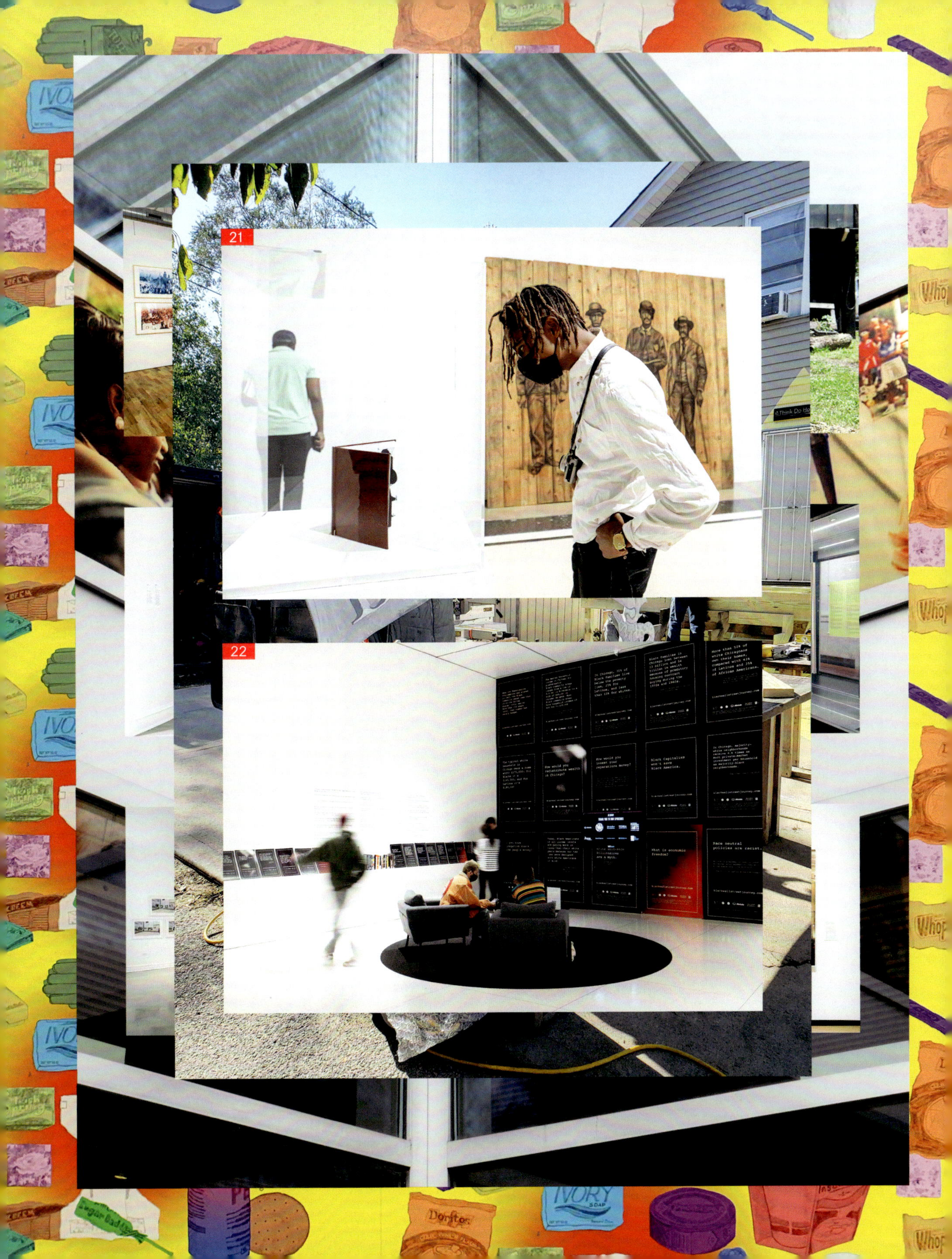
21
22
In Chicago, 30% of Black families live below the poverty line, 23% for Latinos, and less than 11% for whites.
More than 50% of white Chicagoans own their homes, compared with 43% of Latinos and 35% of African Americans.
How would you redistribute wealth in Chicago?
How would you invest your reparations money?
Black Capitalism won't save Black America.
What is economic freedom?
Race neutral policies are racist.
IVORY
Doritos

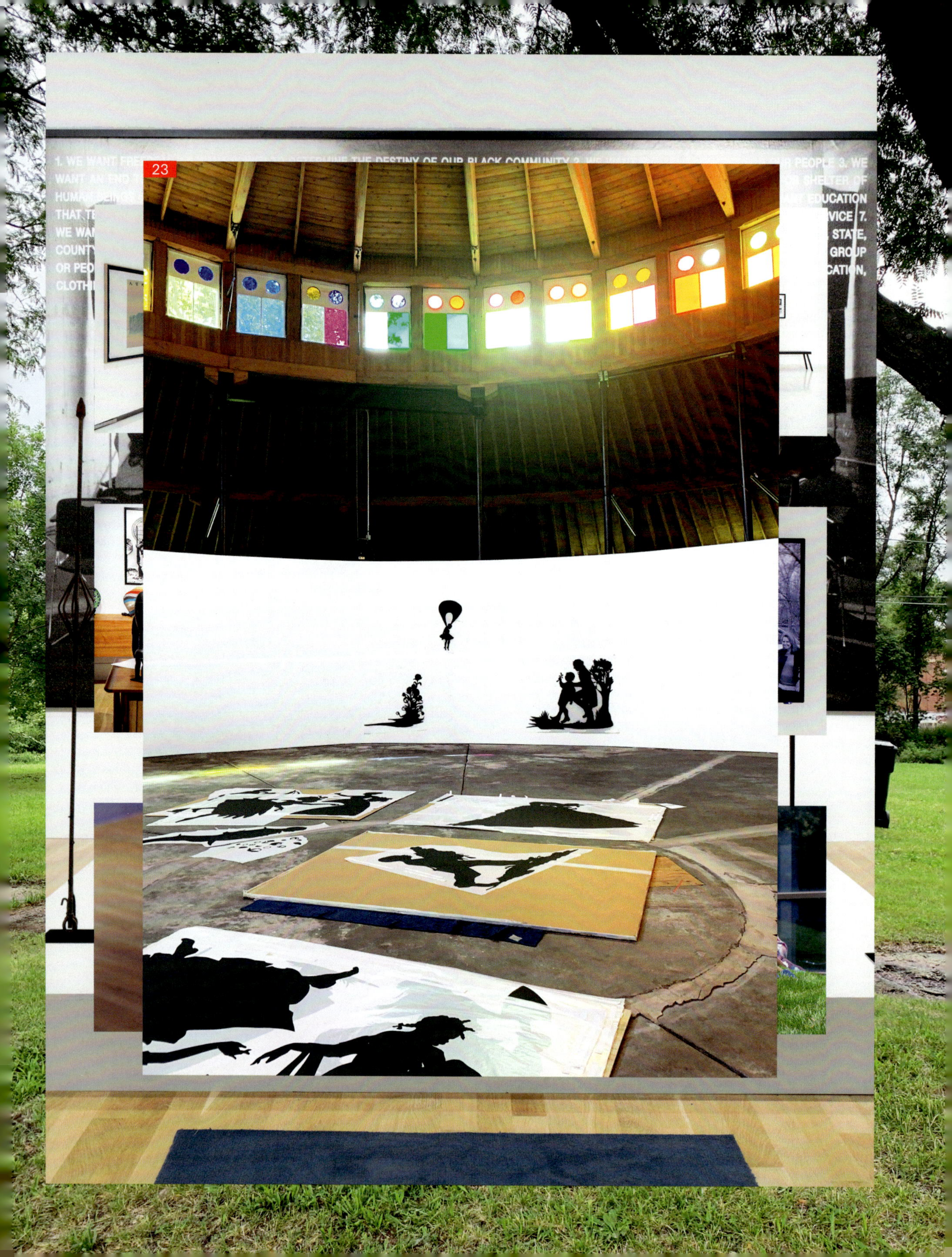

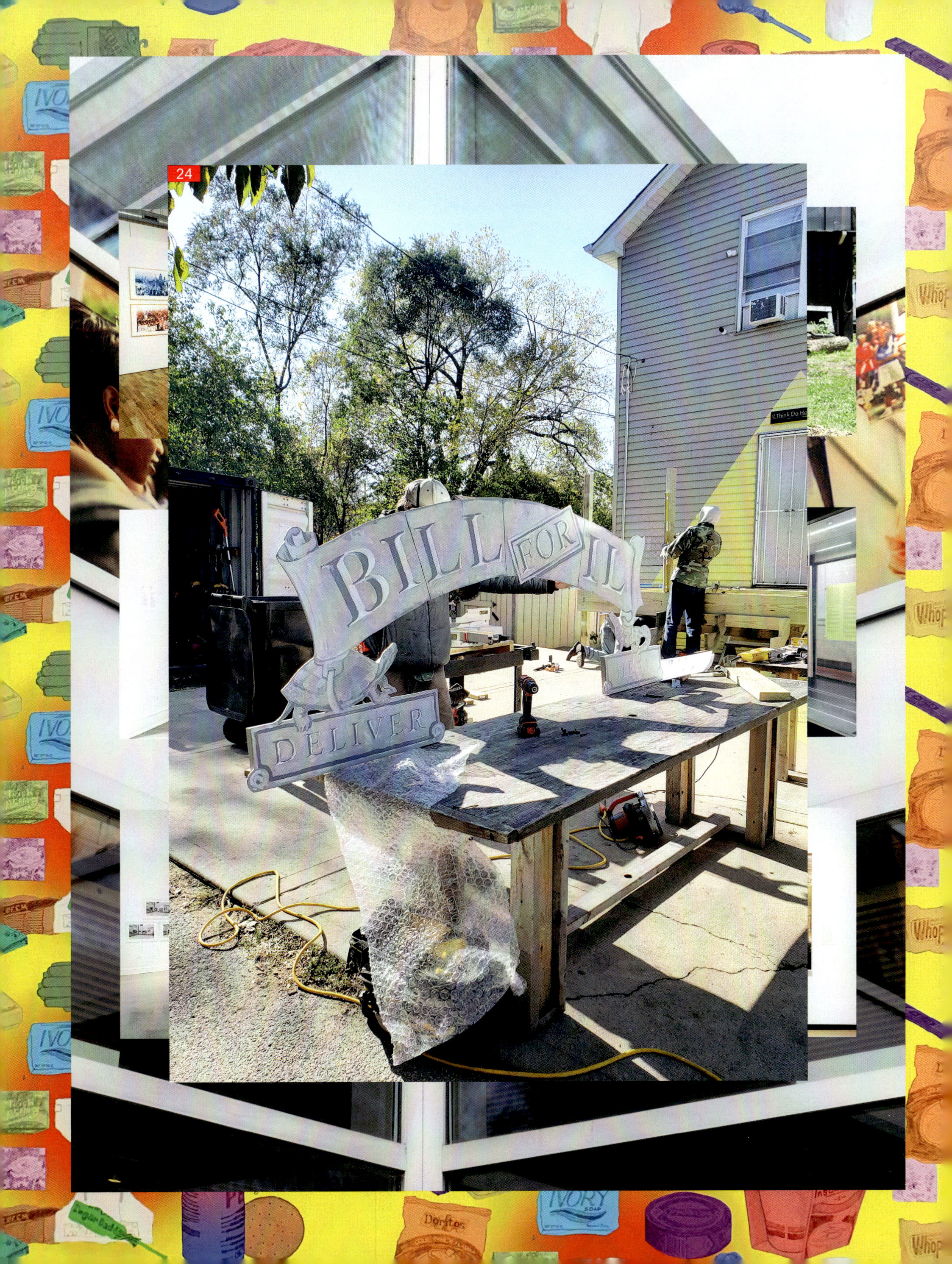
24
BILL FOR IL
DELIVER

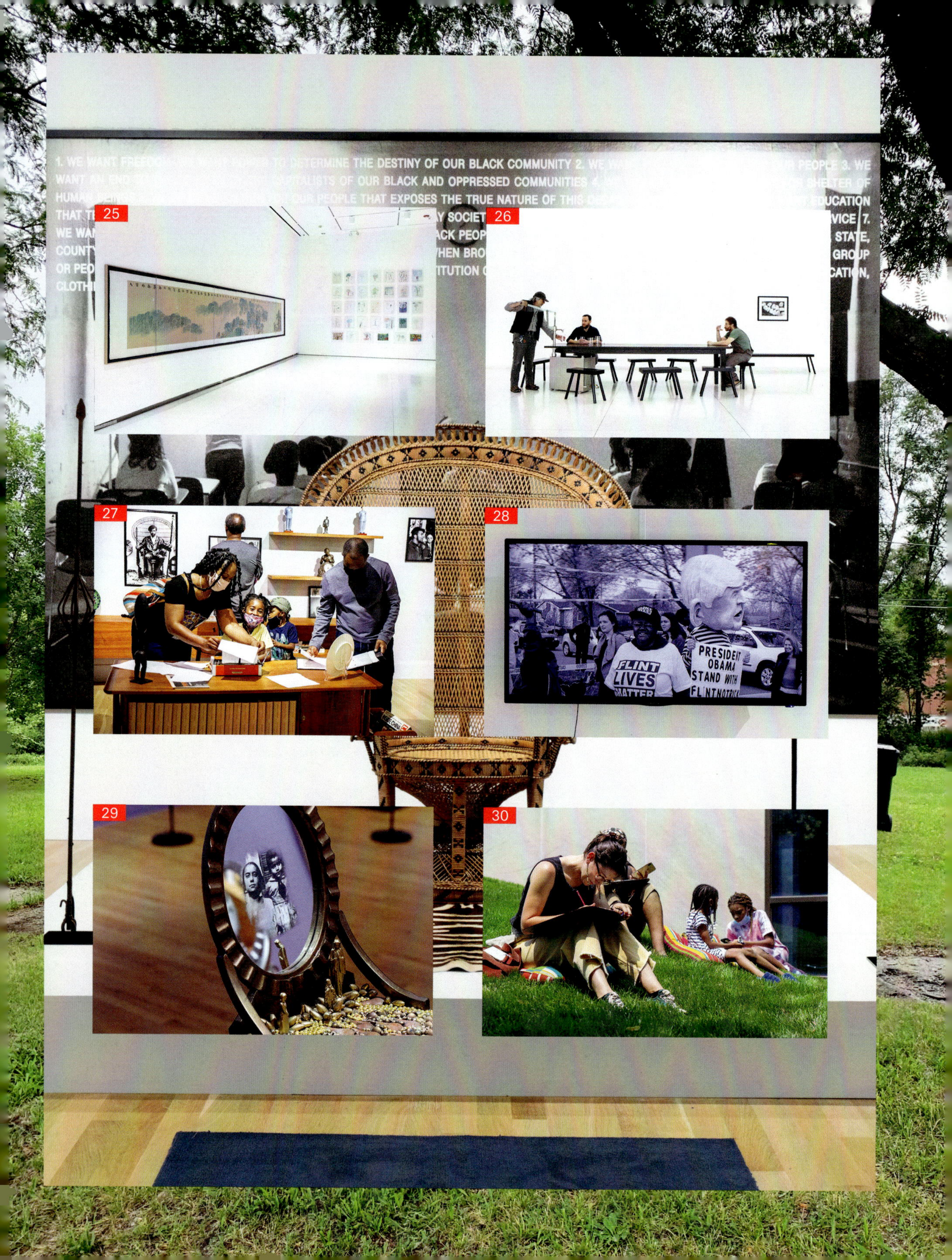
25
26
27
28
29
30
FLINT LIVES MATTER
PRESIDENT OBAMA STAND WITH FLINT

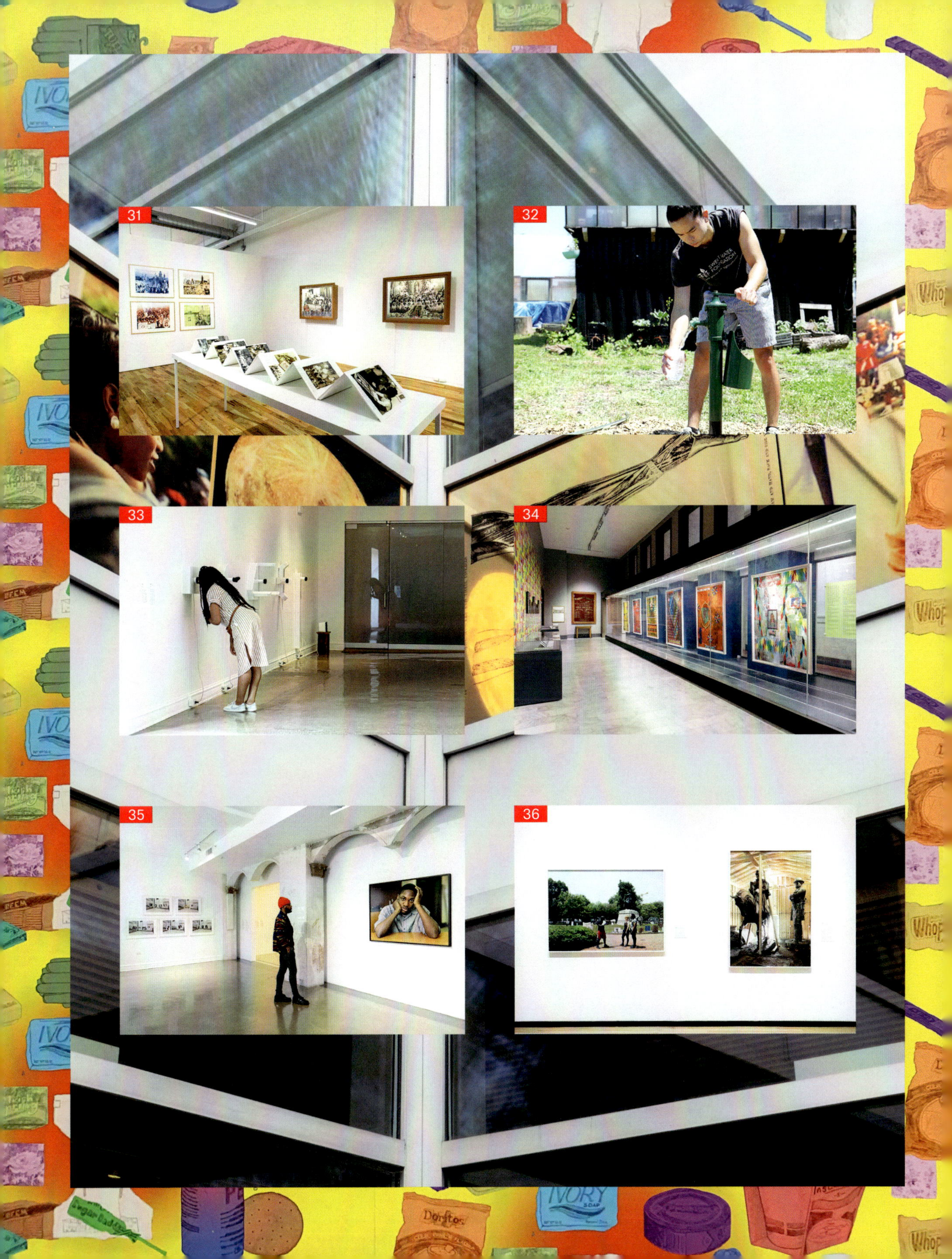
31
32
33
34
35
36

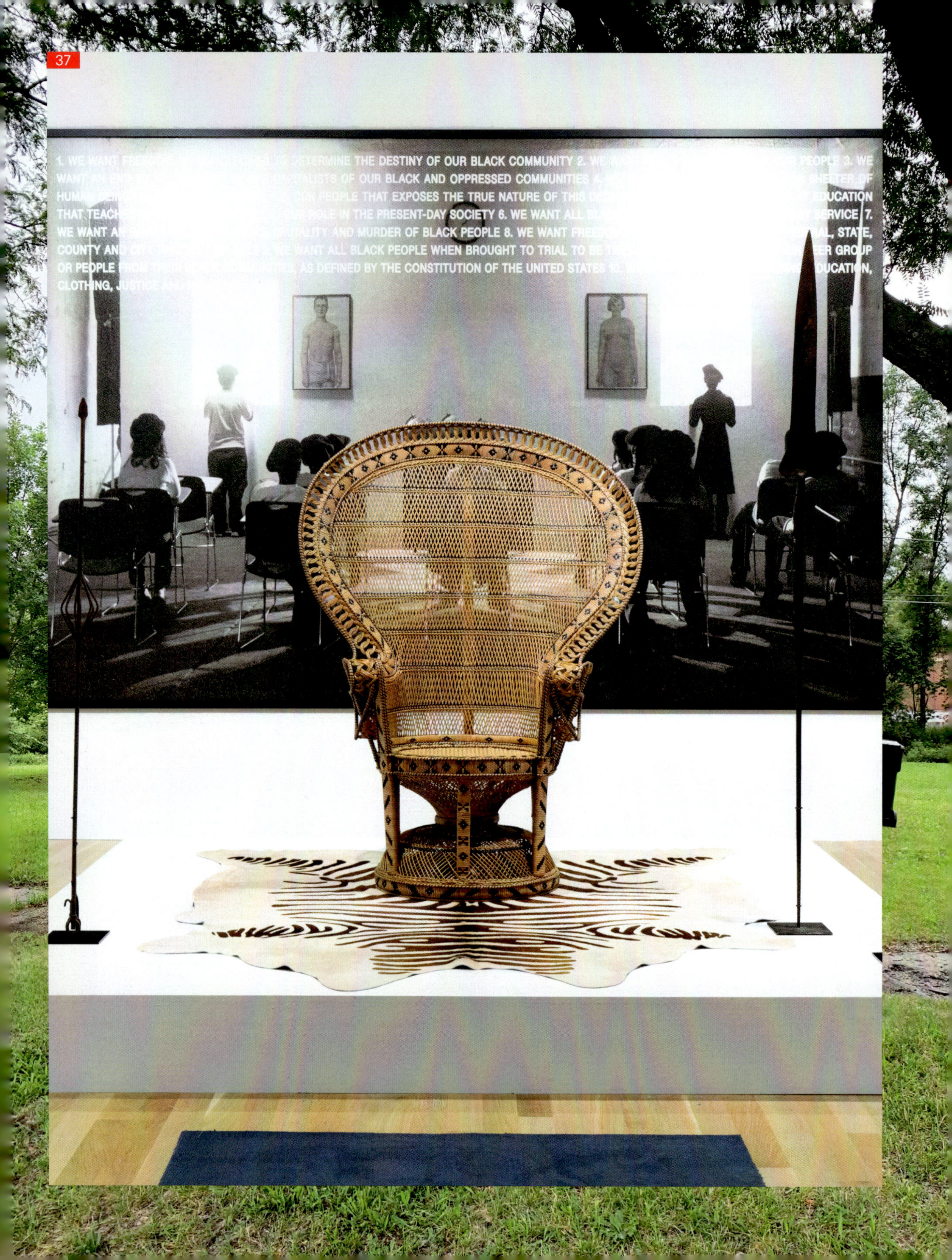
1. WE WANT FREE
DETERMINE THE DESTINY OF OUR BLACK COMMUNITY 2. WE
PEOPLE 3. WE
OF OUR BLACK AND OPPRESSED COMMUNITIES 4.
OUR PEOPLE THAT EXPOSES THE TRUE NATURE OF THIS
EDUCATION
IN THE PRESENT-DAY SOCIETY 6. WE WANT ALL
SERVICE 7.
WE WANT AN
AND MURDER OF BLACK PEOPLE 8. WE WANT
STATE,
COUNTY AND
WE WANT ALL BLACK PEOPLE WHEN BROUGHT TO TRIAL TO BE
GROUP
OR PEOPLE FROM
AS DEFINED BY THE CONSTITUTION OF THE UNITED STATES
EDUCATION,
CLOTHING, JUSTICE AND

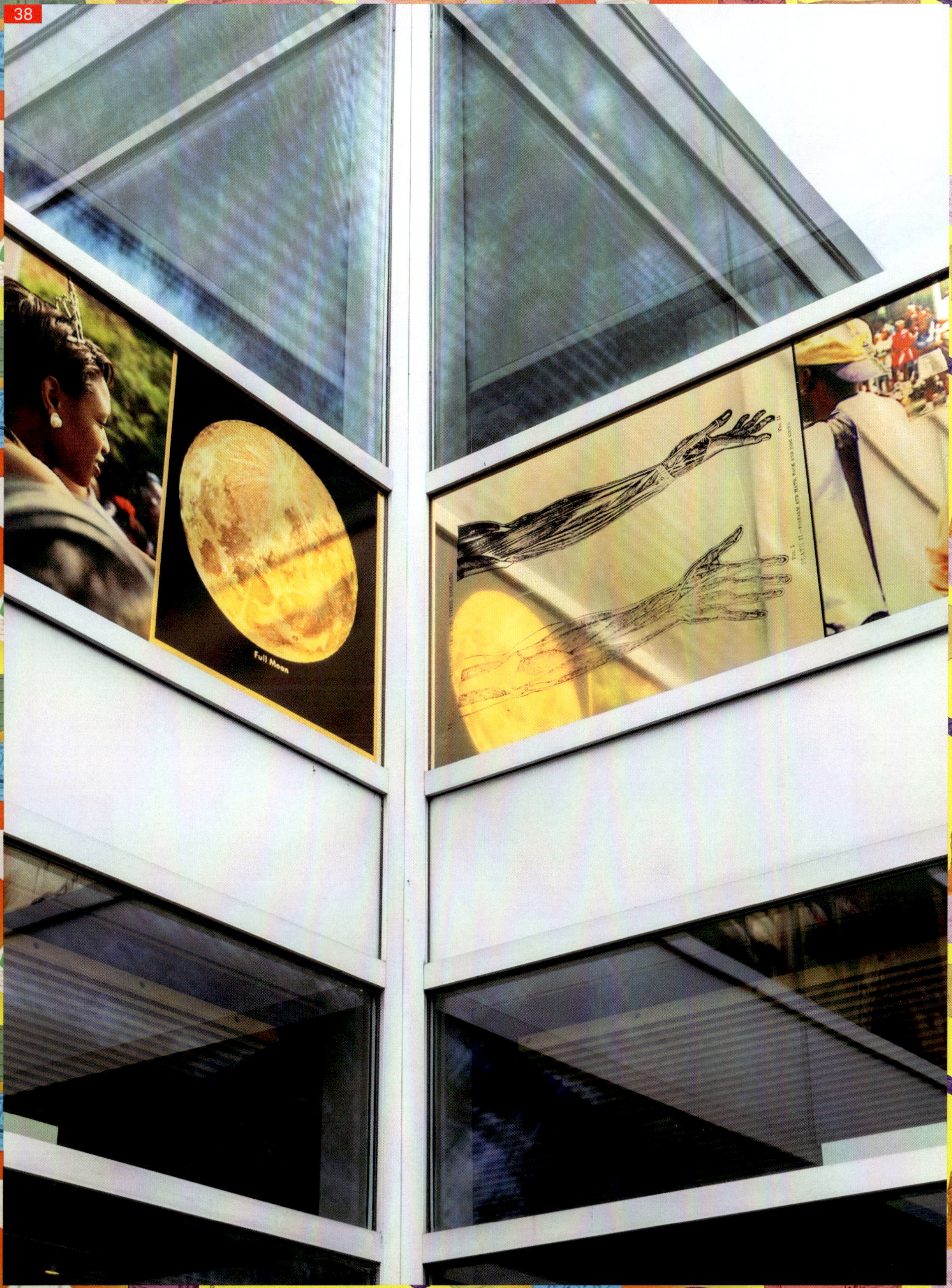
Full Moon

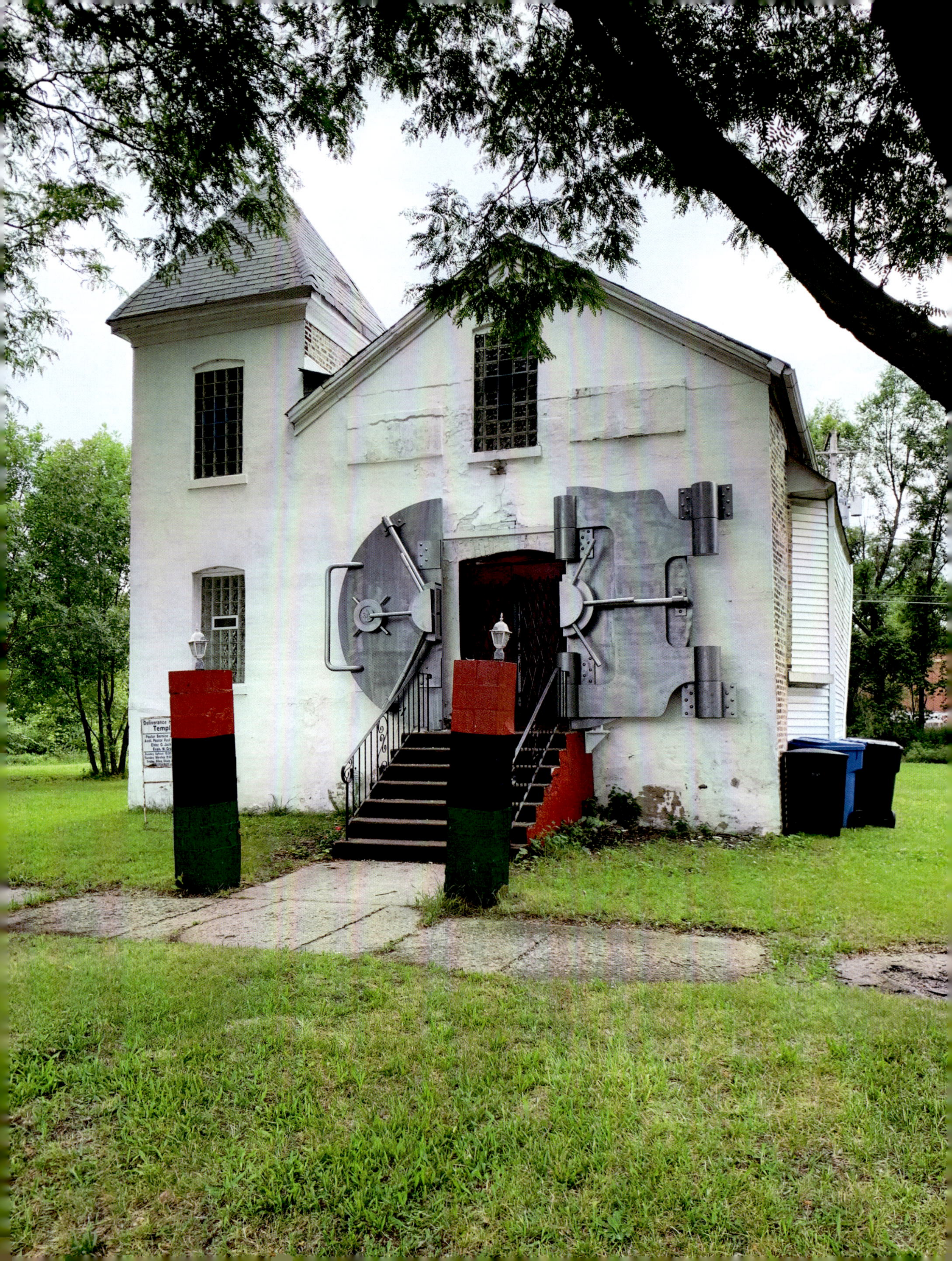
Deliverance

1 Visitors watch Opening Celebration performances in the Smart Museum courtyard, July 17, 2021.

2 Works at the Smart focused on environmental racism. Shown here: Jeffrey Gibson's *STAND YOUR GROUND* and two photos from LaToya Ruby Frazier's series *The Notion of Family*.

3 Mark Bradford's *Dancing in the Street* at the Smart.

4 Alfredo Jaar's *A Logo for America* at the School of the Art Institute of Chicago.

5 Fazal Sheikh's *In Place*—a collaboration between the artist, scientists, and Indigenous communities of the American Southwest—installed at the Smart.

6 At the Stony Island Arts Bank, a Venetian glass mirror from Fred Wilson's *Act V. Scene II—Exeunt Omnes* reflects works by other artists addressing race, gender, and class, including Whitfield Lovell's *Spell Suite*.

7 Kara Walker's *Presenting Negro Scenes* (originally commissioned by the Renaissance Society) at the DuSable Museum, America's oldest African American history museum.

8 Large-scale facsimiles of Njideka Akunyili Crosby's paintings were installed on public housing sites. Here, *The Beautyful Ones, Series #9* at the former Jane Addams Homes (future site of the National Public Housing Museum).

9 The golden frieze of Kerry James Marshall's *Untitled (Circulation)* wraps the courtyard of BBF's glass building.

10 Shahzia Sikander's *Promiscuous Intimacies*, *Flared*, and *Oil and Poppies* at the Museum of Contemporary Photography.

11 Two paintings by Toba Khedoori, *Untitled (Black Fireplace)* and *Untitled (Seats)*, created a space for introspection at the Smart.

12 Ida Applebroog's *Monalisa*—a hut papered with drawings of the artist's vagina—at the Neubauer Collegium, a former theological seminary.

13 Mel Chin's *Philadelphia Footed Fundred Minting Table* at the Hyde Park Art Center.

14 Njideka Akunyili Crosby's *I Still Face You* at the Chicago Housing Authority Riperton Apartments.

15 At the Stony Island Arts Bank, Deborah Willis's *The Clothesline: Women's work never praised never done*, photographs celebrating the activism of women, particularly women of color.

16 Jane Addams's dress and Guillermo Gómez-Peña's sombrero are juxtaposed in *Casa Museo*, the artist's takeover of historic Hull House, now a museum.

17 Whitfield Lovell's *Spell Suite*—Conté crayon drawings with found objects that challenge stereotypes of African Americans—in the historic gallery of the South Side Community Art Center.

18 Mark Bradford's *Tulsa Gottdamn*—a newly commissioned work reflecting on the 100th anniversary of the Tulsa Massacre—at the Smart.

19 Exterior of Weinberg/Newton Gallery: portraits by participants in Centro Romero's youth program in collaboration with Wendy Ewald for *Daily Life and Dreams in the Pandemic*.

20 Nicole Eisenman's commanding painting *The Triumph of Poverty* greets visitors entering the Smart galleries.

21 Kara Walker's *Freedom: A Fable* and Whitfield Lovell's *Missoura* at the Stony Island Arts Bank.

22 Visitors at the Smart engage with Rick Lowe's *Black Wall Street Journey*, installed alongside a poster project by artist Amanda Williams and journalist Natalie Moore.

23 Kara Walker's cutouts reinstalled at the DuSable Museum, with a slideshow of the artist producing the original work. Above: Cauleen Smith's 2017 site-specific window installation *The Right Time, Before and After*.

24 Mel Chin's *Bill for IL* being installed at Sweet Water Foundation.

25 Xu Bing's *Forest Project: The Blue and Green Wonderland* and *Children's Drawings* at the Smart.

26 Iñigo Manglano-Ovalle with *Water Table, 41°47'36.993" N—87°36'0.726" W* at the Smart.

27 Visitors at the Logan Center's Family Arts Crawl, September 18, 2021, during Carrie Mae Weems's installation *A Land of Broken Dreams*.

28 LaToya Ruby Frazier's *Flint Is Family* at the Hyde Park Art Center.

29 Amalia Mesa-Bains's *Circle of Ancestors* at the National Museum of Mexican Art.

30 Visitors make Mel Chin's Fundreds at the Smart's Opening Celebration.

31 Amalia Mesa-Bains's *Dos Mundos: Mexican Chicago* at Weinberg/Newton.

32 A visitor uses Iñigo Manglano-Ovalle's *Hydrant, 41°47'22.662" N—87°37'38.364" W* at Sweet Water.

33 Gary Hill's *SELF (A-F)* at the Stony Island Arts Bank.

34 Jeffrey Gibson's *Sweet Bitter Love* at the Newberry.

35 Deborah Willis's *The Clothesline: Women's work never praised never done* and Dawoud Bey's *Steven, Kenwood Academy High School* at the Stony Island Arts Bank.

36 At MoCP, selections from An-My Lê's *Silent General* series: *Andrew Jackson Statue, Lafayette Square, President's Park, Washington DC* and *Fragment VI: General Robert E. Lee and P.G.T. Beauregard Monuments, Homeland Security Storage, New Orleans, Louisiana*.

37 At the Logan Center, a rattan peacock chair in *A Land of Broken Dreams*, Carrie Mae Weems's homage to the Black Panthers and the legacy of radical Black pedagogy.

38 Kerry James Marshall's *Untitled (Circulation)* at BBF. Background: Jeffrey Gibson's vinyl wallpaper *Acc. 3784* at the Newberry.

Opposite: Mel Chin's *Safehouse Temple Door*—a facsimile bank vault door installed on the facade of the Civic Arts Church, a converted historic Black church on the campus of Sweet Water Foundation—provided a physical instantiation of his *Fundred Project*.

An Open Letter to the Museums of the Future

Guillermo Gómez-Peña

What follows is a transcript of Guillermo Gómez-Peña's live radio keynote "An Open Letter to the Museums of the Future" presented on February 3, 2021, as part of *Toward Common Cause: Art, Social Change, and the MacArthur Fellows Program at 40*. Images are from Gómez-Peña's residency at Jane Addams Hull-House Museum during *Toward Common Cause*, including the installation *Gómez-Peña's Casa Museo: A Living Museum and Archive*; radio broadcasts, presented by Public Media Institute, of *Gómez-Peña's Mex Files: Audio Art & Strange Poetry from the US/Mexico Border (1985–2021)*; and workshops with the artist's performance troupe, La Pocha Nostra.

The images shown here are drawn from the following sources: the San Francisco site of *The Living Archives*; ephemera and objects from Guillermo Gómez-Peña and La Pocha Nostra's practice; the installation of *The Living Archives at Casa Museo*; performances at the Jane Addams Hull-House Museum; an affiliated production at the University of Illinois Chicago; and the live broadcast of Gómez-Peña's keynote address "An Open Letter to the Museums of the Future," February 3, 2021.

(GÓMEZ-PEÑA SPEAKS)

(WHOOSHING SOUNDS)

The original memory.

In August 1492, Columbus departed from the Port of Palos in three state-of-the-art *caravelas*, *La Pinta* for the prisoners, *La Niña* for the child molesters, and *La Santa María* for the religious fanatics. Columbus arrived in the Americas with no documents. Don't we all secretly wish he had been deported right away?

The white art world. The white word—or rather the word "white"—meaning white house, white privilege, white lies, white supremacy, whitewashed, white versus black and brown and red versus white men, white savior, white power, white witchcraft, white dears, white purity. White walls, white gallery walls, white biennials equals the death of the white avant-garde. Tabula rasa. Chromatic change. Black and Brown lives matter forever, whiteout.

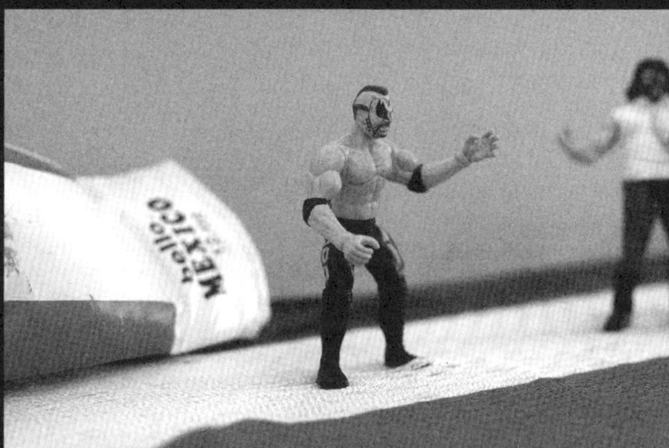

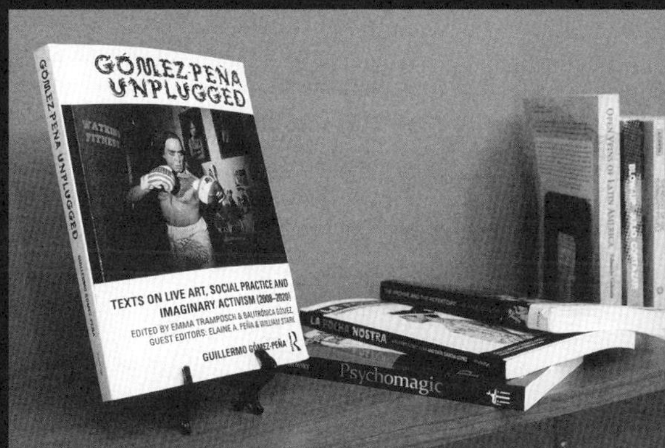

Questions I haven't found the answers for as an artist. After thirty years of being a dangerous presence in the capital, our world, I still haven't found satisfactory answers to many questions. If we were to place secret microphones to record the backstage chatter of the art world, the stuff people talk about in the bathroom during an opening, what would we hear? So, I asked thirty performance artists to respond. Here is a sampling of their answers, rewritten by yours truly. How come people speak with much lower volume when they are inside of a museum? Are we intimidated or merely respectful? Is it so not to wake the ghosts of arts past? Are we embarrassed about not saying something smart unless we take a selfie? Do people have sex in the back galleries of the Tate Modern or documenta, when no one is around? Wouldn't you like to see the surveillance tapes? Is there a codified mental illness or an eccentric sexual taboo that compels certain people to secretly caress or lick the artwork in museums?

Why are most museum guards and cleaning personnel in the US still Black or Latino, even in a Fred Wilson or a Gómez-Peña world?

Why is it that whenever I visit a chic museum with a bunch of chicken necks within minutes, a security guard begins to follow us? Who told him to do it? What exactly do they assume we will do? Attack a painting with spray paint or splatter it with *tapatíos* semen? Steal an artwork? Piss on a sculpture? Hang our own artwork?

Why is it that, with a few exceptions, in the big museums, the educational departments tend to be more adventurous and open-minded than the curatorial staff?

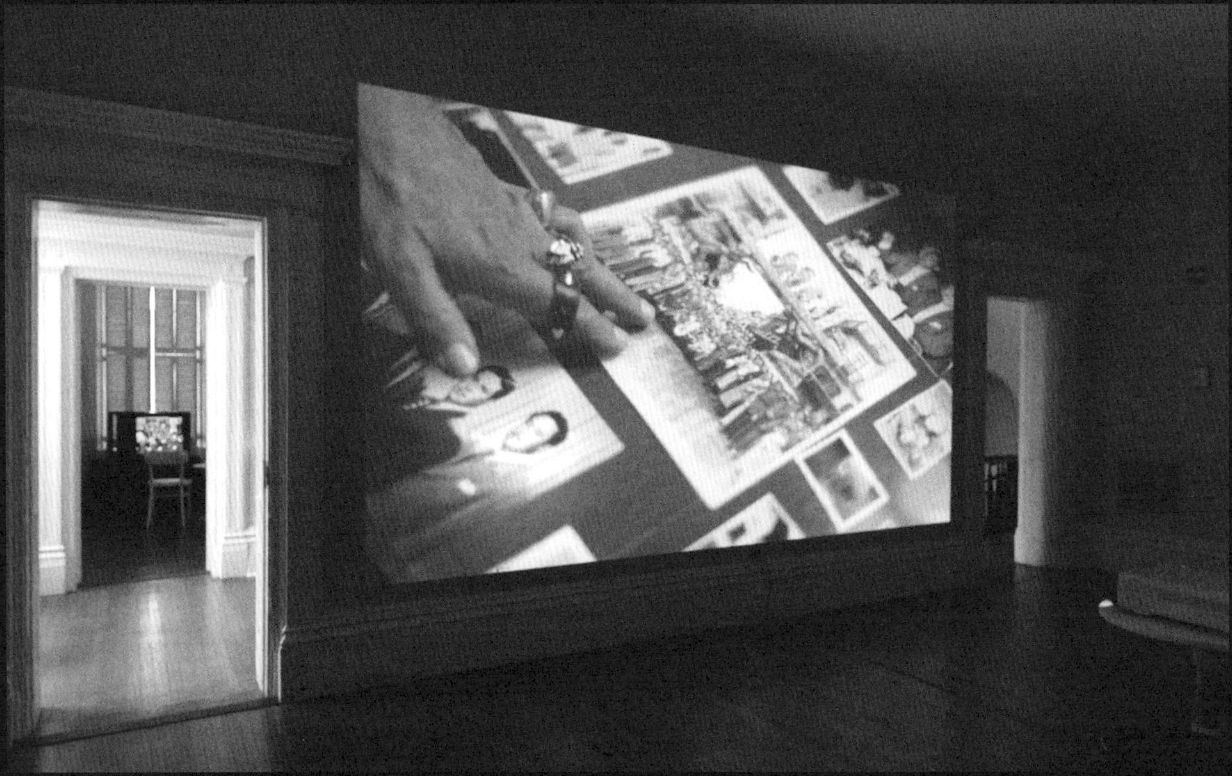

Why do people talk about the art world as a single entity, when, in fact, there are hundreds, thousands of art worlds, some of which overlap and many of which ignore the existence of the others? Which art world are they really talking about? Theirs? What the hell is the international art world? A very exclusive club that only includes a handful of operators and minions from Western countries and a few seasonal, stylish Third World or refugee guests of honor. What's international about these? Is this a branding strategy from the PR department?

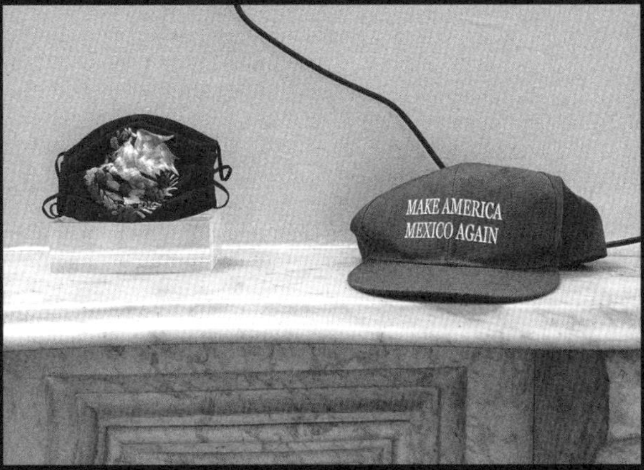

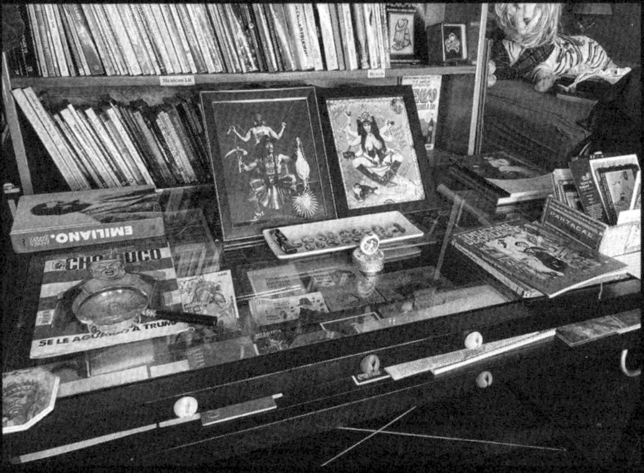

How come curators and producers are there either one year or two and then when you least expect it, they disappear for good never to answer your phone calls again? And you are left shivering like an abandoned provincial bride howling under the rain, wondering what's wrong with your artwork and waiting for the next young, hip, horny curator to discover you. Why is it that after all these years, artists of color are still expected to make community-friendly art? And if we don't do it, we get scolded by the institution that sponsors our project. Are we being infantilized and defanged? Do they think we lack the conceptual prowess to create other forms of art?

(SLOWLY)

Preguntas. Preguntas.

How can we redefine our roles as socially minded artists in a world engulfed in political turmoil, generalized violence, financial despair, and white supremacist delusion? La Pocha Nostra has been developing a series of concrete, practical jobs for utopian artists operating outside of the capitalist art world. By proposing these new roles, we wish to honor art as one of the oldest and most essential human activities.

First proposal: adopt an elder. Our intellectual and artistic elders have been abandoned by society. No one is listening to them. Very few young artists are actually working with them. What if all artists choose an elder from their communities to adopt? Once a week, they could spend time with their adopted elder, listen to their stories. Take them for a walk or a drive to a place of their choice, document carefully their opinions, help them choreograph their latest delusion. Organize their archives—that's important!—and help them make their living spaces more pleasant and vibrant by bringing other artists to talk to them.

We can also extend the service to artists who have been impaired by illness and even to the homeless in your street.

Two: redesign our hospitals. It is no secret that the state of our public hospitals is pathetic: overworked staff, inhuman institutionalized environments trying to service an overpopulation of confused patients, especially those not protected by HMOs or living on the edges of society. So, what if every hospital hires a multidisciplinary group of artists to redesign and redecorate the main gathering and waiting areas? Every central space in a hospital would be treated as an experimental art gallery, starting with comforting lighting and sound.

The same group would also develop a calendar of weekly cultural events for both medical staff and patients, including lectures, performance monologues, interpretive dance jams, poetry readings, and film screenings.

The neighborhood as a work of art. What about hiring a group of artists in charge of making sure that public space in every neighborhood is utilized to its full potential and is conducive to a healthy community life? The role of the group would be to first observe local civic life and talk to neighbors in order to understand their needs and how to improve the overall quality of community life. Then the artists will give concrete recommendations for how to enliven a semi-dead street, where to strategically locate a new cultural center, where to paint a new mural or build an interactive sculpture garden. Mimes could be hired to creatively direct the flow of traffic and performance artists to utilize psychomagic strategies to broker community disputes and animate the spirit of the troubled streets. The group would also provide suggestions to landlords and chambers of commerce to rehabilitate buildings and rooftops for alternative communities of artists. And gardens—rooftop gardens—and strategically plant more trees, whatever possible, and paint in quirky ways the homes of residents. The entire neighborhood.

The neighborhood itself would be the work of art. Just a *pinche* idea.

The Neighborhood Museum. This idea is, in fact, an extension of the last one. Every neighborhood would have a funky and exciting 24-hour museum for live art. It would perform multiple roles beyond presenting both traditional and contemporary art created by artists living in the 'hood. It would be a gathering place to discuss neighborhood politics and culture. Meet other neighbors, and host an active video, audio, and book library. There would be activities for the elderly and the youth, for LGBTQ, the newly arrived immigrants, and the homeless. Every neighborhood museum would also have a great art bar and café for all the local bohemians and eccentrics to conspire, play table games, and have some fun on a daily basis.

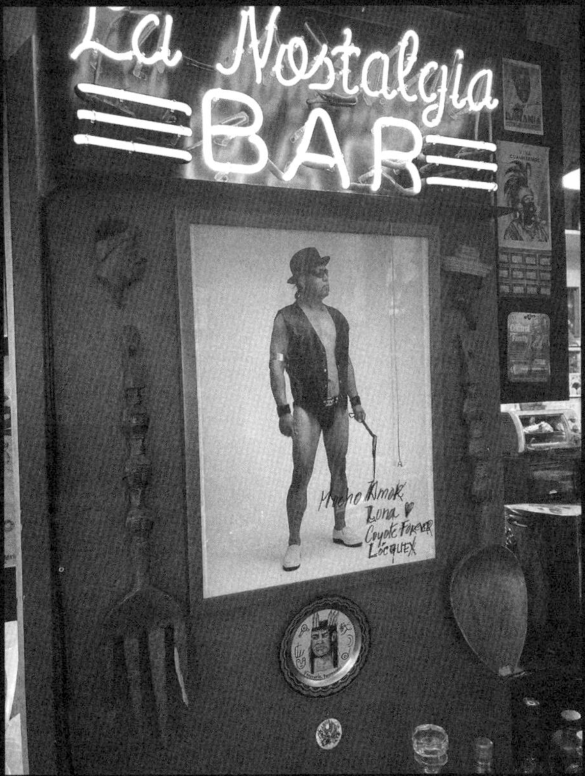

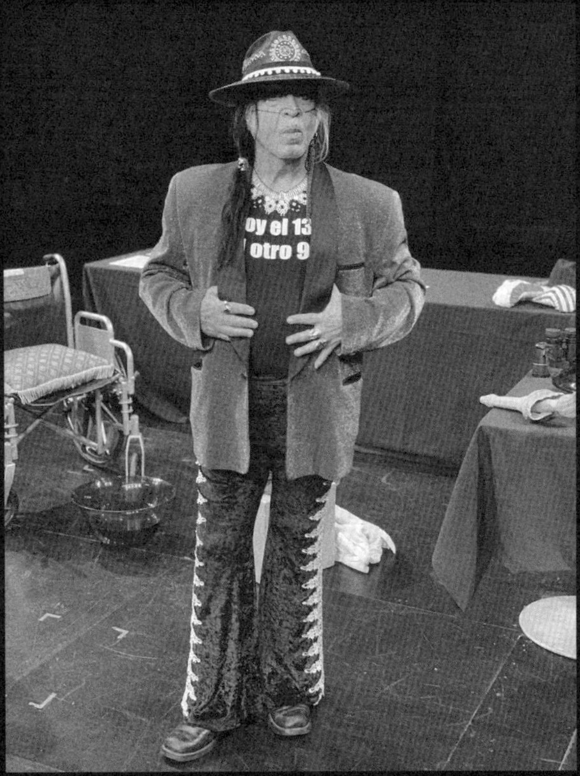

For these proposals to happen, we need to collaborate closely with curators.

I wish to share a letter I wrote to a young, independent curator inspired by the practice of my comrade Francesca Carol Rolla:

"I write to you from the balcony of my personal experience, 35 years of making live art across borders and collaborating with artists and curators from four continents. Yes, I am proud of my artistic practice. And exhausted: for 35 years I helped young rebel artists to fly, and today I can barely open my wings and they are full of insects.

"I write to you with total humility, as a strategic insider-outsider of the art world, appealing to your artistic vision and ethos. And I will. be. bold.

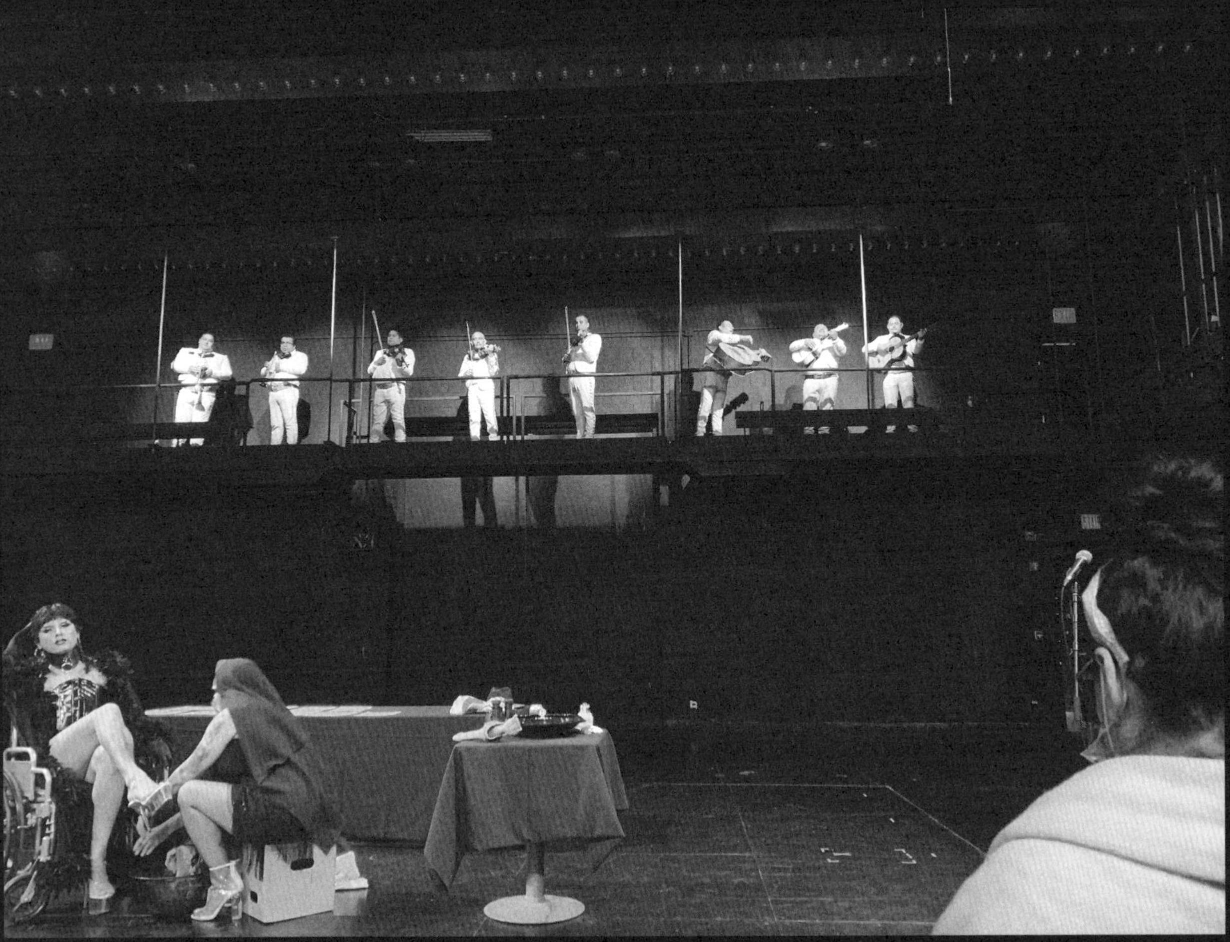

"Are you aware of your power? Do you realize that the life of the artist is in your hands? My dear, this undeserved power, given your age and lack of international experience, cannot be taken lightly. But you can prove yourself that you're worthy of the power that has been given to you by the big institution. I know, it's normal, of course, you want to rise up the ranks in the biggest sexiest art space, it is okay to dance with the devil. But you should try not to get burned. Remember, you are our broker, coyote, and Trojan horse. Don't just follow the latest trend. Follow your critical ideas, even when they go against fashion, money, and recognition. Fight ageism. Be an ambassador between generations. Guide your generation with the knowledge you acquire working with more experienced artists. We need you as much as you need us: we are your memory, you keep us current and visible.

"Listen to the artists and then challenge them to become a better version of themselves. In return, part of our job is to listen to you and challenge you, but please don't get angry when we talk back and question your decisions. *Desparte de rollo*.

"Distrust art magazines, distrust the art market. Don't let them manipulate you. They serve the interests of the commercial art world. You don't. Distrust academia. Find your own voice, be independently minded, always against the status quo, the lingua franca.

"Learn other languages. In the imaginary borderless world we wish to inhabit, it is necessary to be multilingual. Unfortunately, for reasons we all know, English has been the dominant language in the art world and we need to change this. Take a step out of the art world, engage in an ongoing dialogue with all kinds of people, activists, socially conscious scientists and eccentrics in your neighborhood. Have a few criminal friends. Ask the homeless what they think about art. Be prepared to wear multiple hats: cultural DJ, intellectual warrior, researcher, archivist, nurse, cook, hostess,, even chauffeur. They are all equally important. From sweeping the floor and cleaning the mess of the artist to persuading wealthy people and politicians to fund us. Cross that class border regularly, do it with humor. Don't worry, we will clean your mess, blood, and vomit as well. Be also our translator, interpreter, an *abogado defensor*, not our ventriloquist or circus impresario. Please don't treat us as the new specimen you have discovered. Or, if we are aging, as a forgotten artist you have rediscovered, treat us with utmost respect, as peers. We will treat you accordingly. Let's develop a new trust. Step outside of your zone of comfort. Perform with us. Take off your existential clothes. Become part of a live image, and in turn invite us to co-curate the project. Be tender to us. We need it to feel empowered because we're broken humans. We will reciprocate with radical tenderness and powerful art actions.

"Choose the right space to locate the project, a weird space. Create a general steam, build an eclectic community of difference, work horizontally, create your own map. Live outside of the centers, even if only part time. Travel south and learn how other cultures do it. You will be surprised and humbled. Create utopian projects, impossible projects, projects that defy the status quo.

Take us to faraway lands with you and then in reciprocity, we will host artists from faraway lands in our hometown.

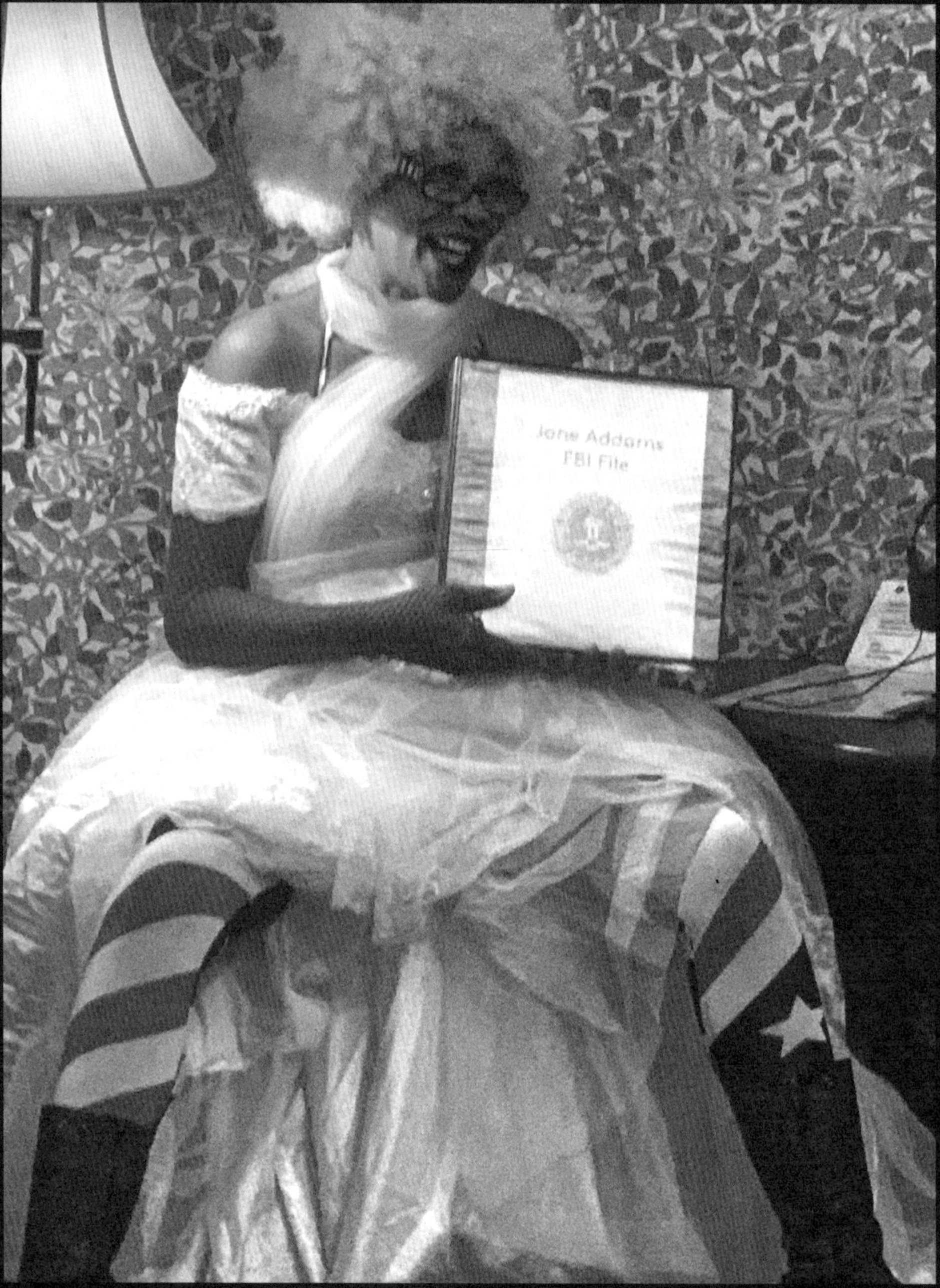

"Write. *Escribe. Todo los días*. Write daily. Writing is a militant act. Write your own script for life, write in dialogue with the artists you are working with. Through this dialogue, you will discover the true potential and possibility of the project. The project will end up being very different from what you originally conceived.

"When you commit to artists: please, I beg you, do not abandon them. It is a love commitment. It is now or never. It is every day and for the rest of your life. It is a lifetime commitment for both artists and curators. Finally, help me to be a better artist than I am. I expect you to look after me. As a curator, I expect you to cure my wounds and help me heal my broken bones because I often fall during the process. I might also get lost in the journey, and you have to help me find the way back to my inner island, *archipiélago,* or *barrio*. Will you feel tired after doing all this? Yes, most likely. It is the nature of the work. It's an impossible task and we are in the business of the impossible."

So maybe now in the terra nova of pandemia, it is the perfect time to set a new ethical groundwork. Here are La Pocha Nostra's new rules for today.

The borders between the old normal and the new uncertainty, between daily despair and hope, between the metropolis and the necropolis: I cross these borders every day.

Dear audience, the only difference between a madman and a performance artist is that the latter has an audience. So, thank you for not letting me go mad.

Psychomagic performance number 69: be a matriot not a patriot. Believe in people and land, not in government or corporations. Walk the walk, perform the performance.

Today's weather report: it's time for Anglo-America and Europe to be quiet, humble, and listen. Listen to nature and so-called people of color. It's your only possible redemption. Advice to a young, live artist. Work with the accident, dwell in the wound, open it, open more wounds on the street. But be hyper careful. The cops and the Proud Boys are out to get us.

Mystery: suddenly old museums have become antiracist, conveniently forgetting their track record of white supremacy? Is the CEO of Taco Bell truly a major Black Lives Matter supporter? Give me a billion breaks. I'll take my *chalupas* to go.

Dear art collector, isn't it time to politicize and retitle those racist and sexist paintings and sculptures in your private collection?

Postscript. Dear performance artist, if you cannot tour the world, tour your *pinche* neighborhood.

Ni pero.

A cruel journalist asked me last week, where are you going next GP? Let me think, an airport, a museum, or a hospital? Shit, I need my project coordinator to give me my existential itinerary. I had forgotten I was in lockdown.

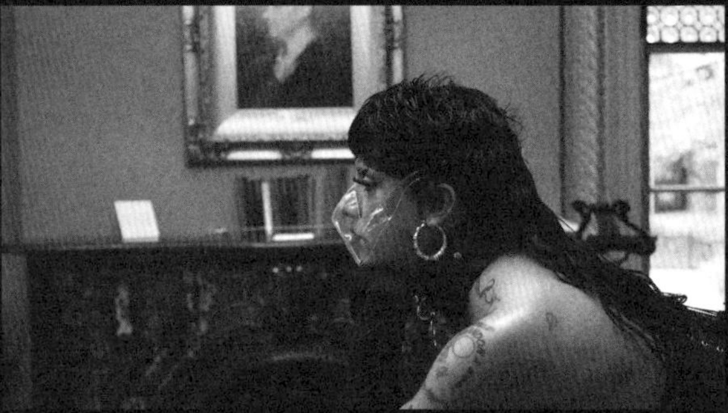

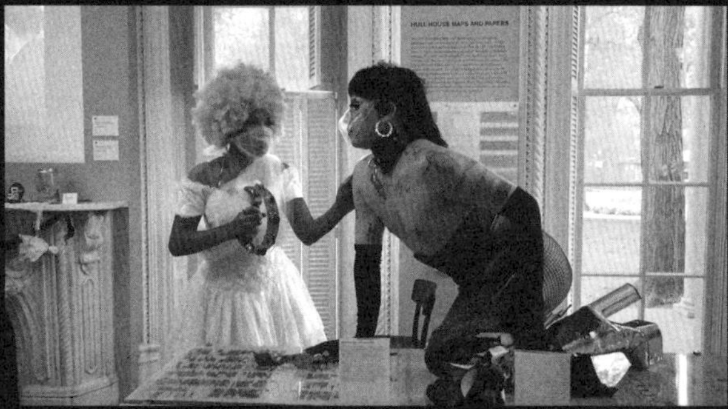

As performance artists, our relationship to the Art World (in capitals) has always been ambivalent and awkward from both sides, a macabre dance with lots of intermezzos and pauses. The art world loves to commodify and exhibit our freedom, our marginality, while we desire to access their funding and infrastructure. Sadly, our desires never truly align.

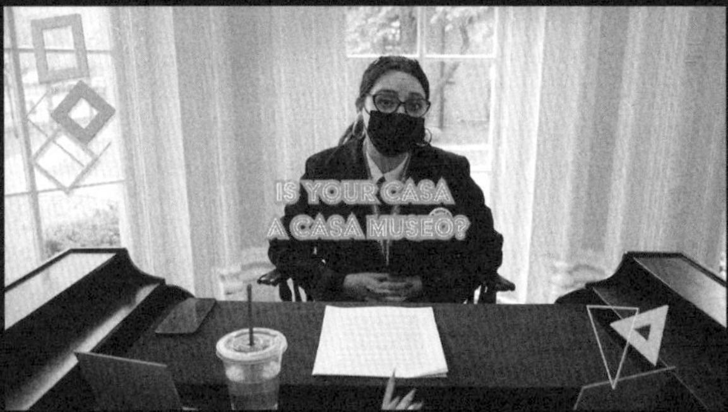

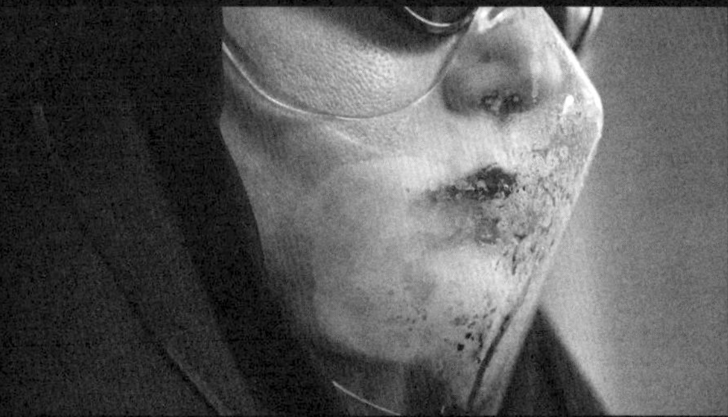

Yes, *The Artist Is Absent*. A Chicano tribute to Marina Abramović. Question: why are they absent? Maybe they are tired of working twelve hours a day for you.

Typical journalist question: why is performance art always shocking? My answer: shocking is war, police brutality, and human rights violations at the US-Mexico border. Shocking is the daily behavior of our politicians.

True, naming my antisocial behavior "art" has saved me from the jaws of the police, the Border Patrol, and the IRS. But I talk about art as critical thought and embodied theory, not as object or market. I talk about art as in uncomprising art practice, not as in the art world. The art world is full of compromises, humiliation rituals, complicated power negotiations. It takes a special skill to survive it. If you comply too much, you lose your voice, your sharp edges, your *culo*. You become someone else you dislike. One day, when you least expect it, they send you back to the margins where you wait and wait for a second chance that rarely comes. So, between being an art world darling, coolie, pronto, and being poor and bitter, I rather choose to be an uncompromising dandy, a *mariachi* with a big mouth, a performing contradiction, if you will.

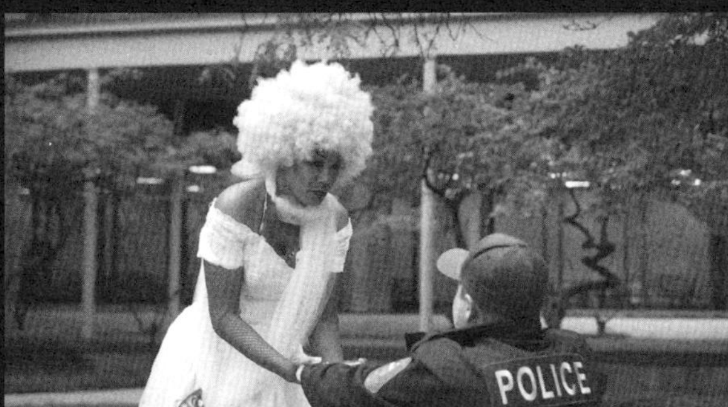

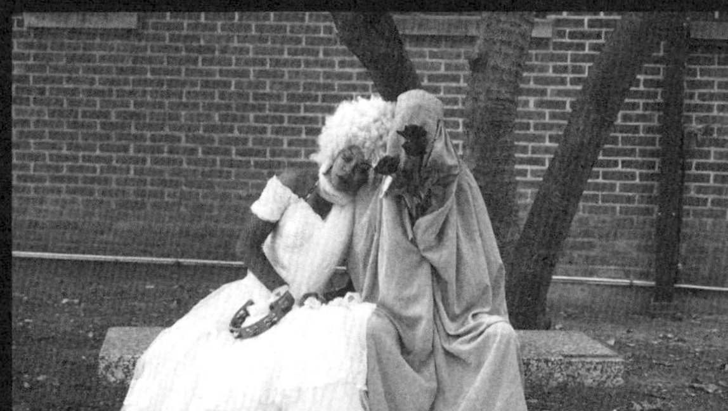

"Contradiction" is the name of my favorite lotion, and my job as a performance artist is to avoid simplistic definitions, trends, and adjectives and to remain as slippery and evanescent while I continue to ask irritating questions in original ways. What a bizarre job, and I get paid for it. Kind of. Merde. Merde! I am so moody tonight, I feel like an existential wolf that went to sleep in the Arctic Circle and woke up on the rooftop of a Manhattan skyscraper.

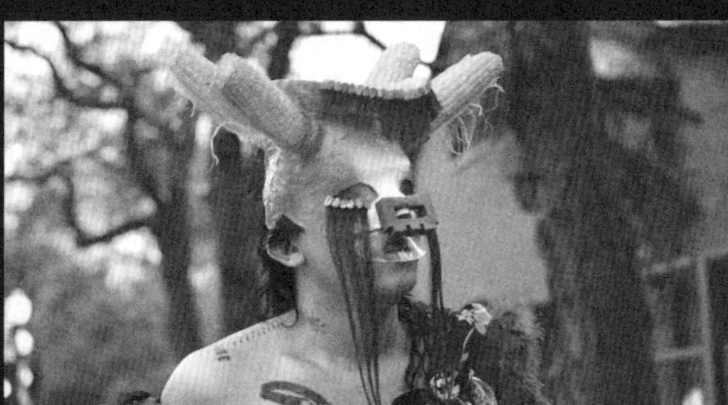

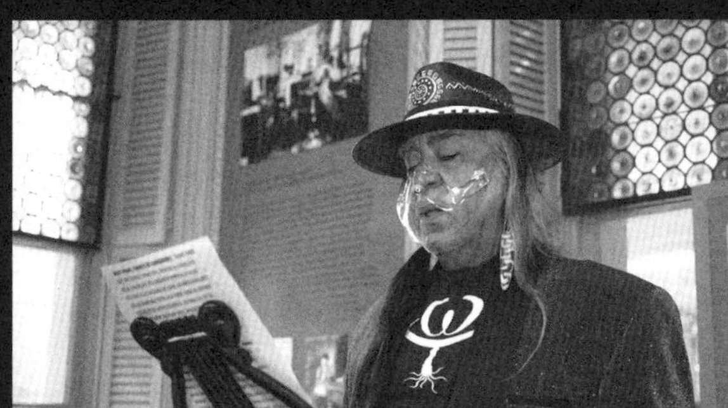

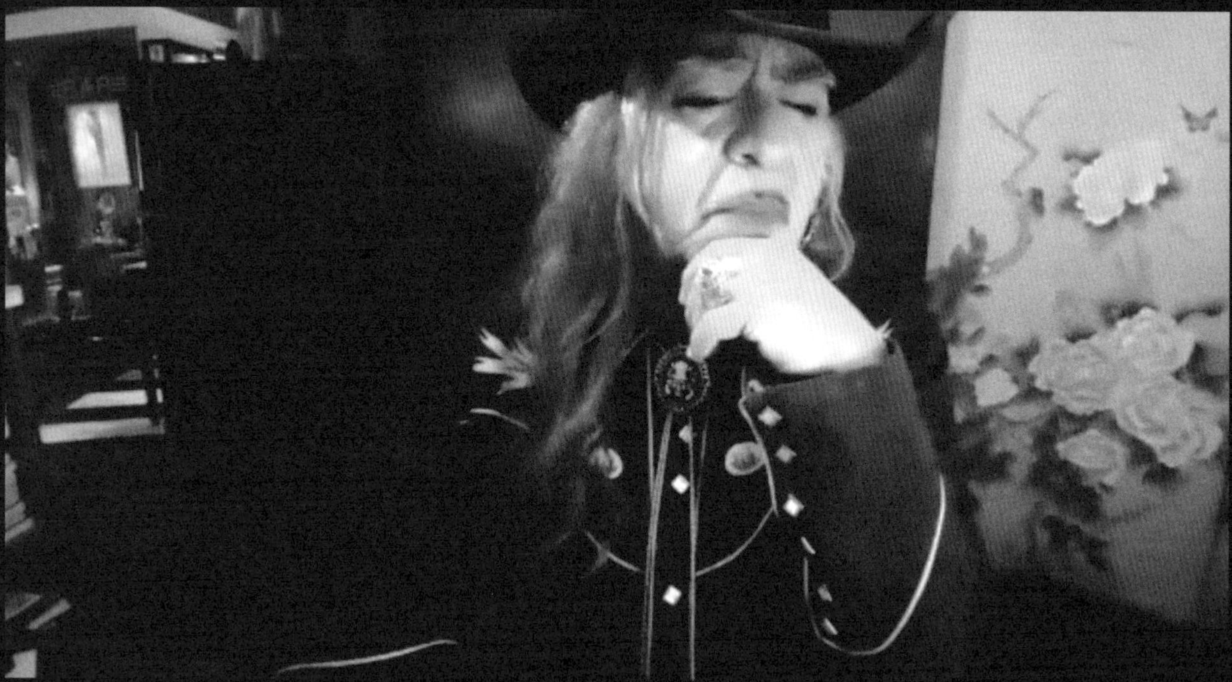

Finale. In the absence of political certainties and human contact, I have been dreaming a lot. I dream of an art world without superstars and mega exhibits about nothing or about something irrelevant. I dream of funding institutions who are race, gender, and class literate, who are truly, *truly* committed to social justice, the word of the month. I dream of museums and galleries as community think tanks and gathering spaces for cultural difference and deviant behavior, as eco, ethno, techno, trans-generational laboratories to envision a better *mañana*, spaces that look and feel like the world I wish to live in. I dream of neighborhood museums made out of adobe, *petate*, mud, tractor tires, found wood trash containers, imaginary architectures in high *rascuache*, proletarian-chic style. I dream of rooftop gardens with outdoor bars and tropical canopies, of amphitheaters performing punk operas, mariachi rock, poetry slams, 24 hours, 8 days a week. I dream of ritual performance spaces made out of stones and metal. High-tech native longhouses and dream circles around the bonfire of collective dreams where elders are telling stories and dirty jokes. I dream of a performance space that looks like my home, where everything is possible, and the call-out culture and the PC patrols are nowhere to be found. I dream of a world beyond the white avant-garde, way beyond the Western canon. A supernova of possibilities. And I invite you, dear foreigner in my performance country, to dream with me and send me your own letters, imagining a better art world or rather a myriad of art worlds coexisting in synergy with nature, radical imagination, and community. Your surrounding multiple communities. Do you have ideas to propose for a Museum of the Future?

(LOW MUSICAL STRING SOUNDS, CHANTING, BIRDCALL)

Photos: Nathan Keay, pp. 35, 36, 37; Courtesy of Guillermo Gómez-Peña, pp. 37, 39; Jill Sterrett, pp. 39, 40, 42.

Images of La Pocha Nostra's activation of *Casa Museo* at the Jane Addams Hull-House Museum are taken from a video produced by Robert Chase Heishman and Robert Salazar, and Public Media Institute's film of the broadcast of "An Open Letter to the Museums of the Future." The following members of La Pocha Nostra performed in Chicago: Guillermo Gómez-Peña, Emma Tramposch, Balitrónica, and Aranza Cortez, with performance assistants Amaya, MahNu, Celeste, Carissa Lee Pinckney, and Robin LaVerne Wilson (aka Dragonfly).

Note to the Reader

A project as complex as *Toward Common Cause* would naturally give rise to an equally complex publication that attempts to document the scope of its activities and honor the multiple partnerships and voices that contributed to its realization. The book is anchored by four thematic essays. These in turn are augumented by annotations (placed in red alongside the main text) and short texts detailing the contributions of partner venues (placed in the outer columns). The annotations, which are preceded by the contributor's initials (see the key on this page), offer differing perspectives on points made in the anchor essay. The anchor texts are accompanied by shorter texts, including discussions among participants relating to the chapter's theme, as well as case studies elaborating the collaborations between artists and partner organizations. Three focused topical texts appear between the longer thematic chapters. The backmatter includes material not typically included in an exhibition catalogue, such as a timeline of the planning process, exhibition budgets, and the metrics that guided outreach to community partners.

Annotators

AB Alyssa Brubaker, former Exhibitions Manager, Logan Center for the Arts

DF Daysi Funes, Executive Director, Centro Romero

DR Dieter Roelstraete, Curator, Neubauer Collegium for Culture and Society, The University of Chicago

ET Emma Tramposch, Executive Director and Curator, Living Archives, La Pocha Nostra

FC Francesca Colussi, conference participant, "Reshaping the Collectible: Learning through Change," Tate Britain, September 16, 2022

HR Heidi Reitmaier, Executive Director, Myseum of Toronto

IF Isis Ferguson, Senior Director of Engagement and Partnerships, Arts + Public Life

JdL Jason de León, Professor of Anthropology and Chicana/o Studies, University of California, Los Angeles, MacArthur Fellow 2017

JG Juan Griego, conference participant, "Reshaping the Collectible: Learning through Change," Tate Britain, September 16, 2022

JJ Jyotsna Jagai, Program Officer, MacArthur Fellows Program

JS Jill Sterrett, *Art in Pursuit of Common Cause* co-editor

JTG Jay T. Goodwin, Senior Program Officer, MacArthur Fellows Program

JW Jiahe Wang, University of Chicago student

KP Krista Pospisil, Senior Program Officer, MacArthur Fellows Program

LF Lori Fogarty, Director and CEO, Oakland Museum of California

LS Laura Scholl, Associate Director, MacArthur Fellows Program

LY Laura Young, Associate, Evaluation and Learning, MacArthur Foundation

MJ Maggie Jensen, artist, *Art in Pursuit of Common Cause* managing editor

NP Nancy Proctor, Chief Strategy Officer and founding Executive Director, The Peale

NYT "Genius at Work: 29 MacArthur Fellows Show Their Art in Chicago," *New York Times*, July 14, 2021

PD Paul Durica, former Director of Exhibitions, The Newberry

PL Pip Laurenson, Professor of Art History, University College London

SB Sanchita Balachandran, conference participant, "Reshaping the Collectible: Learning through Change," Tate Britain, September 16, 2022

"Water, Water Everywhere?" Interdisciplinary course offered through the Pozen Family Center for Human Rights, The University of Chicago, in conjunction with *Toward Common Cause*, fall 2021

WE Wendy Ewald, *Toward Common Cause* artist, MacArthur Fellow 1992

ZC Zachary Cahill, Director of Programs and Fellowship, Gray Center for Arts and Inquiry, The University of Chicago

Uncertainty

Our recent history has been defined by a state of uncertainty. *Toward Common Cause* explored the generative potential of uncertainty by embracing collective engagement to minimize the sway of institutional authority, and to facilitate the participation of venues of varying sizes, types, and budgets.

We are living in the future
I'll tell you how I know
I read it in the paper
Fifteen years ago.
We're all driving rocket ships
And talking with our minds.
And wearing turquoise jewelry
And standing in soup lines.
We are standing in soup lines.

"Living in the Future,"
John Prine

All Flourishing Is Mutual

Abigail Winograd[1]

I know I am not the only one to feel that we are currently living outside of time or that time as we understood it at the end of the 2010s no longer exists. I know this because of the frequency with which people in Zoom rooms preface apologies about lateness or rudeness or forgetfulness with a comment about how time feels stretched or collapsed or just plainly strange "since the pandemic." We seem to have collectively decided to blame the wonkiness of our present on this singular event, which inarguably shook to its very bedrock our understanding of the sturdiness of the world humanity had created. I am often tempted to reach out from my square to comment that we cannot just blame COVID for pushing us through the looking glass. COVID was the perfect vector, painful and bad pun intended, to show us that the certainty we felt about our relationship to the natural world (mastered), the global economy (the triumph of capitalism and prosperity), and history (progressively correcting the wrongs of the past) was a dangerous illusion. By the beginning of 2021, it was clear that environmental catastrophe was here, democracy was under attack, and the neoliberal promise of endless growth was a fallacy. We have all had an epiphanic moment, or two, in the past several years. We found ourselves living in the future, but it was not what we had imagined.

There are those among us who saw this coming, who tried to warn us that the end was nigh. In 2013, the Potawatomi biologist Robin Wall Kimmerer published *Braiding Sweetgrass*, a reflection on the increasingly fragile and disordered state of the natural world, citing the Western notions of private property, individualism, and infinite growth as destructive paradigms driving the planet inexorably toward climate catastrophe. Kimmerer demonstrated that humanity's belief in the possibility of ecological control was an illusion. Indeed, she argued, Western science and our faith in it were forestalling the realization that nature had not slipped our grasp but that we had never been in control of it in the first place. She offered indigenous models of kinship and land stewardship that center mutual aid, one of the buzzwords of 2020, as a potential solution to our current predicament. In 2015, the anthropologist Anna Lowenhaupt Tsing published *The Mushroom at the End of the World: On the Possibility of Life in Captalist Ruins*. She used the matsutake, a rare and highly prized mushroom that only grows in forests disturbed by human intervention, to frame the increasing precarity of the environment and the global economy. Along the way, she explored the tyranny of the notion of progress and called into question the power of individual actors to affect their own circumstances. In 2019, Shoshana Zuboff warned that our democracies and freedoms were imperiled by the sacrifice of privacy to the gods of the internet in *The Age of Surveillance*

Capitalism: The Fight for a Human Future at the New Frontier of Power. Most recently, archaeologist David Wengrow and anthropologist David Graeber argued that virtually everything we have ever learned about history is wrong. *The Dawn of Everything: A New History of Humanity*, published in 2021, explores the dangerous political consequences of a worldview that takes inequity and competition as self-evident truths of human nature. Collectively, these books reveal the inability of our existing intellectual frameworks to account for the social, political, and ecological challenges of the moment.[2]

The inadequacy of existing models had been on my mind for some time when, in late 2018, I returned to Chicago after several years of living abroad, where I had watched from a distance as the United States descended into a kind of madness. The accepted rules of engagement had dissolved, and we were entering a social and political era in which acceptable speech, behavior, and discourse were being redefined. It felt, naively so in retrospect given what was to come, like a moment of extreme urgency. It was at this moment that I received a call from Donny Meyer, a program officer in the MacArthur Fellows Program inviting me to propose an exhibition project to commemorate the fortieth anniversary of the program. The prompt was broad: deliver a concept and a list of artists that the Fellows Program could share with foundation leadership for consideration. A goal of the Fellows Program is to elevate awareness of extraordinarily creative individuals, and the goal of the exhibition should center that value as well. The exhibition also needed to connect to the history and particularities of Chicago, MacArthur's home. Ideally, the project would leave a legacy consonant with the organization's stated commitment "to building a more just, verdant, and peaceful world." There was, at that time, no venue for the exhibition but a hope that the project would be easily accessible to broad audiences. I accepted immediately without asking questions. This was, after all, an opportunity to work with some of the most important living artists but also a chance to activate the interdisciplinarity of the Fellows Program itself, to probe the intersections of art, history, science, etc., and to experiment with institutional and exhibition frameworks. The seeds for *Toward Common Cause* were thus planted.

HR: Throughout history, creative practitioners have led conversations about the world—they create moments, spaces, and works in which audiences can pause, reflect, and question. It doesn't matter if you leave a cultural space knowing the name of an artist or an artwork. If you leave and look at the world differently, engage in a conversation with a new level of personal awareness, and if your curiosity and humanity are heightened, then the artwork has done its job. It sounds utopian, but it happens.

Artists can also be prognosticators. One of the central conceits of *Toward Common Cause* is that the group of artists invited to participate had been pointing to our societal fault lines, offering speculative proposals about how to build community, transform neighborhoods, build coalitions, and heal the earth, long before things began to visibly fall apart. These oracular figures were proposing pathways to different futures. With this in mind, I was compelled to offer a proposal that asked: What is the role of art and museums in such moments of political, social, economic, and environmental exigency?

Over a year into planning what would become *Toward Common Cause*, the global pandemic and associated lockdown had us scrambling to figure out how to proceed in the face of such unpredictability. Artists reconsidered their projects. We considered postponing. Three months into lockdown and the upending of our collective reality, our team wanted to open a space for discussion and reflection for the participating artists. So, on May 28, 2020, I sat in a virtual room with more than a dozen MacArthur Fellows. Reaching out from our own isolation, we found ourselves together a mere three days after George Floyd's murder. The ensuing protests were reminiscent of those that shook the United States in the summer of 1967 and swept the globe in 1968. We were all stunned by the twin realities of the pandemic and the explosion of popular anger in the streets. We shared our sadness, frustrations, fears, and questions and discussed how we might respond individually and as a collective. On that day and every day since, I marvel at the enormity of the moment in which we found ourselves. Following an introspective silence, it was An-My Lê who voiced the question with which we were all preoccupied: What is the value of what we do at a time like this?

Lê's question struck me for several reasons. First, it was precisely that question that had prompted the exhibition concept in the first place. Its resonance was only reinforced by the crises we, and the world, now faced together. Second, the assembled artists were, to a person, consumed by the same question. Finally, it reminded me of a post-it note sitting on my desk on which I had scribbled a passage from *The Mushroom at the End of the World* some time in the summer of 2019:

> Precarity is the condition of being vulnerable to others. Unpredictable encounters transform us; we are not in control, even of ourselves. Unable to rely on a stable structure of community, we are thrown into shifting assemblages, which remake us as well as our others. We can't rely on the status quo; everything is in flux, including our ability to survive. Thinking through precarity changes social analysis. A precarious world is a world without teleology. Indeterminacy, the unplanned nature of time, is frightening, but thinking through precarity makes it evident that indeterminacy also makes life possible.[3]

It was clear that the art world as it existed was not equipped to accommodate the challenges we faced. Yet I was surrounded by a group of artists who had raised questions about structural inequity, class, race, environment, and democracy for decades. We wondered if the art world as we knew it would be forever changed by the events we were witnessing. I think we were trying to envision, to borrow a turn of phrase from my co-editor of this volume, how to build a better mousetrap.

I first met Lê in her studio in Brooklyn in the fall of 2018. Our discussions focused on her ongoing series *Silent General* (2015–), an epic examination of the US present that began as a road trip-cum-artistic journey in 2015, prompted by the murder of nine African American worshippers at the Emanuel African Methodist Episcopal Church in Charleston, South Carolina (Scenes #36). In 2017, Lê was in Louisiana photographing historical reenactments of Civil War battles restaged for the film *Free State of Jones*. By happenstance, she found herself in New Orleans just in time to witness the dismantling of the monument to P. G. T. Beauregard, the Louisiana-born Confederate general who ordered the first shots fired at Fort Sumter (launching the Civil War in April 1861). The removal of this and three other Confederate monuments had been mandated by a city council resolution passed in 2015. When Lê turned her lens to the Beauregard monument's removal, the country had already been in turmoil for some time. After Donald Trump's election to the US presidency, and just before the white supremacist rally in Charlottesville that resulted in the death of one antiracist protester, the controversy in New Orleans reflected the divisiveness and anger of the moment. The opening suite of Lê's photo project *Silent General* powerfully captures the tensions engendered by competing visions of Americanness and foreshadows the turmoil to come.[4]

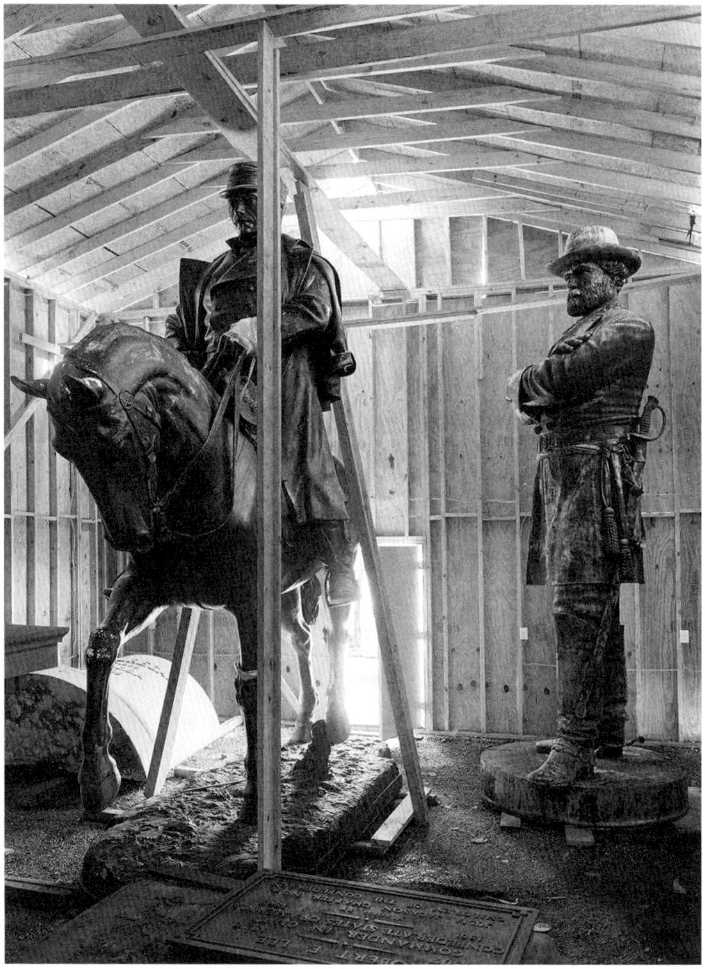

An-My Lê's *Fragment VI: General Robert E. Lee and P. G. T. Beauregard Monuments, Homeland Security Storage, New Orleans, Louisiana*, from the series *Silent General*. Courtesy of the artist and Marian Goodman Gallery

Of all the images in *Silent General*, it was *Fragment II: Restoration of J. M. W. Turner's Port Ruysdael, Yale Center for British Art, New Haven, Connecticut* that struck a particular chord with me. In the photograph, Turner's seascape is pictured in a conservation studio among other paintings, stripped of its frame and propped on a conservator's easel. The tempest and the single seafaring vessel at the center of Turner's canvas evoked for me the institutional crisis consuming museums. Amidst calls for systemic change, museums were struggling to declare and stand up for antiracist principles. The quiet, behind-the-scenes moment captured in Lê's photograph exposed the fragility of museums themselves and their struggle to retain relevance and moral authority in the thick of a storm.

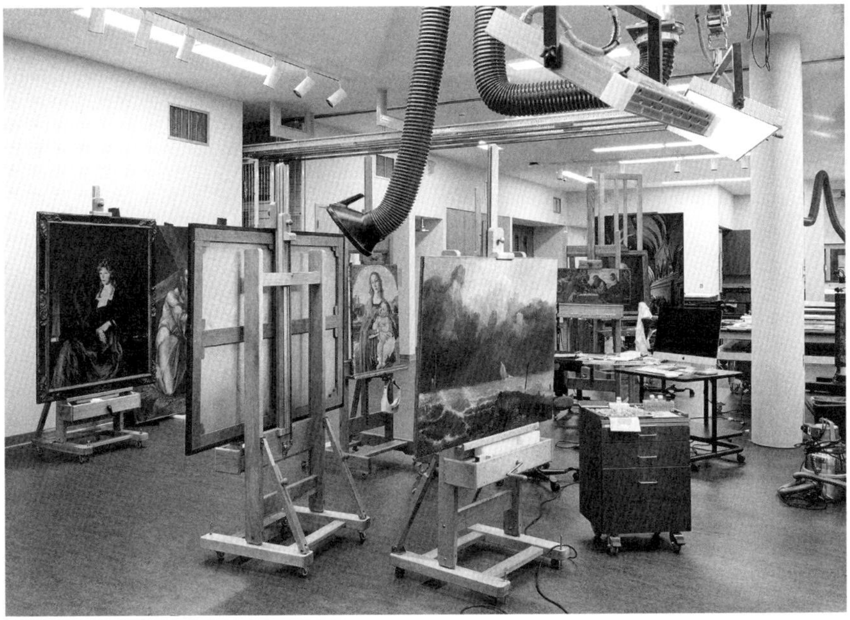

An-My Lê's *Fragment II: Restoration of J. M. W. Turner's Port Ruysdael, Yale Center for British Art, New Haven, Connecticut*, from the series *Silent General*. Courtesy of the artist and Marian Goodman Gallery

Silent General takes its title and structural inspiration from Walt Whitman's *Specimen Days and Collect* (1882). Whitman's final work of nonfiction, *Specimen Days* is a loose, stream-of-consciousness meditation on the poet's life, his experiences during the Civil War, and his feelings about the United States. When asked to describe the book, Whitman called it "a mélange of loafing, looking, hobbling, sitting, traveling—a little thinking thrown in for salt, but very little— . . . Wild and free and somewhat acrid—indeed more like cedarplums than you might guess at first glance."[5] Lê's project, likewise composed of a series of fragments, each reflecting on what it means to live in the United States now, borrows Whitman's architecture, his reverence for quiet moments and minute detail, the documentary impulse, and his tendency to wander. *Specimen Days* was a reaction to, and reflection upon, the political crises of the 1850s, that is, widespread corruption, a growing wealth gap, rising anti-immigrant sentiment, and fragmentation of the political system. (One cannot help but notice the striking similarities to present conditions.) The political theorist Jason Frank asserts that Whitman's work contains deep relevance to contemporary democratic theory because of his insistence on the aesthetic dimension of politics and its role in engendering radical democracy. "For Whitman," he writes, "the popular commitment to democracy requires an aesthetic evaluation, and he aimed to enact the required reconfiguration of popular sensibility through the poetic depiction of the people as themselves a sublimely poetic, world-making power. . . . Through his poetry, Whitman claimed to sing the multitudinous diversity of the vox populi back to the people themselves, thereby enhancing their latent poetic capacity and aesthetically enabling a radical democratic politics of collective revision."[6] If Whitman was right, and I believe he was, this assessment explains much about the visceral responses to a variety of sociopolitical shifts currently upending a visual landscape and attendant power structure that have been in place since times seemingly immemorial.

ZC: The July 2021 opening of the exhibition *Toward Common Cause* was an emergence. An emergence out of the chaos of the Trump years, an emergence out of sequestered life in the wake of the spring 2021 Biden administration vaccine rollout, an emergence into a new set of practices that worked to redress systemic and institutional racism through a lens of social justice–based art. We must continue thinking through notions of opening and emergence in relation to exhibition-making, and prevent the foreclosure of the promise of socially engaged art within our institutions.

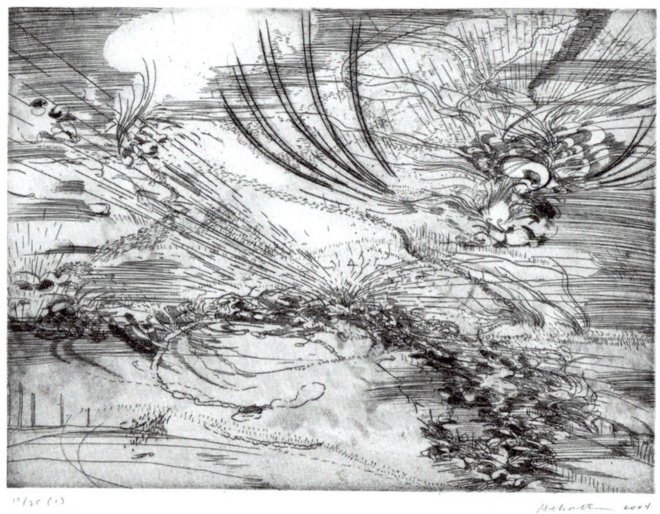

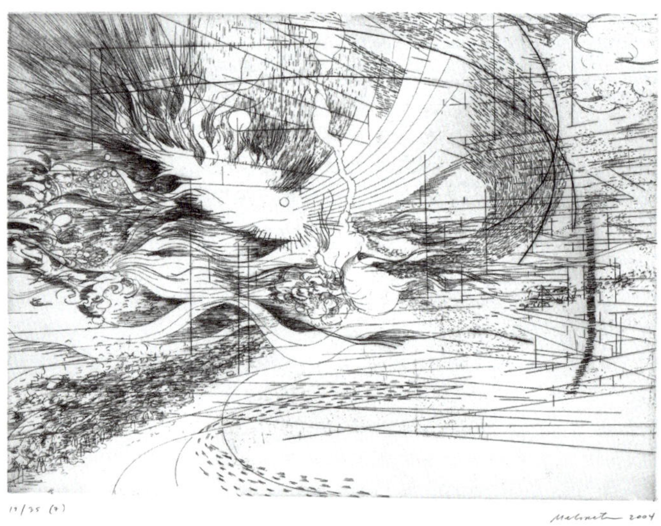

Two works in Julie Mehretu's *Landscape Allegories*, a suite of seven copper-plate etchings shown at the Smart Museum of Art. Courtesy of the artist and Marian Goodman Gallery

Cultural workers are often called upon to defend the value of art. This necessity always strikes me as odd because it is evident that art does matter. This becomes most clear in moments of crisis when artworks that hide in plain sight become sites of controversy. One need look no further than protests in Charlottesville over the removal of Confederate monuments or the events of the iconoclastic summer of 2020 to see how visual art is a battleground for definition. There were some spectacular examples that summer: Jefferson Davis, president of the Confederacy, was dragged off his pedestal in Richmond, Virginia; the seventeenth-century slave trader Edward Colston was dislodged from his plinth and rolled into Bristol Harbor in England; King Leopold II of Belgium, founder and brutal overlord of the Congo Free State, vacated a public square in Antwerp after his enthroned likeness was set on fire in the middle of the night during protests against Floyd's murder. Monuments and objects become targets of protest because we have invested them and the spaces they inhabit with meaning.

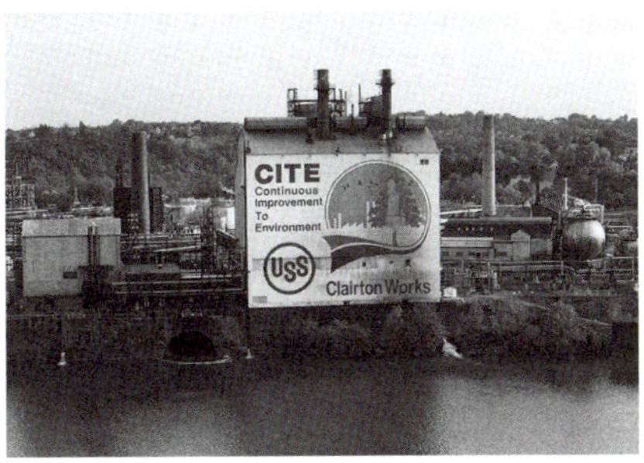

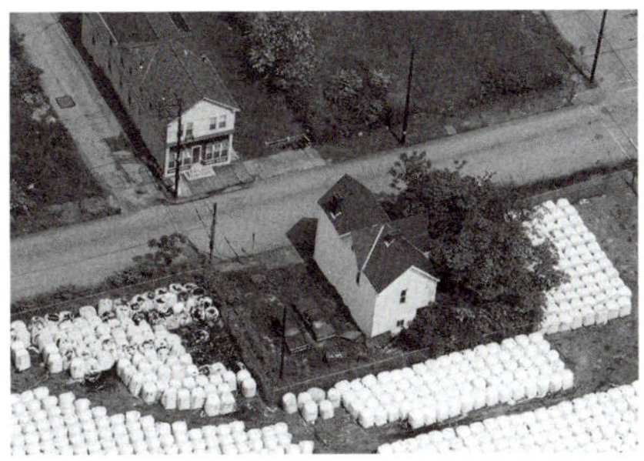

LaToya Ruby Frazier's *United States Steel Clairton Coke Works, C.I.T.E. and Monongahela River* and *The Bunn Family Home on Ninth Street*. Courtesy of the artist and Gladstone Gallery

JdL: I've always been interested in finding ways to give people the tools to tell their own stories, relinquishing control as gatekeeper. The visual is accessible because it transcends language barriers.

Exhibition-making is storytelling, a three-dimensional narrative built of objects. The proposal I delivered to the MacArthur Foundation in 2018 leaned on two theoretical texts: Lewis Hyde's *Common as Air: Revolution, Art, and Ownership* and Stefano Harney and Fred Moten's *The Undercommons: Fugitive Planning & Black Study*.[7] *Common as Air* argues for the need to protect the cultural commons against its steady and continued enclosure. Hyde's history notes that, the literal timbre of that which is "held in common" notwithstanding, resources such as air, land, water—and, crucially, for my understanding, *art and culture*—are not always "free," that is, *freely available*: all commons involve obligations and are, to some extent, exclusionary. For the purposes of our exhibition, this notion of a precarious commons made an ideal lens through which to explore the current sociopolitical moment, in which questions of inclusion, exclusion, ownership, and rights of access are constantly being challenged and redefined across a wide range of human endeavor.

In their aptly titled and hugely influential pamphlet *The Undercommons*, Moten and Harney describe the myriad ways in which the commons are continuously besieged. Their point is a critical injunction to vigilance at a moment in time when our understanding about what human beings share (culture, values, rights, duties) is being undermined by new barriers erected

The David and Alfred Smart Museum of Art
The University of Chicago
5550 S. Greenwood Ave.
Chicago, IL 60637

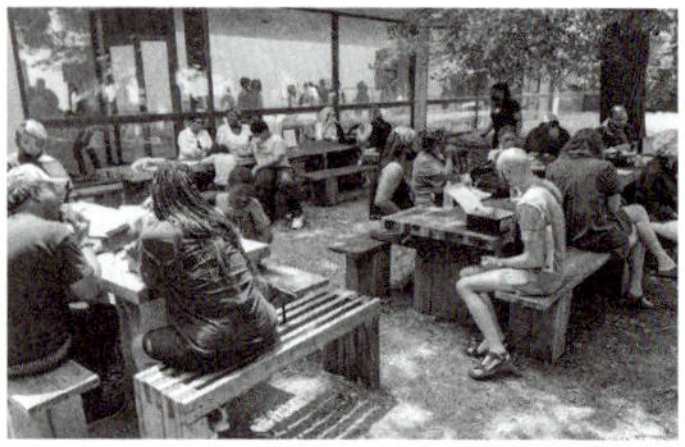

The installation at the Smart, on display from July through December 2021, provided the most complete overview of *Toward Common Cause*'s themes and goals. It opened with Nicole Eisenman's tragicomic commentary on humanity's tendency to fumble its way into disaster, and concluded with Toba Khedoori's vast canvases exploring the art-historical premise of landscape as a social and political construct. Both were perfect vehicles for considering one's relationship to the power structures and social inequities highlighted by the constellation of projects on view (Scenes #20, #11).

Toward Common Cause was conceived in a moment of transformative potential at the Smart. Alison Gass, who served as director from 2017 to 2019, fueled bold possibilities for the museum and its role in public and academic engagement. The Smart's Public Practice team, led by Michael Christiano, had for years been doing productive work with the Chicago Housing Authority's Summer Youth Program. The team brought this experience to the collaboration between Njideka Akunyili Crosby, the Smart's Teen Program, and the CHA to create outdoor murals wrapping the sides of two housing high-rises (the Minnie Riperton Apartments and the National Public Housing Museum) (Scenes #8, #14).

Many consequential partnerships were realized between artists and UChi-

(continued on opposite page)

to enclose those very rights once considered universal. The authors make the case for the possibility of resistance within the confines of an increasingly corporatized scholarly universe. It follows that art can play a crucial role in this call to vigilance, precisely because of its universalist appeal as a platform for the exchange of values and ideals. It seems evident that these questions are also pertinent to a critical appraisal of museums and the contemporary art world as a whole. Taken together, Hyde's history and Moten and Harney's blueprint for acts of clandestine opposition provided an intellectual framework for an exhibition that sought to explore the role of art as a vital social resource.

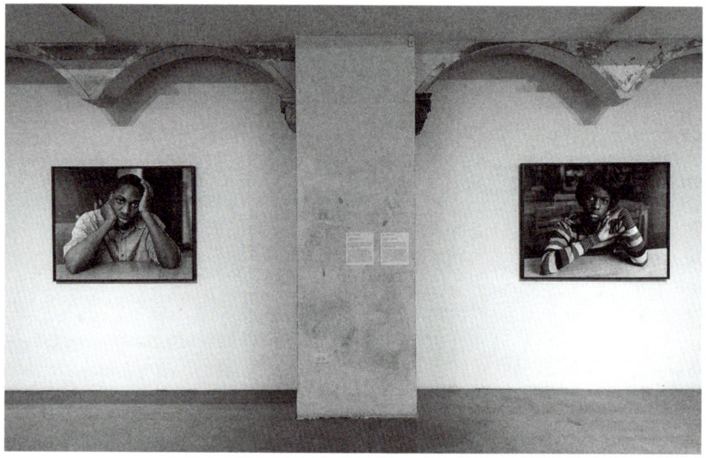

Dawoud Bey's large chromogenic prints *Steven, Kenwood Academy High School* and *Theresa, South Shore High School* from the artist's *The Chicago Project*. Both works were commissioned by the Smart Museum and were included in *Toward Common Cause*'s presentation at the Stony Island Arts Bank. Photo: Nathan Keay

Likewise, Chicago and its local art history were critical points of departure. *Toward Common Cause* paid homage to the city's status as the capital of community-based art in the United States. The activation of art on the part of its marginalized communities is a tradition that stretches back to the 1940s. Social practice, as a recognizable movement, emerged in the 1980s and was fostered by a combination of factors—cultural (a wealth of art schools), social/political (the ethnic diversity of the city), and economic factors (working-class roots)—unique to Chicago.[8] In a city as segregated as Chicago, access to art is concentrated in predominantly white and affluent communities.[9] Lowering the barriers of access to art became a central tenet of the exhibition, and meant prioritizing free venues located in areas outside the circuit of traditional art audiences.

ZC: Almost thirty years after Mary Jane Jacob's groundbreaking exhibition *Culture in Action* in Chicago, *Toward Common Cause* rethought notions of site and took up the mantle of Jacob's curatorial methodology and enlivened and expanded on its legacy.

The list of artists to be included in *Toward Common Cause* ultimately comprised twenty-nine MacArthur Fellows. All have worked in a manner that can be described as socially engaged, though the project was rooted in the premise that all art is a form of social practice. The selections encompassed a broad spectrum of media, from artists working in painting and photography, like Kerry James Marshall, Nicole Eisenman, and Carrie Mae Weems, to those who produce community-based social sculpture, such as Rick Lowe, Fazal Sheikh, and Wendy Ewald.

Each venue of *Toward Common Cause* and its patchwork of installations across the city functioned as part of a whole story. Many of the artists' works appeared in multiple venues. However, each individual display had its own internal coherence, an issue or question at its center. The most complete overview of the exhibition appeared at the Smart Museum of Art. The constellation of objects there considered questions of natural and built environments. They engaged the scourge of environmental racism and its disproportionate impact on communities of color in both urban and rural areas. The artists and artworks considered how race and class shape our rural and urban spaces and also took up art-historical questions about the history of landscape photography and painting. Together, these works questioned embedded power structures and social inequities that plague contemporary society, a reality thrown into stark relief by the global pandemic. Together, they called for a critical interrogation of the purported neutrality of landscape in the history of art.

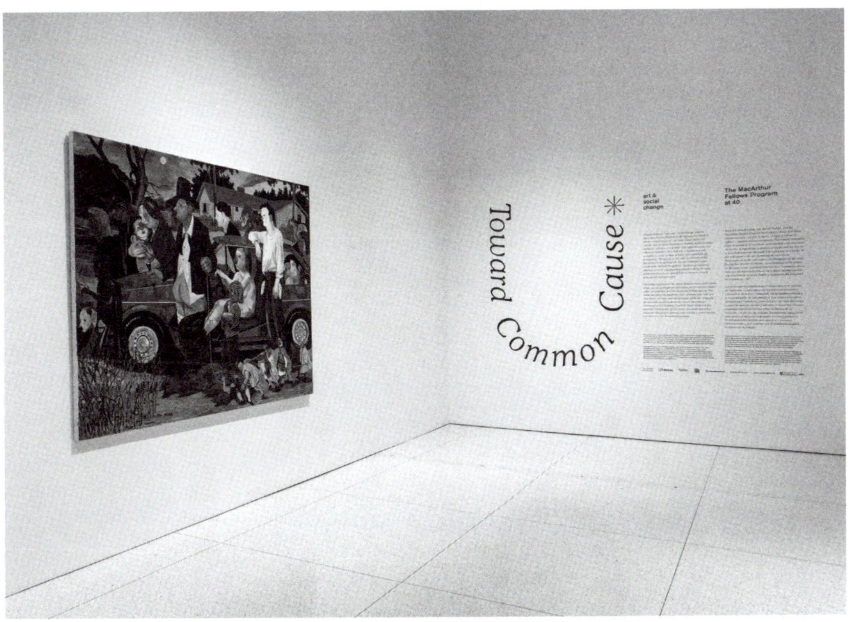

Nicole Eisenman's *The Triumph of Poverty* greets visitors to the Smart as they enter the first gallery. Photo: Michael Tropea

DR: Eisenman's painting contains another art-historical reference (bottom right corner) to a near-contemporary of Holbein, namely Pieter Bruegel the Elder's *Blind Leading the Blind* (1568).

The exhibition opened with *The Triumph of Poverty*, Nicole Eisenman's tragicomic commentary on wealth and poverty, painted in the wake of the 2008 financial collapse (Scenes #20). Based on Hans Holbein the Younger's work of the same name, Eisenman's painting depicts a motley human assemblage following a rich man, a bedraggled figure dressed in a wrinkled tuxedo and drooping top hat, his tie undone and pants around his ankles. Having lost his trousers, we can see that the rich man is also the ass-backwards man. He holds a flashlight to illuminate the way forward, but it is turned upward toward the night sky, rendering him as blind as the gaggle of blind men at his feet, adding a link in the chain of the proverbial blind-leading-the-blind. Eisenman's work is a reminder of the circular nature

cago academic departments, centers, and schools during *Toward Common Cause*. The Gray Center for Arts and Inquiry supported Iñigo Manglano-Ovalle and the making of sculpture in his *Well* series that became a site for gathering, conversation, and reflection on water in the lobby of the Smart Museum (Scenes #26). As a fellow of the Neubauer Collegium for Culture and Society, Rick Lowe embarked on *Black Wall Street Journey* to document the actions of innovative people who have contributed to making Chicago a hub of Black prosperity (Scenes #22). Lowe's research included partnerships with the Mansueto Institute for Urban Innovation and the university's Department of Sociology. The Harris School of Public Policy was a program partner for Mel Chin's *Chicago Fundred Initiative: A Bill for IL*. As part of this partnership, Mona Hanna-Attisha's first-hand account of the Flint water crisis, *What the Eyes Don't See: A Story of Crisis, Resistance, and Hope in an American City*, was selected as the Harris Common Read for returning students and faculty in the 2020-21 academic year.

Finally, it was the Smart team that made possible the mounting of *Toward Common Cause* around the city of Chicago. Thinking outside the walls of a museum was what architect Edward Larrabee Barnes had in mind when he envisioned an Arts Quad on the northern edge of the university in the late 1960s. The Smart Museum sits, to this day, at the heart of this arts nexus alongside Court Theater and across Cochrane Courtyard from the Department of Art History. Since opening its doors in 1974, the Smart has remained free and open to students and the public. Its location, reputation, and accessibility are but a few of the qualities that made the museum an ideal hub for *Toward Common Cause*.

Photo: Spencer Bibbs

Museum of Contemporary Photography
Columbia College Chicago
600 S. Michigan Ave.
Chicago, IL 60605

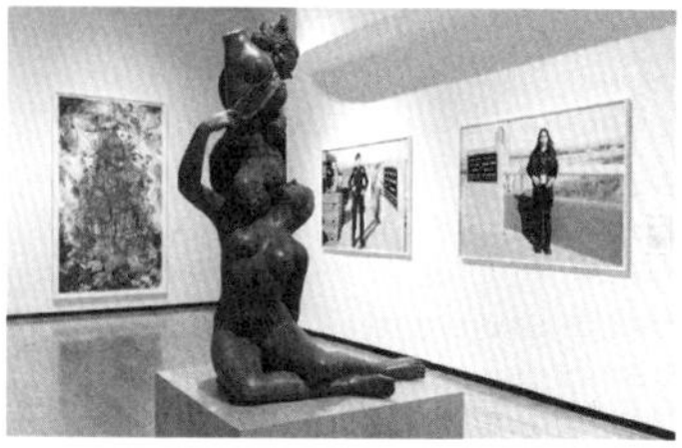

Founded in 1976 as the successor to the Chicago Center for Contemporary Photography, the Museum of Contemporary Photography is an academic museum focused on emerging artistic practices in Chicago and the world. The museum is dedicated to generating ideas that provoke dialogue among students, artists, and diverse communities through exhibitions and programming. MoCP's mission is to "cultivate a deeper understanding of the artistic, cultural, and political roles of photography in our world today."

In the years leading up to *Toward Common Cause*, many contentious conversations about who—and what—should represent the United States revolved around monuments. This reimagining of how we visualize and relate our collective history served as inspiration for *Much Unseen Is Also Here*, an exhibition of works by An-My Lê and Shahzia Sikander. Both artists explored the monument as a key to understanding the episodic and fragmented way history is embedded in our present. Their installation told the story of two Asian American women examining their relationship to America in the midst of a collective national upheaval and long-overdue reckoning.

With the photographic series *Silent General*, Lê probed the ways in which both identity and history are projected onto landscape as she negotiated the tradition of the American

(continued on opposite page)

of the human predicament, our seeming inability as a species to learn from previous human-made disasters. In the context of the exhibition, it was also a provocation, as was *Toward Common Cause*, to see artists as offering novel ways to understand the realities we inhabit.

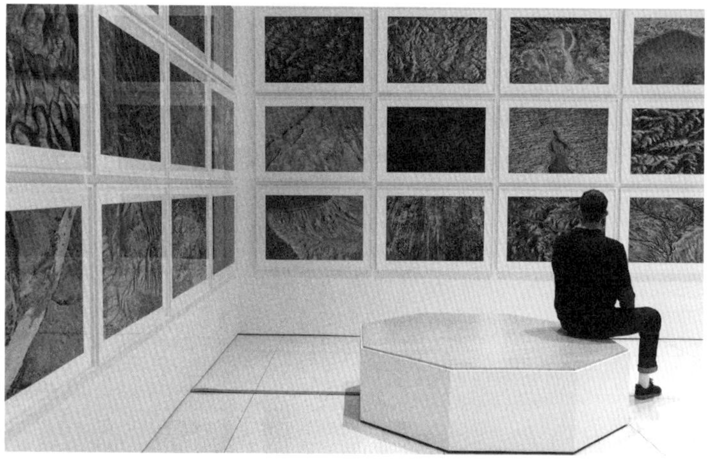

Fazal Sheikh's *In Place (Four Corners region, Utah, Arizona, New Mexico, and Colorado)*. Photo: Nathan Keay

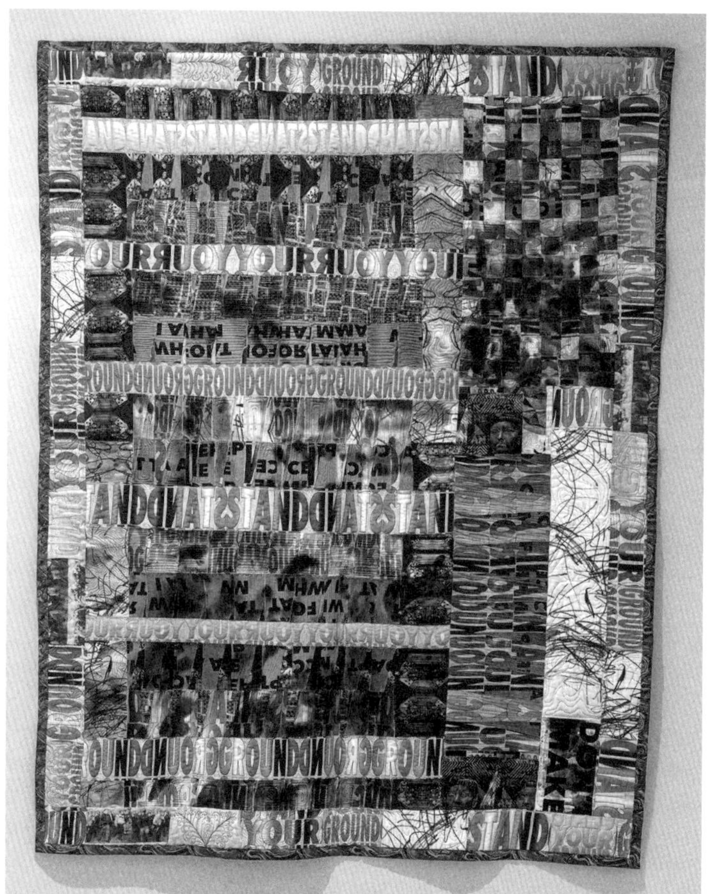

Jeffrey Gibson's large-scale *STAND YOUR GROUND* is part of his *Quilt* series in which intricate patterns are stitched together with pieces of printed fabric. Photo: Michael Tropea

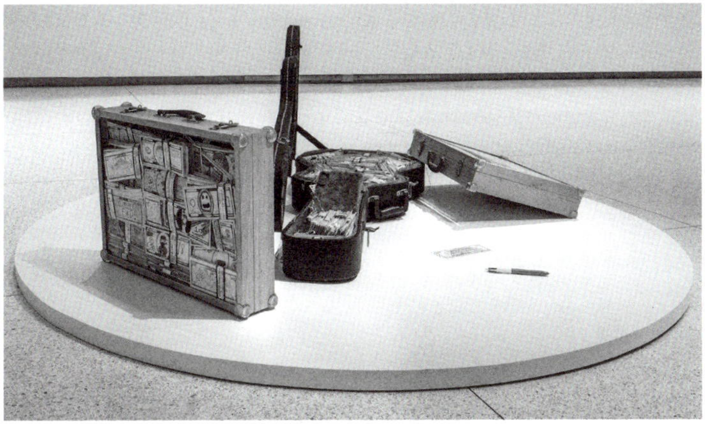

A display of Mel Chin's *Fundred Project*. A collection of the hand-drawn bills fills a guitar case and several glass-sided briefcases. Photo: Michael Tropea

MJ: This grouping of works recalls for me Lauren Berlant's discussion of the way the "figure of infrastructure" can "block seeing its contingency and creativity." Each artist's strategy to displace the static figure creates a new ecosystem to think through.

The rest of the Smart's galleries were divided into three sections. The first section included works by Jeffrey Gibson, LaToya Ruby Frazier, Mel Chin, Julie Mehretu, and Fazal Sheikh (Scenes #2, #5). Their works highlighted contemporary environmental crises (the Dakota Access Pipeline, mineral extraction, postindustrial pollution, and extinction) as factors shaping the landscape. These threats exacerbate existing infrastructural inequalities, including access to healthcare, healthy food, and clean drinking water, realities shared by abandoned and disenfranchised communities across the globe. The dire consequences of these deprivations were laid bare when COVID-19 ravaged the very communities left most vulnerable by their exposure. Aside from illuminating these problems, the artists offered proposals to ameliorate them. Gibson, for example, celebrated the Native women and water protectors standing between the sacrifice of sacred lands for profit. Chin proposed the production of creative currency to fund the infrastructural retrofits to end the plague of childhood lead poisoning.

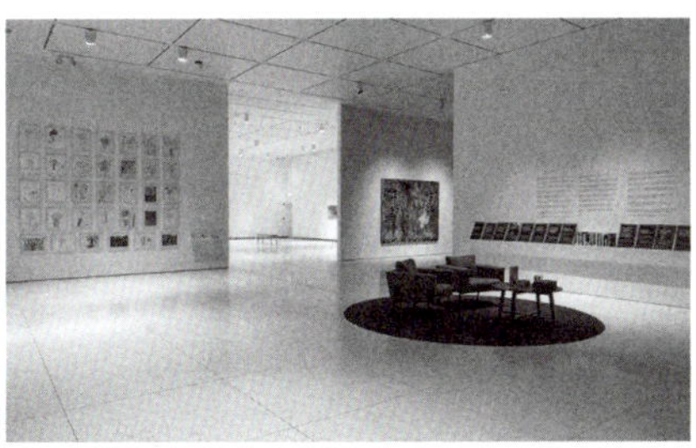

Installation view of *Toward Common Cause* at the Smart. Photo: Michael Tropea

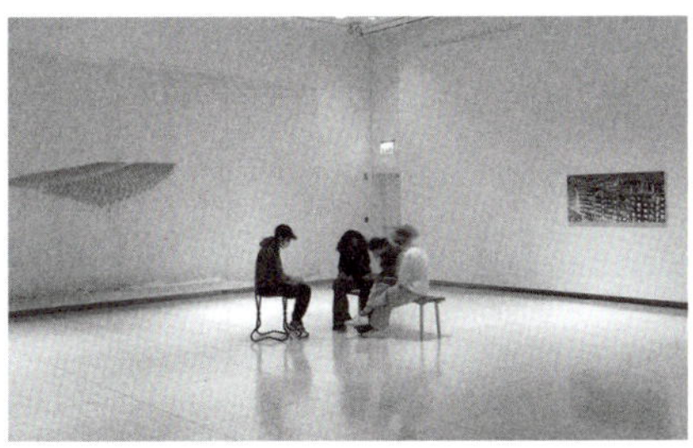

Students at the Smart discuss Toba Khedoori's paintings. Photo: Nathan Keay

The central galleries included paired works by Rick Lowe and Mark Bradford (Scenes #18, #22). In preliminary conversations with the artists, we considered Chicago's history as a destination for migrants fleeing the South, and the disenfranchisement they experienced in Northern cities through police brutality, redlining, and urban renewal. In response, Lowe and Bradford produced new works for the exhibition, taking the hundredth anniversary of the Tulsa Massacre, a tragedy driven

road trip to confront the political conflicts and rhetoric of the moment (Scenes #36; p. 66). Captured in large-format photographs, her sweeping survey of the political and geographical terrain of contemporary America takes in protests, migrant work, the state of the landscape, Confederate monuments to the Lost Cause, as she made her way across the country from the Atlantic to the Pacific.

Sikander's work investigates the interstices of power and gender, empire and self, and her work for the MoCP installation focused on the vagaries of representation and monumentalism as well as the investigation of traditional art forms. The show included her *Promiscuous Intimacies*, a heavily patinaed bronze antimonument depicting two intertwined female figures—a Greco-Roman Venus and an Indian *devata* (deity) (Scenes #10; p. 66). The artist first expressed a desire to produce such a work during a 2019 research trip to Chicago. *Promiscuous Intimacies* was the apotheosis of Sikander's many lines of inquiry and streams of thought, brought together in a single three-dimensional expression of the kaleidoscopic reality we inhabit.

Photo: Nathan Keay

Hyde Park Art Center
5020 S. Cornell Ave.
Chicago, IL 60615

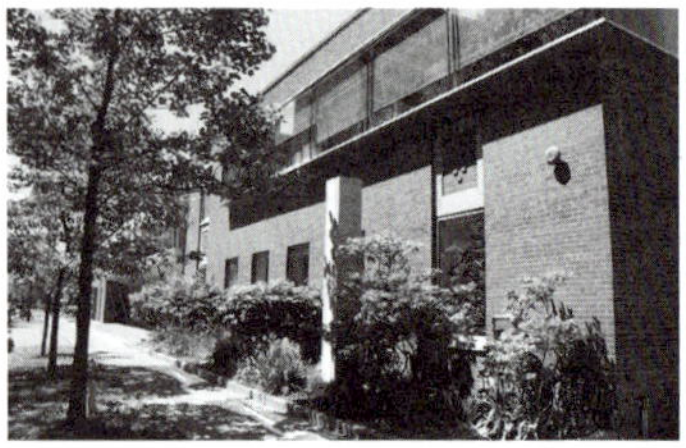

The Hyde Park Art Center is a mainstay in the Chicago art community. Created by a guild of artists in 1939, the DNA of this South Side art gallery and makerspace stems from a Depression-era drive to sustain social systems for care and learning. HPAC rests on the foundational thinking of Jane Addams on the West Side (p. 98) and John Dewey at the University of Chicago who, for decades, were devoted to educational and social structures for citizenry.

Quirky from the get-go, HPAC has always maintained direct links to the present. When the Chicago Imagists emerged at the School of the Art Institute in the 1960s, it was HPAC that brought them to public view. Decades before the center moved to its current home on South Cornell Avenue, it offered studio classes to the Hyde Park and greater Chicago community. Those offerings continue today through summer camps, teen programs, classes for lifelong arts enthusiasts, and artist residencies. HPAC's public exhibition space opens onto South Cornell Avenue via a giant garage door that literally removes the barrier between the white cube and the street to create an interspace for public gathering. The ongoing biennial project *Ground Floor* showcases emerging artists in the city. HPAC has offered many local artists their first institutional showing, and marked turning points in their careers.

(continued on opposite page)

as much by greed as racial animus, as a point of departure. Bradford's *Tulsa Gottdamn*, inspired in part by cartographic views of Tulsa during the riots of 1921, suggests the violence and destruction unleashed by the white rioters, and the winding river of blue in the center of the canvas evokes the movement of people. Lowe's project, *Black Wall Street Journey*, considers the past and future of Black economic power.[10]

DR: Rick Lowe and Mark Bradford were both born in 1961, four decades after the deadliest racist massacre in American history, and they have greatly influenced each other's takes on the social-practice paradigm.

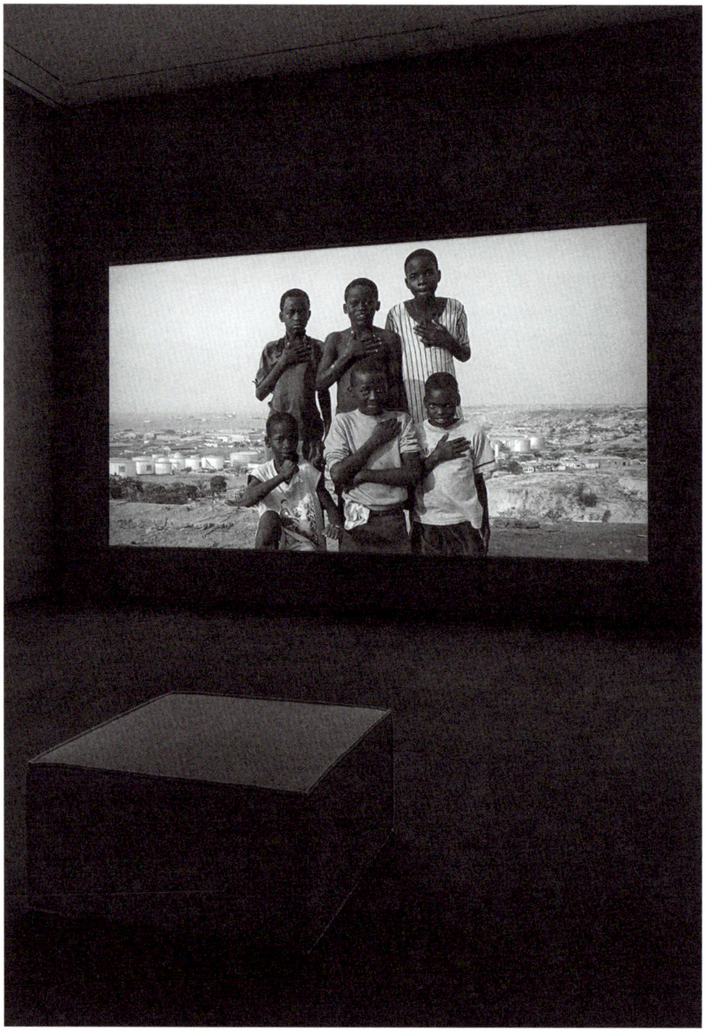

Installation view of Alfredo Jaar's film *Muxima*. Photo: Michael Tropea

Though many of the works at the Smart focused on local concerns—i.e., challenges that US communities are facing—Xu Bing, Alfredo Jaar, and Julie Mehretu broadened the exhibition's perspective (Scenes #4, #25). In 2005, in partnership with UNESCO, Xu Bing traveled to Kenya to teach drawing to children aged seven to thirteen in communities enduring the impacts of deforestation. The students' drawings of trees were sold to raise funds for replanting, thereby collecting revenue from citizens of wealthy nations. A collection of these drawings was installed near Xu's *Forest Project: The Blue and Green Wonderland*, a scroll depicting trees that echo the outstretched branches in the student drawings and recalls an archaic style of Chinese ink painting, balancing washes of color with quick, short brushwork. Mehretu's etchings of fantastically abstract landscapes layer references to architectural designs, airport diagrams, maps, and even plans for failed utopias (p. 56). They evoke the increasingly interconnected, globalizing world in a way that does not collapse different locales into sameness, but instead foregrounds their complexity. The three films by Jaar included in the exhibition call attention to the ways in which we excuse our own ignorance and inaction in a world saturated by information and images. He argues that our refusal to see, at home and abroad, is a collective cultural failing that allows abuses of power and atrocities to take place in plain sight.

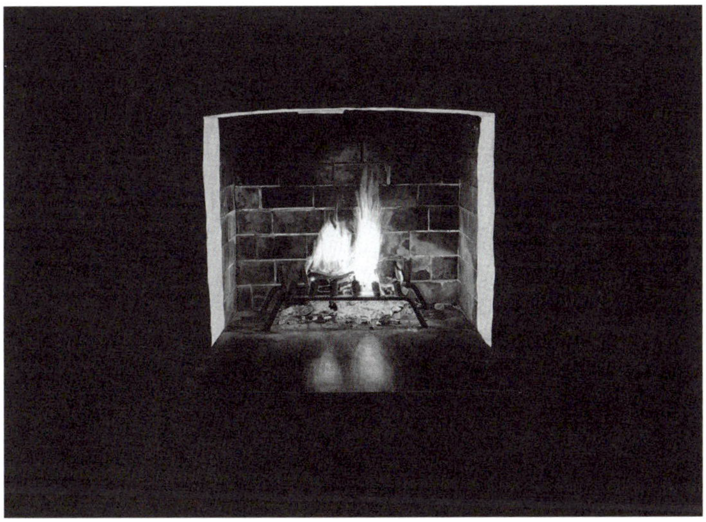

Detail of Toba Khedoori's *Untitled (Black Fireplace)*. Photo: Nathan Keay

The last works in the galleries, a trio of paintings by Toba Khedoori, are meditations on the alienation and fragility of the contemporary landscape devoid of human presence. The global pandemic and the isolation it had wrought lent Khedoori's haunting and enveloping paintings an added sense of urgency in 2021, forcing us to question what it means to live in a twenty-first-century urban environment (Scenes #11).

Toward Common Cause started with big questions. How does art illuminate what we have not seen before? How does it create space for dialogue and exchange? The more we worked, the clearer it became that there were no easy answers to any of these questions. In fact, offering solutions felt like an act of hubris. Instead, we established a model rooted in the certainty that collaboration with partners across the city was essential to challenging hierarchy and expanding the horizons of what our work could accomplish. Rather than starting from a determined outcome, we elected to remain open to change and circumstance. We live in a disinformation age—one in which volatile facts and rhetoric are wielded as weapons by those in power. Human beings intentionally or accidentally miss what happens just below the surface, at the periphery, in the gaps between what we know and what we refuse to acknowledge. The exhibition posited a belief in artists and artworks as catalysts.

JS: In moments of crisis, isn't it striking to watch art be so many things for people, ranging from spark to salve?

The art of Mel Chin, LaToya Ruby Frazier, and Fazal Sheikh was on display at HPAC for *Toward Common Cause* (Scenes #13, #28). From distinct geographic locales—New Orleans, Flint, Michigan, and the Negev Desert in Israel—the focus was environmental racism and insufficient access to safe drinking water, food, and healthcare. HPAC was the perfect place for Chin to supply his handcrafted cherry tables and colored pencils for people to produce Fundred dollar bills because, in his own words, places "that show this work have to join the action." This is the same instinctual commitment to action that has motivated Frazier's ongoing work about pollution in the industrial Midwest and selections from Sheikh's landscape photography from the *Erasure Trilogy*, which examines the displacement of Bedouin communities and its connection to colonization and desertification in the Middle East.

An interdisciplinary class at the University of Chicago's Gray Center for Arts and Inquiry delved into the questions surfaced by Chin, Frazier, and Sheikh. Led by Iñigo Manglano-Ovalle, Abigail Winograd, and Susan Gzesh, "Water, Water Everywhere?" explored the "aesthetics, environmental racism, and a human rights approach to the Commons to inform our perspective on the politics and aesthetics of water." Students read texts that had informed the thinking around *Toward Common Cause*, such as Lewis Hyde's *Common as Air* and Fred Moten and Stefano Harney's *The Undercommons* (pp. 57-58). Manglano-Ovalle introduced his work produced for the exhibition and his larger practice around questions of water access, bringing students to HPAC for discussion.

Photo: courtesy of Hyde Park Art Center

In *Braiding Sweetgrass*, Kimmerer considers the role of fungus in supporting trees in their production of nuts:

> The mycorrhizae may form fungal bridges between individual trees, so that all the trees in a forest are connected. These fungal networks appear to redistribute the wealth of carbohydrates from tree to tree. A kind of Robin Hood, they take from the rich and give to the poor so that all the trees arrive at the same carbon surplus at the same time. They weave a web of reciprocity, of giving and taking. In this way, the trees all act as one because the fungi have connected them. Through unity, survival. All flourishing is mutual.[11]

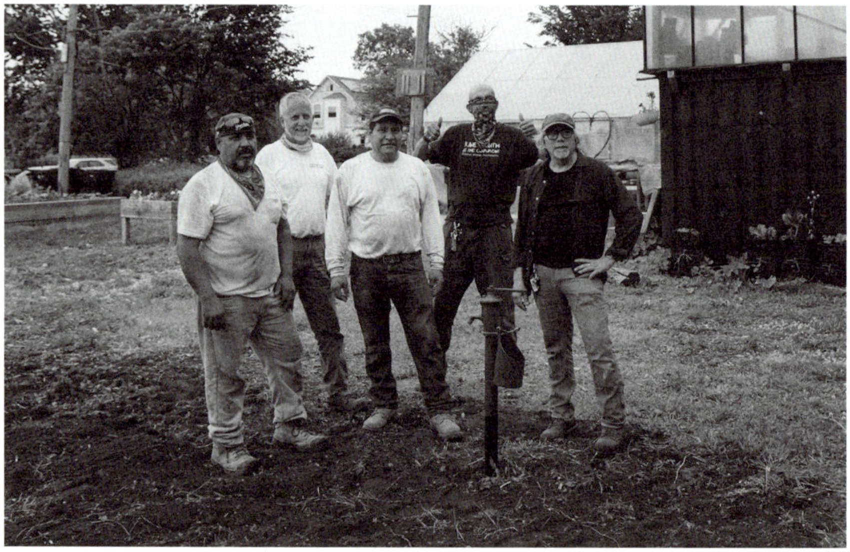

Iñigo Manglano-Ovalle poses with staff of Kerrigan Brothers Plumbing after installing his *Hydrant, 41°47′22.662″ N—87°37′38.364″ W* at Sweet Water. Photo: Iñigo Manglano-Ovalle

Mutuality and gifting—these notions are at the center of Iñigo Manglano-Ovalle's *Water Table, 41°47′36.993″ N—87°36′0.726″ W*, the first or the last object at the Smart depending on your perspective (Scenes #26). *Water Table* was handmade out of reclaimed ash wood, stained black, and surrounded by a collection of hand-turned benches installed in the museum's lobby. Apart from an unusual leg, the table was indistinguishable from any other piece of museum furniture. Its fourth leg consists of a hand pump attached to a stainless-steel reservoir. When activated, visitors to the museum could pump a glass of water. The water came from Manglano-Ovalle's *Hydrant, 41°47′22.662″ N—87°37′38.364″ W*, his gift to Sweet Water Foundation and installed on the SWF campus (Scenes #32). *Hydrant*'s primary function is to provide potable water for consumption, irrigation, and other purposes at SWF's Community Gardens. At the Smart, the water was, in turn, a gift to museum visitors. These twin installations are part of Manglano-Ovalle's *Well* series—a project based in reciprocity. *Water Table* bound the two sites of the exhibition together, linking a community development organization to the architecture of a museum and vice versa.

NYT: [Manglano-Ovalle's] wells become the property of their owners once installed, but "the wells cease to be a work of art if any money changes hands for the water," he said.

"Water, Water Everywhere?" syllabus: The U.S. Constitution does not contain a "right to water." But the UN recognizes that a "right to water is indispensable for leading a life in human dignity. It is a prerequisite for the realization of other human rights."

It was a platform for conversation, for action, and for exchange. Both works were rooted in place, connected to the ground and to the water—that elemental substance beneath all our feet that is becoming increasingly precious by the minute. *Water Table* was an act of hospitality, an invitation to sit, stay a while, and share. It is a reminder that artists, artworks, and the institutions that house them, like trees, are part of an ecosystem that exists in a changing world.

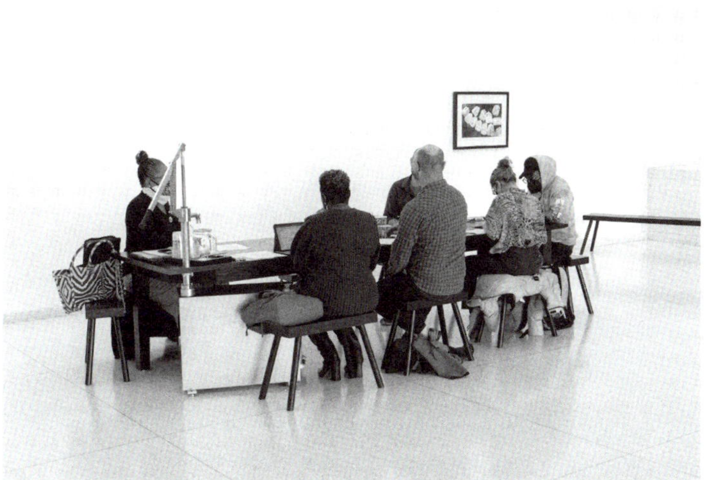

Staff meeting at the Smart around Iñigo Manglano-Ovalle's *Water Table, 41°47'36.993" N—87°36'0.726" W*. Photo: Nathan Keay

1 The title of this essay is borrowed from a repeated refrain in the Potawatomi botanist and author Robin Wall Kimmerer's *Braiding Sweetgrass: Indigenous Wisdom, Scientific Knowledge, and the Teachings of Plants* (Minneapolis: Milkweed Editions, 2013). Passages from this essay are drawn from other writing produced for various aspects of *Toward Common Cause*. In particular, I borrow heavily from my essay, "It Remains to Be Seen," written to accompany the presentation of An-My Lê and Shahzia Sikander at the Museum of Contemporary Photography. Likewise, the curatorial description of the exhibition and the discussion of its theoretical underpinnings appear in various locations. Both texts are available on the exhibition's website.

2 Anna Lowenhaupt Tsing, *The Mushroom at the End of the World: On the Possibility of Life in Capitalist Ruins* (Princeton: Princeton University Press, 2015); Shoshana Zuboff, *The Age of Surveillance Capitalism: The Fight for a Human Future at the New Frontier of Power* (New York: Public Affairs, 2019); David Graeber and David Wengrow, *The Dawn of Everything: A New History of Humanity* (New York: Farrar, Strauss & Giroux, 2021).

3 Lowenhaupt Tsing, *The Mushroom at the End of the World*, 20.

4 New Orleans Mayor Mitch Landrieu responded to critics decrying the move as a historical outrage by defending the decision as a long overdue historical correction. The monuments, Landrieu pointed out, were erected decades after the Civil War not to memorialize Confederate losses but as *sculptural expressions* of the so-called Cult of the Lost Cause. Proponents of this cult had long sought to recast the Civil War as a heroic and ultimately tragic stand against Northern aggression rather than a defense of the enslavement and exploitation of African Americans. Their effort to enshrine the cause of white supremacy was wildly successful: some 700 such monuments were erected across the United States, the majority between 1890 and 1950. Mitch Landrieu, "We Can't Walk Away from This Truth," *The Atlantic*, May 22, 2017.

5 Whitman quoted by Leslie Jamison in her introduction to *Specimen Days and Collect* (Brooklyn: Melville House, 2014), ix.

6 Jason Frank, "Aesthetic Democracy: Walt Whitman and the Poetry of the People," *The Review of Politics* 69 (Summer 2007): 403.

7 Lewis Hyde, *Common as Air: Revolution, Art, and Ownership* (New York: Farrar, Strauss & Giroux, 2010); Stefano Harney and Fred Moten, *The Undercommons: Fugitive Planning & Black Study* (Wivenhoe, N.Y.: Minor Compositions, 2013).

8 Dieter Roelstraete, "South Side Story: A European Curator's Adventures in Chicago," in *Institutions and Imaginaries*, ed. Stephanie Smith (Chicago: School of the Art Institute and University of Chicago Press, 2015), 45–55.

9 The Chicago Metropolitan Agency for Planning's Community Data Snapshots and publicly available IRS data from 2022 show that the majority of Chicago's cultural offerings were, at that time, located in community areas where the median household income is above $51,074 and the population is predominantly white.

10 See my forthcoming essay, "The Informer: Rick Lowe's *Black Wall Street Journey*," in *Rick Lowe* (Chicago: Neubauer Collegium for Art and Society and Gagosian, 2023).

11 Kimmerer, *Braiding Sweetgrass*, 20.

An-My Lê and Shahzia Sikander ruminate on a prompt from Abigail Winograd

MUCH UNSEEN IS ALSO HERE

My work with the artists Shahzia Sikander and An-My Lê was critical in the years leading up to *Toward Common Cause*. Our long-running conversation took place amidst a particularly fractious phase of America's confrontation with what constitutes Americanness. Much of our discussion, as well as the artists' work at the time, was focused on monuments. *Much Unseen Is Also Here*, the installation that we produced together for *Toward Common Cause* at the Museum of Contemporary Photography, was about two immigrant women artists of color seeing America and picturing America seeing itself (Scenes #10, #36).

While assembling the installation, I kept coming back to Walt Whitman. Sikander had recently collaborated with the novelist Ayad Akhtar on a series of illustrations for his novel *Homeland Elegies*, in which the protagonist meditates on Whitman as a means of processing his own relationship to the United States. Lê's *Silent General* took inspiration from the observations of Whitman's miscellany *Specimen Days and Collect*. I returned again and again to his *Democratic Vistas* and its eerie resonances:

> I say we had best look our time and lands searchingly in the face, like a physician diagnosing some deep disease. Never was there, perhaps, more hollowness at heart than at present, and here in the United States. Genuine belief seems to have left us. The underlying principles of The States are not honestly believed in, (for all this hectic glow, and these melo-dramatic screamings), nor is Humanity itself believed in. What penetrating eye does not everywhere see through the mask? The spectacle is appalling. We live in an atmosphere of hypocrisy throughout.

I processed the geopolitical events in the run-up to *Toward Common Cause* through Sikander's and Lê's work, itself informed by their own reckoning with the times. It was critical for me precisely because neither artist totalized or summarized the state of current affairs. Instead, their work provided a space for reflection without rhetoric or prescription, which lent their project within the larger exhibition such striking power.

In the fall of 2022—a year after the installation at MoCP closed—I reached out to the artists to ask that they reflect again on Whitman's statement above, and on monuments, meaning, and history. Their thoughts, shared via email, follow.

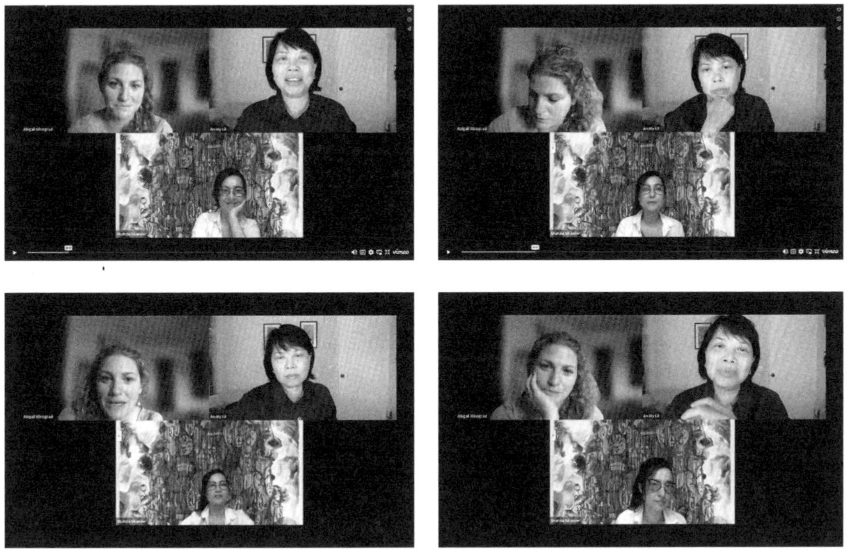

An-My Lê and Shahzia Sikander discuss their exhibition *Much Unseen Is Also Here* at the Museum of Contemporary Photography in a Zoom conversation, July 22, 2021. Courtesy of MoCP

An-My Lê

Monuments figure prominently in the history of photography. You have Maxime du Camp's photographs of the Great Sphinx of Giza from 1849; Eugène Atget's allegorical take on the statues in the Tuileries and the gardens at Saint-Cloud; Lee Friedlander's *The American Monument* project; and iconic images of the toppling of Saddam Hussein's statue.

Photographing monuments is not new to me. I did it very early in my career when I was working as a staff photographer for a guild of craftsmen who specialize in the restoration of France's architectural patrimony. I certainly didn't consider the monument with the same urgency and awareness that I do today.

Monuments are erected to create an account of history. That account is a narrative within a narrative that is chronicled in a public space. Monuments are examples of civic architecture that endeavor to honor achievements and progress but often attest to an individual's dream or delusion of grandeur. Their goals can devolve to articulate notions of dominion, colonialism. In their own ways, monuments help to create or reinforce myths. But as history tells us, with time, opposing cultural and social forces will contest, and the monument may become a target of dissatisfaction. In the same breath, the act of taking down monuments becomes an attempt to create another narrative.

Though monuments may be necessary to tell an important story, in the end they often fail. If not kitschy, they are follies. One of the few exceptions for me is Maya Lin's *Vietnam Veterans Memorial*, perhaps because it is a humble gesture inspired by failure itself: diplomatic, military, and geopolitical disaster. In the shadow of that exceptional monument, one must consider Judith Joy Ross's extraordinary portraits of people visiting or mourning there in 1983–84, the first years after it was built. The memorial itself is alluded to in the photographs. It looms large in the background but is cropped out or blurry. Ross's focus is on the people. With her large-format camera, she freezes them in time and in space and singularizes them. They become statue-like. But unlike most monuments, which tend to simplify or tell only one story, Ross's portraits wrestle with and embrace the complexity of human experience as we are reminded of a dark period in our history and the pain and loss we incurred.

My work from 2020 and 2021 had begun during the 2016 contestations over Confederate monuments and the upheavals of the presidential election campaign, followed by the deadly 2017 rally in Charlottesville during the Trump presidency in which white nationalists marching with burning tiki torches protested the proposed removal of a statue of Robert E. Lee. The simplification of the critical issues we were confronted with—whether about immigration, race, religion, women's rights, LGBTQ rights, medicine, patriotism—was infuriating. Everything was inflamed. There was a lack of regard for facts and logical reasoning that we had never experienced before. One could not simply disagree with someone else and still have a civil discussion. I realized that a war front had come to the home front, and I needed to do something urgently. I don't want someone else to tell my story. I don't want to be served a reductive account of history. So I hit the road with my camera. Photography, with its descriptive power and its trenchant specificity, can function as a counterpoint against scale, against fantasies of power.

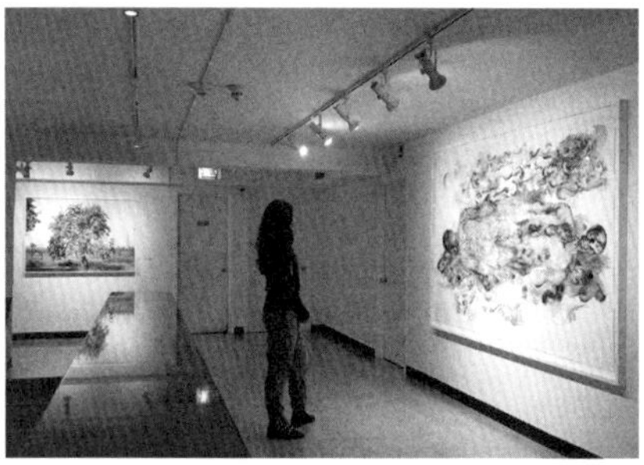

Visitor with Shahzia Sikander's ink-and-gouache *Kinship* (foreground) and An-My Lê's *Fragment IV: Citrus Tree, Fowler, California*, from the series *Silent General*. Photo: Nathan Keay

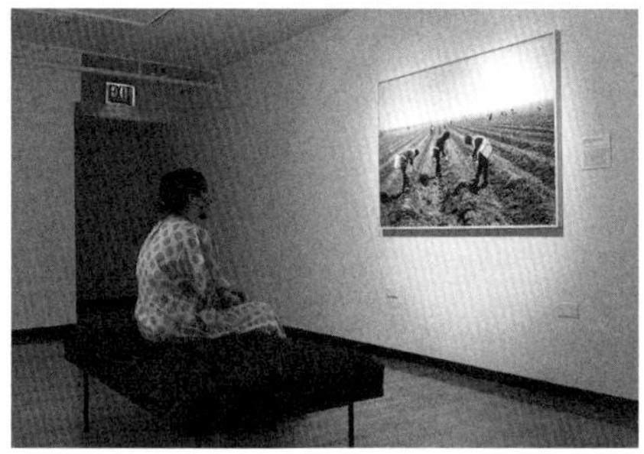

Visitor with An-My Lê's *Fragment II: Migrant Workers Harvesting Asparagus, Mendota, California*, from the series *Silent General*. Photo: Nathan Keay

Shahzia Sikander

In 2017, my service on the New York City Mayoral Advisory Commission on City Art, Monuments, and Markers exposed me to tension-ridden situations around public monuments, their complicated histories, historical reckoning, and conflicts between competing visions of history. That year, charged and even violent public demonstrations around the removal of Confederate monuments resulted in a moment of crisis and reflection, fueling debate around race; monuments' limitations on representation; the glorification of the Confederate defense of slavery in the Civil War; who gets to decide what is removed and what is retained; and what is to be done with the statues after removal.

The debates of that year became my touchstone for reflections on the interface of people and public art, and the complexity of and capacity for centering art on our shared humanity. The discussions around erasure and lack of historical and cultural diversity paralleled the ethos of my work, in its engagement with colonial and orientalist histories and their reductive representations of the other.

My intent as an artist is to create something wondrous, with many possible associations—something that can generate thought and produce difference. I think through my hand. Thinking collectively with the mind and hand creates an armature of research, clarifies ideas, and connects thought to gesture, to action, to practice. Critical thinking, creativity, and collaboration are the three tenets on which I have built my entire understanding of being an artist. How culture, society, and economy intersect, and how communities coalesce, play a role in how art functions in overlapping spaces. I like to believe that the function of art is to allow for multiple meanings and possibilities, to open up space for a more just world.

Societies are not static, nor histories one-dimensional. A common cultural belief is that art survives time. But art can also fade out of relevance, while some art remains invisible—expunged from the annals of recorded history. Art is alive, moving, and changing. How we experience art, how we respond to it, and how we interpret it are open-ended processes.

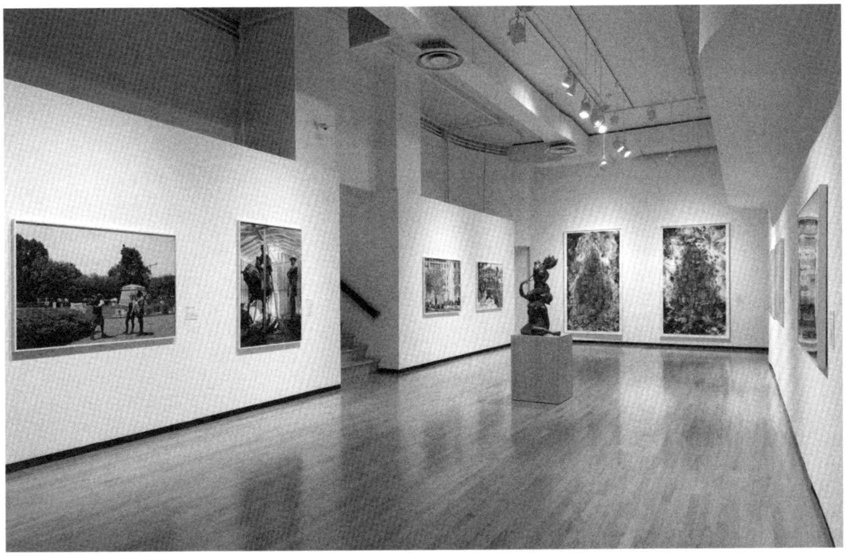

Installation view of An-My Lê and Shahzia Sikander's exhibition *Much Unseen Is Also Here* at MoCP. Photo: Nathan Keay

Most of my work engages the past without glorifying it. It doesn't lay claim to grandiosity. It is often ephemeral. There are works on paper, murals, installations, and animations. These types of work are rarely seen through the lens of the antimonument. To remedy that, I thought, "All I need to do is turn the drawing into a sculpture."

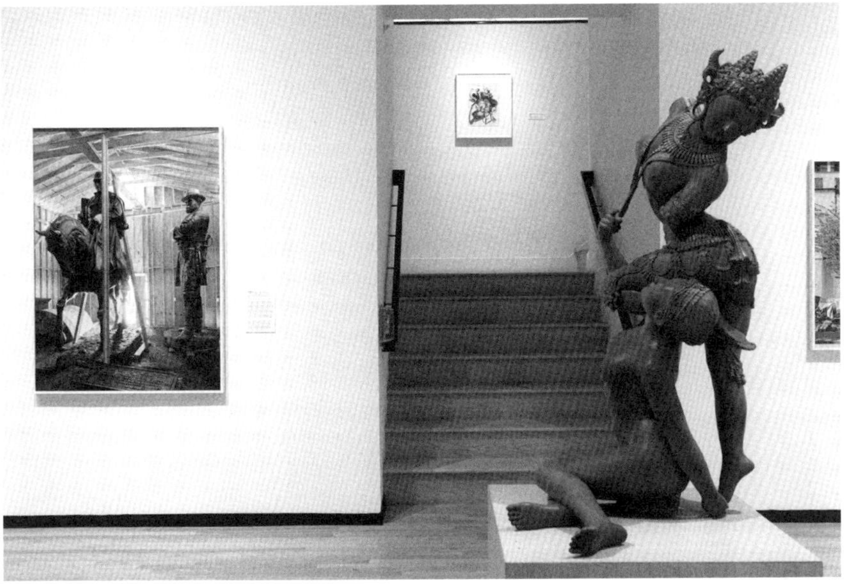

Shahzia Sikander's bronze sculpture *Promiscuous Intimacies* (foreground) and An-My Lê's photograph *Fragment VI: General Robert E. Lee and P. G. T. Beauregard Monuments, Homeland Security Storage, New Orleans, Louisiana*, from the series *Silent General*. Photo: Nathan Keay

The questions at the core of my interest in shifting painting into the realm of the sculptural revolved around the issue of time: How can art remain valid over time, across different languages, geographies, and histories? Where does the power lie in an image? How is time visualized in an artwork? Does art create new ways to experience time? How can a painting erode its historically produced reality, its value-giving mediated structures? Can it determine how and what we see? How are beliefs tied to the reproduction of cultural knowledge?

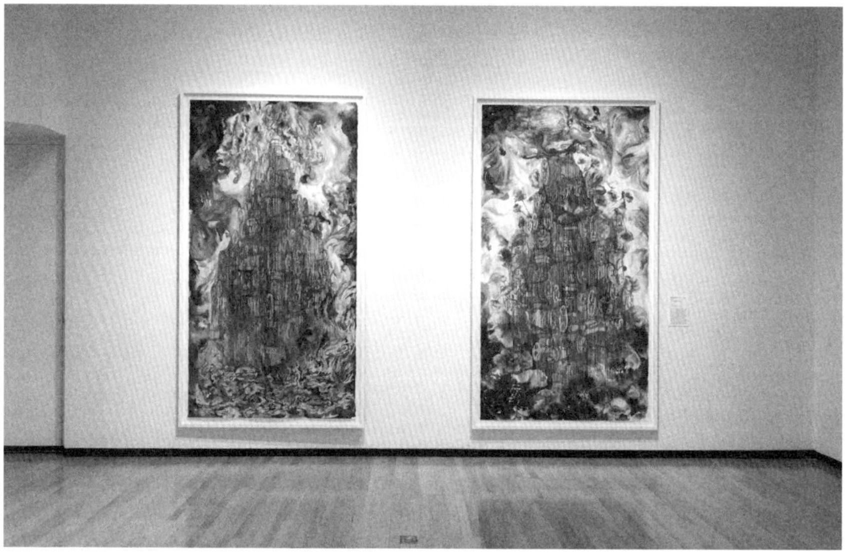

Shahzia Sikander's large-scale works on paper *Flared* and *Oil and Poppies*. Photo: Nathan Keay

Women in my art function as agents of resistance, change, nurture, and power. They are centered as symbols of endurance and transformation within vast global histories of empire to offer redemptive possibilities as a counternarrative to exploitive and extractive forces. There are two female figures in *Promiscuous Intimacies*: the Greco-Roman goddess Venus and an Indian *devata*, or celestial dancer. The work is in bronze, colored in various brown patinas to highlight the fact that classical painted statuary was polychromatic and not lily white, as constructed over time in the popular imagination. I'll quote Gayatri Gopinath's elegant description of the sculpture:

> *Promiscuous Intimacies*, with its sinuous entanglement of the Greco-Roman goddess Venus and the Indian devata, explores the promiscuous intimacies of multiple times, spaces, art-historical traditions, bodies, desires, and subjectivities. In their suggestive embrace, the intertwined female bodies bear the symbolic weight of communal identities from multiple temporal and geographic terrains. They evoke non-heteronormative desires that are often cast as foreign and inauthentic but here challenge the viewer to imagine a different present and future. This backward glance demands that we understand "tradition," "culture," and "identity" as impure, heterogeneous, unstable, and always in process, disrupting taken-for-granted national, temporal, and art-historical boundaries.[1]

The *devata* figure references a truncated temple sculpture formerly in the collection of the Metropolitan Museum of Art.[2] The dancer flirtatiously entwines with a figure drawn from the Italian Mannerist painting *An Allegory with*

Venus and Cupid by Bronzino.[3] By entangling Mannerism—an anti-Classical impulse of the Western tradition—with Indian art, as accomplice to and witness of a one-sided history, I was pushing back at the polarizing East-West binary. I also hoped to highlight art history's lingering Classicism and ethnocentric reactions to Indian art in the tradition of Johann Joachim Winckelmann. In the sculptural iteration, the protagonists take on new roles. Which of them is in a position of power? Is the *devata* unattainable or is the Venus lifting her up? Who wants whose gaze? What is the nature of the relationship? You question one thing, and another thing comes up. It's open-ended while being extremely precise. The details are carefully thought out; for example, the intimate enmeshment of the Venus's head and the *devata*'s foot, or the tug at the necklace. The choice of the patina coloring, too, creates a palette that draws the figures closer to a geographical-historical relationship between Greece and India and their overlapping sculptural traditions.

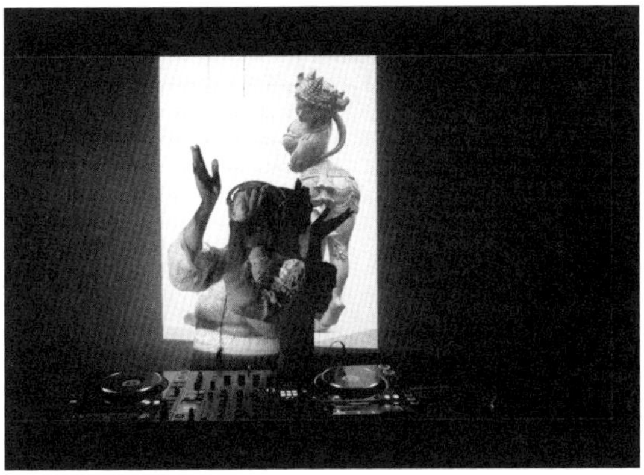

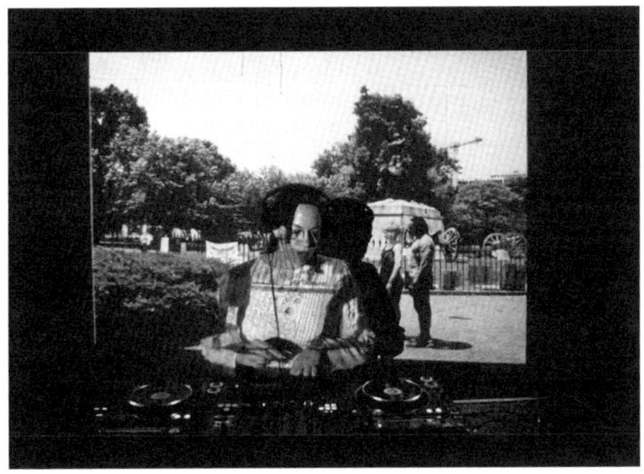

DJ CQQCHiFRUIT performs in front of a slideshow of Lê's and Sikander's work at the virtual opening of *Much Unseen Is Also Here*, June 3, 2021. Courtesy of MoCP

My practice involves working with colonial archives, visual traditions, manuscript histories, Western art histories, writing, poetry, and calligraphy, combined with syncretic sculpture. It knits together these references and mythologies, along with more private inner encounters, dreams, memories, and fantasies, and gives rise to my explorations of feminine power, with the desire to be multivalent. I explore the specific narratives surrounding race, empire, diaspora, gender, sexuality, and politics. The women in my work are always complex, proactive, confident, and intelligent, and in their playful stances they are connected to the past in imaginative ways without being tied to a heteronormative lineage or conventional representations of diaspora and nation.

In my visualization of a new and different future of American cultural landscapes that are not only white, or binary, but white and black and brown, too, that draw non-Western symbols into the public sphere, I have activated broader conversations outside of the confines of the art world and have been diminished and censored for doing so by certain media outlets. Such ruptures are an indication of the fear that lurks when women are perceived to have power, real or imagined. They also expose and project underlying anti-immigrant and anti-Muslim sentiments.

1 Gayatri Gopinath, "Promiscuous Intimacies: Embodiment, Desire, and Diasporic Dislocation in the Art of Shahzia Sikander," in *Shahzia Sikander: Extraordinary Realities*, ed. Sadia Abbas and Jan Howard (Munich: Hirmer, 2021).

2 The sculpture, originally thought to be an 11th-century work from Madhya Pradesh, has been removed from the Met's collection due to its suspect provenance.

3 Bronzino (Italian, 1503–1572), *An Allegory with Venus and Cupid*, ca. 1545. Oil on wood. National Gallery, London (NG651).

Chicago Housing Authority
Minnie Julia Riperton Apartments
4250 S. Princeton Ave.
Chicago, IL 60609

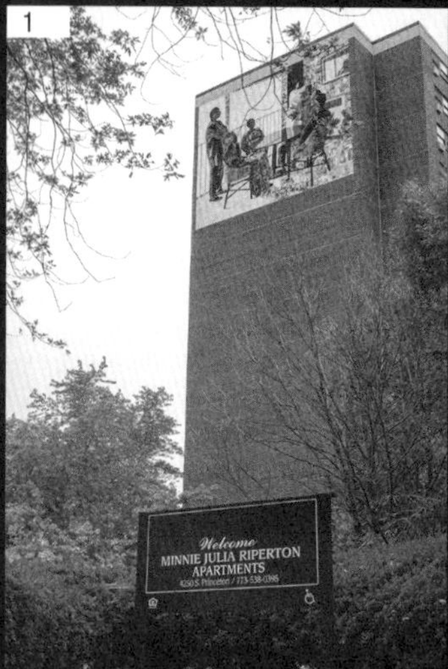

1

National Public Housing Museum
1322 W. Taylor St.
Chicago, IL 60607

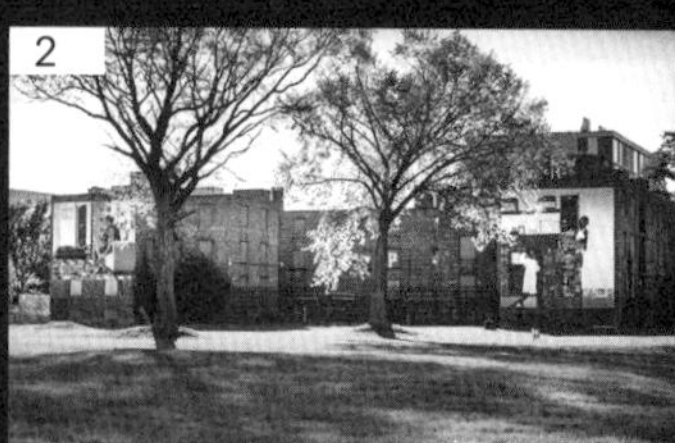
2

The National Public Housing Museum is the only cultural institution in the United States dedicated to documenting the history of subsidized housing and collecting the stories of its residents. A member of the International Coalition of Sites of Conscience, NPHM believes that collecting and telling stories is a critical tool for advancing its mission to "preserve, promote, and propel the right of all people to a place where they can live and prosper." NPHM occupies the last remaining three-story building of the Chicago Housing Authority's Jane Addams Homes—originally thirty-two buildings containing 987 units built in 1938 on Chicago's Near West Side. The Minnie Julia Riperton Apartments occupy the corner of West 43rd Street and South Princeton Avenue in Chicago's Fuller Park neighborhood, across the street from Thomas A. Hendricks Elementary School. The last residents of the Jane Addams Homes departed when the buildings were closed in 2002, but the 335 units at the Riperton complex are rented to seniors by the CHA.

In the summer and fall of 2021, four pictures by the Nigerian-born, Los Angeles-based painter Njideka Akunyili Crosby were installed on the facades of the future site of NPHM and the Riperton Apartments. In recent years, Akunyili Crosby had placed facsimiles of her paintings in public spaces in London, New York, and Los Angeles. In our conversations about her participation in *Toward Common Cause*, she explained that her enthusiasm for this new direction in her practice stemmed from her own anxieties about who had access to her work in galleries and museums. She recalled the affirmation she had felt when a Nigerian taxi driver, while delivering her to LA MOCA, the site of her most recent mural installation, described details of her images with pride and delight. We decided to follow this path in Chicago.

Our original plan was to place the murals on the exteriors of participating exhibition venues, a strategy that we came to see as conflicting with our goal of spreading the exhibition throughout the city. Even with nineteen venues across Chicago, we would still miss large sections of the city. It occurred to me that these tales of domesticity and familial love would make sense outside of the circle of traditional art spaces.

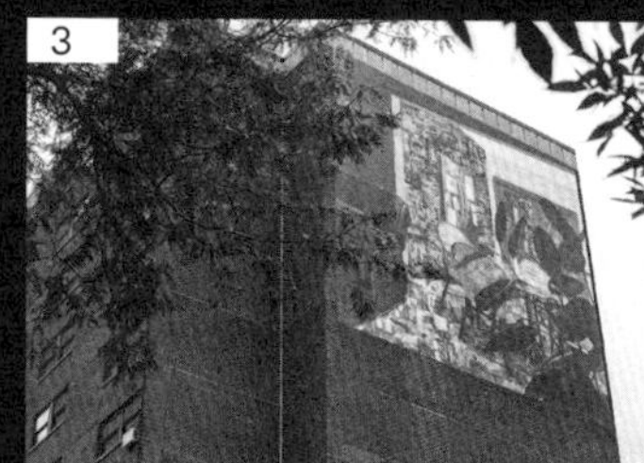
3

We turned to the Smart's Public Practice team, which was recognized for their groundbreaking work in establishing relationships with organizations in the South Side community. One such relationship was with the Chicago Housing Authority, which we tapped for a collaboration with the Smart's Teen Program. The idea to place Akunyili Crosby's paintings in and on public housing sites appealed to the Curatorial and Public Practice teams, to an eager group of Teen Program participants, and to the artist, who would explain to the youth participants that her work was driven by a desire to share her home and her transatlantic journey with audiences:

> I almost want people to feel like the door is open and they're walking by a scene into someone else's life, because that really is what I'm doing ... mining my life to tell a story that is global but really wanting people to feel like they're getting a glimpse into my world.

I suggested to Akunyili Crosby that we surrender curatorial control of site and image selection for the project to the youth participants of the Teen Program and ask them to find CHA properties to host the works.

4
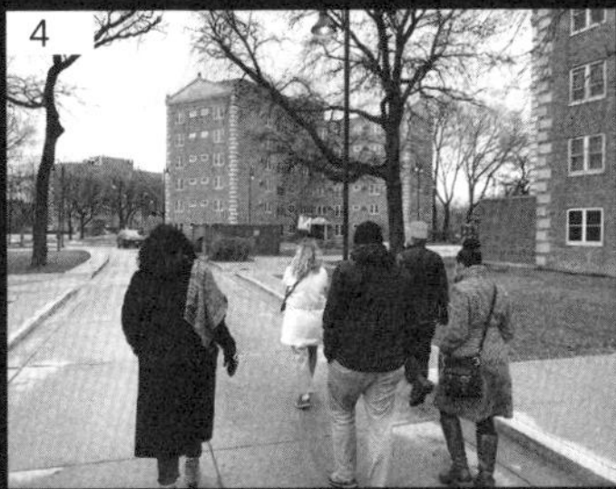

In many ways, the historic arc of the promise and tragic demise of public housing is embedded in the history of Chicago. The Jane Addams Homes was the first federal housing project in the city, one of three demonstration projects built by the Public Works Administration, and opened its doors in 1938. The legal framework for public housing was part of Franklin D. Roosevelt's New Deal, the realization of decades of Progressive Era advocacy. The failures of public housing became synonymous with Chicago by the mid-1990s, when eleven of the fifteen most impoverished communities in the nation could be found in Chicago Housing Authority properties. Statistics about crime and poverty erased the stories of family, community, ingenuity, and joy that existed alongside the other painful realities. In 2002, the city of Chicago vacated the Jane Addams Homes and demolished all but one of its thirty-two buildings, as part of the CHA's Plan for Transformation.

Our first conversations with CHA took place in the summer of 2019, and the project was provisionally approved nine months later. Beginning the following summer, the participants in the Smart's Teen Program began what would become an eighteen-month dialogue and collaboration with the artist that took place against the backdrop of the global pandemic. Their work included designing and executing a community engagement proposal; identifying potential sites; and coordinating visits to determine feasibility. After finalizing the venue selection, the works were chosen through a balloting process that included project participants and residents of the Riperton Apartments (Scenes #14). The young people also trained as oral historians with the team at the National Public Housing Museum, collecting stories of Riperton residents that are now part of the NPHM oral history archives.

5
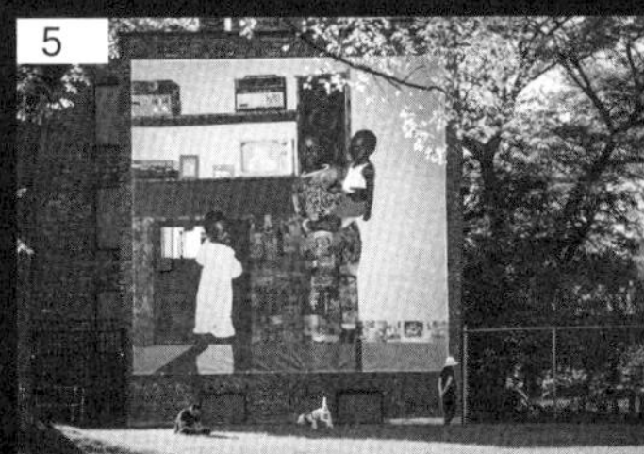

The young people wrote the text that accompanied the murals at both sites. They asked, "What does the inside of your home look like? What does it say about you, your family, community, the world, the past, present, or dreams of the future?" The murals at both sites have become a familiar sight to neighborhood denizens, and they remained in place years after their scheduled deinstallation. They were there because the residents of the Riperton Apartments and the NPHM staff wanted them there.

— Abigail Winograd

1 Njideka Akunyili Crosby's *I Still Face You* at the Chicago Housing Authority Minnie Julia Riperton Apartments. Photo: Nathan Keay

2 Installation view of Njideka Akunyili Crosby's *Mother and Child* and *The Beautyful Ones, Series #9* at the National Public Housing Museum. Photo: Jonathan Loïc Rogers

3 Njideka Akunyili Crosby's *Home: Say It Loud* at the Riperton Apartments. Photo: Nathan Keay

4 Site visit of *Toward Common Cause* team members to the Riperton Apartments. Photo: Michael Christiano

5 Njideka Akunyili Crosby's *The Beautyful Ones, Series #9* at the NPHM. Photo: Jonathan Loïc Rogers

Toward Common Cause sought to engage the entwined political, racial, economic, and environmental crises engulfing the world before and throughout the COVID emergency.

WAYS TO WALK IN BEAUTY

Abigail Winograd (AG) in conversation with Tommy Rock (TR), Fazal Sheikh (FS), and Jonah Yellowman (JY)

In Place is an installation of sixty-six photographs of Utah landscapes in Bears Ears National Monument (established in 2016 by President Barack Obama) and Grand Staircase-Escalante National Monument (established in 1996 by President Bill Clinton), accompanied by seismological sound recordings of the buttes depicted in those landscapes, footage of methane gas emissions, and an offering from Jonah Yellowman (Scenes #5). The work, included in *Toward Common Cause*'s installation at the Smart, emerged from Fazal Sheikh's artist residency with the Utah Diné Bikéyah, the land-conservation organization that successfully lobbied the Obama administration to declare Bears Ears a National Monument. Sheikh trained his camera on the ancestral home of the Hopi Tribe, Navajo Nation, Ute Mountain Ute Tribe, Pueblo of Zuni, and Ute Indian Tribe—a landscape of tremen-dous cultural diversity and spiritual importance. He began this work in 2017 as the Trump administration announced its intention to reduce the area of the National Monument, reopening protected areas to extractive industries and real-estate development—a decision the Biden administration reversed during the course of the exhibition. The intended outcomes of the project were threefold: an admonition about the sacrifice of public lands and sacred spaces to extrac-tive industries; a document of the environmental injustices suffered by Indigenous peoples and downwinders;[1] and the capture of the sensorial experience of place. Sheikh's plans for his contribution to *Toward Common Cause* changed drama-tically in response to shifting political sands. The pandemic—and its devastating impact on the Navajo Nation—also moved the work toward the spiritual and healing powers of sacred spaces, resulting in a work focused more deeply on collaboration.

In Place is part of Sheikh's ongoing collaboration with individuals and institutions in the Southwest and beyond. Jonah Yellowman, spiritual advisor of the Utah Diné Bikéyah Inter-Tribal Coalition, placed an offering for protection and reverence of this sacred landscape at the center of *In Place*. Dr. Tommy Rock, a geoscientist studying the impact of uranium mining on Native communities in Arizona, worked with Sheikh and Yellowman to collect data. We asked Sheikh, Yellowman, and Rock to discuss their collective work and how they use art as a vehicle for advocacy.

AG The three of you collaborated to make an installation at the Smart for *Toward Common Cause*. How did you meet each other?

JY As a spiritual advisor for Utah Diné Bikéyah at Bears Ears, I look after what we still have, our medicines and the things that are sacred to us, the offerings that we make. That means we look after the land and study it and what's happening on it. We ask, why is this happening today? Somewhere along the line, Fazal came into the picture. And from there on, we started traveling to different areas. Tommy is from this place. I'd never met him, though.

FS I have a very specific set of memories. In 2016, Jonah was part of the Inter-Tribal Coalition that had approached the Obama administration about turning Bears Ears into a National Monument. I came to Utah at a critical moment when this decision was at risk pending the outcome of the presidential election in 2016. While I'd been to this area many times, what was different this time was that I was invited to be part of the coalition's annual meeting in Bluff. Something that is etched in my mind is this idea that I was entering a room filled with members of many different communities, all of whom were extremely well regarded, and all of whom had put historical differences aside in the service of this wonderful thing that became Bears Ears.

There were members of five tribes sitting around a table, men and women. Writer Terry Tempest Williams, who is from a family deeply impacted by life as downwinders from nuclear testing, was with me. I saw myself among a mixture of various communities, and this resonated with what a lot of my work is about—the idea is to reach across distance to collaborate, and uncenter the ego of being a singular artist.

TR Having completed postdoc work as a research fellow in earth sciences and environmental sustainability at Princeton University, I came back to Utah in 2019. I was working with grassroots organizations gathering data on uranium ore in abandoned mines at Bears Ears. Fazal reached out to me and came to Utah with two undergraduate students from Princeton working on topics related to environmental exposure—oil, fuel, gas, air quality, and water quality. We went to Bears Ears with a Geiger counter to look at native ore. I explained that a lot of tribal compensation comes from uranium mining, specifically uranium ore, but what's not well known is that where there's uranium you will also find beryllium, thorium, and radium.[2]

FS What Tommy's not saying is that on that day, at that spot, the Geiger counter was humming. To spend the night in this spot is to put your life at risk.

The super-simple synopsis of what followed very organically was a collaboration with the elders at the intersection of the sciences and the humanities. The aim was to attend to the voices of the elders while thinking about the science and the legacy of environmental racism. And then it grew again to become an activist rebuttal to stripping the monument. So Jonah has a perspective, Tommy has another, and I offer my two cents. We learn from each other.

AW Jonah, the invitation to Fazal to be part of *Toward Common Cause* was also an invitation to consider two questions: How does art respond to a crisis? And can art do something different than other modes of problem solving? What do those questions mean to you?

JY My dad, my uncles, my brother-in-law all worked in the mines. I was just living my life day-in and day-out. I didn't think about Bears Ears preservation. As time went on, they got sick and they're no longer around.

Here's what I am learning from work at Bears Ears. Public Lands Initiative (PLI) is going to start digging into the ground. They're going to start looking for uranium and potash, or whatever, to make something, a profit, out of it or to live off of it. It makes me think back, back to when I was young. It makes me think about all my relatives that used to work there, how the water was being contaminated. We've seen how things are over there, the oil. When it gets really hot, it smells over there. I thought about that. I lived that. We don't want this any more. We've seen what happened.

Preserving what we still have, what little we have, means we have to study it. The plants that were there, and the medicine that was there. Food, everything, was nearby. We need to preserve this. Most of our ceremonies stem from that area. A lot of stories were gathered just being there, just being part of the place.

Fazal came, and then Tommy, and they started taking me around to these areas that Tommy was studying and talking about. It made me think about things that we never really thought about when I was young. I guess we just wanted everything to be okay. It wouldn't bother us until later on.

This place, the monument, is sacred. It is where our prayers are and where our medicines are. We want to preserve it. That's the way I think about this work together, that is its purpose, why we work together. I think about what we're going to preserve, what we're looking after. How are we going to fix some of the things that are still out there making people sick? How are we going to tell our people? Anyways, that's some of the way I understand.

FS Don't forget this was all unfolding during the pandemic, an intercession that had a profound impact on this community. What we started making together shifted. A kind of aggressive insistence on environmental racism shifted to making a space for healing and solace. Smaller, place-based projects focused on the wellbeing of people became more important than anything else.

TR I'm invited to attend a lot of meetings about risks associated with environmental exposure. They can be contentious meetings, highly political. It took me some time to realize that they were the perfect opportunity to say what I have to say coming from my Indigenous community. The science will be hotly debated, but I can tell a personal story that cannot be denied. Our project operates in the same way. The personal cause-and-effect cannot be denied.

It has to do with trying to give back. And that's what I've been working on. Working with Fazal on the water project empowers the community as well. The knowledge I've gained as a scientist goes back to the community, there's power in the knowledge that I give back. They learn and they realize that what I've done and what I've experienced and what I'm offering doesn't only benefit me, it benefits the community.

AW Jonah, how do you share your work with the community?

JY I went to a boarding school and experienced all kinds of trauma. As a spiritual advisor, I look back on that, and it makes me think about our language, are we really losing our language? Are we really forgetting who we are? Trauma and genocide could have made that happen [but we can try to] go back to the way we used to live.

So we started an apprenticeship program to relearn our languages and relearn our traditional ways of medicine, being a medicine man. That started a year ago. So far, we have one apprentice who became a medicine man. Another one is still an apprentice, and we're still working on getting the funding. That's how I'm sharing my work with the community, relearning our languages. If we lose all that, how are we going to survive? How are we going to remember our stories, how this National Monument became what it is? And if you preserve something, there's something that's there that we can learn from. And we can relearn our ways of being, our Native perspective. Our creation stories say we were the stewards of this land. We are supposed to be the ones here looking after this. If we forget about that, then what do we have?

That's what I've been telling my relatives. We are getting back to our way of life, learning how to talk, learning who we are, and what our plan is. And from that, where we come from, where we are going.

That's one of the things that I teach my community. That's what I do.

Fazal and Tommy are doing their part, making people realize by looking at how harmful the way things are and what we can do.

AW And that's a way of telling stories as well.

FS That's one of the most interesting things about our project—it happens at the intersection of traditional knowledge and scientific rigor. Tommy embodies both of those, he was raised in the traditional household and brings scientific rigor back to the community. We are trying to nurture a conversation between the sciences and Indigenous knowledge that is at risk of being lost—knowledge that could be tapped into usefully. How can we resituate these forms of knowing so they are not in opposition with each other, but rather in productive dialogue?

Jonah, do you remember when we gathered together to ask, why are we giving over all of the decision-making abilities to the outside? What I heard you saying was let's not forget about our own traditional knowledge. We've seen things like this before. Why are we looking to Western medicine to heal us? We can be looking to our traditional healing processes. We don't know with certainty what will move us forward, but why would we throw out or forget the extraordinary resource of our traditional knowledge?

AW And so, is there an outcome you have in mind from this project?

TR There are three.

First, it's air and water quality: the community's oversight for regulation, maintaining jobs, improving the quality of life, reducing the number of health effects. And that's not just for Aneth but for the community out by the Chaco Canyon area as well.

Next, it's uranium and the dust here in Monument Valley: looking at the dust that's on top of the cliff that wasn't addressed before. By finger-printing that dust, you can trace it as a source of groundwater contamination. For instance, I've traced groundwater contamination in Sanders, Arizona, to Church Rock, some fifty miles away. Such studies would allow us to get federal dollars to address health issues.

Third, making access to potable water inside Monument Valley Tribal Park a reality while demonstrating how tribal federal regulators can address preserving a culture and not altering it. Because personally I think that safe drinking water strategy is based on population densities, putting all these people together in one community and providing water, but it's not preserving our way of life in a traditional sense. I will define as success having policy incorporated into our tribe, and other tribes realizing that there are alternative ways of doing things that will benefit them as well.

JY For me, it's mostly applying how the medicine men look at things alongside these two and how they see things. Together it helps protect what we're preserving, and the way we talk about things back home. Myself and some of my relatives are very traditional in what we believe in, and we want it to go forward, to see if we can learn our old ways of living, our old ways of doing our ceremonies and what we did through our ceremonies and through faith.

It got us to where we are today. So I know that in the future time, what we try to do to be successful is through our languages, or relearning some of the ceremonies. And some of the artifacts are out there that need to be brought back, and a lot of other things that we talk about that we can do. There are a lot of things on my mind every day. So that's my belief, I guess, and telling my people that we can go forward with this. That's in the plan.

AW How do you want people to respond to the work, to the photographs, to the portraits, to the testimonies, to the film of methane emissions? What do you want people to experience when they see this work in a public exhibition space?

JY I want people to look and understand something that we still have as Natives, to see the way we see things. Despite all that has come before, we still hold on to our traditional ways to be clear to walk in beauty. That's what it is all about. The way the basket is with the medicine items inside. For us and for everybody's protection, it's worth looking at, understanding, and respecting.

FS I hope it's a clear marker for a history of environmental racism that hasn't been properly addressed, a signpost in collaboration with these communities, working with them, giving over the voice. We're standing together in a collaboration. When you take the testimony, advance the portrait, make an exhibition, those are all investments in conversation that insists on attending to what has happened historically in order that it not happen again.

1 Downwinder is the term used for communities and individuals who experienced fallout from nuclear testing in the American West.

2 Uranium, beryllium, thorium, and radium are all highly toxic, radioactive elements. Exposure to any of these materials poses myriad short- and long-term health risks.

Experimentation

Key principles underlying the MacArthur Fellows Program–embracing risk, accepting the potential for failure, and encouraging open-ended engagement and adaptation–guided the project planning of *Toward Common Cause*.

Beyond What We Know: Philanthropy, Experimentation, and the Support of Creativity

Don Meyer

PHILANTHROPY AND EXPERIMENTATION

Private philanthropic foundations are defined by their intent to serve a public purpose. They are where privately held resources meet commitments to common cause.

The John D. and Catherine T. MacArthur Foundation was established in 1978 by John Donald MacArthur, who amassed a fortune growing the Bankers Life and Casualty insurance company into an empire. From the start, the MacArthur Foundation embraced a spirit of experimentation and trust. "I made the money, now you figure out what to do with it," MacArthur is said to have told the first board of directors he assembled to guide the work of the future foundation. The son of a coal miner turned Baptist preacher, Mr. MacArthur himself grew up in poverty. He was a self-made man, a protagonist in an American dream, in the manner of a character from a Horatio Alger story, like the philanthropist and steel magnate Andrew Carnegie, who pioneered large-scale philanthropy as we know it today.

The MacArthur Fellows Program, where I have served as a program officer since 2013, announced its first class of fellows in 1981. Along with the foundation's enduring commitments to journalism, media, and the city of Chicago, where the foundation is headquartered, the Fellows Program is among its longest-running programs and for many people its best known. MacArthur Fellowships, often referred to as "genius grants," are awarded annually to exceptionally creative individuals doing groundbreaking and timely work in any field. The fellowship comes with a no-strings-attached cash award, currently $800,000, paid out over five years.

LS: The Fellows Program does not use the term "genius grant," which can be awkward and burdensome for recipients, with its connotations of solitary pursuits and high IQs. Fellows themselves often point to the contributions of others that have made their work possible.

The program does not shape its classes of fellows around a particular topic or theme or to achieve a specific agenda, aiming instead to celebrate the broad spectrum of human creativity. The MacArthur Fellowship is not project-based, and no reporting is required, the hypothesis being that: (1) an award of this nature, free from restrictions, can provide the conditions for creativity to flourish; (2) creativity generates new ideas, experiments, works of literature and art, and institutions and organizations; and (3) all these have the potential to benefit society broadly.

Like the MacArthur Foundation as a whole, the Fellows Program began as an experiment in philanthropy. What would result from a funding mechanism of this sort? Would it lead to major scientific advancements? Would it enable the writing of a literary masterpiece or a new way of working in the visual arts? In the humanities, would it support difficult and extended archival research enabling scholars to press beyond prevailing assumptions? In any case, would it not at least allow for unformed ideas and emerging lines of inquiry to percolate and germinate over the course of the fellowship period and beyond? By focusing on creativity—a broad concept that takes many forms and changes with time—the MacArthur Fellows Program was designed to make space for testing these possibilities and more.

LS: The fellows named here offer a small sampling of endeavors recognized over the years. The examples of creativity could go on and on, to include a midwife, a landscape architect, a computer scientist, a blacksmith.

Creativity can advance disciplines as traditionally defined in unexpected ways, as Yuval Sharon has done with opera, or Michelle Dorrance with tap. Creativity drives the combination of methods and approaches from different fields to produce original results, the way Dani Bassett draws from physics and neuroscience to provide new insights into how the human brain works. Creativity finds innovative and effective solutions to seemingly intractable or poorly understood problems, as has Ai-Jen Poo, who is leading efforts to improve working conditions for domestic workers. And at a basic level, creativity is inventing something new, as Manu Prakash and Peidong Yang have done in bioengineering and inorganic chemistry, respectively.

Creativity also characterizes the work of a figure like Bryan Stevenson, who founded the Equal Justice Initiative (EJI) in 1989 to provide legal representation to people who have been wrongfully incarcerated. Since its founding in Montgomery, Alabama, EJI has expanded its scope and grown into an organization with national reach and a fortified commitment to "changing the narrative about race in America," opening the National Memorial for Peace and Justice in Montgomery in 2018.

The MacArthur Fellows Program is still quite unique in philanthropy in the United States, and after four decades, the program's founding experiment continues. We learn from it in real time, attentive to new areas of inquiry, and responsive to societal needs in a changing world.

ON THE FELLOWS PROGRAM PROCESS AND PHILOSOPHY

One cannot apply for the MacArthur Fellowship. The selection process of the MacArthur Fellows Program relies on an extensive and ever-expanding network of nominators, evaluators, and selectors. Nominees are suggested to the program by a large, revolving, and geographically diverse group of nominators with experience and expertise in an unlimited array of fields who are well positioned to recognize creative potential. Nominators serve confidentially, and nominees can be under consideration for many months or years.

The evaluation process is comprehensive: a broad range of individuals are invited to share their thoughts on a nominee's work and its significance based on their familiarity with it.

We aim to include a multiplicity of voices and insights coming from within a nominee's field and beyond. In the next stage of our process, an external selection committee—comprised of around a dozen individuals representing a breadth of expertise across disciplines and fields—reviews nominees' work and considers recommendations from nominators and evaluators.

LS: This participatory process is a feature of the award that recipients often find most affirming and humbling. The vote of confidence comes not just from a foundation in Chicago, but from a chorus of voices from within and beyond a recipient's community of practice.

Finally, after intensive deliberations by the selection committee, potential MacArthur Fellows are presented to the foundation's board for final approval. The work of the Program Staff is to coordinate and accommodate the many voices and viewpoints that reach us through our networks of nominators, evaluators, and selectors, and to safeguard the confidentiality of all participants and nominees. Honesty and candor are critical to the success of our process, and establishing trust between the program and its wide-ranging participants is essential to our work. In short, our process is a participatory one that values the perspectives and insights of individuals representing innumerable fields who are positioned to know much better than we are what stands out as exceptionally creative in their respective areas of work and expertise.

In 2012 and 2013, the Fellows Program underwent a review—part of the foundation's cyclical evaluation process—to assess its impact and to identify opportunities for change and growth. During the review, MacArthur Fellows were surveyed, and many expressed interest in having the Fellows Program provide more opportunities for awardees to connect with each other as well as with the foundation. Since then, the program has responded. For our thirty-fifth anniversary in 2016, the Fellows Program worked with local organizations and institutions to bring MacArthur Fellows to Chicago to present their work in public-facing performances and events, connecting fellows with each other, with Fellows Program and other MacArthur Foundation team members, and with the city of Chicago. Building on the activities of the thirty-fifth anniversary, the Fellows Program also introduced a new mechanism for making small grants to organizations nationwide for free public programming that brings two or more MacArthur Fellows together to share their work with new audiences.

KP: Over seven years, the Fellows Program has funded nearly sixty events through its X-Grants program. These events—talks, panels, performances, exhibitions, workshops, a documentary film—engage fellows across areas of endeavor.

The successes of the thirty-fifth anniversary activities inspired an even more ambitious project for the Fellows Program's fortieth anniversary, the exhibition that became *Toward Common Cause: Art, Social Change, and the MacArthur Fellows at 40*. It began with the notion of celebrating our fortieth anniversary with an exhibition of artwork created by MacArthur Fellows spanning the program's history. Just as the MacArthur Fellows Program originated as an experiment in philanthropy, the anniversary project developed as an experiment and a challenge. In this case, the challenge was to share the work of MacArthur Fellows equitably across communities in Chicago. Over the course of more than three years, the exhibition would acquire a name, grow into a multisite, cross-institutional project, and in the process bring surprising new insights to both the Fellows team and the MacArthur Foundation.

In the spirit of the Fellows Program's embrace of multiple perspectives and openness to ideas, a small group of MacArthur colleagues drawn from other programs and departments at the foundation was convened to offer insights on engaging with communities and organizations in Chicago and share their thoughts on the prospective exhibition. The group quickly foregrounded the urgent need to address disparities in access to resources in Chicago, stressing the necessity of extending the exhibition's presence to communities where there are few opportunities to engage with art. It became clear that the projects, installations, performances, and programs that would constitute the exhibition would need to be responsive to the organizations that hosted them and the people they serve.

LY: Understanding the characteristics of place-based grantmaking and the desired change we seek there requires place-based information and analysis. Maps are an important tool to provide spatial analysis for data-informed decision-making.

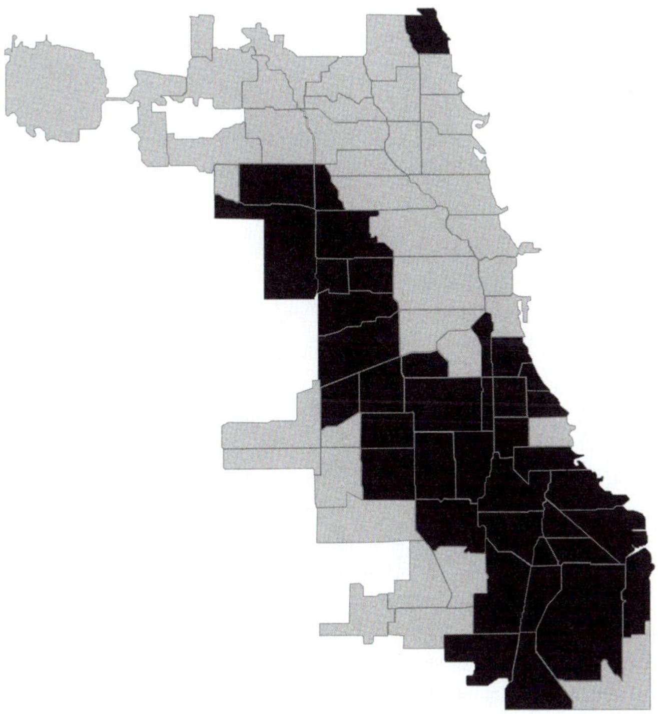

Areas of Chicago where median household income is < $51,074 (in black).[1]

Given the scope of work involved in planning and producing an exhibition that would reach communities across the city, the Fellows Program determined that an organization with expertise in exhibition-making would be best equipped to realize the nascent vision. The Smart Museum of Art at the University of Chicago expressed strong interest in meeting the challenges such a vision presented. They proposed a framework for producing an exhibition involving the participation of organizations all around Chicago while allowing each to pursue its own mission and decide for itself what its participation might entail. In adopting this framework, *Toward Common Cause* grew beyond

DuSable Black History Museum and Education Center
740 E. 56th Pl.
Chicago, IL 60637

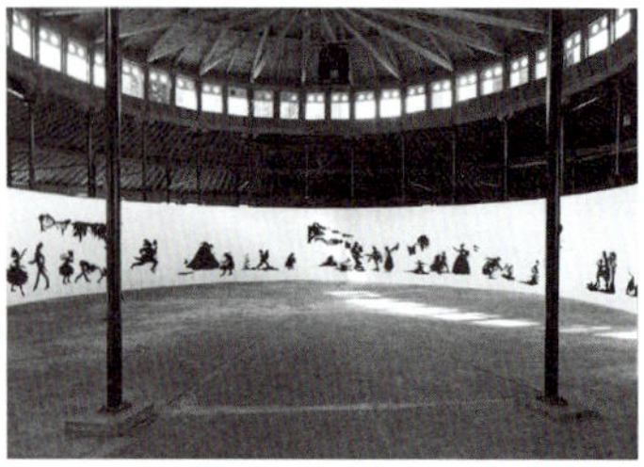

When the DuSable Black History Museum and Education Center opened in 1961, it was known as the Ebony Museum of Negro History and Art. Born in the home of Dr. Margaret Taylor Burroughs and her husband Charles Burroughs, it has always been dedicated to Black history, art, and culture. Located today on the eastern edge of Chicago's Washington Park, the DuSable campus comprises a museum, the Roundhouse—an indoor horse arena designed in 1880 by architects Burnham & Root for the Chicago Park District—and an outdoor plaza where live music plays throughout the summer months. The Roundhouse was the *Toward Common Cause* venue for Kara Walker's *Presenting Negro Scenes Drawn Upon My Passage Through the South and Reconfigured for the Benefit of Enlightened Audiences Wherever Such May Be Found, By Myself, Missus K.E.B. Walker, Colored* (Scenes #7, #23).

Kara Walker's 150-foot silhouette narrative has been displayed multiple times across the city of Chicago. It premiered in 1997 at the Renaissance Society, a space that for more than a century has engaged new ideas in the arts (p. 91). Walker's work was acquired by the Museum of Contemporary Art Chicago and displayed there and in North Michigan Avenue galleries in 2013. For *Toward Common Cause*, it was installed at DuSable's Roundhouse in a circular

(continued on opposite page)

a museum exhibition to include community art centers and foundations, research centers, social-service organizations, and the Chicago Housing Authority.

Toward Common Cause poses a question about resources. The exhibition treats the work of MacArthur Fellows as a common resource to be made accessible to local communities and the general public. After all, art is created for an audience. Through this overarching concept, which raises pressing questions about the relationships between creativity, access to resources, and societal change, *Toward Common Cause* models what sharing can look like. *Sharing* is more complicated and messy than simply *giving*. Equitable access involves accommodating multiple parties—meeting them where they are, both literally and figuratively—which requires listening and open dialogue, the outcomes of which cannot be known in advance.

NYT: A show of artists celebrated for their individual accomplishments is intentionally diffuse, collaborative and community-oriented, but that fits the theme, an exploration of how resources can be shared.

PHILANTHROPY AND MEASUREMENT

As cultures and societies change, the line between the public good and private interest gets redefined and renegotiated. Existing at this nexus, foundations navigate this shifting terrain.

Let me pause here briefly to consider the role philanthropy plays in the arts and culture. The history of philanthropy is intertwined with social hierarchies of the nineteenth century. The American myth of the self-made man originates from a social matrix that validates notions of individualism and assumes the superiority of some groups of people over others. Today, the concentration of wealth in private hands poses threats to equitable access to resources necessary to thrive. Representative governments are designed to deliver power to the people they represent, but when they fail to do so, the public good is increasingly entrusted to private entities that control access to vital resources.

JS: How will philanthropy adapt to root meaningful change in the bones of 21st-century institutional practice?

At the turn of the twentieth century, recognizing the needs of a society afflicted by a grossly uneven apportionment of wealth, Andrew Carnegie articulated a new mode of cultural support that would become a key model for modern philanthropy. Carnegie believed that accumulated private wealth should be left neither to heirs nor to the state but instead should be directed to the establishment of institutions that would benefit the public good. He went on to found 2,509 libraries around the world, over half in the United States. He also established universities, museums, and concert halls. In Carnegie's philanthropic model, private foundations can reconcile differences in access to resources that governments cannot or will not address.

For Carnegie, exposure to cultural achievement was a vital means to achieving self-improvement. He compared libraries and cultural institutions to ladders leading to higher levels of thought and refinement of taste. He understood that education, science, culture, and art cannot thrive without the resources to support them. However, Carnegie's model of philanthropy assumes a top-down approach unchallenged by twenty-first-century values of transparency and equity. Histories of Western art are also histories of inequitable ownership, colonialism, and industrialization. A challenge of philanthropy today is to embrace the best impulses of Carnegie's model while retooling our practices for a new century.

The Question of Impact

LY: Relating demographic, population, and other data with spatial data provides an important piece of knowledge in understanding patterns, relationships, reach, and impact, in order to make informed decisions on wide-ranging complex issues.

MacArthur Fellows have contributed to the development of knowledge and culture in numerous ways demonstrable by traditional measures of success and achievement: scientific breakthroughs, humanistic research that reorients a field, works of art that push artistic traditions in new directions. The work of the fellows is impactful in ways we can readily grasp. But the MacArthur Fellows Program also recognizes that impact may manifest in ways we are not yet able to measure, discern, or even know. The definition of impact is treated provisionally by the program since the extent of impact only reveals itself over time. The experiment is ongoing.

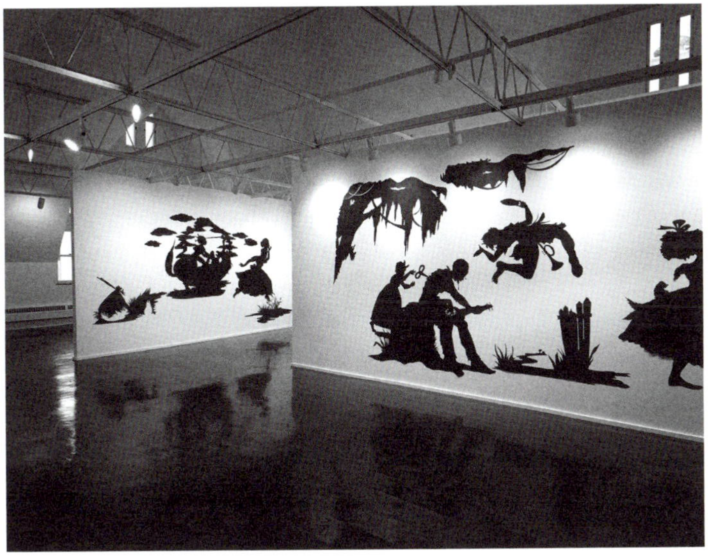

Kara Walker's 1997 installation of *Presenting Negro Scenes Drawn Upon My Passage Through the South and Reconfigured for the Benefit of Enlightened Audiences Wherever Such May Be Found, By Myself, Missus K.E.B. Walker, Colored,* at the Renaissance Society. Photo: Tom van Eynde

When Kara Walker was awarded a MacArthur Fellowship in 1997, she was twenty-eight years old, with only a few solo exhibitions to her name. Nevertheless, her early work is mesmerizing and challenging. Already there were the black silhouettes of scenes from the history of American slavery for which she is now so well known. Walker's approach to representation in both form and content has since played a critical role in reorienting the field of contemporary art toward questions of racialized power and subjugation. But how can one begin to quantify that impact? Exhibition histories, bibliographies, awards and and other forms of recognition, and holdings in public and prominent collections

room within the 64,000-square-foot arena. Thus situated, *Presenting Negro Scenes* occupied a Black space with a predominantly Black audience on the city's majority Black South Side at a remove from the white cubes and predominantly white institutions in which it had previously been shown.

Presenting Negro Scenes' debut in the Roundhouse also placed the work in exquisite dialogue with artist Cauleen Smith's *The Right Time, Before and After* from 2017. Sited perfectly on the north-south-east-west axis, one of the building's architectural elements is a circular ring of windows atop the roof. Smith installed colored filter gels on these windows to create dynamic, luminous pockets of colored light on the Roundhouse floor that divide north from south, an axis that maps redlining and racial division in the city of Chicago. Warm gel colors point north, and cool colors point south. Walker's silhouettes were animated throughout the course of the day by this reminder of the city's enduring racial divides.

Photo: Nathan Keay

Stony Island Arts Bank
6760 S. Stony Island Ave.
Chicago, IL 60649

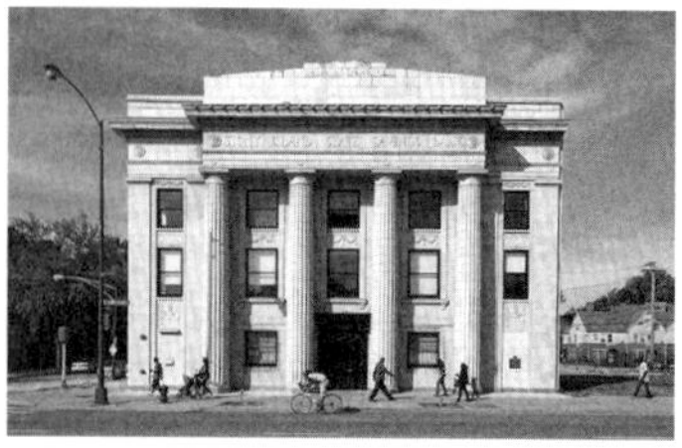

The Stony Island Arts Bank sits at the corner of East 68th Street and South Stony Island Avenue on Chicago's South Side. The Neoclassical building first opened in 1923 as the Stony Island Trust and Savings Bank, part of what was once a thriving ecosystem of community banks across the city. The building is situated within the Greater Grand Crossing neighborhood, immediately adjacent to the communities of Woodlawn and South Shore and mere blocks from the site of the soon to open Obama Presidential Center in historic Jackson Park. The bank building was abandoned in the 1980s and sat vacant for decades until Chicago-based artist Theaster Gates purchased the property from the city in 2015 and transformed it into the Stony Island Arts Bank.

The Stony Island Arts Bank serves as the headquarters for Rebuild Foundation's network of properties on the South Side and as a home for the foundation's archives and collections. Founded by Gates, Rebuild supports artists and strengthens communities by providing free arts programming and creating new cultural amenities on the South Side of Chicago. Their mission is "to demonstrate the impact of innovative, ambitious, and entrepreneurial cultural initiatives and is enriched by three core values: Black people matter, Black spaces matter, and Black objects matter."

(continued on opposite page)

provide the framework for a story, but they cannot account for the actual encounters between millions of viewers over the decades and Walker's arresting, haunted images, which prior to her controversial interventions had never before been so frankly displayed in art galleries and museums (p. 144).

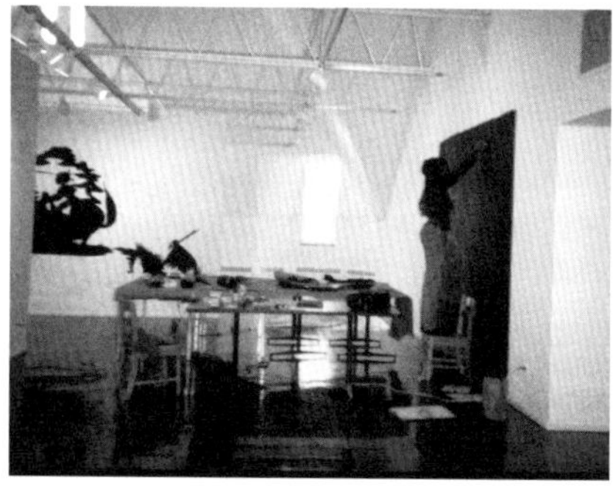

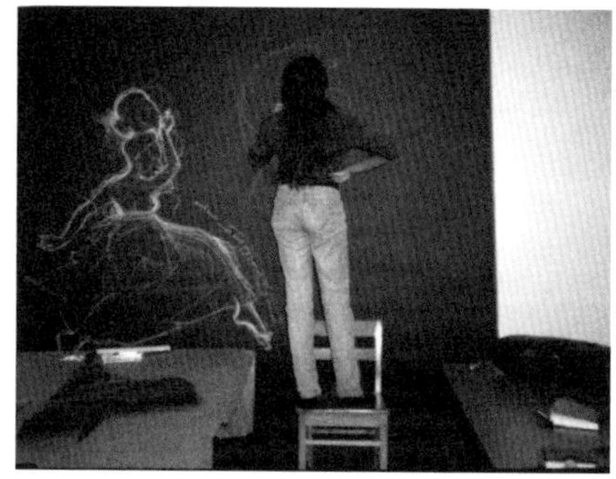

Kara Walker preparing her 1997 exhibition at the Renaissance Society. Photo: Renaissance Society at the University of Chicago

Metrics, Quality, and Quantity

Foundations and philanthropy are interested in impact. They exist to benefit the public good and must demonstrate that they do so. Thus, metrics are devised and employed to measure and understand the impact of the work a foundation supports. But metrics cannot capture all forms of impact and account for only what we already know how to measure.

In academic fields, publication and citation records serve as a means to gauge impact, but they are of limited use when trying to understand the unique nature of scholarly contributions that chart new patterns of thought and open onto new areas of inquiry. Exhibition and performance histories, bibliographies, and awards and fellowships all serve as indicators of aesthetic value within the realm of artistic production, but they capture little in the way of actual, individual aesthetic experience. Likewise, exhibition attendance figures fail to shed light on the lasting impact that works of art leave in the minds and memories of individual viewers.

Challenges arise when it comes to finding metrics capable of capturing the impact articulated in a statement like this one from Jerrold Herman, a resident of the Minnie Riperton Apartments where Njideka Akunyili Crosby's mural project was installed: "They wanted to put out something that the general public notices these buildings were here. You could see it, but there wasn't any reason to *notice* it. Then there's you coming home to a plain place versus you coming home to a place with a mural. That's where you stay. It's an extra incentive to look up. If you look up, your head is high and your shoulders are back and all's right with the world." Impact of this kind is deeply meaningful but exceedingly hard to quantify (Scenes #14; p. 182).

The Fellows Program recognizes that impact can take many forms, many of which cannot be known in advance. This openness to not presupposing to know the extent of creativity's manifold forms and its impact on society has guided the mis-

NP: Funders have traditionally defined the metrics of success. Trust-based philanthropy turns that system on its head. Trust is powerful, but also fragile, particularly between people who have been locked in relationships of conflict and inequity for generations.

sion of the MacArthur Fellows Program from the start. One of the hypotheses of the program is that creativity and freedom are linked. The no-strings-attached aspect of the fellowship is there to provide fellows maximum freedom to pursue any line of inquiry, activity, or endeavor they so choose, in any way they see fit. It is intended to offer the freedom to explore untried ideas and new lines of inquiry, the freedom to fail, try again, and refine. Freedom is a condition for critical reflection, which fosters creativity—and freedom of this sort is premised on trust.

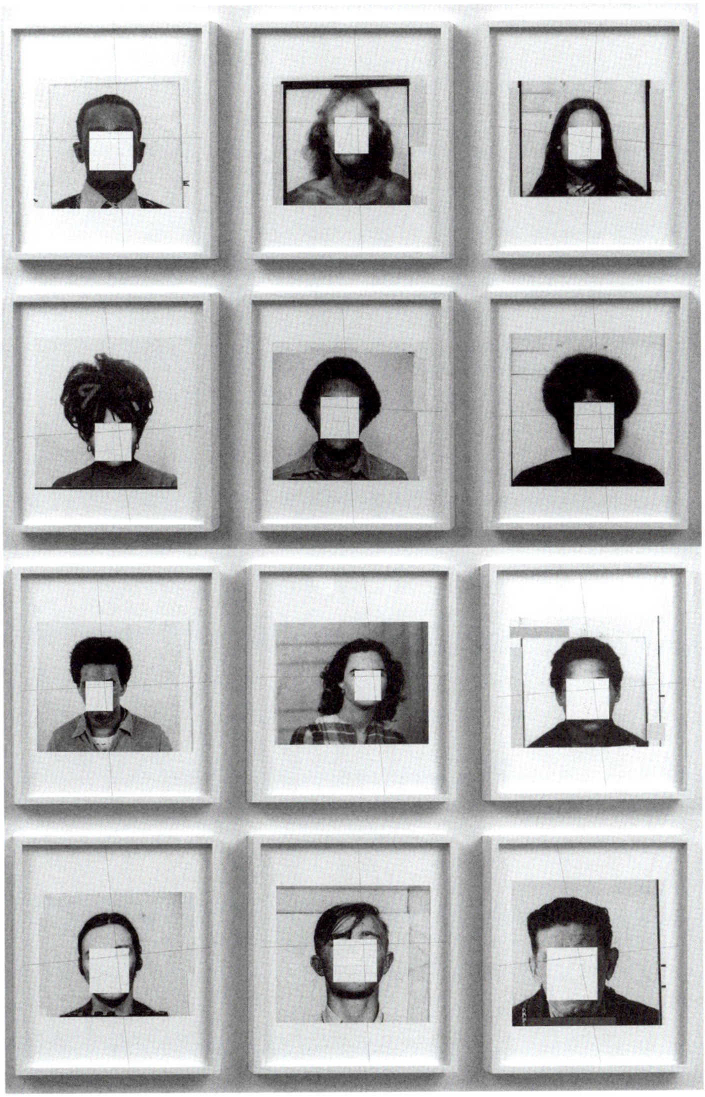

Trevor Paglen's *They Took the Faces from the Accused and the Dead . . .*
Photo: Courtesy of the artist, Pace Gallery, and Altman Siegel, San Francisco

During *Toward Common Cause*, the Stony Island Arts Bank hosted the work of Dawoud Bey, Nicole Eisenman, David Hammons, Gary Hill, Whitfield Lovell, Kerry James Marshall, Trevor Paglen, Carrie Mae Weems, Deborah Willis, and Fred Wilson (Scenes #6, #15, #21, #33, #35). This group of objects offered artistic reflections on how we see others, how we see ourselves, and how our view of others is inflected by race, gender, and class, among other considerations. These are questions that currently preoccupy the art world. Yet they are questions that the artists included in this exhibition had been raising for decades.

The presentation at the Stony Island Arts Bank featured several works from the Smart's permanent collection. This represented an opportunity to share works by the likes of Marshall and Weems with audiences who may not have felt welcome on the university campus. This included a remounting of Bey's *Chicago Project* commissioned by the Smart in 1992. Bey's first Chicago-based project with young people, it is comprised of portraits and interviews with students from four local high schools (p. 58).

Photo: Tom Harris

INTERDISCIPLINARITY

As *Toward Common Cause* developed, alignment between the values of the Fellows Program and the methods of the exhibition team came into clearer view. With its themes of inclusion, visibility, access to resources, and environmental justice, *Toward Common Cause* demanded an interdisciplinary approach, reflecting the MacArthur Fellows Program's embrace of multiple perspectives.

The space of the work of art shares affinities with the space of scientific experimentation. Both present models of provisional worlds, constituted within designated frameworks. The experiment's procedures are analogous to the artwork's processes of creation. The scientific method and the act of making art both begin with conjecture—a hypothesis, a sketch—then proceed to assess validity, promise, potential. The knowledge thus gained becomes new ground for further experiments and creative work.

JTG: We need to increase fluency in both STEM and the arts, integrating them as Leonardo da Vinci said for "The Development of a Complete Mind": Study the science of art. Study the art of science. Develop your senses—especially learn how to see.

An essential feature of the MacArthur Fellows Program is interdisciplinarity. We use the metaphor of the bouquet to conceptualize the interdisciplinary composition of our classes of fellows. Interdisciplinarity broadens perspectives through representation of multiple bodies of knowledge and methodologies within a shared framework. It establishes conceptual space for insights from fields typically far removed from each other to inform thinking in new contexts.

Fellows themselves have reported that the MacArthur Fellowship is particularly meaningful to them because it reaches beyond the disciplinary and professional limits of their specific areas of work and connects people across a multitude of fields. As one fellow put it, "boundlessness" is what the program represents to them.

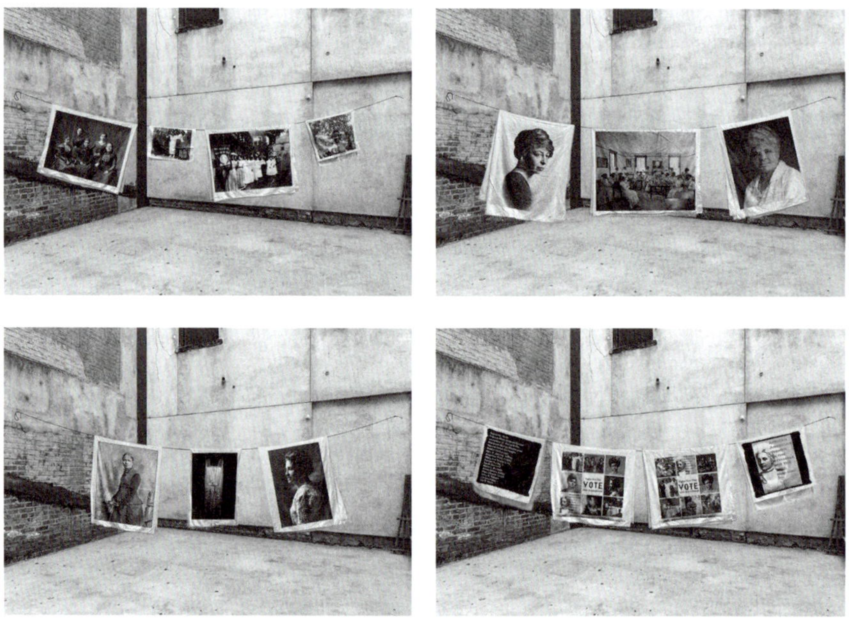

Deborah Willis's *The Clothesline: Women's work never praised never done*. Courtesy of the artist and Kalia Brooks Studio

Take Trevor Paglen, whose work crosses boundaries between art, geography, investigative reporting, and human rights. He is finding ways to make secret operations visible, to expose systems of surveillance and abuses of power that determine the lives of everyday people. Trained as a geographer,

Paglen mobilizes photography's intertwined documentary and aesthetic capacities to give original visual form to his research findings. In his 2019 work *They Took the Faces from the Accused and the Dead . . .*, he exposes how facial recognition software is trained on archives of mugshots in an alarming violation of privacy. The social and political dimensions of Paglen's work are established and solidified through interdisciplinarity.

Deborah Willis, too, has developed an artistic practice underwritten and enriched by interdisciplinarity. The academic study of the history of photography informs her own photographic work, and she utilizes photography's capacity to hold and convey social meaning to make foundational contributions to our understanding of how Black women have been represented in history (Scenes #15).

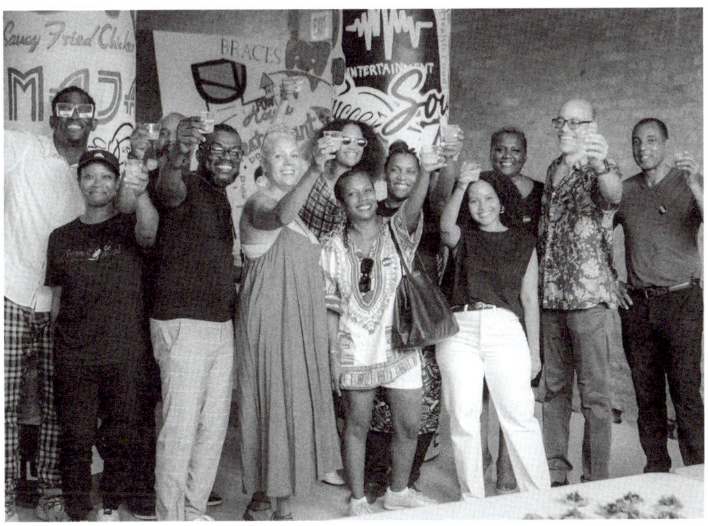

Opening event for Rick Lowe's *Black Wall Street Journey* at Urban Juncture Foundation, July 17, 2021. Photo: Nicolette Stanton

LS: Rick Lowe's social sculptures embody another important form of creativity. They aim to activate and shine light on the value and creativity of entire neighborhoods and communities.

But how is one to measure the impact of artwork that addresses social issues? By what criteria does one assess a project like Rick Lowe's *Black Wall Street Journey*, which finds precedent in his Project Row Houses. Begun in 1993, Project Row Houses transformed five city blocks in a transitional Houston neighborhood into a vibrant and essential community center. Still thriving today, the project offers a vast array of art programs, community enrichment services (including tutoring, support for small business development, community markets and food distribution), and neighborhood development activities that pair preservation work and affordable housing. For *Toward Common Cause*, Lowe chose to focus on the promise and the tragedy of another once-thriving Black community, Tulsa, Oklahoma's Greenwood neighborhood, known as "Black Wall Street," where generations of Black wealth were destroyed in a two-day race riot in 1921. In Chicago, Lowe's work was a collaborative endeavor that engaged audiences with the far too little-known story of Black Wall Street, but this is only one part of a project with a long-term goal of creating Black wealth in Black communities (Scenes #22; p. 142).

Jane Addams Hull-House Museum
800 S. Halsted St.
Chicago, IL 60607

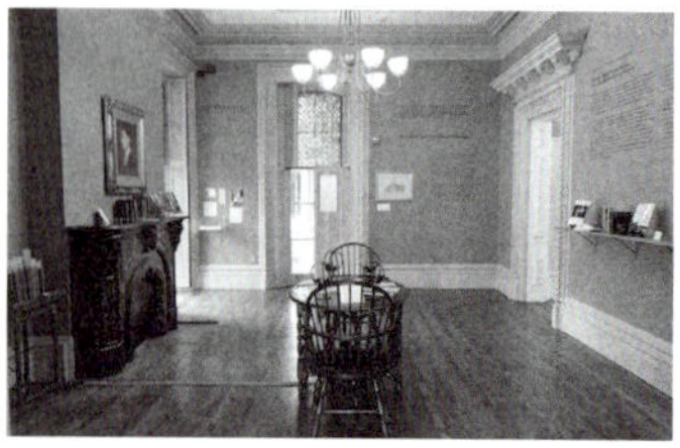

In 1889, Jane Addams and Ellen Gates Starr opened Hull House on Chicago's Near West Side. Hull House was the first settlement house in the United States. Its mission was to provide social services to the city's immigrant and working-class communities, including child care and kindergarten, an art gallery, employment support, citizenship classes, language courses, and access to arts and cultural courses and events. Hull House grew to encompass more than a dozen properties, was home to dozens of activists and visionaries, and became a hub for Progressive activism and reform in Chicago, the country, and the world.

Jane Addams Hull-House Museum draws upon the legacy of international peace activist and feminist Jane Addams and other social reformers who lived and worked alongside their immigrant neighbors to create social change on the Near West Side. The museum is located in two of the original settlement house buildings: the Hull Home, a National Historic Landmark, and the Residents Dining Hall. The museum connects the histories of the Hull-House Settlement to present-day social-justice issues. Exhibitions and public programs highlight histories of activism, progressive education, and democratic principles of participation and exchange.

With *Gómez-Peña's Casa Museo: A Living Museum and Archive*, pioneering conceptual-performance artist

(continued on opposite page)

When my colleagues and I began iterating ideas that eventually became *Toward Common Cause*, I did not anticipate an exhibition that would lead to projects with such ambitious goals as imagining forms of economic development in communities historically deprived of opportunity. I did not at the time of the exhibition's inception have the vision to foresee how art could play such a galvanizing role in bringing people together at a time of pandemic-induced isolation. *Toward Common Cause* helped me understand that art is a source of inspiration that nourishers all kinds of human endeavor.

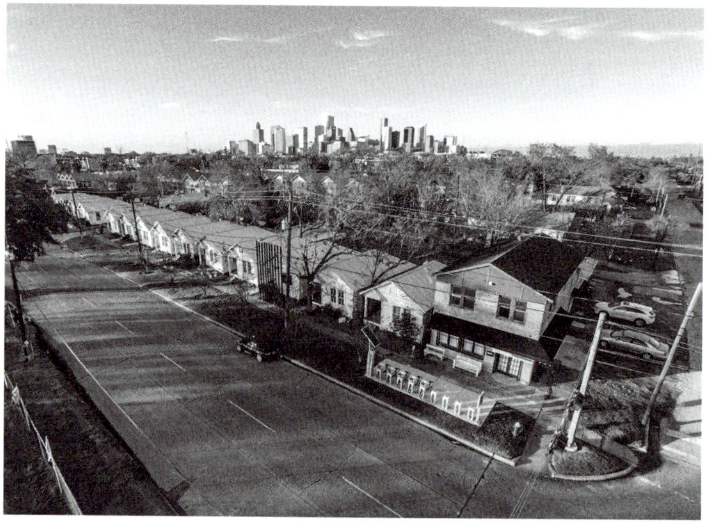

Project Row Houses, Houston. Photo: Peter Molick/Project Row Houses

How does one evaluate the success of Wendy Ewald's photography workshops with young students at Centro Romero, which culminated in two exhibitions in different neighborhoods? Is success measured in terms of the experiences of the students? Or does it depend on the critical reception of the exhibition and artworks? Three years later, the program and relationships built through this project are ongoing, and Centro Romero has since secured funding to support a gallery space focused on youth participation. Totaling attendance numbers would hardly measure the impact of a permanent new art space in a neighborhood historically lacking access to resources (Scenes #19; p. 108).

WE: Who has the right to speak, the right to speak for themselves? What value is attributed to work? I think the images produced by the kids are as valuable as any other artist's. It relates to power, those barriers between what gets appreciated and what doesn't.

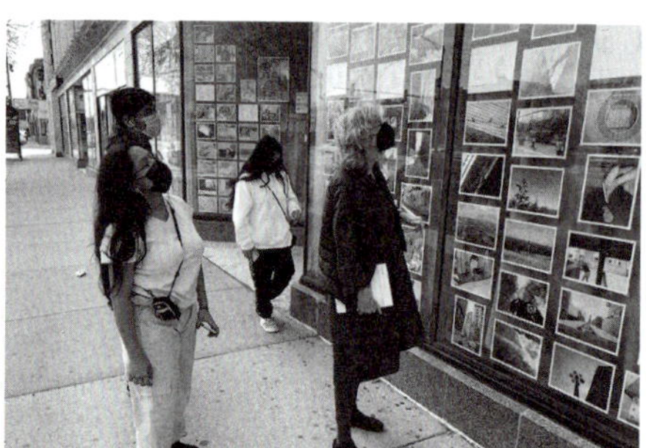

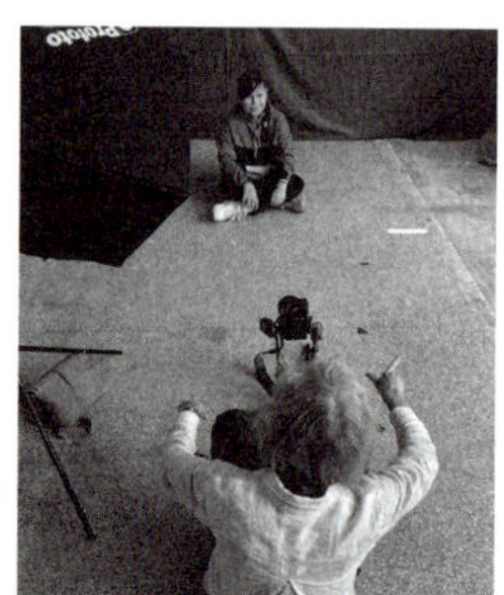

Left: Wendy Ewald and young artists at Centro Romero. Right: Wendy Ewald and Cyntia working on a portrait project. Photos: Wendy Ewald

How does one gauge the meaningfulness of *Carrie Mae Weems: A Land of Broken Dreams*, which brings together objects and images that capture the spirit of the Black Panther movement? Weems's presentation merges learning with looking. Learning perhaps more than anything else describes my experience working to bring *Toward Common Cause* to fruition (Scenes #27, #37; p. 158).

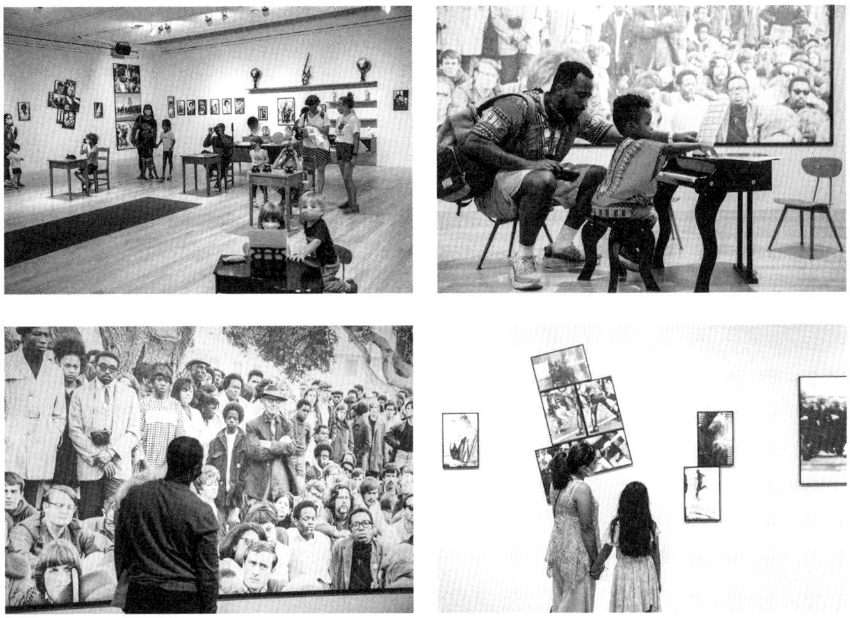

Family Arts Crawl event during Carrie Mae Weems's installation *A Land of Broken Dreams* at the Reva and David Logan Center for the Arts, September 18, 2021. Photo: Amber Marie Green

TRUST

Philanthropy has evolved significantly since the days of Andrew Carnegie and his top-down approach. The MacArthur Fellows Program and its no-strings-attached award is an early and shining example of trust-based philanthropy. Trust is a throughline connecting the origins of the MacArthur Foundation to the philosophy of the Fellows Program to the working methods of *Toward Common Cause*.

Toward Common Cause and this volume are the outcomes of a series of experiments in philanthropy. I close with questions about impact because answers to such questions can be formulated only provisionally. Impact unfolds over time. It manifests in the future. This volume has been created in anticipation of a future readership interested in the collaborative work of *Toward Common Cause*. As the exhibition's impact becomes clearer with time, here is a resource documenting how it began.

Guillermo Gómez-Peña took up residence in Jane Addams Hull-House Museum (p. 34). The exhibition layered one historic-house museum on top of two others, in San Francisco and Mexico City, highlighting the many affinities between the ideological and social commitments of Gómez-Peña, Addams, and Hull House. Gómez-Peña's homes in San Francisco and Mexico City are conceptualized as living archives—binational hubs of cultural activity, artistic creation, and domestic experimentation. A new film exploring his home was commissioned for the exhibition, which also included items from the residences deposited throughout the Hull-House Museum, a Pochafied Library, archival recordings of live performances and radio broadcasts, and a Pochx Soundtrack (Scenes #16). Virtual and live performances took place during the run of the exhibition.

Gómez-Peña's participation in *Toward Common Cause* began with a radio broadcast early in 2021. *Gómez-Peña's Mex Files: Audio Art & Strange Poetry from the US/Mexico Border* is a multilingual live radio and archival audio program addressing "the multiple pandemics of racism, sexism, xenophobia and neo-colonialism on steroids in the Trump Era." Throughout his life, Gómez-Peña has worked in audio art and radio across multiple genres, from poetic journalism to Spanglish spoken word, and from radical storytelling to collaborations with musicians, poets, and activists. This ongoing series presents samples of his previous work (1980-2015) and newly recorded material created in the last two years and during the pandemic lockdown. The *Mex Files* began broadcasting on Chicago's Lumpen Radio in February 2020 as an initiative of the exhibition (p. 168).

Photo: Nathan Keay

1 Chicago Metropolitan Agency for Planning, July 2021 Community Data Snapshots (https://www.cmap.illinois.gov/).

Texts by Jane Addams (JA) from her 1930 essay, "The Play Instinct and the Arts,"[1] and responses from Peter Fitzpatrick (PF), Victoria Nabor (VN), and Susana Salgado (SS)

AT THE INTERSECTION OF DAILY LIFE AND IMAGINATION THERE IS AN ART STUDIO: A CONVERSATION ACROSS TIME BETWEEN JANE ADDAMS AND STAFF AT PUEBLO UNIDO GALLERY

Jane Addams—co-founder of Hull House, the first settlement house in the United States—is a towering figure in Chicago, a city that has long been a destination for immigrants and refugees. This is largely because of the history of Hull House as a beacon of hope and succor; the powerful imprint of Progressivism on Chicago politics; and Addams's untiring advocacy on behalf of immigrants, women, and peace. Her work earned her the Nobel Peace Prize in 1937, and her ideas endure through her lectures, papers, and publications. Many organizations in Chicago continue to live her legacy, among them Centro Romero, a program partner for *Toward Common Cause* (p. 108). This virtual conversation places Addams in dialogue with the team at Pueblo Unido Gallery, an art space at Centro. Representing Pueblo Unido and Centro are Peter Fitzpatrick, Special Advisor for Community Engagement in the Office of the Provost, Columbia College Chicago, and Co-Director of Pueblo Unido; Victoria Nabor, Teen Leadership Coordinator for the Centro Romero Youth Program; and Susana Salgado, Director of the Youth Program at Centro.

JA

Because the modern industrial city is so new, we are as yet ignorant of its ultimate reactions upon human life, and we know little of the impressions and even of the scars which this new type of living makes upon that most highly sensitized material, the body and mind of the young at the moment they are most acutely alive to their surroundings. We only know that young people, with their newborn instincts, whether walking in crowded streets or in the open fields, continually test the achievements and shortcomings of the life about them by standards of romance new to them but as old as the world. . . .

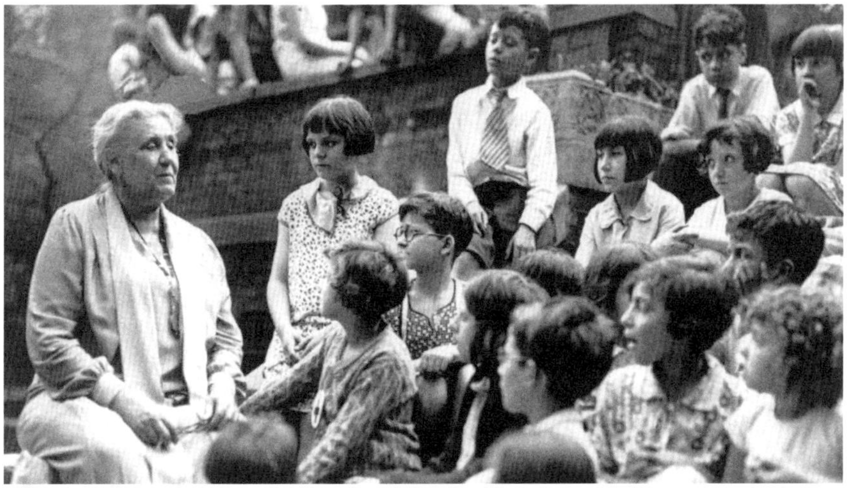

Jane Addams speaks to Hull House visitors in 1935. Photo: Wikimedia Commons

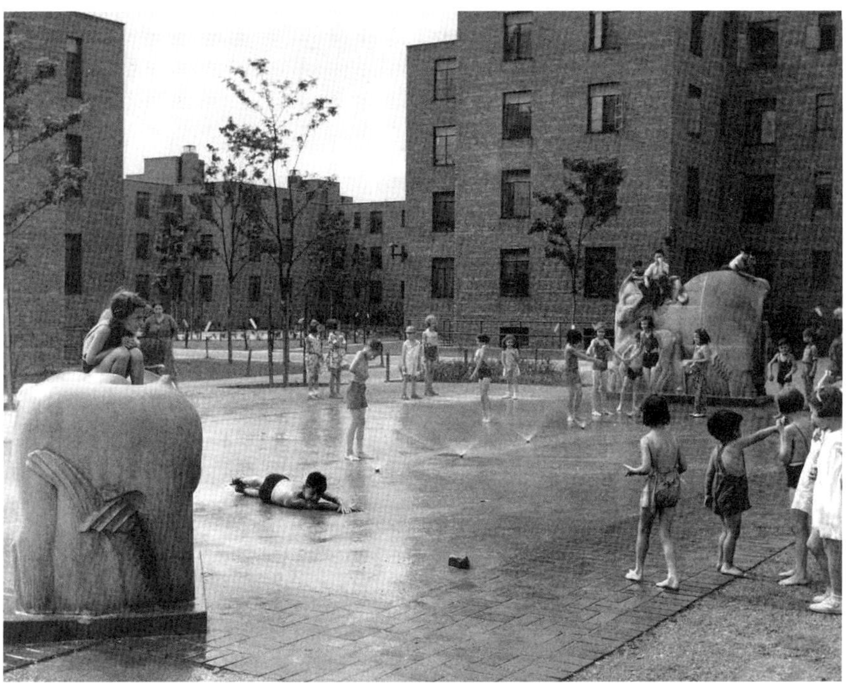

In this historic photograph, children play in fountains and on animal sculptures in the courtyard of the Jane Addams Homes—Chicago's first public housing project—built in 1938 by the Public Works Administration. Photo: Taken for the US Housing Authority, via Wikimedia Commons

We realize afresh that it is the business of youth to reaffirm the beauty and joy in the world that such spontaneity may become a source of new vitality, a wellspring of refreshment to a jaded city.

PF Chicago's a very interesting city because we have a variety of communities in the Southwest and North Sides. In one way, it's hard to navigate, but at the same time, there's so much potential to bring communities together through a project like the gallery and other types of visual arts activities. Sometimes it's hard to navigate to the right people to create the relationships and then keep those links happening because we all are dealing with our immediate community's issues, needs, and desires, although there are so many common causes we are dealing with across this city.

The scale of the city is a factor to overcome, but I think it's also the barriers that have been put up over years, the hierarchy of things within the city. Community organizations working with institutions? How do you get those two different types of entities together? You have to find the right people, risk-takers within the city, that can actually challenge and also use the systems that they're in to create something that is better for more people. Often the youth are the ones who can help reverse hierarchies.

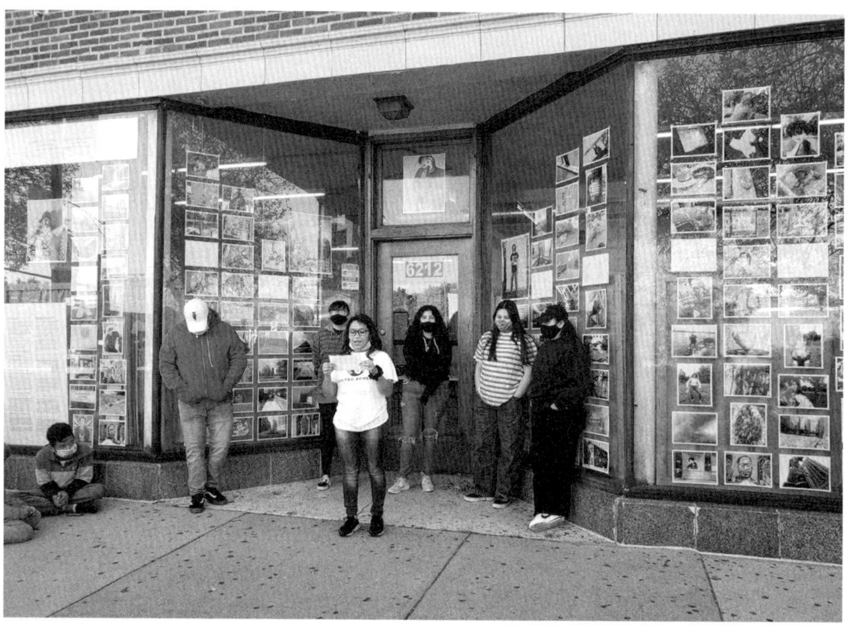

Opening of the Pueblo Unido Gallery (6212 North Clark Street) at Centro Romero. Photo: Wendy Ewald

SS I think that for me, it still is a challenge to work with the Latinx youth in this specific neighborhood on the far north of Chicago. We're not located in a zip code typically associated with high-risk youth or a high rate of violence, but we're nearby.

Securing grant funds can be challenging. Let me give you an example. There are funding sources that say, "Okay. You guys provide academic support, and the measure for success will be the number of students with A's at the end of the term." But what about youth that have IEPs, that have different ways of learning? Through art, they have been able to express themselves even though they might not be able to write a seven-page essay.

JA *[Dr. John Dewey] demonstrated that a child after an historic period had made itself at home in his imagination would wholeheartedly live in it for weeks at a time. He energetically dug, built, wove and cooked, sometimes according to his need in a primitive hut, at other times in a medieval castle surrounded by a moat. But because this fresh imaginative life with its instinct for play is, in a sense, the mission of art itself we have found at Hull-House that our educational efforts tend constantly toward a training for artistic expression; in a music school, a school of dramatics, classes in rhythm and dancing and the school of the plastic and graphic arts.*

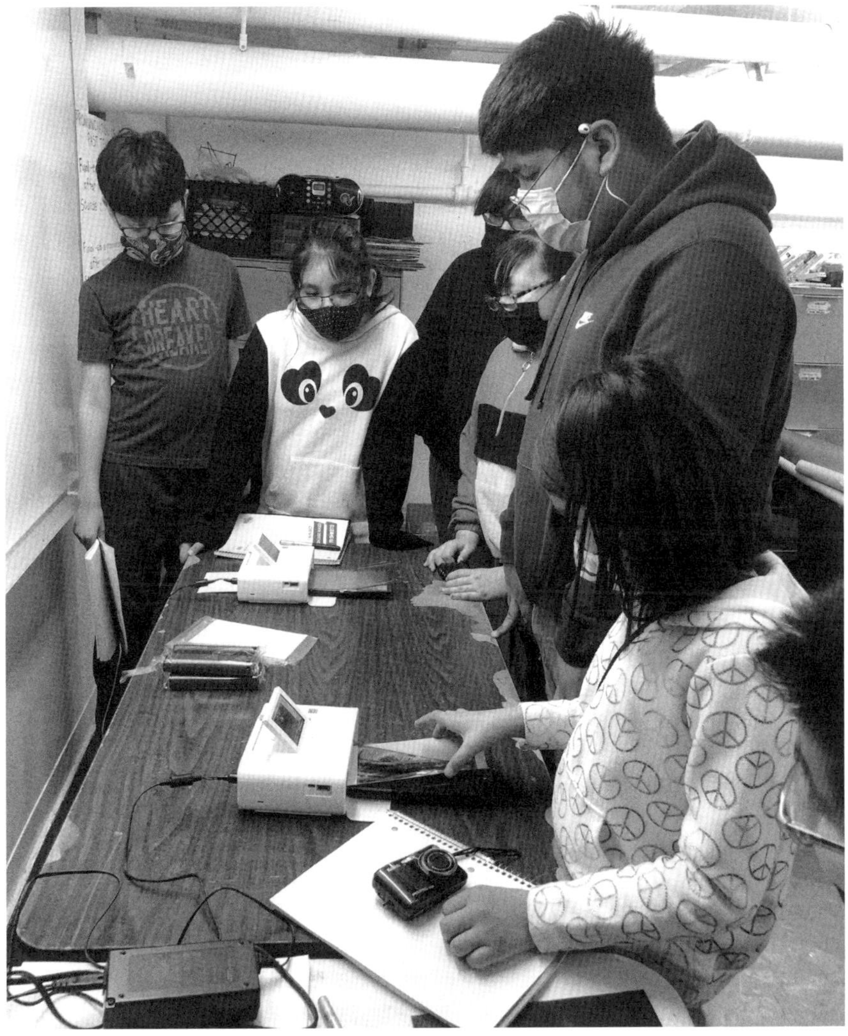

Students working with Canon mini printers at Centro. Photo: Wendy Ewald

SS If you ask our youth "What do you want to be when you grow up?" many will answer police officer or soccer player because they have seen those roles in their community. But with the art gallery at Centro, now their vision is broader, they can see that, "I can be a professor at the university. I can work in a museum. I can be a photographer. I can do all these other things when I grow up." With Wendy Ewald's project, it was also about access to cameras and exposure to new things and other parts of the city.

JA *Because Hull-House is in an immigrant district, we have the great advantage that children in the art school are of many races and nationalities and to a surprising degree they are familiar with the backgrounds of culture which their parents represent. . . .*

It is to be hoped that such experiments as are carried on in the art school at Hull-House and in many other places in America, including the advanced public schools, will at last influence the entire system of public education. . . .

Social life and art have always seemed to go best together at Hull-House. This is shown in what has been called the Big Studio, the large room where young people come year after year. . . . Between them all, there seems to be created an atmosphere in which each can find his own way in art.

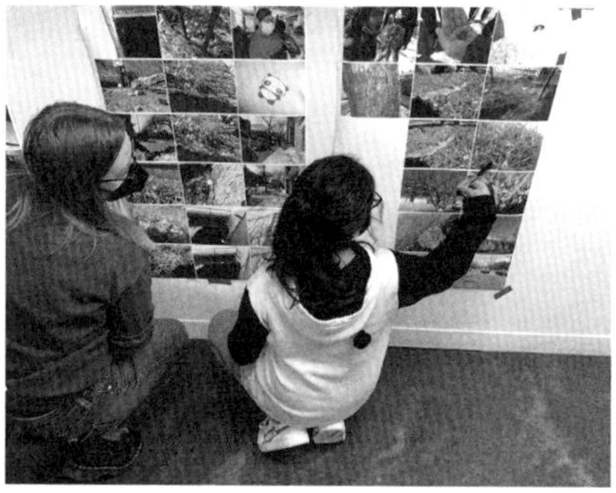

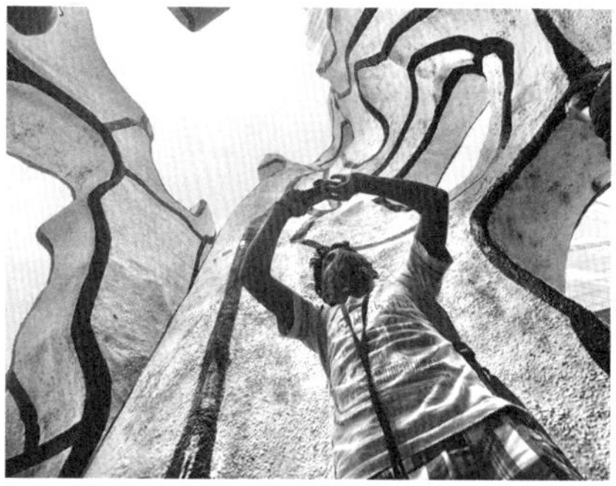

Left: Photographer Ali Stanton working with a Centro student. Right: On a field trip to downtown Chicago, a Centro student photographs Jean Dubuffet's public sculpture *Monument with Standing Beast*. Photos: Wendy Ewald

VN Arts and crafts were always a part of our program at Centro in the classrooms, but we started focusing more on art as a kind of therapy. We worked on a mural by the train station, and then through Jackie Seward, our After School Matters coordinator, they also got more involved in the arts. They also painted those murals that are by the windows.

We see a lot of talent in the arts with the students. Sometimes they will push back on doing the art activities, but in the end their own creativity comes through. When the photography program started, there were lots of questions because it was something new. Entire families were interested in knowing more about the program. We needed ten students to get it off the ground. Eight students have been with us in the photography project since the beginning.

Students tell us they like the field trips, taking pictures in different parts of the city, from downtown to Pilsen. They liked how Peter and Ali Stanton, Peter's former student who helped on workshops during *TCC*, showed them how to see from different angles and perspectives. The students really enjoyed their company. More students got interested, and then we were able to offer it also to younger students. Like Susi said, they express themselves through another way (other than writing), and I feel that's what art does.

JA *[We want] to give every child in our schools the ability to use his hands with ease and pleasure, not upon the narrow basis of fitting him for factory life . . . but in order to retain that power of unfolding human life which is implicit in the play instinct. If it had a natural expression, [this instinct] would normally develop into the art impulse with that power of variation which industry so sadly needs to redeem it from its extreme mechanization. . . .*

But if the play instinct has been ignored in industry, it has also failed to assert itself in large areas of social life. After all, the city is made up of an

infinitely varying multitude, working their way, through much pain and confusion, toward better social relations. . . .

Perhaps one of the most notable expressions of the play instinct in these later times has been connected with the amateur drama. Many years ago a little theater was built for Hull-House which has sheltered many interesting plays in many tongues. . . .

The arts have, I think, always been embodied in the ultimate aims of Hull-House. From time to time in moments of depression or of exhilaration over some public undertaking to which the residents were committed, we have urged Miss Smith to phrase in music the social compunction which at the moment it seemed impossible to express in any other way.

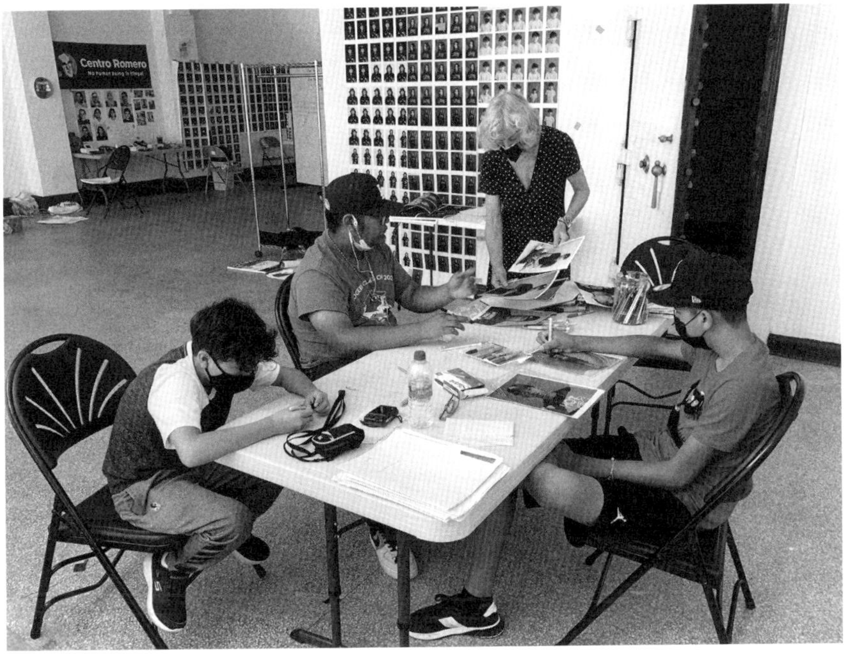

Wendy Ewald discusses portraits taken in collaboration with Centro students. Photo: Wendy Ewald

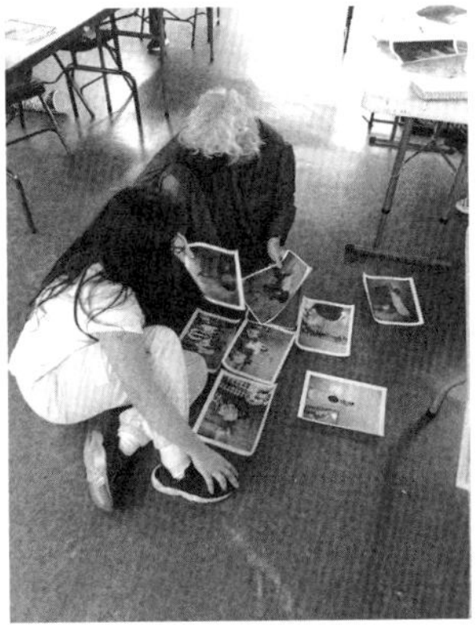

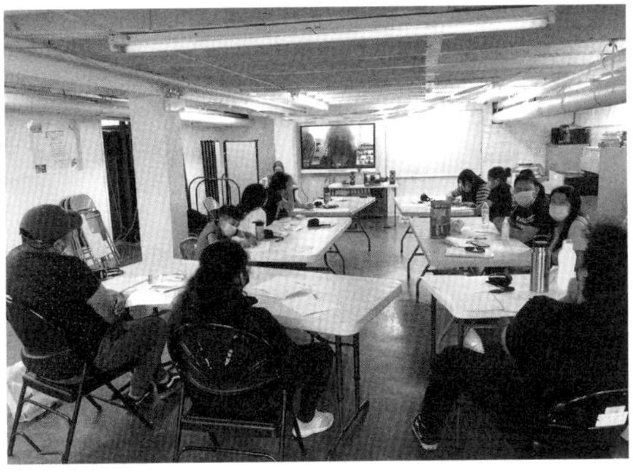

Left: Wendy Ewald and a student discuss their work. Right: Students at Centro in a Zoom meeting with Wendy Ewald. Photos: Wendy Ewald

PF Photography is a really good tool. It breaks down that fear of creativity. The way that we deliver photography, especially with Wendy Ewald and the programs that I do, we make it very accessible, very simple. And then if you want to grow technically, that's fine but it's not necessary. The point is to get people comfortable with their creative ideas. At Centro, while we're having photography class, we're also talking about music and playing music and learning guitar and so on. It's all part of that initial engagement with the creative process. Even though I'm a professor of photography, taking pictures is just a tool to open up that creative mindset.

That's what has been wonderful at Centro—it's not all about photography, it is about expression. Now some of the photographers are talking about filmmaking, so they want to do video. They want to go beyond. One has just formed a band. All kinds of creative activities happen from picking up a camera. At Centro, you can see this working in real time. Two students from Venezuela came one day and they couldn't speak English. Basically, they were placed in the camera club two days after they arrived in America. Communication was difficult but the picture-taking process brought them into the group quickly. It was pretty amazing to experience how effectively looking at pictures, sharing pictures with each other, brought them together.

ART AND COMMUNITY

JA *The Art Center considers the whole of Hull-House as its laboratory. . . .*

Doubtless our scientific advance depends more upon disinterested intellectual curiosity than upon any other human trait but we may be faced at this moment with an opportunity to so revitalize our own experiences that we may score as never before in the very Art of Living itself.

VN We teach our youth to advocate for themselves, to stand up for themselves and their communities. For example, every year we do the peace walk. High schoolers and middle schoolers in 2022 were exposed to social media, and in preparing for our walk last year, they included recent events on their peace signs. For example, one of the students wrote the names of people who have died due to police brutality. She was very passionate about that. When she went to Pilsen with Wendy, she took pictures of the George Floyd portraits and they became part of her installation in the exhibition. She wrote about that.

As they get older, they start seeing other issues they care about and they start advocating for their community. The gallery is helpful for that because art is a way of expressing their own ideas.

SS I remember a conversation about how not-for-profit organizations support causes. Centro Romero's fundamental mission is to help people become self-sufficient, which comes with responsibilities like once you're a US citizen you need to go out and vote, and like talking to your elected officials about the things that impact your community.

As an organization, we focus a lot on advocacy, providing youth with the tools to change their own lives and contribute to their community to make things happen and change. For example, one of our youth went to a rally with a sign that read, "Today we march, tomorrow we vote." Then, in the 2020 election, we took a picture of him voting. We did not tell him who to vote for, but when we asked him, "How do you feel about the elections?" he said, "We won!" His voice counted.

A couple of our other high schoolers volunteered for the campaign of a public school teacher who was running for Chicago alderman. He didn't win, but it was really close. It also gave us an opportunity to address that and say, "What are the things we can do differently next time?" As an administrator at Centro, I see the gallery as a place for kids to explore where they want to go.

JA *Thus, as a result of the broad scope of the activities of the Art Department, the workers in the [Hull House] are becoming increasingly interested in the subjects of housing and community-planning.*

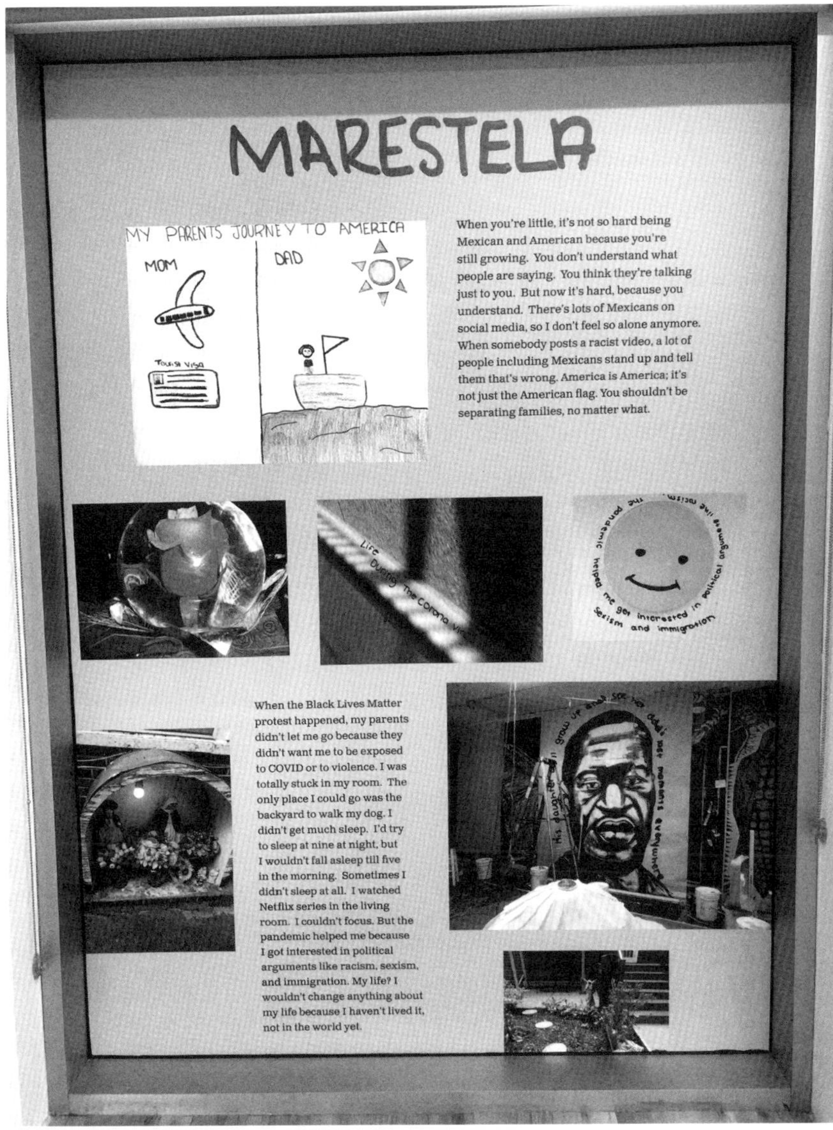

Work by Centro student Marestela with Wendy Ewald appears in a window installation at Weinberg/Newton Gallery as part of the project *Daily Life and Dreams in the Pandemic: A Project with the Centro Romero Youth Program*. Photo: Wendy Ewald

PF The fantastic things about the space that became the Pueblo Unido Gallery were very basic. The location of the space: it's right next door to the headquarters of Centro Romero. That was just a gift. Susi talked the landlord into giving us access to that space for Wendy Ewald's workshop, and then the gallery became an idea we couldn't let go of. With large windows on the street, it's creative practice on view.

While working with Wendy and doing the initial portraits of the youth, we kept having walk-ins—people coming in randomly. They just felt welcome somehow, and they would come in and ask questions. That was the signal, I think, to myself and Wendy that we needed to hold on to this space. Even now, people come to Centro through those doors of the gallery. I don't know why, but they come to us even though they're looking for Centro support. They come first to the gallery and then we guide them to headquarters. I think there's still more potential to bring people in, and I'm looking forward to strategizing with Abraham, from the gallery staff, on some things that we could do to invite people in. It's an accessible space—whether you're in a car or on foot, you can look through the windows and see what's going on. It's too good an opportunity to pass up.

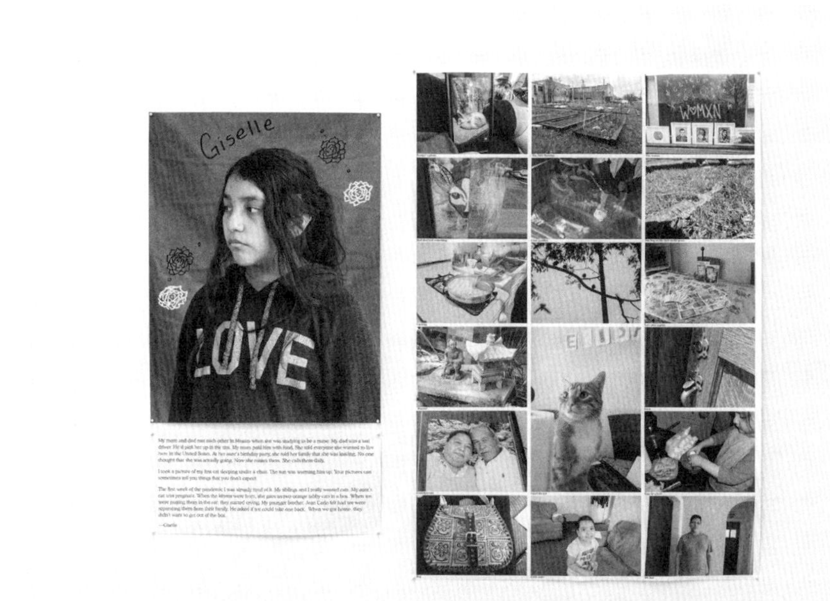

Installation with Wendy Ewald's portrait of student Giselle and a compilation print of Giselle's photographs and text, part of *Daily Life and Dreams in the Pandemic*. Photo: Wendy Ewald

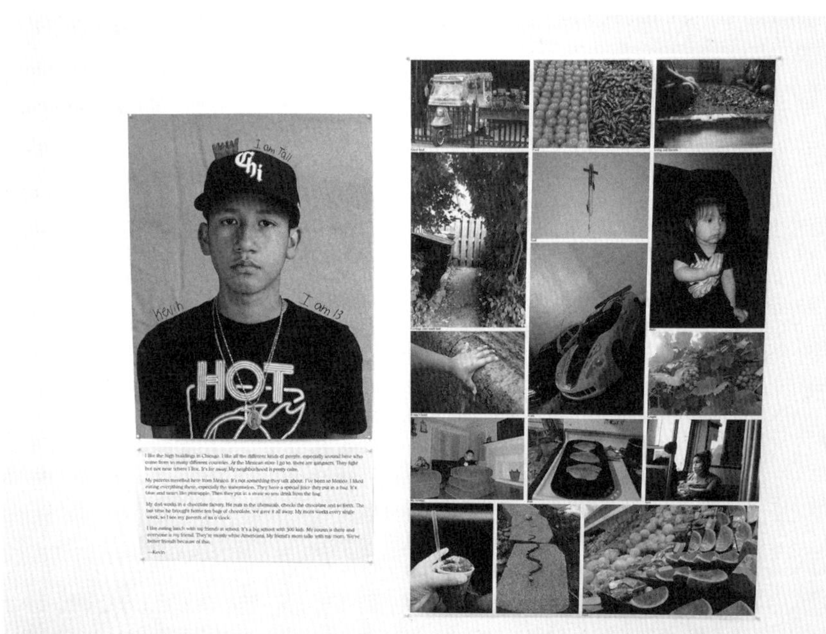

Installation with Wendy Ewald's portrait of student Kevin and a compilation print of Kevin's photographs and text, part of *Daily Life and Dreams in the Pandemic*. Photo: Wendy Ewald

Centro has been really invested in the gallery. That's not always the case. Sometimes organizations will take on an art program because they need more people to look after the kids. But for Centro, it was very obvious that there was a much deeper investment in actually having art and creative practice going on within their community. And there's potential to reach beyond the youth, to reach adults as well. That's probably stage two of the project.

SS The gallery has brought us a lot of people who say things like, "I didn't know Centro existed until I saw this." "What are you guys doing?" "Where were the kids taking these pictures?" It's a different exposure. Typically, people come to Centro looking for a service. But now we have a gallery, and it reaches a different population. One lady shared a story that when she saw my picture outside, she actually came inside because she recognized me. We had been in programs together at Centro when we were young, and now she lives two blocks away. She said, "Every morning that I go out for a walk, I say 'Hi Susi.'" I think that it raised awareness about Centro Romero, for not only the community that needed our services but for those who can support the work that we do.

I'm really happy to hear when individuals encounter this work and bring their entire families back to see it. It's a new activity for our youth and a way to open communication between parents and their children about their experiences. I didn't know I was undocumented until I was graduating from high school. My mom said, "Well, we didn't want you to feel different." But at the same time, I feel that with this project, our youth got ownership of who they are and don't feel ashamed or shy about why they're immigrants. They might be undocumented, but don't we bring more to our community than our immigration status?

Fifteen years after I graduated from high school, I grabbed my DACA and thought, "Wait. I've been doing all this work without a document and now I have it. Can I go back to school to do more?" I wanted it also so that our youth can begin conversations with their parents, take ownership and feel proud of where they're from, the work that they're doing, and about their families. You see it in the stories that parents were sharing with their children during Wendy's project, it was an opportunity for them to actually tell their kids, "This is the reason why I immigrated." A lot of times, it was for their kids. At the same time, the kids could appreciate more the struggles that their parents have faced here in the US.

JA *From the standpoint of the [general aims of Hull-House], the Arts are vastly important for the same reasons which make them important to civilization. The Arts nourish and integrate the individual. The group and the community are also affected when art goes beyond theory and techniques and is related to the environment. Furthermore, art practice itself is democratic, being no respecter of race or station and being within the capacity of all. . . . Lack of aesthetic experience is a form of starvation detrimental to a society.*

In addition to giving the individuals an opportunity for congenial work and industrious recreation, it has been the concern of the department to relate its activities to community interests and needs. . . . This offers a newer approach to the arts, whereby students design for use—for the needs of our age and environment—and produce by means of the tools of our age.
[From Hull House at the Fiftieth Year]

1 Jane Addams, "The Play Instinct and the Arts," in *The Jane Addams Reader*, ed. Jean Bethke Elshtain (New York: Basic Books, 2002), 416–31.

Centro Romero
6216 N. Clark St.
Chicago, IL 60660

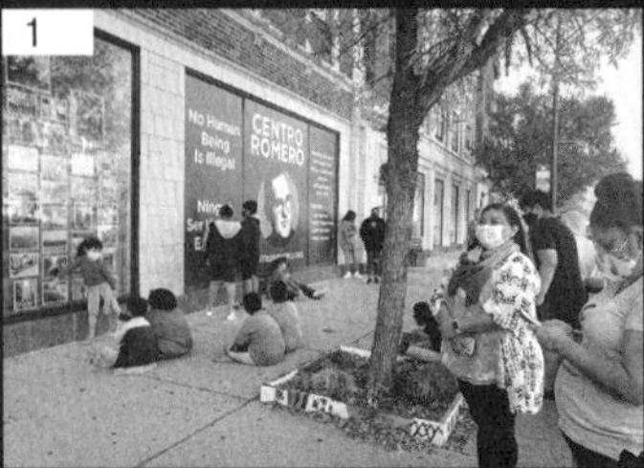
1

Weinberg/Newton Gallery
688 N. Milwaukee Ave.
Chicago, IL 60642

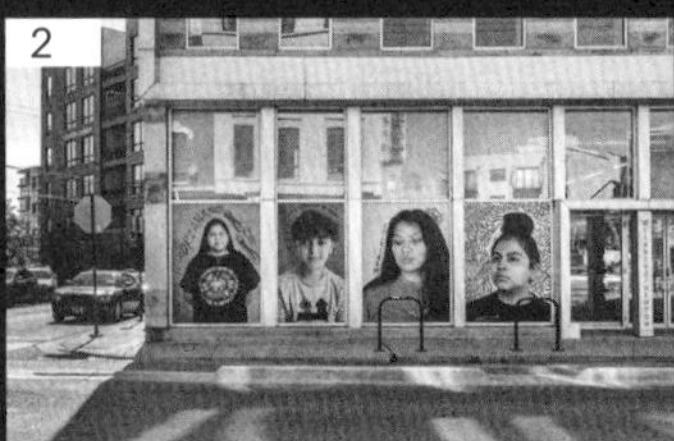
2

Centro Romero was founded by Salvadoran refugees to assist community members. Over the course of the past four decades, it has grown to include departments for legal services, adult education, family services, and a youth service and leadership program that serves a multiethnic community numbering in the thousands.

Weinberg/Newton Gallery, which sadly closed in 2024, was a noncommercial space dedicated to educating and engaging the public on social-justice issues. Through artwork and programming, the gallery provided a vital space for open discourse on critical contemporary issues facing our communities. Connecting artists with social-justice organizations, the gallery worked to drive change and cultivate a culture of consciousness.

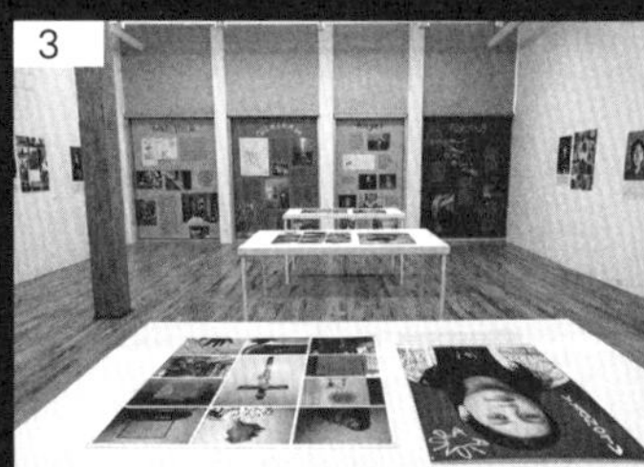
3

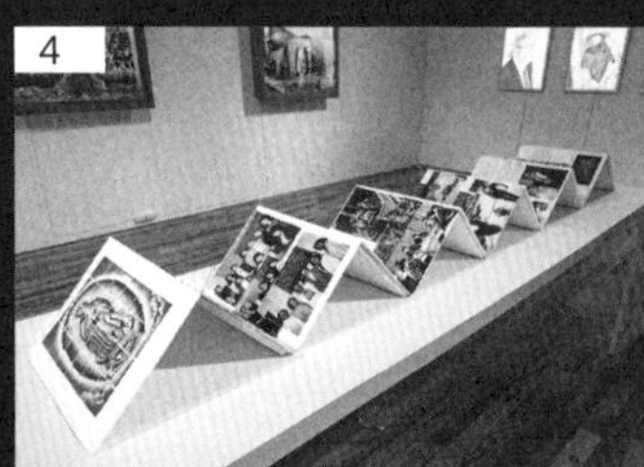
4

The national debate about the immigration crisis and the Trump administration's treatment of refugees at the southern border exploded during exhibition planning. Wendy Ewald and Amalia Mesa-Bains contributed complementary projects focusing on Latinx migration in the city of Chicago. Mesa-Bains took a historical and very personal look at Mexican migration to the city through the lens of her own family, while Ewald worked with middle and high school students, encouraging them to use cameras to reflect and record their stories of contemporary immigration. Together these projects presented a comprehensive, transhistorical picture of the Latinx immigrant community in Chicago. They bridged temporal and geographic distance to connect the historical and contemporary Latinx communities and present local immigration stories within and beyond the immigrant community.

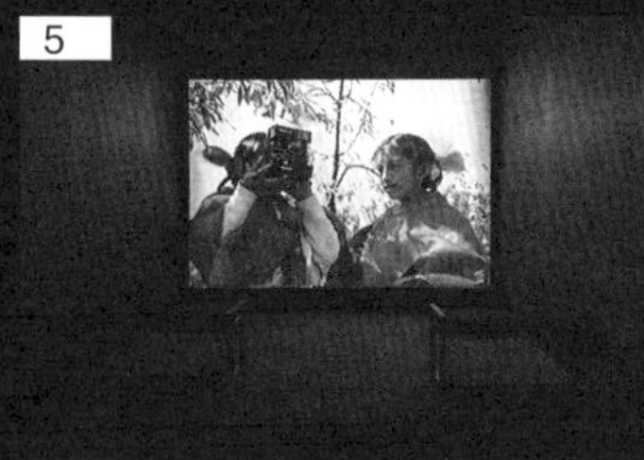
5

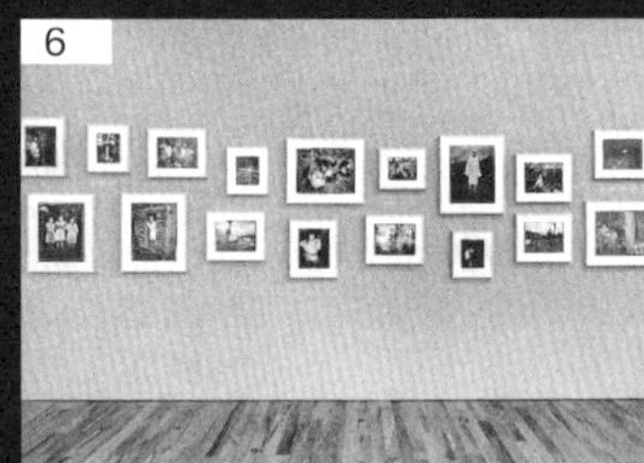
6

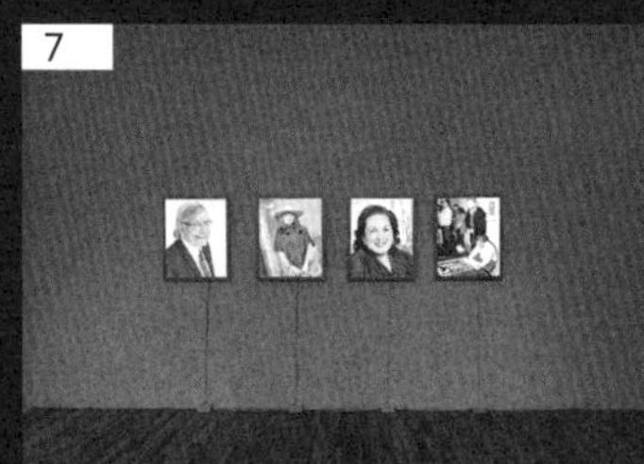
7

Mesa-Bains's contribution, *Dos Mundos*, investigates the social history of the larger Mexican community in the history and building of Chicago, beginning with the wave of migrants that arrived in the city in the mid-1900s (Scenes #31). She approached this history from two perspectives; the private and the public, using public records, research in new scholarship, personal mementos, and interviews with her own family. As laborers in the steel mills, slaughterhouses, and packing plants, Mexicans are a historic community that has contributed to the prosperity and culture of Chicago both in their neighborhoods and throughout the city. From their earliest years, Mexican communities have developed fraternal organizations, sports teams, churches, and community festivities. Often-unrecognized leadership in the Mexican community helped create protective organizations, establish immigrant support structures, and organize protests against discrimination and prejudice. Simultaneously the affirmation of cultural practices in art, music, cuisine, and festivals helped to solidify a sense of shared community (p. 130). Mesa-Bains's project was presented at the National Museum of Mexican Art and Weinberg/Newton Gallery.

8

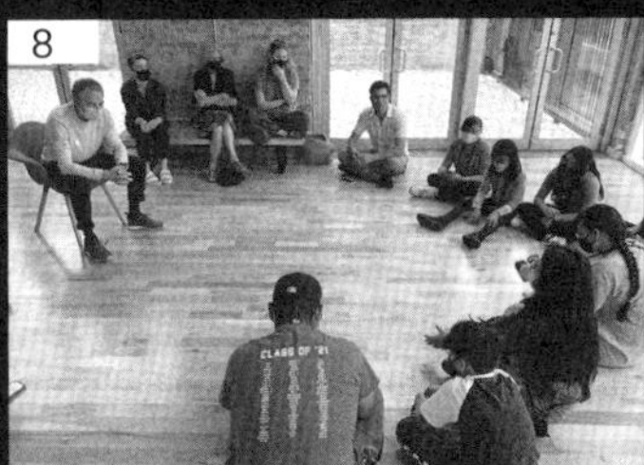

9

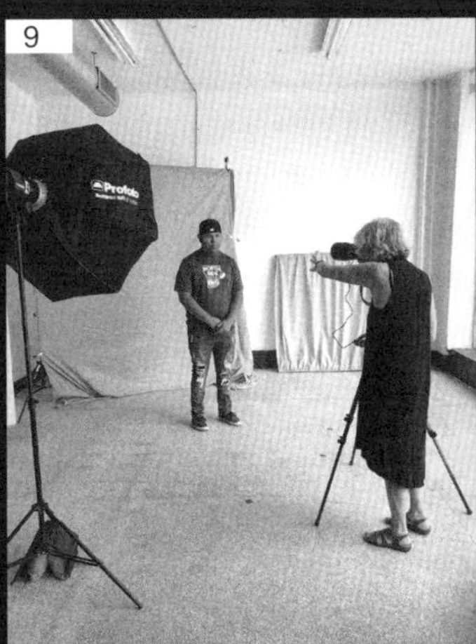

Ewald partnered with the Youth Services team at Centro Romero (Susana Salgado and Veronica Nabor), with the support of Professor Peter Fitzpatrick and Colombia College's Diane Dammeyer Initiative. Over the course of two years, they worked closely with fifteen students. The pandemic forced them to work in a hybrid mode: Ewald present digitally, Fitzpatrick and the Centro team in person. Together, they and the students created *Daily Life and Dreams in the Pandemic: Photographs by Youth in Rogers Park*. The work was featured in a walk-by exhibition mounted in October 2020 at Centro Romero and again as part of *Toward Common Cause* at Weinberg/Newton Gallery in Chicago's River West neighborhood (Scenes #19).

10

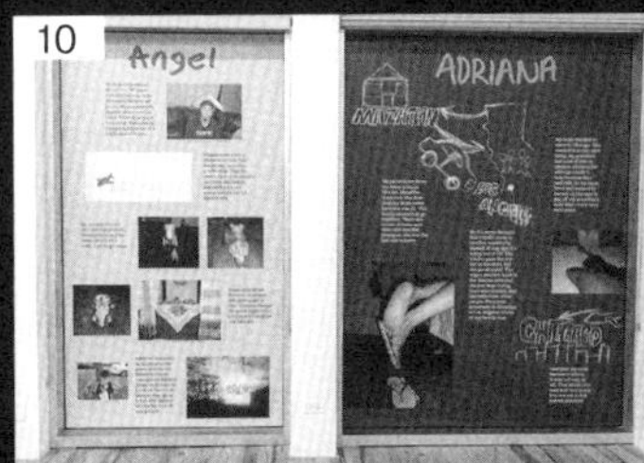

Ewald's yearslong collaboration with Centro was the genesis of the Pueblo Unido Gallery. The mission of the gallery is to highlight the stories and issues faced by refugees and immigrant communities, and the space will be used to elevate the creative works of Centro Romero and similar communities across Chicago.

1 Student work is presented at the Centro Romero opening event. Photo: Wendy Ewald

2 Exterior view of Weinberg/Newton Gallery with portraits by participants in Centro's youth program in collaboration with Wendy Ewald for *Daily Life and Dreams in the Pandemic*. Photo: Evan Jenkins

3 Installation view of works made by Wendy Ewald and students from the Centro at Weinberg/Newton Gallery. Photo: Nathan Keay

4 Installation view of Amalia Mesa-Bains's series *Dos Mundos: Mexican Chicago*. Photo: Nathan Keay

5 Installation view of Amalia Mesa-Bains's 1992 video *Untitled*, made in collaboration with Tom McDonough, at Weinberg/Newton. Photo: Evan Jenkins

6 Installation view of Amalia Mesa-Bains's series *The Devil Is Leaving His Cave: Photographs by Children from Chiapas*. Photo: Evan Jenkins

7 Lightboxes in Amalia Mesa-Bains's *Dos Mundos: Mexican Chicago* (left to right: Carlos Tortolero, Sandra Cisneros, Juana Guzman, Carlos Cortéz with César Chávez). Photo: Nathan Keay

8 Wendy Ewald and students plan the exhibition at Weinberg/Newton. Photo: Wendy Ewald

9 Wendy Ewald and Ernesto work on portrait-making. Photo: Wendy Ewald

10 Weinberg/Newton installation view. Photo: Nathan Keay

Reciprocity

Toward Common Cause prompted artists, the exhibition's institutional partners, and their Chicago communities to explore a mutually beneficial programming model. Sustaining it will require accepting deliberation, differences in points of view, and compromise as part of the process.

Be Water

Michael Christiano

Though *Toward Common Cause* was designed as a multivenue initiative, it nonetheless required an institutional catalyst that was committed to the project's values and that would situate it within a network of allied organizations. The Smart Museum at the University of Chicago was that institution—mostly. Long before its involvement with *Toward Common Cause*, the Smart had been cultivating its relationship with Chicago's South Side community in work that—in recent years—was largely driven by the Public Practice team but which had important precedent in endeavors initiated by previous education and curatorial staff. Warming relationships with South Side organizations and community members activated the university's relatively recent commitment to becoming a better citizen of its South Side community, and *Toward Common Cause* provided an opportunity to test that commitment and the strength of the university's bonds with potential partners (p. 58).

Historically, the university's relationship with surrounding neighborhoods has been tenuous, due in large part to programs such as the mid-twentieth-century urban renewal initiatives that displaced many people of color and disrupted historically Black communities. For the Smart, working in community meant acknowledging these histories and actively seeking to build trust. Achieving an authentic partnership would ideally create a strategic platform on which to build. However, the degree to which the Smart could devote itself to community-based endeavors as part of its mission still felt unresolved at the time of *Toward Common Cause*. University-based museums can be the site of convergence of multiple publics, both campus and broader communities. And while convergence is optimal, there is often a tendency in academic institutions to prioritize some audiences over others. *Toward Common Cause* entered the Smart at a time when there was a heightened commitment to community-centered work, although the nature of that work was not yet fully legible for all stakeholders, and its level of priority remained in question.

HR: This trust is fragile, for sure. It assumes that partners bring an awareness of their power to the conversation. What is also at play is the recognition that each individual within this complex relationship—the producer, the artist, the funder—has skills, and that these skills and knowledges are of equal value. Relying on and respecting each other's expertise is fundamental to making change.

I surface this dynamic, in part, because it will likely feel familiar to many. I also raise it in the spirit of reflection and lessons learned. Community-centered and socially engaged work can sometimes live happily in the fringes of an institution, thriving in cracks like a tenacious flower. But when endeavoring to center this work in an institution, especially a nested organization like a university-based space, it becomes critical to create pathways to investment for all those who share a stake in that space, from co-workers in other departments, to institutional leadership, board members, and funders, to faculty, staff, and students. This was the essential work leading up to *Toward Common Cause*, and it had varying degrees of success and failure. But from my current position, this is the work—the work of institutional culture building—that will ultimately determine the sustainability of community-centered work; work that demands the museum be decentered, is iterative, defies easy categorization, and is often messy. It is about the process and the people. Encouraging a culture that embraces this will undoubtedly shape the potential for success.

DR: It is interesting to note, in the context of Lee's aquatic wisdom, that the politics of water was a substantial undercurrent (pun intended) in *Toward Common Cause* as a whole. Furthermore, as a city notoriously sited on a river that saw its course reversed for economic purposes, Chicago has a charged relationship with the very notion of flow.

In our planning meetings, Mel Chin would often invoke a famous Bruce Lee quote—"Be water, my friend"—to remind us that socially engaged work demands the flexibility to respond to partners and adapt to an ever-shifting context. The full quote is a reminder of the malleability and dynamism of culture itself: "Empty your mind. Be formless, shapeless, like water. Now, you put water into a cup; it becomes the cup. You put water into a bottle; it becomes the bottle. You put it in a teapot; it becomes the teapot. Now, water can flow, or it can crash! Be water, my friend."[1]

Culture moves in and through museums, schools, youth centers, parks, gardens, apartments. Museums have tended to dam that water of culture rather than letting it flow into, through, and beyond their walls. Culture takes shape at the Smart Museum differently than it does at the South Side Community Art Center; its form is different at Sweet Water Foundation, and different again at SkyART.[2] Respecting these differences while creating channels to connect the institutions allows the water to flow, creating space for the exchange of ideas, practices, imaginings, and resources; a network of canals that enables people to travel between, bringing culture with them.

What I've learned, perhaps more than anything else (and the reminders always come from those who I work alongside, especially Dorian Nash and Jason Pallas) is that we must bring our full selves to our work, for it is people who shape culture, who shape institutions. In *Emergent Strategy*, adrienne maree brown shared these powerful prompts for reflection that I'd like to offer here. "Do you already know that your existence—who and how you are—is in and of itself a contribution to the people and place around you? Not after or because you do some particular thing, but simply the miracle of your life. And the people around you, and the place(s), have contributions as well? Do you understand that your quality of life and your survival are tied to how authentic and generous the connections are between you and the people and the place you live with and in?"[3]

It seems shortsighted to think about the health and vitality of a single organization without considering the wellbeing of the broader cultural landscape. If the soil is sick, none of us can thrive. It can be difficult to embrace this broader framework when museums have historically considered success as that which happens inside their building. It can be tougher still to think of the broader network when you lack resources at your own institution to operate equitably and/or sustainably. I only offer that we consider all of our resources—our selves, our people power and expertise, our collections, our buildings, our dreams—as opportunities for collective stewardship, growth, and mutuality.

South Side Community
Art Center
3831 S. Michigan Ave.
Chicago, IL 60653

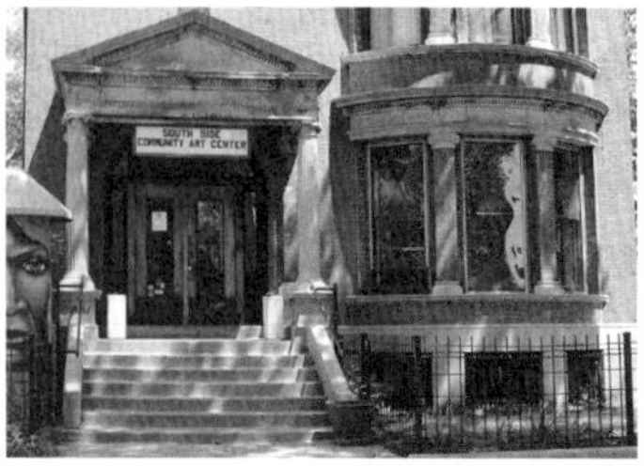

It was impossible to imagine *Toward Common Cause* without the participation of the South Side Community Art Center (SSCAC). Since 1940, it has been a Black-led force of cultural production and preservation. Operating in a nineteenth-century brownstone on South Michigan Avenue, it remains both a "home" and a "hub" to the community it serves. Founding director Dr. Margaret Burroughs lived across the street.

SSCAC was one of the last community-funded WPA projects in the nation, and the cedar wall paneling in the living-room gallery dates to a contemporaneous Bauhaus remodel. These dark, wide planks of wood caught the eye of artist, curator, and former executive director Faheem Majeed (2007-11). He noticed that every extant nail hole was the trace of art on display. Majeed made rubbings of the walls to make visible the physical touch of generations of artists who shared their work here. The gallery at SSCAC—a gallery that never succumbed to white-box conventions—was a fitting context for *Whitfield Lovell: The Spell Suite*.

Lovell's work is testament to untold stories of everyday African American life. For *Toward Common Cause*, he shared six of his exquisitely rendered Conté crayon portraits of anonymous people (Scenes #17). Lovell drew from vintage vernacular photographs and, as is his practice, incor-

(continued on opposite page)

WORKING IN COMMUNITY

A Conversation between Michael Christiano (MC), Dorian H. Nash (DN), and Jason Pallas (JP)

In the following conversation, we consider two projects from *Toward Common Cause*: one predicated on a long-term relationship between the Smart Museum and the Chicago Housing Authority and developed by the Smart's Teen Program in collaboration with Njideka Akunyili Crosby, and the other built on a new partnership between the museum and Urban Juncture Foundation and developed in collaboration with Rick Lowe. The conversation mirrors the working practice of the Smart's Public Practice team.[4] Through the lens of these projects, we discuss conceptual, ethical, and tactical considerations of working in community, and address questions of shared values, advocacy, positionality, continuity and duration, and power dynamics that inevitably arise when working toward reciprocity in cultural production.

Our hope is to suggest a few points of practice that will prove useful to others engaged in cultural work. The nuance of what we have learned from these projects will likely continue to reveal itself over time; with that in mind, we are immensely grateful to have been part of the collective that lifted up *Toward Common Cause* and to all those who helped shape us in the process.

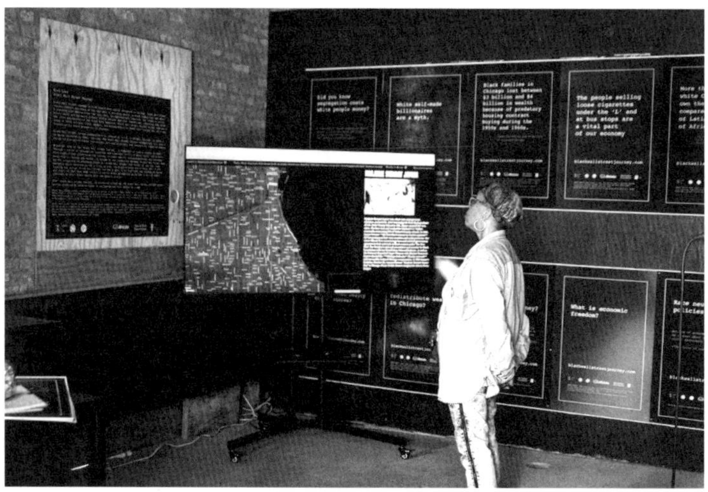

Rick Lowe's installation of *Black Wall Street Journey* at Urban Juncture included a 24-hour video stream and posters by artist Amanda Williams and journalist Natalie Moore. Photo: Nicolette Stanton

BACKGROUND: PUBLIC PRACTICE AT THE SMART AND THE PARTNERSHIPS

The Public Practice Department at the Smart Museum of Art at the University of Chicago has cultivated a practice focused on cultural and social impact across campus and the South Side. Always seeking to understand the museum's position in relation to the network of community and cultural organizations with whom it shares space, the Public Practice team grounded their efforts in long-term partnership. The team played an essential role in situating *Toward Common Cause* projects within this network of partners—brokering relationships between artists and across communities to help define mutually beneficial goals and processes. In addition, the team helped to establish new relationships to expand the scope and geographical reach of the project.

Black Wall Street Journey

In his first Chicago-based "social sculpture," Rick Lowe developed *Black Wall Street Journey*. The multifaceted project pays tribute to the economic resilience of Black communities in Chicago and beyond. It builds on the connection between Chicago and Tulsa, home to the prosperous Greenwood neighborhood known as Black Wall Street and target of the 1921 Race Massacre, which killed more than 300 Black Tulsans and sent 10,000 looking for refuge, many to Northern cities like Chicago. *Black Wall Street Journey* highlights the innovative minds and entities that have made Chicago a hub of Black prosperity, using public art to inform the general public about the building of Black wealth and business on the South Side.

porated found objects—stuffed birds, wooden fruit bowls, American flags, books—to evoke the qualities that make us human. The portraits are suffused with individuality, restoring personal histories that had been forgotten, erased, or reduced to stereotypes of Black culture. Near the fireplace in the back of the gallery, the faint sounds of the *Beulah* show played from Lovell's vintage radio sound sculpture *After an Afternoon*. The reductive mass-media stereotypes of African Americans (like those perpetuated through this radio and television sitcom from 1945 to 1954) were present but overwhelmed by the dignity of Lovell's portraits. The walls of SSCAC can talk, and Lovell's *Spell Suite* was an invitation to join the conversation.

Photo: Courtesy of the South Side Community Art Center

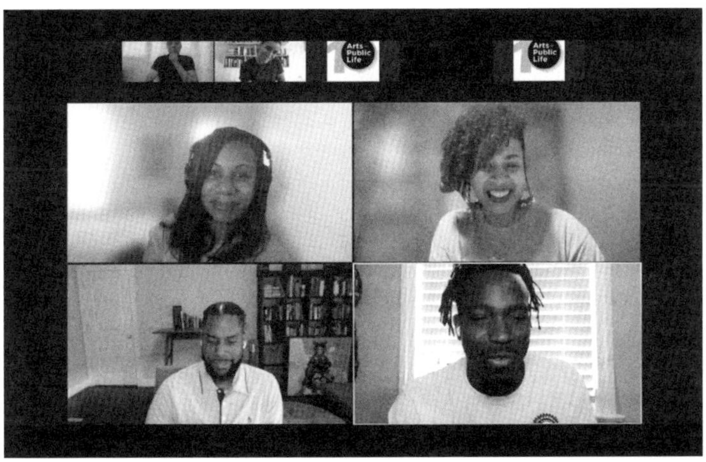

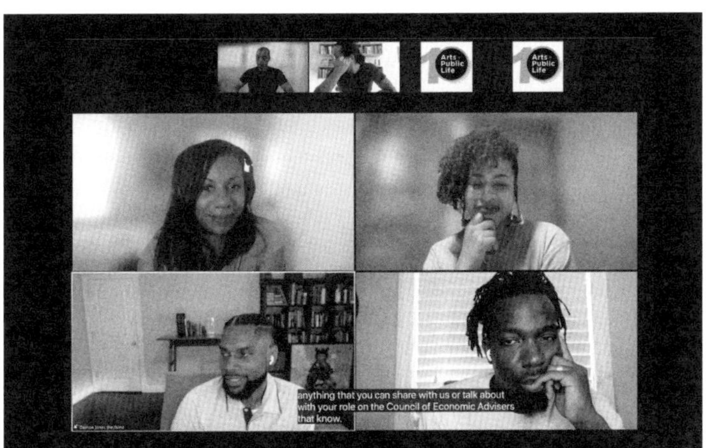

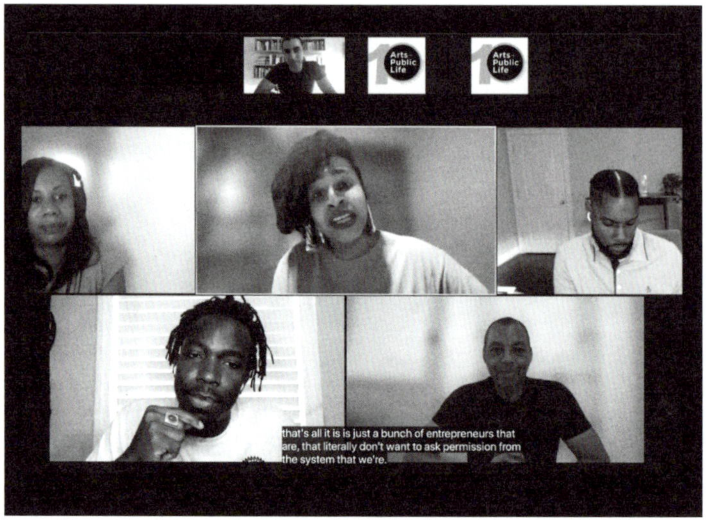

In an episode of Rick Lowe and Natalie Moore's live-streamed conversation series *CHOP IT UP: Black Wall Street Journey (Part I)*, June 9, 2021, guests Keewa Nurullah (Kido Chicago), Richard Wallace (Equity and Transformation), and Damon Jones (University of Chicago, Harris School of Public Policy) weigh in on Black ownership, business, self-reliance, determination, and mutual aid. Screenshots (above and p. 115)

Black Wall Street Journey's content is structured around two themes, art and technology. During *Toward Common Cause*, it was activated through multiple venues across the city, with murals by Dorian Sylvain; a 24-hour Black wealth video stream called *Black Wall Street Journal*, featuring local Black-owned businesses; poster installations with curated texts by Natalie Moore; and discussions on Black wealth at the Neubauer Collegium for Culture and Society in collaboration with the Mansueto Institute for Urban Innovation and the university's Department of Sociology (p. 142).

Njideka Akunyili Crosby and the Chicago Housing Authority

The Chicago Housing Authority's Minnie Riperton Apartments on the South Side served as a public venue for *Toward Common Cause*, with two paintings by Njideka Akunyili Crosby reproduced as large-format murals on the building's facade (Scenes #14). The installation of the murals resulted from a collaborative curatorial process led by young people from the Smart and CHA teen programs. Starting in the summer of 2020, these students, all residents of CHA housing, made several virtual studio visits with Akunyili Crosby, narrowed in on a selection of images, and then worked with the Riperton community of senior residents to select two works: *I Still Face You* (2015) and *Home: Say It Loud* (2017) (p. 72).

NYT: "The teens carried this project." Akunyili Crosby said that for exterior works that would be up for months, she knew she wanted to have a "partnership with Chicagoans. They would have a say."

Throughout their engagement with the artist, and working through the COVID-mandated lockdown, the teens explored themes of home and community empowerment. Akunyili Crosby's images were chosen by popular vote among the residents, who responded to the recognizable domestic interiors and familial interactions depicted in the paintings.

MC Each of these projects required extensive partnership with civic and community organizations. How and why did you identify the partner(s) you engaged for this work? Can you talk about your approach to building those relationships and reflect on the value of the partnership(s) for those involved?

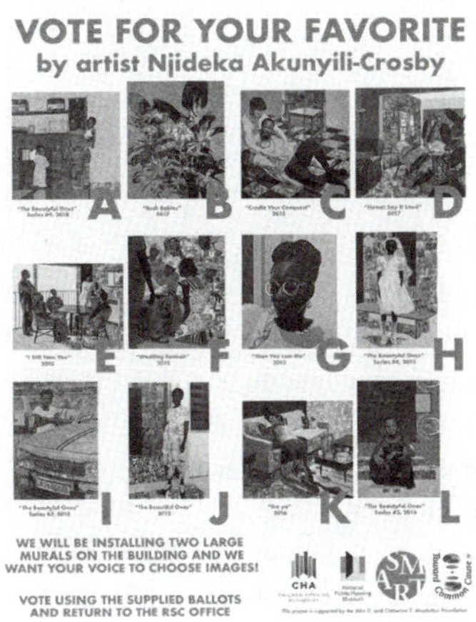

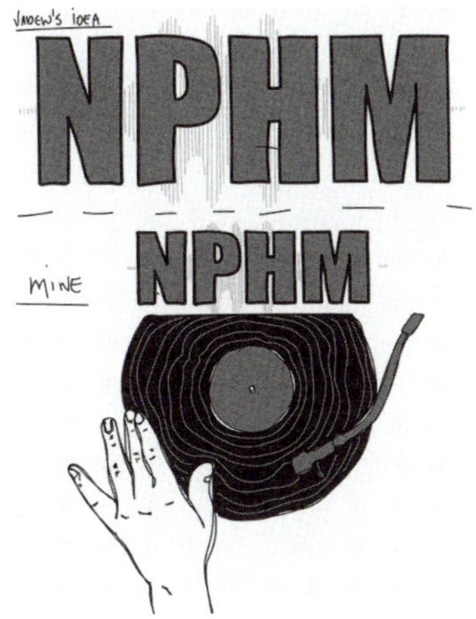

Left: Voting ballot developed by the Smart Teen Program (all CHA residents) to engage the community in selecting works by Njideka Akunyili Crosby for the Riperton Apartments and the National Public Housing Museum. Photo: Smart Museum. Right: Drawing by Jaden Roundtree and Tech Nix (Smart Teen Program) for the National Public Housing Museum. Photo: Tech Nix

IF: The Arts + Public Life gallery is in the residential, predominantly Black neighborhood of Washington Park. Pedestrians could see through the large windows that Black and Brown youth are valued and have worth—respected subjects showcased in a university/community arts venue.

DN So many conversations were had when we started to think about who needed to be a part of this project. Who are our state representatives in Chicago? How best do we identify the cultural, political leaders that should be involved from within the community, in Washington Park, in Englewood? Can we pull from previous relationships? Who are some of the community leaders in these areas? Once we began to pinpoint the areas that we wanted to engage, then we were able to identify the people we needed to engage within those areas. Many people helped. Certainly the graduate interns who did a ton of research and who worked in partnership to get the website and the visualization of *Black Wall Street Journey* off the ground—shout-out to Jennifer Etienne and Ashley Truehart. Obviously the staff here at the Smart; when I think about all the work done by C. J. Lind (associate director of communications), and the fact that he still has hair . . . We all benefited from his expertise, his patience, and the support that he gave the project. I think about some of the work that we did with Natalie Moore, the Chicago journalist who curated the amazing poster series within the exhibition. I think about being intentional about the vendors we hired, Cajun Cafe Chicago and Chef Lashon Burrell. The *CHOP IT UP* series we co-hosted with Arts + Public Life. Working with Urban Juncture, where *Black Wall Street Journey* was situated for about a year, and their neighbor, Boxville, was a great reciprocal partnership that allowed people to come in and learn about the effort.[5] This was all born out of being intentional about the neighborhoods that we wanted to engage with, and then identifying the civic leaders, artists, and practitioners in those areas.

Washington Park Arts
Incubator, Arts +
Public Life
The University of Chicago
301 E. Garfield Blvd.
Chicago, IL 60637

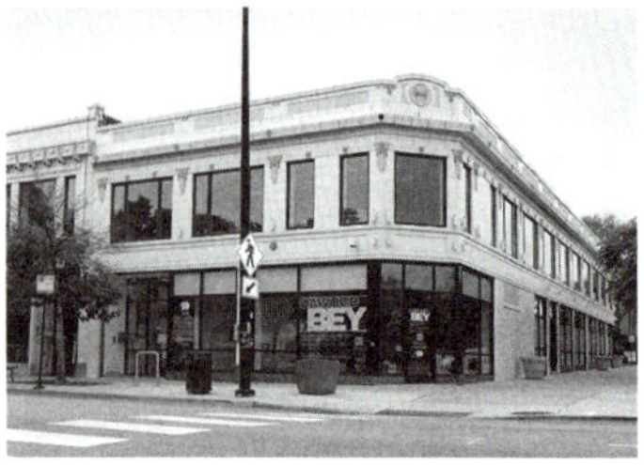

The Arts Incubator, located near Washington Park on the corner of East Garfield Boulevard and South Prairie Avenue, is a destination for communities interested in South Side cultural production across the creative spectrum. Opened in 2013, the Arts Incubator is one of three venues under the umbrella of Arts + Public Life at the University of Chicago. Housed in an Art Deco building that has been beautifully restored under the direction of Theaster Gates, it has developed a network of professional South Side artists, high school creatives and apprentices, community audiences, and university partners. APL's Arts Incubator venue builds on the strong cultural heritage of Washington Park, centering people of color committed to accessible, public space activated by the arts.

During the run of *Toward Common Cause*, COVID restrictions posed challenges to the Arts Incubator's gallery presentation of Dawoud Bey's portrait photographs of young people: it was not possible to have an opening or closing reception, and entry to the space was limited. Happily, the venue's large glass windows on heavily trafficked Garfield Boulevard allowed passersby to catch views of the work. Following the exhibition, the Arts Incubator noted that this

(continued on opposite page)

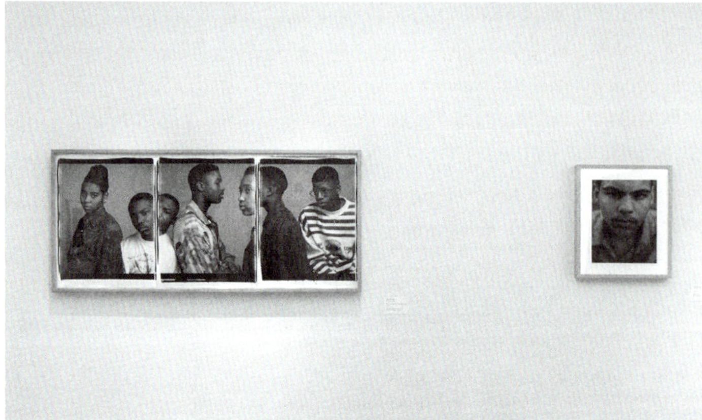

Dawoud Bey's installation at Arts + Public Life, (left) *Sharmaine, Vincente, Joseph, Andre, and Charlie*, (right) *Carlos*. Photo: Nathan Keay

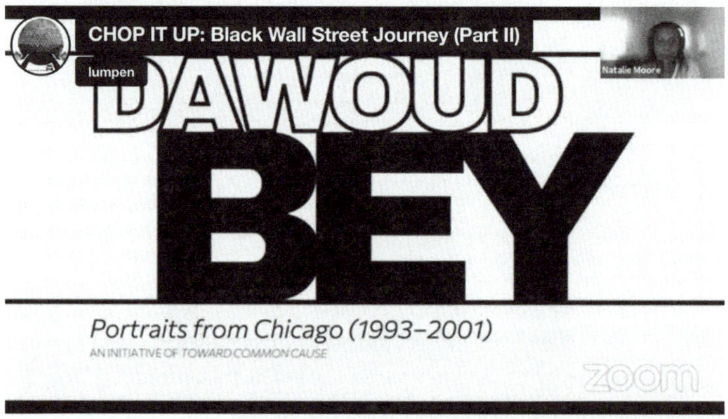

Rick Lowe and Natalie Moore's *CHOP IT UP* series. Photo: APL and screenshot

As for value, well, one of the things that keeps floating through my mind is how Rick [Lowe] was adamant about not continuing the trauma. We know the trauma, we understand the horrific history. We understand how a lot of news stories cater to the fear of violence in Chicago and focus on all the things that are supposedly wrong within the Black community. Rick would say, "I want you to find the *gold*. I want you to bring inspiration to the community." That was our lead when we talked with people. Yes, we wanted people to be aware of the tragic history of the Black Wall Street massacre, but we also wanted to give people

IS: We kicked off the CHOP IT UP series with a Black Wall Street descendant, Keewa Nurullah, owner of the popular children's boutique Kido. She shared that her great-grandfather had a tailor shop on Black Wall Street in Tulsa. During the massacre, he escaped with his wife and two children aided by a customer who hid them in a wagon. Keewa's ancestors came to Chicago, and their story is one of resilience. Her great-grandfather reopened his tailor shop and taught his son (Keewa's grandfather) the business, resulting in family tailor stores on 47th and 63rd streets in Chicago. She is a proud third-generation Black entrepreneur.

hope and to inspire them. I remember having an impromptu kind of sharing of *Black Wall Street Journey* with one family—a young woman with four children. And the youngest child asked me, why did they do this to this town? That's a big question. And what I tried to share with her was that it's important to not focus solely on the violence, to also see the resiliency of the community, the fact that we're celebrating that community a hundred years later, and that she is part of that legacy. So again—to walk away with hope, to walk away with inspiration in spite of the violence, was the guiding light of this project. Black Wall Street can and should be replicated throughout this country, and we get there by showing the resilience of Black people.

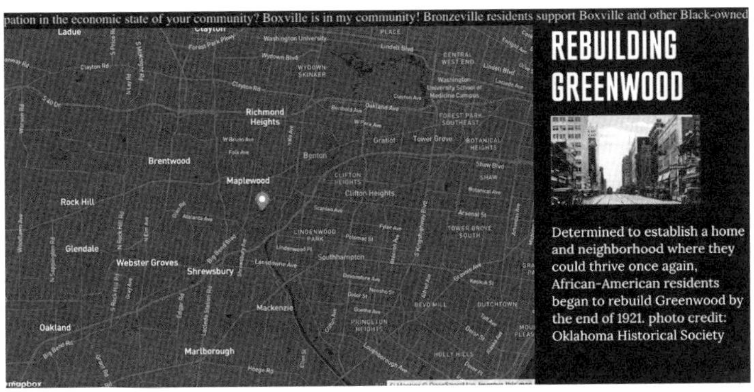

A ticker on the *Black Wall Street Journey* website contributed to the project's efforts to develop a roadmap for assessing and enriching disenfranchised communities. Screenshot

JP So much of this project had to do with squaring the pedagogical practicalities of working in a social-practice modality. If you want to work with students in a way that extends beyond the sketchbook and into the community, it absolutely cannot be fey or feigned. There's an actuality to working with communities and marginalized individuals that doesn't allow for mishaps or mistakes. Likewise, you cannot truly learn about that practice in a studio or lab environment. The dictates of the work demand authentic engagement with people, places, and politics.

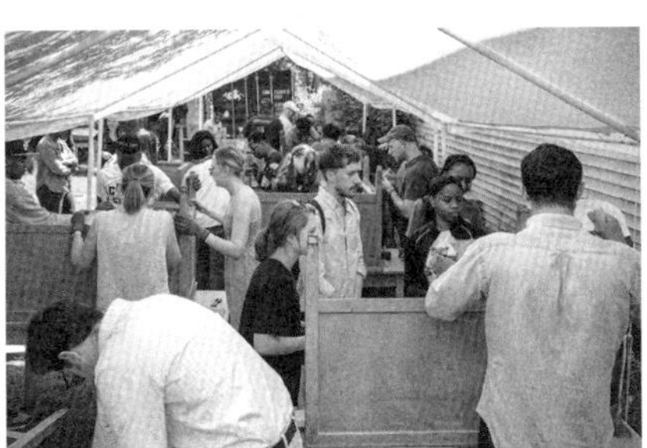

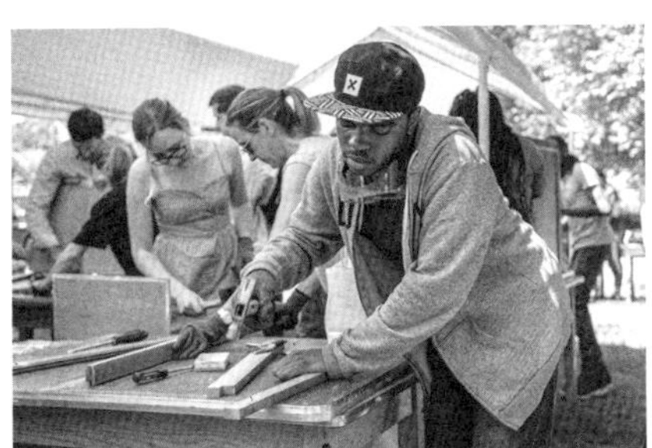

Summer 2019 workshop held at Sweet Water Foundation with Smart and CHA teens and staff to deconstruct and reclaim furniture as part of a project by artist John Preus. Photos: Garret Garcia, courtesy of the Smart Museum

We were able to set up a system for success by working within a framework of long-term partnerships and the trust engendered from years of growing those relationships bit by bit.

material transparency enriched the meaning of Bey's portrayal of Black and Brown youth for the immediate community and resonated with the young people who participate in APL's Teen Arts Council and its various programs (design apprenticeship, community actors, and backstage production).

Navigating the possibilities of remote programming, APL partnered with artist Rick Lowe and journalist Natalie Moore for the series *CHOP IT UP: Black Wall Street Journey Edition*, a demonstration of APL's commitment to supporting local talent, expertise, and resources whose impacts reverberate far beyond Chicago (p. 118).

Photo: On the Real

We had worked intensely with CHA for five years by the time we started this project, each year increasing the depth and ambition of our collaborative endeavors. So we were both accustomed to ratcheting up the intensity after several summers of bigger and bigger projects. *Toward Common Cause* took it into another gear, but we were already moving at a speedy clip.

We also had an established practice of dissolving traditional power dynamics in the program. So the roles of *teacher*, *curator*, and *building manager* took a back seat to the agency and empowerment of *teens*, *residents*, and *community*. And then, crucially, so many of the artists—Njideka [Akunyili Crosby], Mel [Chin], Rick, many others—were incredibly generous with their time and their spirit.

HR: This is absolutely necessary when working with communities whose stories are not part of the hierarchical canon. Our work needs to increasingly create spaces and places for those who have been absent or ignored by bringing their stories to the center. Their stories will change the narrative and the power.

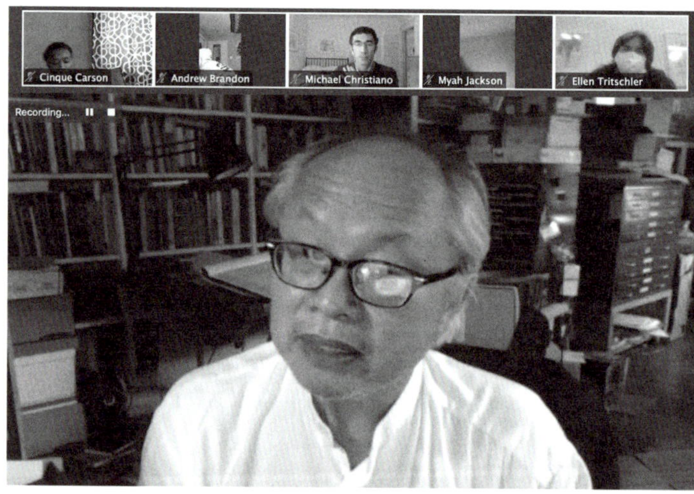

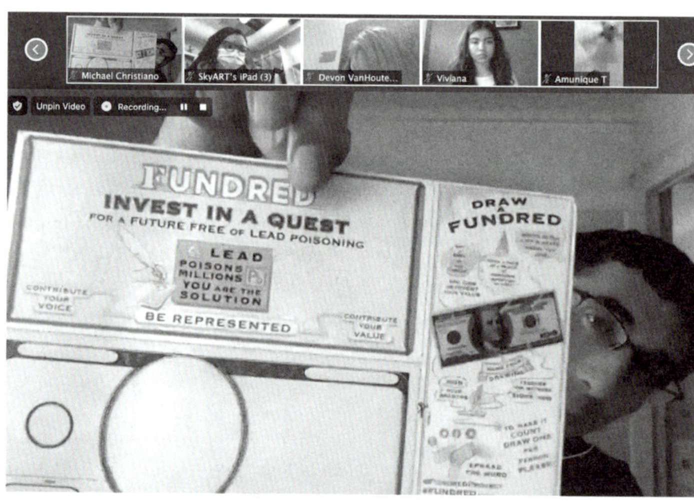

Zoom session with the Smart Teen Program, SkyART, and Mel Chin, July 29, 2020. Photos: Jason Pallas

As for values, I think CHA appreciated Njideka as an artist, but what they were really interested in was the youth voice and that the initiative was teen-led and provided an opportunity for young people to make a positive contribution to the beautification of this building and this community. Those were the values that they aligned with, probably more than the art itself.

MC We've often talked about how to characterize the type of exchange found in different partnerships, which can range from transactional to fully reciprocal (and whether true reciprocity is achievable). Where on this spectrum would you locate the projects you were involved in and why? What did you learn from the partnership?

NP: This is the same old patronage system, simply with new faces in power. Until the museum stops seeing itself as a curator and arbiter of cultural value and instead serves as a platform and stage for the creativity of its communities, it cannot be more than a benevolent dictator.

JP I always find this question funny, because the museum (in the larger sense, not limited to the Smart) will pride itself on giving over some power to a community advisory panel or a youth group but then, in actuality, just about all of the benefits accrue to the museum in terms of social capital, fundraising, and moral (grand)standing. In this case, I know the Smart has extracted as much value from the project as possible, which I note with no shade. But I've been heartened to see the impact on the participants and community beyond the institution.

The students developed personally and professionally in ways that we could not have achieved without being involved in this project. Upon reflection with CHA colleagues, it's apparent the project pushed their boundaries, but it has also cleared a path for future engagement in cultural practices like this. And perhaps we collectively established a model for resident engagement in the issues that most directly affect where and how they live.

DN So, to be honest with you, I don't know if true reciprocity (long term) is ever achievable. I do think there are *moments* of reciprocity. And what I mean by that is that reciprocity is only as good as the relationship itself and the partnership that you've built. And that can move at different points. With *Black Wall Street Journey*, I think we covered the spectrum from uneasy partnership to transactional partnership to reciprocity to now building a new partnership. And rebuilding can look like different things. For example, the relationship that we had with Urban Juncture has changed, but what might look like a dead end can turn around at a moment's notice if you're willing to engage differently.

When you're working in partnership, as we were with Urban Juncture, I have to say that there was the intention and then there's the reality. The intention—or the expectation, I should say—was that Urban Juncture would house and incubate *Black Wall Street Journey* for a minimum of three years. The reality is that it lasted about a year. And now we're reimagining where the work will be housed. It's a change in direction on the side of Urban Juncture that we were not anticipating, but we know that *Black Wall Street Journey* will continue in a different iteration.

JP I was also thinking very much about reciprocity and ambiguity. I love that it allows a lot of space for everyone to enter and mold and shape the work and say what it can and should be. One of the things I had to learn throughout the process was to transparently communicate the structure of the museum and how decisions and timing happen on our end. And then I had to learn to be aware of those same things for everyone else's organization. My engagement for five years with CHA was through youth opportunities. And we produced this great program. Now, all of a sudden we're getting into conversations not just about organizational structure, but the different personalities people might have and the demands on their side.

MC The co-creation of community-based projects requires a great deal of trust; trust in each other and trust in a process that will move things in an interesting direction. Often that process is iterative, messy, and can be frustrating as you work toward a shared vision. Can you talk about how you shaped and navigated the project development process? What helped to build trust and common goals, and what threw a wrench in the works?

DN That's a tricky question for me because so much of my work during *Toward Common Cause* and with *Black Wall Street Journey* in particular was complicated by the relationships between the community and the university. Trust was built slowly. I'll give you an example. I had meetings with community leaders addressing where we could situate *Black Wall Street Journey* outside of the Smart. My initial conversations were met with an absolute no, not doing it, they were not going to sacrifice their time, energy, or their resources, because the Smart was tied to the university. Fast forward three months: we respected the initial no but continued to engage in smaller ways, and then we brought in Rick Lowe to talk with specific partners. It didn't hurt that he came with grant money. There's something to be said about literally putting your money where your mouth is. People, partners, want to see investment that serves the community beyond the scope of the project. Sometimes when you're building trust, you have to be willing to accept an initial no but keep returning. Financial backing is important, yes, but just as important is having the willingness to demonstrate the value in what you're doing and why partnership is so necessary. It's like flying a plane, you must have two wings. You cannot fly without the right infrastructure and the financial support.

Humility is crucial when dealing with community members. You must be willing to acknowledge when mistakes are made, and also to share the vision about why their input is so important. And you must be prepared to have multiple conversations.

JP The entities requiring trust in the CHA project were: the artist, her studio, and gallery; the curatorial team and the museum leadership; the teen participants and their families; our longstanding program partners within CHA, but also staff up and down their administrative hierarchy; the Minnie Riperton community of residents and building management; and the larger arts ecosphere to support this kind of production method. So we were constantly code-switching and running game between all these different constituencies. We had to leverage a dynamic understanding of everyone's shifting motivations, competencies, connections, and timelines.

From some corners, we had a great deal of leeway because

it was an educational and empowering endeavor for our teens. People understood that it would be messy and stop-start. Other times, we operated far above our abilities and pay grade, trying to navigate city bureaucracies to make the project happen. Ultimately, I think our constancy and consistency solicited the ongoing efforts of all the different communities involved.

The pandemic also complicated efforts to build relationships, especially with the residents. There was a yearning for connection. Everyone was isolated. But when working with senior residents, there was such an imperative on their health and wellbeing that we couldn't even enter the building. They often weren't able to leave their units. So ordinarily in the planning phase of a project, I'll just go hang out in the community room or the cafeteria and meet people where they are. Which is a principle of community-based work—meet people where they are, get to know them, build those relationships. The whole process of relationship-building becomes, when there's that physical and psychological distance, so stunted or stifled it doesn't always feel authentic or natural.

HR: Community-centered artwork is often siloed inside the museum. It focuses on people but doesn't contribute to significant audience growth and, in most situations, doesn't generate an object that becomes part of a collection. Focusing on and working *in* communities with integrity and care takes significant resources. These resources can't be easily identified or justified within the economic engine that keeps institutions going.

MC Museums still struggle to define and measure success in relationship to community-based projects, especially when that work happens largely outside of the museum. Conventional metrics also feel inadequate if the goal is to co-develop goals and allow the process to iterate as needed. What did success look and feel like for those involved in the CHA project and *Black Wall Street Journey*? What do you hope that might suggest for how museums understand the value of this work?

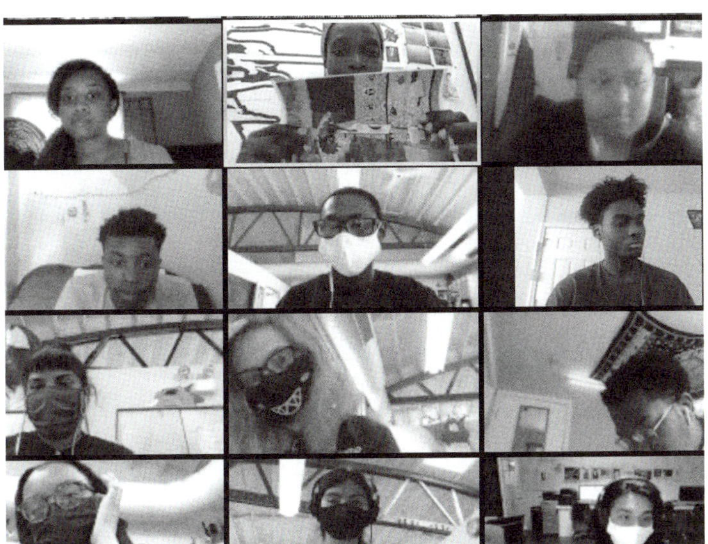

Zoom session with the Smart Teen Program, Jason Pallas, and Njideka Akunyili Crosby, June 8, 2020. Photo: Jason Pallas

JP Community-based projects, by nature, cut against the established grain of museums, which privileges notions of academic expertise and cultural protectionism. So when you propose engaging people in a multimodal project that extends beyond the bounds of curation, registration, etcetera, it can be difficult to quantify impact or even accrue support within the institution.

In the case of Njideka working with the teens, success looked like time and generosity. She took the time with us, whereas we know she has a global practice. I'm sure there are all sorts of demands on her time and energy, but then, also, the time and pacing of her work were visible to us: we'd do studio visits spread out over months and see that she was working on the same painting. And she'd be like, I kind of did a few trees and that's what I accomplished. Her candor was so empowering. She's in there plugging away every day. So the type of labor, what constitutes labor, really exploded open for the teens.

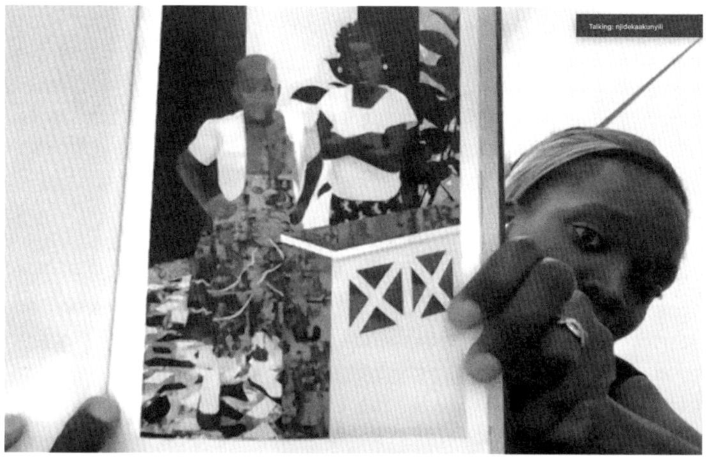

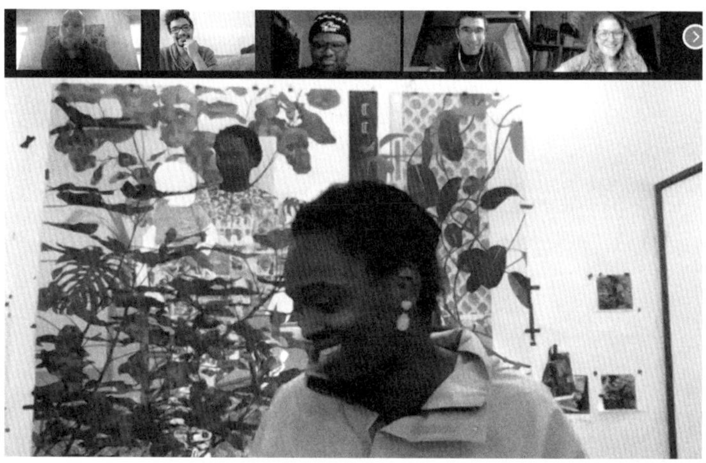

Zoom session with the Smart Teen Program, Jason Pallas, and Njideka Akunyili Crosby, June 8, 2020 (top), February 27, 2021 (bottom). Photos: Jason Pallas

And the timelines of these projects lay like a blanket over the neatly defined fiscal years required for budgeting and grant reporting. We have a practice to understand exhibition research and production, but marshaling the support of broad coalitions to create authentic and iterative practices can cut against those practices. We need to reimagine those administrative structures to make them more nimble so that they can bend and pivot as a project adapts, while still maintaining accountability to the use of funds and staff time.

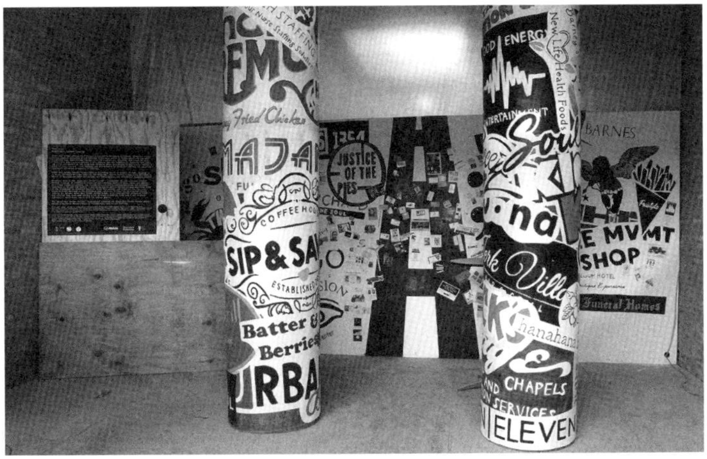

Black Wall Street Journey murals by Dorian Sylvain for Urban Juncture. Photo: Smart Museum

DN The first step toward success has always been to deal with setting the vision. Rick did a really good job of building collective buy-in for *Black Wall Street Journey*, creating an opportunity for everyone involved to make it their own. His practice was about, you have a stake in this project in terms of success. And that investment came from different areas of the community—for example, Dorian Sylvain created the *Black Wall Street Journey* murals with hand-painted logos representing more than a hundred Black businesses. And so when we tried to pin Rick down and ask, okay, what is this project?, he would throw it right back to us: what do you want it to be?

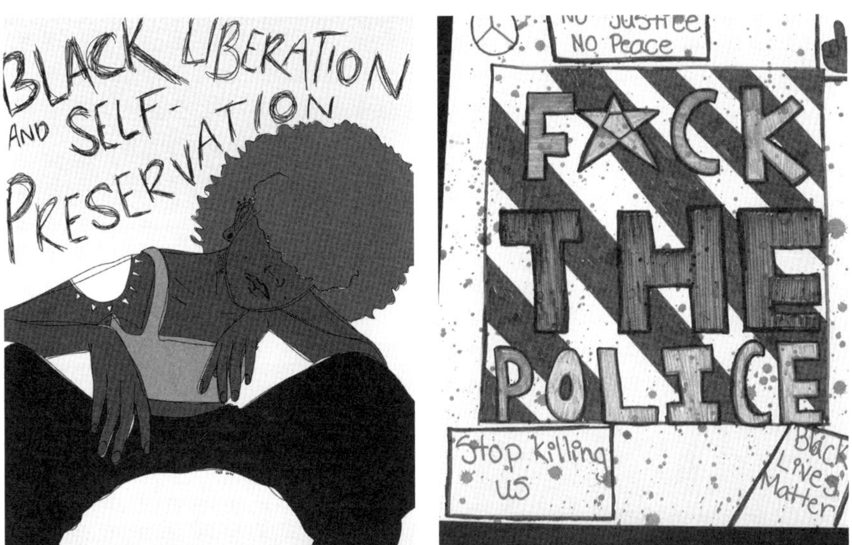

The exhibition *When Revolution Roars the Unacknowledged Speak* at Urban Juncture featured contributions by Smart Teen Program members Anthony Ruffin, Asia Handley, Doncae Long, India Mitchell, Ivan Williams, Jada Jackson, Jamal Watkins, Jamaya Hagerman, Jaden Roundtree, Jahlyn Gaither, Lakyla Banks, Marquise Blakely, Milan Jackson, Nevaeh Nichols, Shatara Dunbar, Tech Nix, Trinity Treadwell, and Xavier Proctor. Photos: Jason Pallas

Beyond collective investment, another important measure of success is making something that can stand beyond the scope of the exhibition. For *Black Wall Street Journey*, that has changed since our relationship with some of the partners has changed, but it has still forced us to really think about what success looks like beyond these four walls.

It's not always easy to sustain partnerships because the temptation is always to be on to the next thing. There has to be a continued effort to maintain those relationships and to include them as best you can in other projects. So one measure of success would be whether these partnerships have been reinforced through additional collaborations.

We can look at attendance numbers. The opening was amazing, and the foot traffic in all of the venues was very successful. But to me, the better measure would be the teacher that came to Urban Juncture for one of the *Black Wall Street Journey* discussions and from that discussion worked with us to develop a curriculum about the history of Black Wall Street for her sixth graders. That's success.

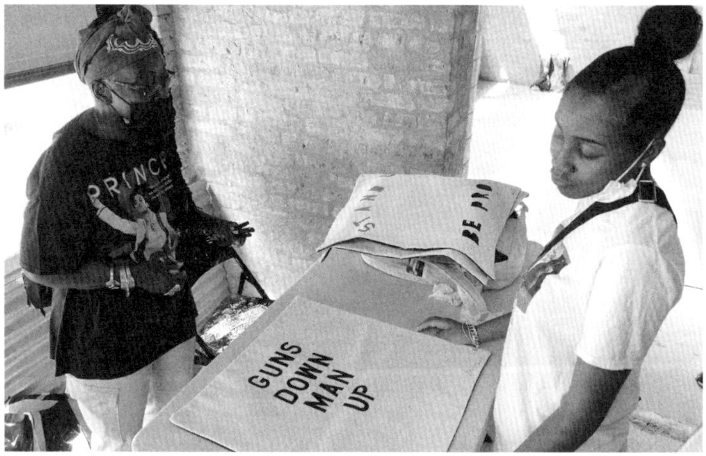

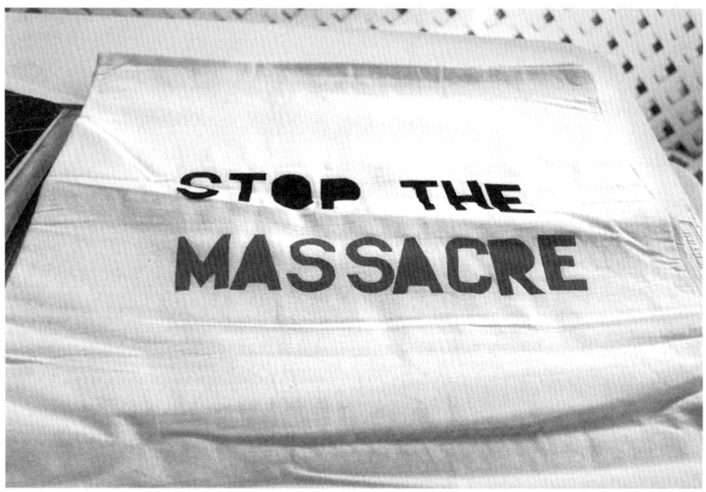

Opening day of *When Revolution Roars the Unacknowledged Speak* at Urban Juncture. Photos: Jason Pallas

MC What will you carry forward from your work on these projects?

DN Intentionality is critical in all that we do. Cultural

National Museum of
Mexican Art
1852 W. 19th St.
Chicago, IL 60608

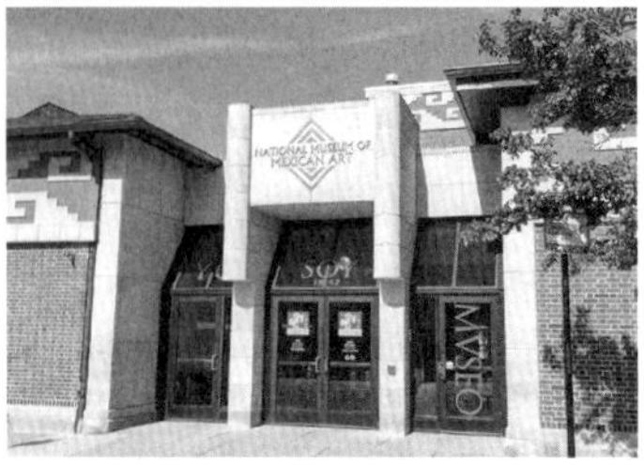

The National Museum of Mexican Art opened in 1982 as the Mexican Fine Arts Center Museum, an initiative of a group of Mexican American public school teachers organized by Carlos Tortolero, who served as the museum's founding director. Their goal was a cultural center dedicated to social justice, education, and community accessibility. Moving into its current location in Pilsen in 2006, the museum holds one of the largest collections of Mexican art in the US, from antiquity to the present. Every fall, it mounts a Day of the Dead exhibition. The thirty-sixth, *Día de Muertos: A Time to Grieve & Remember*, commemorated deaths caused by COVID-19. *Toward Common Cause* commissioned an ofrenda from Amalia Mesa-Bains to be included in that exhibition. *Circle of Ancestors* was part of her two-part project *Dos Mundos: Mexican Chicago*, the other half of which was presented at Weinberg/Newton Gallery (Scenes #29, #31; p. 139).

Mesa-Bains's project engaged the history of Mexican immigration to Chicago through the very personal experiences of her own family. The artist is the child of undocumented immigrants; her maternal family settled in South Chicago. *Dos Mundos* made visible the contributions of the Mexican community to the building of Chicago. As laborers in the steel mills, for instance, they were, in the artist's

(continued on opposite page)

institutions have a stake in understanding and sharing history, in stopping the erasure of history and helping people to formulate critical ideas and thoughts on their own using the tools they already have. Yes, I think that our cultural institutions are instrumental in maintaining that, especially at this time.

The guiding principle of this project was that we should not focus solely on the negative parts of this history: not to diminish the racial violence or negate the importance of making the history of Black Wall Street known, but to continually build self-awareness beyond the massacre. A self-awareness among Black people that focuses on our humanity and demands that others see that humanity. I take it personally, it's part of the reason why I moved back to the city. I am now living and working in the city that I serve. To me, Chicago is a beautiful city. I could focus on all of the things that Chicago isn't. But I choose to focus on the things that Chicago is. Chicago is resilient, Chicago is a great city for artists, musicians, poets, theater. It is a great town to eat in. Chicago has a vibrancy that is unlike any other place in the country. Chicago is all these things because of the people who live and work here. When Black people fled Tulsa for their lives, some were able to build new lives in Chicago, most notably J. B. Stradford, businessman and activist, who was considered to be one of the richest men in Tulsa. Whose great-grandson, J. W. Rogers Jr., founded Ariel Capital Management in Chicago. It's that resilience, that legacy, that I'm going to share with other people.

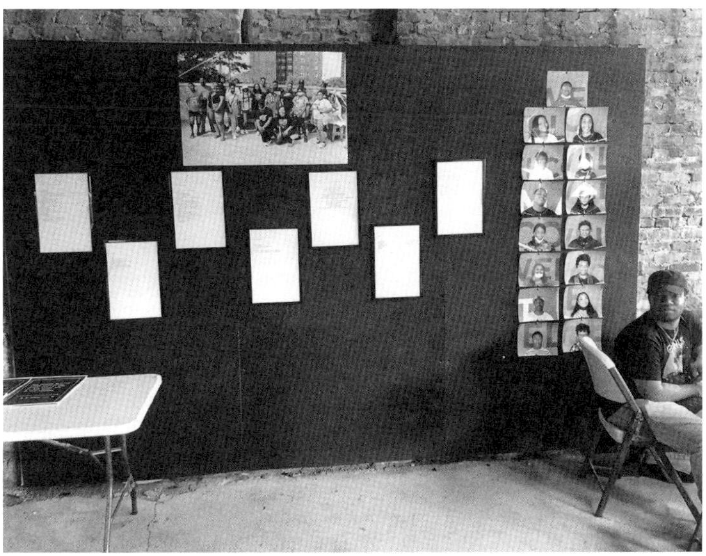

Installation of *When Revolution Roars the Unacknowledged Speak* at Urban Juncture. Photo: Jason Pallas

JP My takeaway is the power of collective action to enact change in our communities. So much of our learning leads us to focus on the "great men through history," the individuals that presumably have pushed culture forward. But in actuality, bigger tables really are the key to better meals. I would much prefer to eat a slice of pie with as many brilliant people, from as many different political identities, as possible.

words, "the invisible infrastructure of this city." The project was dedicated to Mesa-Bains's mother Marina Cornejo Gonzalez Mesa and her Cornejo family, who were active in Chicago's Mexican communities.

Photo: Wikimedia Commons

Can we talk about what brought joy or meaning to us through this work? I'll throw that to you first, Dorian, if you don't mind. Where was your joy in this?

DN I really appreciated Rick's determination that we not focus on trauma. We were in a meeting—Abigail [Winograd], myself, our interns—looking at some of the footage and data that we had gathered for the *Black Wall Street Journey* website. It was only maybe two minutes of material, about the Stradford family who had fled Tulsa to Chicago, but we walked away from that moment feeling that we had learned so much. In going through that material, I was really struck by the resiliency of that family to rebuild and to not let the Tulsa Massacre be the final word. Their story gave me hope that no matter what, if you continue to just keep putting the next foot forward, you may not have the answer for the next ten years, but you could still impact and change the world. I really appreciated that part of the legacy. And then that helped inform the ways in which we interacted not only with our community partners but our business leaders. Because that was really important too.

JP That's beautiful. How about you, Michael, where did you get joy from *Toward Common Cause*?

MC I'm thinking about a moment at an early partners meeting at the MacArthur offices. It was one of the first, so it was pre-pandemic. I think it was the last time that all of the partners came together in person to talk about the project before its launch. The Smart and MacArthur teams introduced the project and framed our conversation before we broke into small groups to discuss. At some point, Carlos Tortolero from the National Museum of Mexican Art, in his critical and generous way, was asking why the geographical scope of the project wasn't broader. It was a really good question. And then someone else asked a question and someone else asked a question. And then Rick Lowe started doing his thing. The idea of the project left the museum and it started to circulate among the community of practitioners with whom we were sharing space. And it became our idea, or at least it became our potential. So those moments where it felt like there was community forming in the shaping of the thing brought me great joy.

What about you, Jason?

JP Specifically, it was researching the possible building sites for Njideka's work. One of the things we had been talking about with CHA is that a lot of the teens aren't aware that they have a connection to CHA because they're on housing choice vouchers and they don't actually live in an apartment building. And for some, where they live is just a building, it doesn't have a political identity. But then, when they researched the buildings and the histories of the sites, they became agents and avatars for not just the artwork but also the representation of public goods and housing as a right, and as an identity, and as a thing that should be in the world.

And by the time they put together the ballots for the residents, they cared deeply. Those kids knew every painting Njideka ever made, and they could tell you why this painting was the best one she ever made. So in a way, in all of my time teaching in a museum, trying to figure out ways to get young people to care, this was one of those magic gallery teaching moments.

1 *Longstreet*, season 1, episode 1, "The Way of the Intercepting Fist," aired September 16, 1971, ABC.

2 SkyART, one of the key cultural partners for Mel Chin's *Chicago Fundred Initiative: A Bill for IL*, offers free visual arts programs to young people in the South Chicago neighborhood.

3 adrienne maree brown, *Emergent Strategy: Shaping Change, Changing Worlds* (Chico, Calif.: AK Press, 2017).

4 Christiano is former deputy director and curator of Public Practice at the Smart (currently director of Visual Arts & Museum, Colorado Springs Fine Arts Center at Colorado College); Nash is former manager of Public Programs at the Smart (currently director of Learning and Cultural Workforce Development at the National Public Housing Museum); and Pallas is former associate director of Public Practice at the Smart (currently fine arts faculty, University of Chicago Laboratory Schools).

5 Boxville is Chicago's first shipping container marketplace to use modified shipping containers for commerce in place of traditional brick-and-mortar spaces. Boxville is located on East 51st Street and the Green Line, next door to Urban Juncture.

Abigail Winograd (AW) in conversation with Amalia Mesa-Bains (AM), Jeffrey Gibson (JG), and Carrie Mae Weems (CMW)

WE HAVE TO INSIST

This conversation was inspired by another, "Deaccessioning after 2020: What Does Diversifying the Collection Mean to Artists?" The panel, moderated by Carrie Mae Weems, was part of a virtual conference organized by Syracuse University. Weems asked the panelists, "In what context would you like your work to be viewed and understood? How do you want your work to be positioned?" I have been thinking about that conversation ever since. What was revelatory about Weems's questions is that, though it should be obvious, museum professionals seldom ask artists how they wish their work to be seen, how they want it to be talked about, in what ways they would like institutions to shift.

AW I want to start by asking Carrie why she asked those questions?

CMW Well, thank you. At the moment, I don't remember why I asked the questions. But I think about it a lot. This issue of context seems so important to the work. I think about what I'm hoping to make, what I've made, how to share it, where and under what conditions it should be shared. As much as I love institutions and museums—or at least have a great deal of respect for them—I know they do not always provide the best context for work to be viewed or understood. Sometimes, my work needs to be taken out of the white-box context and pulled into another kind of space.

I remember an exhibition I did for the Havana Biennial several years ago where I invited a group of younger artists to participate with me. We were in this old funky house, this old, crazy, wonderful house, and together we turned this house into our space of contemplation. There were dozens of exhibitions going on in every conceivable gallery space in Havana during that time, but nobody wanted to leave our space. People kept coming, and nobody would leave. It was just this old house with a certain kind of spirit. Somehow the work was able to infuse and broaden and give specificity to the house, in a way that no museum, no other institution could match. Work doesn't have to be shown in an institution to be validated.

When work is shown in institutions, how is it shown? So often when work is shown—particularly for people of color—it's shown in relationship to other people of color, which I find problematic. Not that they shouldn't do that, but rather museums should do considerably more. For instance, how is Jeffrey's work, Amalia's work, my work, related to all of these other huge ideas around modernism? Often we're left out of that context completely.

I don't think I've ever been shown alongside white men. Literally at this moment, I cannot remember a time. My work has been considered in a very narrow band that doesn't really consider the breadth of the work and how the work functions, how it should be understood and perceived. I think that has a lot to do with the narrowness and the limitations that curators have often placed around it. It's something that I'm very aware of and something that I'm always trying to figure out how to crack.

AW So Amalia, when Carrie asked the questions originally, you gave a rather pessimistic answer. You were extremely skeptical of the museum's ability to change, to represent your work, and you were vocal about your decision to take an active role in controlling how and where you show your work.

AMB Well, I have to say that for large portions of my art life, I wasn't just making art. I was an educator in public schools for almost thirty years. I was of course writing about it, and also confronting what I saw as boundaries and limitations. And especially for us on the West Coast, especially as a Chicana, for the first twenty years we wanted and made our own spaces. We had our own *galería*, we had our own "Brown box." We called our places *galerías*, but they were not commercial galleries—the point was not to make something to be sold. The Galería de la Raza in San Francisco was like that crazy house Carrie describes.[1] You could go there any Saturday of the week for years and years and years. And anybody passing through from Cuba, from Latin America, from Paris, from England, they knew this little place. People would run out and get beer and quesadillas from the little restaurant next door. They would just hang out there all day. It could be journalists, it could be anybody, because it was a place that was always alive.

I soon realized that the art world had many misconceptions about us.

On every level of my life, I felt the weight of those misconceptions. I kept hitting that thing that was there, the misunderstanding, the distortion, the neglect, the inability to even see us. So for a long time, I felt I had to do the job of translation.

In 1990, Marcia Tucker brought us all to the Art Institute of Chicago for the annual meeting of the Association of Art Museum Directors. It was myself, Skip Gates, Jack Chen, Tomás Ybarra-Frausto, Irene Winter, and others. They produced a volume from it, *Different Voices: A Social, Cultural, and Historical Framework for Change in the American Art Museum*.[2] They were asking us, "How should museums behave in order for you to be able to be there?" I spoke about the social reality of not being greeted, of not feeling welcome.

That experience in Chicago was one of the ugliest I've ever had. If those old white men had had rotten tomatoes, they would have thrown them at us. The panelists I invited, the facilitators, all of us left in the middle of the day in tears because it was so rude and terrible. I left thinking, this is cancerous. I'm not going back there anymore. I went home and started my ReGeneration Project through the Galería de la Raza to try to build a new generation. Because one thing was really clear to me: you do not ask white men in their sixties or seventies to change the way they look at art. Their intellectual and financial investments have been in a particular kind of work, and they're just not ready to make that change.

And now I see what has happened, exactly what we imagined. I finally got a show at the San Francisco Museum of Modern Art in 2022, after living in that city, being a commissioner of art, starting three organizations there. Why? Because Maria Castro was there, a young Latina curator. She is evidence of generational change and that is why I would say museums can change. However, change is constantly running up against the concerns we have already mentioned: lack of curatorial experience, absence of knowledge or curiosity, the marketplace, etcetera. From its earliest inception, Chicano and Chicana work was tied to activism that museums are still not ready to embrace. There's a part of me—that Chicana sort of idiom, the mentality we grew up with—that is sometimes extremely rageful, and the rest of the time it's just turbulent.

Thirty years ago, we were advocating for institutional change by arguing that decisions about collections and acquisitions be based in research and historical concerns and be separated from the concerns of the market and patronage. We were naive. Now, thirty years later, we are confronting another reality. I recently did a panel with Rashida Bumbray. She referred to this moment as a period of recovery because the art world is currently awash in retrospectives or major shows of women of color aged 80 (my age) to 101. I thought, "recovery, what a strange word," and I've been mulling it over.

So if I were to respond to Carrie's questions now, my answer wouldn't be so extreme, but I would say that museums are still plagued by ignorance. They are not spaces where there is a free exchange of knowledge. Museums are still connected to the market and are supported by those invested in it. Exhibitions are tied to those market concerns. It is extremely difficult to compete with that.

AW Jeffrey, I would like to give you a chance to answer the same questions. Because I wish I had asked you this question when I first reached out to you about *Toward Common Cause*. I realized, well into our work together, that I put you in a difficult position, one with the potential to trigger historical trauma. I did the thing that curators do so often lately—I asked an artist of color to engage with a collection that relates to his community and his history. I asked you to provide a critical lens, to correct the historical record. At the time, I did not fully appreciate how onerous that request might be and in time had to apologize for my insensitivity. So I want to ask you the questions that Carrie asked: In what context would you like your work to be viewed and understood? How do you want your work to be positioned?—because that's what I should have started with.

JG Thinking about this made me think more about how I've been shaped by the art world that has been available to me. I have spent the last twenty years trying to find ways to make the best work I can—to be vulnerable and emotive, to resist compromise within an existing system. In the last ten years, I've realized how pervasive racism and the fear of other cultures are. They remain deeply embedded in institutional thinking. This realization does not scare me. I don't know if it's because I am a queer person of color, which comes with a kind of acceptance that wherever you are in the world people are afraid of you: you are going to judged and dismissed and misread. By necessity, I've built up a lot of strategies to deal with that.

So with institutions, I ask how can we do things differently, what can we do? Who's the community I want to speak to? The Native community does not have a single point of contact. It's hundreds of micro communities. There are Indigenous arts organizations for sure. There are queer organizations of Indigenous people, but that is not the bulk of who the culture is. The bulk of these communities of people live outside cultural hubs. My question is always how to reach the young artist on the reservation in South Dakota? How does my work become available to the communities that I am speaking to and speaking of? How does that happen? For me and for many artists of color, it always comes down to programming, because programming connects us with educators and those tasked with community outreach. Unfortunately, all too often there is little to no knowledge and bandwidth for creating programming that would support an exhibition. These efforts are critical and important, but this responsibility is not shared by my white peers. They can show an abstract painting without being asked to justify or contextualize it or program alongside their exhibitions.

I have come to the end of my optimism about my relationships with institutions. However, I don't know where else to go. I completely understand what Carrie is talking about, as far as who you're shown with and how that extends your work or doesn't. I often tell curators and institutions just how rare it is that Indigenous artists are included in group exhibitions with non-Indigenous artists. It just doesn't happen. There remains a perception that our world is so far removed from theirs that it can only be shown separately in exhibitions of only Native artists. More and more, Native artists are declining to be included in large group exhibitions, and rightfully so. On the other hand, that does not mean we *are* being included in topical exhibitions without an exclusive Native focus.

CMW It seems the way museums work and young curators are trained are diametrically opposed to our positions as artists. Young curators are building their careers. They are looking at, writing about, doing PhDs on artists that they believe will allow them to advance. In a very fundamental way, the problem begins at the university level. Being open to new ideas and new artists, well, that involves incredible imagination, chutzpah, and determination to push past these narrow avenues. As a teacher, I was always talking to young artists and museum professionals about the kinds of questions that they might start asking now, as opposed to doing one more document or a PhD on Rothko or

Warhol. I made the decision early on to chart my own path through and around institutions. I realized it was my responsibility to myself, that I couldn't simply allow the institution to tell me what to do. Institutional thinking is shallow when it comes to people like us, people of color, because it is predicated on fear. We have to insist that institutions engage with us. Doing so is a part of my responsibility to myself, to art, to the institution, and to the field.

AMB It was inevitable that artists of color would be the ones to change museums. We were historically excluded from museums and slotted into natural history museums or "halls of man." I remember when I went to London for the first time. I went to the National Gallery looking for the Mexican mosaic skulls. I asked a guard who told me, "Well, they wouldn't be here. This is classic art. That would be in a hall of man and there's one down the block."

The idea that there are two separate spaces—the museum, on one hand, full of masterpieces made by artists, and the hall of man, on the other, filled with artifacts made by anonymous artisans—is disrupted when we appear. When Fred Wilson appears or when Jaune Quick-to-See Smith appears, the masterpieces and the hall of man collide. Artists like these, like us, scare museums because we explode these neat categorizations, we challenge the distinction between fine art and folk art, previously anonymous, but now made by artists who insist on defining themselves and identifying with their communities.

In my case, I was moved forward by my community. I was asked to speak for them to challenge this kind of thinking. It was not just me. When Carmen Lomas Garza had her first big show, she rebuffed a VIP reception and a cocktail hour. She insisted instead that the opening be moved to a Sunday, that it be open to the public, that children be welcome, that there be free food. Carmen did this throughout the 1980s, repeatedly demanding the "Family Sunday" in every institution she worked in. She made it up, the Family Sunday. I remember those events so well. I remember the grandmothers with the grandchildren, standing in front of work and telling stories. It was not just our people but lots of people with families that had suffered, that had struggled.

I have been waiting eighty years for the recognition that I am receiving now. Before, I only appeared in group shows about spirituality or feminism. I'm in there with people, white men, but major players in that field of what is called spirituality. Or I would get dropped into feminism because what I made was about *mujeres*, women. It wasn't feminist in its intention but ironically it was in its practice.

You're right, Jeffrey, about shouldering a burden of representation. Carrie, you've been able to do it because you've also tied your life to caring for young people, mentoring. This is a crucial part of building the new generation that will not stand for the shit that we've had to put up with, frankly.

AW Speaking of the next generation—what do you think will be different or is different for the artists coming up behind you?

CMW About five or six years ago, I pulled together a panel at the Ford Foundation with Amalia and other artists I admire as critical thinkers. Each person was asked to invite two or three younger people who they felt were on a certain track, going back to this idea of knowledge accumulation and bringing younger people forward.

Amalia, you are one of the great gifts of our generation, how you think and the way in which you really work. You're not only talking about yourself as an artist, you're an activist and an educator who has also started organizations.

You've moved into the institution at Monterey in order to build a program that grows not only artists but critical thinkers and museum professionals as well.[3] You have been at the forefront of this movement.

AMB We stand where we are because people have been there for us and we represent something to them. It is a very reciprocal experience. We have been at this for fifty years, my *compadres* and I. We've gotten sick. We've gotten older. Our communities have gone under in some places. We've lost some of our institutions. And yet, we are still there. Part of what is so special about our communities is that they defy the hyper-individualized notion of becoming an artist that is part of artistic training now. It really can't be done alone.

I think about you Jeffrey, you're part of what I consider a new generation. I worked with the Native artists who were part of my generation, Jaune Quick-to-See Smith, Peter Jemison, and Kay WalkingStick. They came to these big events. We gathered together. Over time this burden wears you down, but then someone like you comes along and everything feels possible again. You have brought up materials and ways of being that have been absent in the bigger picture for many, many years. Your perspective is so important as a queer person, as a Native person. You can open doors for the next generation.

JG I worry about the two or three generations coming up behind me because I worry they will drink the proverbial Kool-Aid. We are in a moment where I would say more Native artists—young, contemporary Native artists—are showing than I've ever experienced. My fear for the younger generation is that they remain in the thrall of a problematic art world. From the vantage point of an older person, I can look with some distance and know what's important to me and understand the necessity of setting boundaries.

Jaune Quick-to-See Smith is one of my mentors and has been since the 1990s. I've learned so much from her. One of the remarkable things about Jaune is her work ethic. I wonder where I would be if I worked as hard as she has. She raised children, drove across the country to pick up artwork, organized multiple exhibitions of her peers. She did it to make sure that these artists were seen. She hasn't stopped. Edgar Heap of Birds was very kind to me. James Luna was very kind to me. Rebecca Belmore was very kind to me. Jaune, Peter Jemison, Kay WalkingStick: I thought about that generation, with their work ethic of sacrificing everything for the importance of being an artist and bringing up other artists with them, the toll that it takes on your psyche, on your family, on your mental health, on your physical health. I had to make a decision. I have two small children. I'm married to my husband. I've really tried to be a grounded person—a father and a husband and a teacher and a mentor and a son. But it means that I have to put real boundaries on my professional life in many ways.

I made the decision that I need to walk on from what they've achieved. My job is not to go back and to continue being the educator, the curator, the translator, the community outreach person, and the artist, but just hold the line at "I'm an artist." I'm an artist and that's what I'm going to do.

AW To all three of you, have you achieved a status that allows you to demand change? Are you treated differently now? We know that the art world loves its fads. For example, there was a clamor for Latinx art and Latin American art in "celebration" of the Columbus Quincentenary. Do you feel you are in a place to challenge that kind of tokenism? Do you feel empowered to demand something different for yourself or for the next generation?

AMB Or maybe *command.*

AW Command, yes.

JG I think the success that I've had is also institutional success, which is still very much a Western and European definition of success. Success of this nature isolates me from my community, which is primarily in Mississippi and Oklahoma, because I'm having an experience that the majority of my family and my community cannot access. There are no museums there. They're not looking at contemporary art. What I make doesn't really make sense in the context of that lived reality. They're very proud of me, but they would be proud of me regardless of what I did. It's just familial love and support.

To answer your question, yes, I am surprised that in recent years I am able to tell people what I want to do and that they are on board. I am in a position that I can challenge the market, and more and more I feel it is important to make work that is difficult to sell. That's been my prize, but I tend to self-fund those parts of my practice. I use the market to raise money for myself to be able to do the multimedia performances, which can involve music, collaborations with Native writers and performers. It takes time for the institutions to get on board. Lately, they tend to come around and agree to fund them.

CMW Well, I have fascinating relationships with people and I cherish them.

I really hear you, Jeffrey. I hear what you're saying about the borders and the boundaries that you set for yourself. My boundaries are very open. I have had to be selfish because I want to make my own work. I want to produce it at a certain level. I've had to elbow my way in and find the pockets and inroads that make that possible.

At the same time, I started my career going to various museums saying, "You really need to know about these artists. You need to be looking at these photographers. You need to do something really exciting with them," or "This is something you can do with them." I've just been working in this way for over fifty years. I care deeply about the field. I don't want to be in it by myself. I want to be in it with you and Amalia, with Abigail, with a host of other people really advocating for change because I know that it makes a difference. I have developed a way of asking questions in such a way that people are willing to listen. I think of it as one of my gifts, of being able to frame a question in such a way that I am not intimidating, that I'm not scaring the pants off you, but I'm actually offering you something of great value that you can take and run with.

So in recent years, I do ask very direct questions. I have asked some of my white male colleagues and curators, "Why?" They have finally been honest with me, that they simply didn't know what to do with me. They were fearful that I would not be open to working with them. This goes back to Jeffrey's early comments about the institution being afraid of otherness. I am trying to push through that fear to have some really important conversations. It is necessary for me, not just for me as a woman of color, but I hope for those coming up behind me.

This also goes back to what Amalia was saying earlier, this idea of conflict and confluence. They simply didn't know what to do with us, right? So a part then of the way that I function as an artist-educator is to lay out the agenda, the program, the look, the feasibility, the catalogue, the work: this is how you deal. This is how you deal with me and by extension any number of artists that are around me and coming behind me.

I'm actually very excited about the moment. I'm not disheartened. I understand what museums are. I understand in some way, not deeply but in some way, how they work. I see it as being an extraordinary opportunity to get really important work done, not only for myself but for others. So the kinds of convenings that I've been doing, for instance, in the last ten years, these convenings have become models for how convenings might be constructed. I use that really as a platform for a deeper engagement. And yes, it's an extraordinary amount of work, but I would rather be doing this than almost anything else that I can imagine. I'm very excited about being in the room and being at the table and trying to make shifts and changes in those locations that really matter.

AMB I've been in many of your convenings, Carrie, and one of the things that I realized eventually is that you are an institution unto yourself. So many of us came up through institutions like the Galería or SPARCC or the National Museum of Mexican Art. You also created an institutional world in a very loving and proactive way that allows other people to come together, to create a network.

I have spent a lot of time lately trying to understand why this is happening. Why are people interested in our work, why *now*? I am thinking about this from the vantage point of my own community. Black Lives Matter, without a doubt, shook them up. Those little black squares they kept putting on Instagram told you. To me, the black square wasn't solidarity. The black square was, oh my God, what should I do? Museums had to respond. Their response was, of course, DEIA—Diversity, Equity, Inclusion, and Accessibility.

Leave it to institutions to find a formula that won't work. The truth is that change is incremental, but in their anxious efforts to look proactive, they make up a new thing. Sometimes I think we operate in parallel universes, and sometimes we manage to find a way to cross over. I make jokes about the *viejas*, the age of discovery of old ladies, but it really is very profound for me. Carmen Herrera got her first show at the Whitney at the age of 100, 101. Louise Bourgeois's recognition came in her eighties and nineties. Now, people like Jaune Quick-to-See Smith, Lorraine O'Grady, Faith Ringgold, and Betye Saar are getting big shows. These were the women I looked up to. The first time I saw a Betye Saar piece was in a group show, and I stood in front of it and cried. I thought, "Oh my God, you can do this."

What we were doing in those early years was reclaiming our heritage and traditions. We were really operating profoundly from the recapturing of traditions. It didn't have anything to do with the art world. It was just somehow bringing your everyday life into a way of making art. Even when we managed to get our work to be seen within a larger context, there was always backlash. For a long time, I stopped even thinking about it, but I always really wanted it for us, and that is what kept me going.

I remember Amiri Baraka coming to one of the gatherings for a new organization that I was helping to build, the Center for the Arts at Yerba Buena Gardens. There was a lot of discussion and concern about the nature of the organization we were building—the people who would run it; if you build this, will our organizations lose out? At one of those meetings, Amiri said, "You have to think about it this way. It's like twin poles. One is self-determination and that's what we do. These are our communities, our families, our organizations. And the other one is democracy. We pay fucking taxes. We elect people. We want our fair share, and they need to give it to us." It was so simple. And from that point on, I kept this duality in my mind because we still have not gotten our fair share. It is why I persist now despite my ambivalence and my frustration with this moment of "discovery."

I have been forced to confront this now with my retrospective. I realize that all of my work has been made to show the world who we are, to insist on our value. At the same time, I have had to confront how I have neglected my body. I have thought about precisely what Jeffrey said about Jaune or my dearly beloved Hung Liu, who died a month before her retrospective. This all takes a toll. I have been sick for forty years while making art and having a full-time job. I guess what I'm saying is that it's hard now to look at this (retrospective) moment, this opportunity, with a completely positive attitude. I have paid for it. I mean, in every sense of the word, I've paid for it. Knowing what we have all been through, it is really hard to visit these very, very grand spaces and not be angry. However, I know I need to do it because I'm a model for my next generation and the generation after. If I don't take this opportunity and do it the right way, then what will happen is exactly what Jeffrey was talking about—they'll get caught in that machine. I have to do it the right way or it won't mean anything.

1 The Galería de la Raza opened in 1970.

2 Carol Becker et al., *Different Voices: A Social, Cultural, and Historical Framework for Change in the American Art Museum* (New York: Association of Art Museum Directors, 1992).

3 Mesa-Bains was the director of the Institute for Visual and Public Art at California State University, Monterey Bay, from 1997 to 2014. She was instrumental in designing a program that placed community partnerships and social justice at the center of arts education.

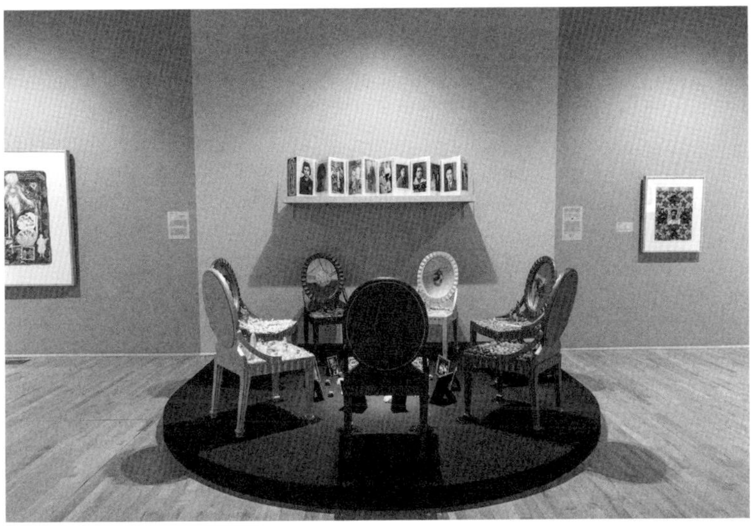

Installation of Amalia Mesa-Bains's *Circle of Ancestors* at the National Museum of Mexican Art. Photo: Nathan Keay

BBF Building Brighter Futures Center for the Arts
1512 S. Pulaski Rd.
Chicago, IL 60623

1

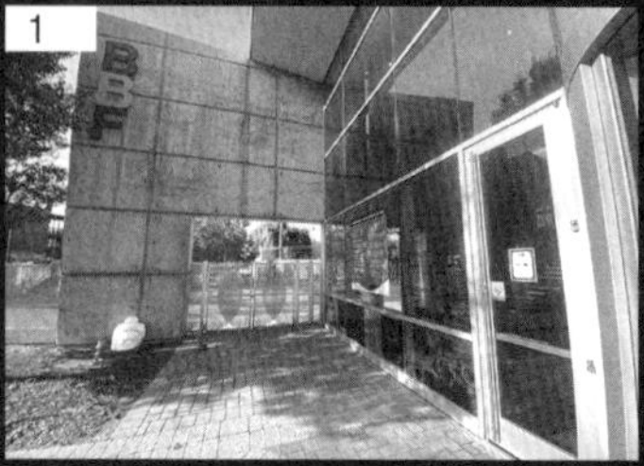

Kerry James Marshall is one of the most influential artists in the world. He is also a longtime resident of the city of Chicago and a prolific contributor to the city's public art landscape. It was impossible to consider *Toward Common Cause* without a contribution from Marshall; at the same time, finding an appropriate venue for a new public project was challenging. Just as our exhibition planning kicked off, the city of Chicago announced its intention to auction Marshall's *Knowledge and Wonder*, a large canvas painted for a branch of the Chicago Public Library in West Garfield Park in 1995. Marshall went public with his disappointment over the city's plan to capitalize on his skyrocketing market value by offering a public work for private sale, and the auction was ultimately canceled.

I credit Marshall with much of what I've learned about the importance of opening the museum to diverse communities through diversity of representation on the walls. I had the privilege of working closely with him as he prepared for his retrospective exhibition *Kerry James Marshall: Mastry*, first as a fellow and then as a research assistant at the Museum of Contemporary Art Chicago. His paintings feature figures whose faces, activities, and environs are unequivocally Black. I saw firsthand the significance to museum visitors of recognizing their own lives in his subject matter—from the guerrilla weddings taking place in front of his paintings to the consternation his figures elicited in people.

It took me more than eighteen months to find a location that Marshall would embrace for a public project. I asked him to consider a site-specific installation at BBF Family Services, formerly the Better Boys Foundation, an idea that he received with enthusiasm. Entrepreneur Joseph Kellman founded BBF in 1961 in North Lawndale, where he was born and raised. Concerned about rising crime and the future of children in his community—then predominantly Jewish—Kellman opened a boxing gym to provide afterschool activities to local youth.

2

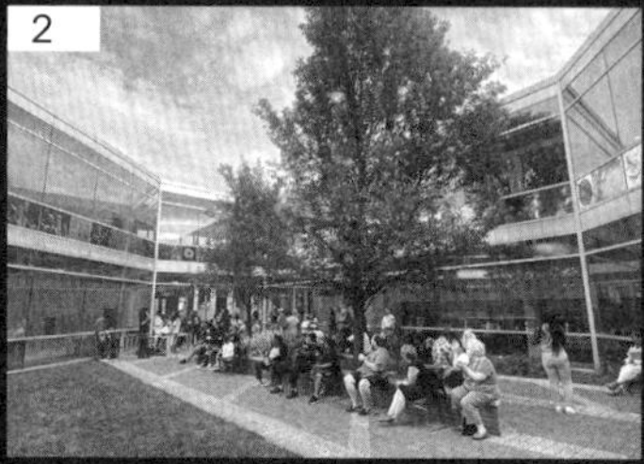

3

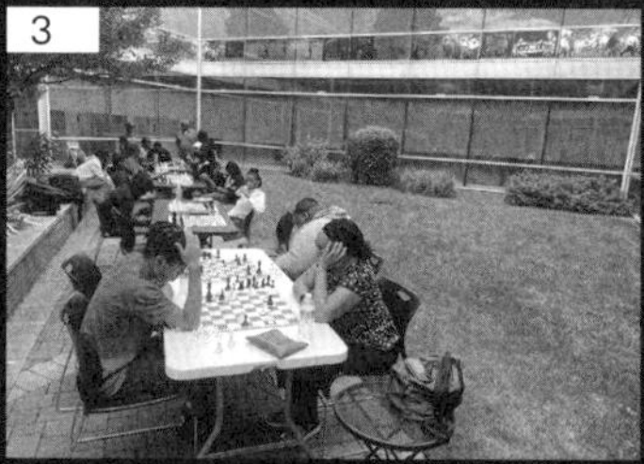

By the time I approached BBF to serve as a partner venue for *Toward Common Cause*, it had been in continuous operation for almost sixty years and had shifted from being an afterschool sports center to a comprehensive, human-services organization for children and adults, boys and girls, men and women. BBF helps the neighborhood's current low-income, primarily African American community "move from a place of impoverishment, educational challenges, joblessness, marginalization, and trauma to stability, academic success, employment, inclusion, and wholeness. It coordinates resources that meet the entire family's needs, from reentry services for ex-offenders to parenting classes for single mothers, from mentoring and tutoring for youth in at-risk situations to job readiness training for the unemployed."

Art has always been a focus of BBF's programming. BBF's art advisor Clinee Hedspeth notes that, while "most people might not think of BBF as being cultural stewards … 'cultural steward' doesn't mean just being great preservers and interpreters of art. It means actually encouraging people to engage with art and culture and giving them the opportunity to do that." The organization does just that with its temporary exhibitions, artist talks, and student museum/gallery tours. For many years, it was also the home of the Lamont Zeno Theatre, an award-winning theater arts program that showcased the talents of young people in the community.

4
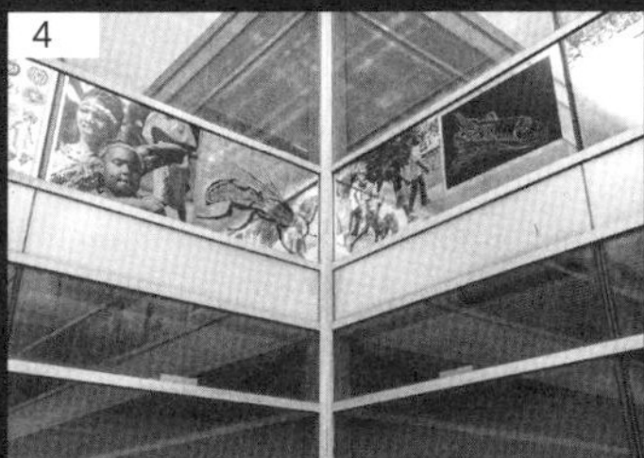

5
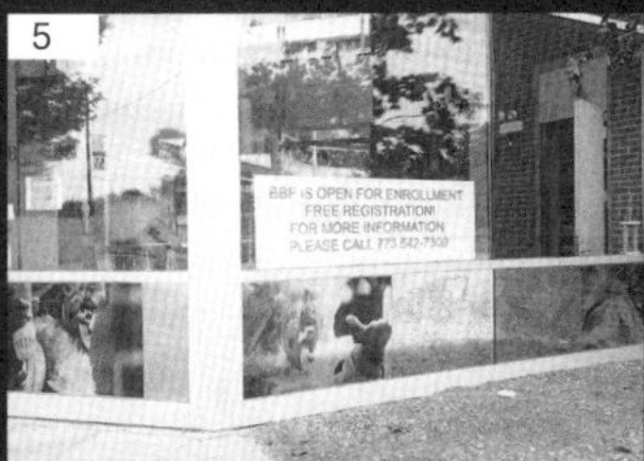

from various disciplines including astronomy, architecture, engineering, biology, chemistry, and medicine. Together, they are a celebration of Black joy and the unlimited avenues for Black achievement.

6
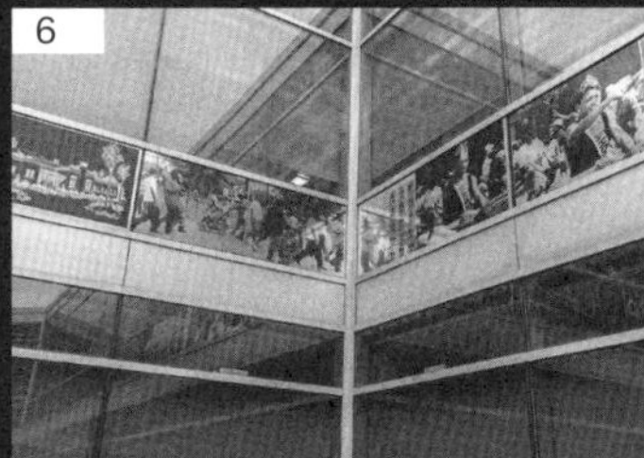

7
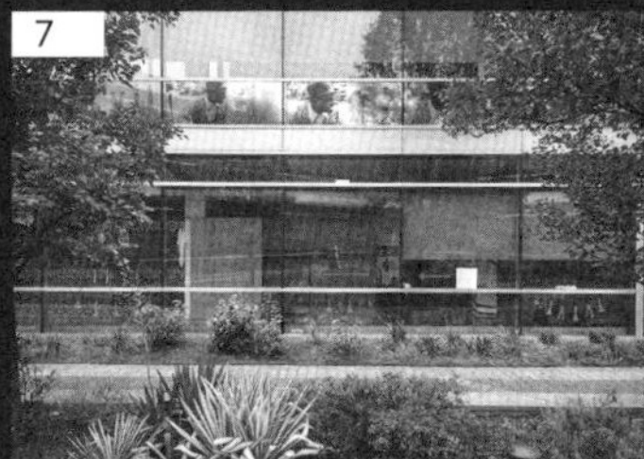

The installation exceeded Marshall's expectations. He was so pleased with it, he agreed to let it remain indefinitely in place. It is a constant backdrop to the learning and community-building that takes place on a daily basis at BBF. It is also open to the public and visible from the street. For Hedspeth,

1 Exterior of the BBF Building Brighter Futures Center for the Arts Photo: BBF

2 Kerry James Marshall's site-specific *Untitled (Circulation)* frames daily activities in the courtyard of BBF. Photo: BBF

3 Chess players in the courtyard of BBF. Photo: BBF

4–7 Installation views of *Untitled (Circulation)*. Photos: Nathan Keay

Urban Juncture Foundation
300 E. 51st St.
Chicago, IL 60615

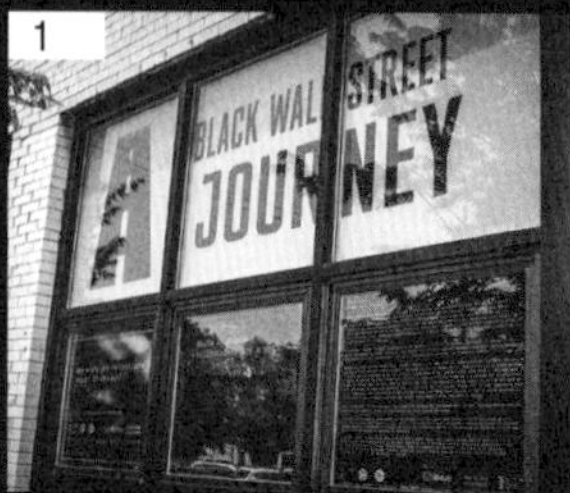

1

School of the Art Institute of Chicago
37 S. Wabash Ave.
Chicago, IL 60603

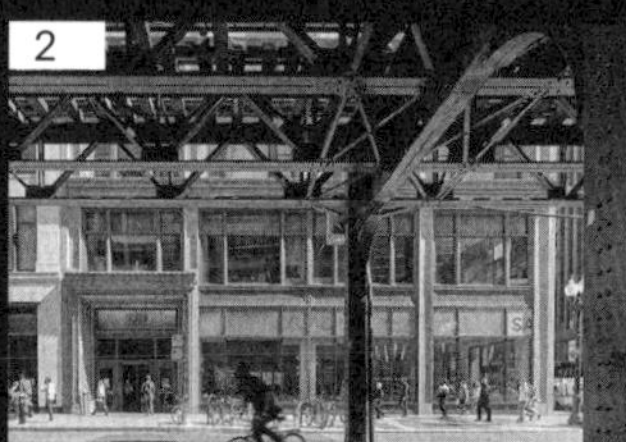
2

Black Wall Street Journey is Rick Lowe's first social sculpture in Chicago and an expansion of a project begun in Tulsa, Oklahoma. Lowe had been invited by the Tulsa Race Massacre Centennial Commission to help define an art project commemorating the centennial of the 1921 Tulsa Massacre, which destroyed the city's Greenwood neighborhood, devastating what had come to be known as Black Wall Street. Chicago, as home to the descendants of Tulsa's Black Wall Street "founder," as well as its significance as a center of African American economic and cultural life, was an ideal city within which to imagine a contemporary Black Wall Street. Lowe's goal was to challenge existing "underclass" narratives of Black communities and to instead reflect upon their resilient entrepreneurial, creative, and inventive spirit. *Black Wall Street Journey*'s mission was to highlight the innovative minds and entities that have made Chicago a hub of Black prosperity.

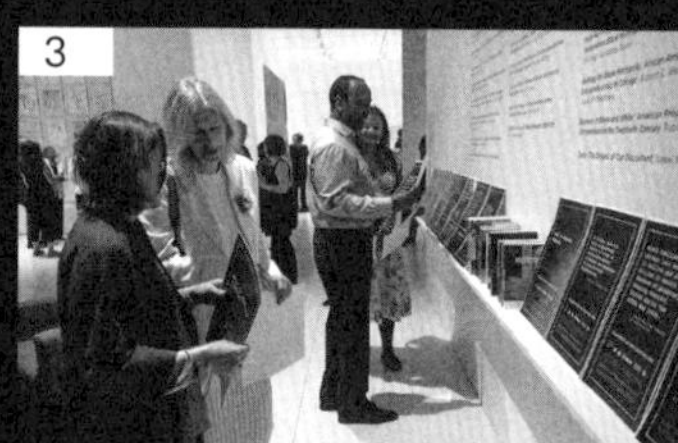
3

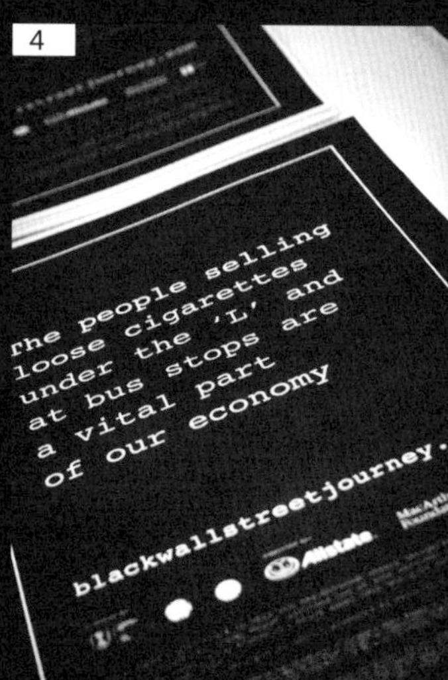

4

Through the project, Lowe developed a roadmap for assessing and enriching disenfranchised communities. *Black Wall Street Journey* launched simultaneously at the Smart Museum of Art (Scenes #22), the LeRoy Neiman Center at the School of the Art Institute, and Urban Juncture Foundation. All three installations featured Lowe's *Black Wall Street Journal*, a 24-hour Black wealth video stream. The journal was the realization of the "ticker," an iterative, ongoing digital project that celebrates the history of Greenwood, recognizes the Tulsa Massacre, and tracks the movement of people from Oklahoma to Chicago. To populate the ticker, Lowe engaged a research team of computer scientists, sociologists, data scientists, and artists to better understand the economic and social health of the African American communities in Chicago's historic Bronzeville and Washington Park neighborhoods. At the Smart, Lowe debuted the *Black Wall Street Journey* library—a collection of books focused on questions of Black economics on a local and national scale. The installation solicited feedback from visitors asking them to share what gave them hope about the future of Black communities. The space was papered with the *Black Wall Street Journey* poster project, a collaboration between artist Amanda Williams and journalist Natalie Moore.

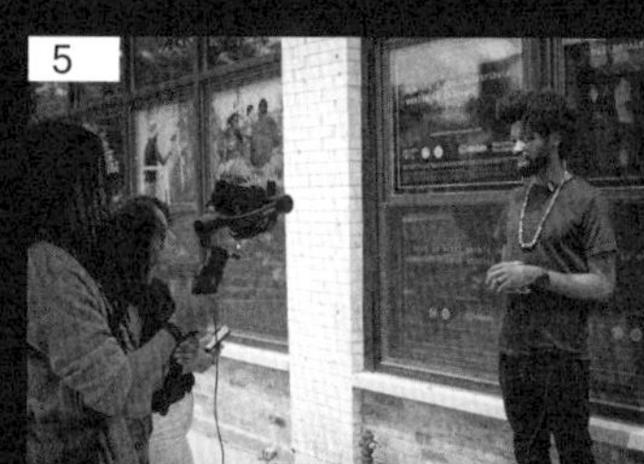
5

The symbolic connection to Wall Street and its publications was well-defined and intentional. Financial information has largely been opaque to communities of color and designed to maintain structural economic imbalances. The goal of the journal, for instance, was to invert this power dynamic by conveying different information using what has become an iconic indicator of economic inequality. In the context of *Toward Common Cause*, *Black Wall Street Journey* sought to be a source of information that contrarily constitutes value and facilitates action and decision-making, not by bankers, but by residents of low-income, historically divested communities in South Side Chicago and beyond.

6

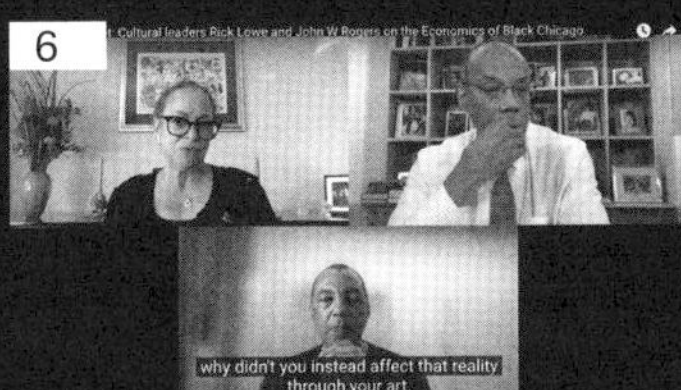

Black Wall Street Journey is an ongoing project for Lowe, who, working with collaborators, continues to seek avenues through which to share information and interrogate received notions. Might *Black Wall Street Journey* function as its own Bureau of Labor Statistics? The answer to this question involves understanding what data exists, how data is used, and how it might be leveraged differently. Can data be a source of empowerment? Can it be responsive to local concerns? What does it mean to make data "accessible"? Can an art project help reshape and reorient the narrative about the economic fortunes and misfortunes of Black communities?

1 Window display of Rick Lowe's *Black Wall Street Journey* at Urban Juncture Foundation. Photo: Nicolette Stanton

2 Installation of *Black Wall Street Journey* at the LeRoy Nieman Center, SAIC. Photo: Nathan Keay

3 Guests with *Black Wall Street Journey* flyers at the Opening Celebration of *Toward Common Cause* at the Smart Museum. Photo: Spencer Bibbs

4 Close-up of *Black Wall Street Journey* flyers. Photo: Nicolette Stanton

5 *Black Wall Street Journey* opening event. Photo: Nicolette Stanton

6 "The Economics of Black Chicago: Past, Present, and Future," with Rick Lowe and John W. Rogers Jr., and moderated by Valerie Van Meter, October 20, 2021, a provocative discussion of the topic of Black wealth-building in Chicago. Photo: Smart Museum

An artwork is seen through many lenses: the artist's intent, curatorial interpretation, critical reception, audience response, institutional needs—and these different points of view are often at odds. *Toward Common Cause* embraced this complexity by inviting artists, critics, audience, community members, funders, and institutional partners to play unorthodox roles in the selection and presentation of artworks.

The exhibition *Presenting Negro Scenes Drawn Upon My Passage Through the South and Reconfigured for the Benefit of Enlightened Audiences Wherever Such May Be Found, By Myself, Missus K.E.B. Walker, Colored* was commissioned by the curator Hamza Walker and the Renaissance Society at the University of Chicago in 1997. The now-iconic work consists of 67 cut-paper silhouettes and 21 watercolors, which were installed in the Renaissance Society's gallery on the fourth floor of Cobb Hall, a nondescript building on the west side of the university's Neo-Gothic main quadrangle. Ultimately, the work found a permanent home on Chicago's "Gold Coast" when it was acquired by the Museum of Contemporary Art Chicago.

1997 was a significant year for Walker. She became the second-youngest recipient of a MacArthur Fellowship, while a controversy focused on the content of her work brewed: some artists in the Black community thought it trafficked in negative racial stereotypes and should not be shown at all. The contention over Walker's work prefigured the kind of disputes that roiled the art world in the aftermath of George Floyd's murder.

Accompanying the exhibition in 1997, Hamza Walker wrote an essay exploring the artist's and the audience's relationship to the ghosts of the past, and addressing the complexity inherent in navigating the space between history and collective memory and the attendant feelings of propriety that give rise to feelings of discomfort. Walker's essay, prescient in anticipating the rancor of our current discourse, insists on the value of looking directly at the consequences of history by championing Kara Walker's inspiration and her decision to visualize the explicit and unspeakable truths of America's racial legacy.

Presenting Negro Scenes Drawn Upon My Passage Through the South and Reconfigured for the Benefit of Enlightened Audiences Wherever Such May Be Found, By Myself, Missus K.E.B. Walker, Colored

Hamza Walker, 1997

> *Which of us has overcome his past? And the past of a Negro is blood dripping down through the leaves, gouged out eyeballs, the sex torn from the socket and severed with a knife. But this past is not special to the Negro. The horror is also the past, and the everlasting potential, or temptation, of the human race. If we do not know this, it seems to me, we know nothing about ourselves, nothing about each other; to have accepted this is also to have found a source of strength—source of all our power. But one must first accept this paradox, with joy.*
>
> *—James Baldwin*

It was from a personal perspective that James Baldwin arrived at the question: What does it mean to be human? As a Black gay man who took pride in his skill as a polemicist, Baldwin felt obliged, if not entitled, to address the question of humanity. He immediately understood that the question was accountable to race and sexuality, making the stakes at once both personal and social. The question of humanity, however, allowed Baldwin to consider the past outside of an historical context. Not only do the words "past," "potential," and "temptation" establish a trajectory that transcends history, they also paint a dark picture of human nature by calling into question the idea of moral progress. But Baldwin's comment was far more than a condemnation of this country's inability to come to terms with its historical underbelly of racial violence.

Implicit in his suspicion of moral progress was a critique of the question. Baldwin knew that the use of the word *human* was rhetorical in that the question of humanity could never yield answers universal in scope. It is a question whose answer ultimately depends on who is doing the asking and what period is under examination. In short, Baldwin understood that the question would always falter before history, making it a paradox rather than an inquiry capable of resolution.

In light of this quote from Baldwin, one could without reservation characterize Kara Walker's imagination as joyful. That is a scary thought for an artist whose work often includes sexually explicit images which at their most harrowing have depicted acts of pedophilia and bestiality. Then again, some imaginations are more active than others. As black paper cut-outs adhered directly to the white walls of the gallery, Walker's work is put forth in no uncertain terms. Her world is quite frankly black and white. In fact, it is shameless. The work's refusal to acknowledge shame when dealing with issues of race and desire set within the context of slavery allows Walker to challenge, indeed taunt, our individual and collective historical imaginations. From Baldwin's generation to Walker's, the issue as to how to come to terms with a painful past persists. How does one write oneself into a painful history without first inquiring into the human capacity for lust, disgust, and violence? And if one is African American, as is Walker, where does one begin this task amidst the pickaninnies, sambos, mammies, mandingos, and mulatto slave mistresses depicted on sought-after flotsam and jetsam hiding in the back of antique stores, bric-a-brac that goes by the name of bygone Americana? As bizarre, beautiful, or violent as her imagery may be, Walker understands that an historical imagination is a prerequisite for genuine ownership of the past. And if the task of writing oneself into history is conducted at the level of Baldwin's paradox of what it means to be human, then this task must take into account pain, parody, pleasure, poetry, and ultimately the perverse.

Although her cutouts have been likened to the literature of Toni Morrison, Alice Walker, and Toni Cade Bambara, Kara Walker's work actually shares more in common with dimestore historical romances that use the antebellum as a backdrop. With human chattel as part of the historical mise-en-scène, it begs to be asked to what extent a romance could follow conventions of decency before the specter of perverse power relations would come into play. For Walker, this extent certainly is not great. Her vignettes are designed to upstage the entire genre. But Walker's work exceeds parody. Using her artistic hindsight, slavery could just as easily have been dubbed "the perverse institution" by Sigmund Freud as it was "the peculiar institution" by Frederick Law Olmsted. Her vision is a skewed triad of race, history, and desire, that when it avails itself to a reading, avails itself to one of such surreal and psychological dimension that perhaps it is better to call it a diagnosis.

Shame, the psychic force of prohibition, is a good place to begin. Walker's work is shameless three times over. In her choice of imagery, she has abandoned the historical shame surrounding slavery, the social shame surrounding stereotypes, and finally a bodily shame regarding sexual and excretory functions. To put it bluntly, as the legibility of her imagery warrants, Walker's installations are a freak scene *à la* de Sade. Lick, suck, devour. Prod, poke, puncture. Shit, fuck, bludgeon. They are a psychosexual mess of Looney Tunes proportion. Needless to say, it is the 200-year history of a shameful act conducted squarely within our consciousness that makes it possible for Walker to not only refuse shame but to blur the distinction between forms of shame. Even more important, Walker is aware that to speak of shame is simultaneously to speak of disgust, the overcoming of which is a prerequisite for sexual pleasure. Given the volume of shame, it is no wonder that the pleasures derived by her characters are often Sadistic in nature. Even her victims victimize, as is the case with the detail from *The End of Uncle Tom and the Grand Allegorical Tableau of Eva in Heaven*, in which an amputee stabs one child and through some perverse polymorphous gluttony is attempting to ingest another whole. The psychology behind this perpetuated cruelty recalls a scene cited by Frantz Fanon from the film *Home of the Brave* in which a Pacific War veteran turns to an African American and says, "Resign yourself to your color the way I got used to my stump; we're both victims."

Walker, however, is capable of more subtle forms of confounding, as is the case when the economy surrounding slavery is overlapped with that surrounding sex. As Walker's baby-plopping pickaninny in her 1994 installation *Gone: An Historical Romance of a Civil War as It Occurred b'tween the Dusky Thighs of One Young Negress and Her Heart* suggests, slavery was a labor force meant to reproduce itself. If sex is theoretically defined as an economy whose poles are reproduction—read work or utility—on the one hand, and pleasure—read play or surplus—on the other, then slavery would fall into the former category. The tier of breast suckling from *The End of Uncle Tom and the Grand Allegorical Tableau of Eva in Heaven* depicts the transition of sex from reproductive utilitarian ends to an erotic surplus that stands outside the ends of slavery. In short, sexual pleasure becomes the locus of an individual bodily sovereignty, pleasure as a form of power. But pleasure should not simply be equated with power. As theorist Michel Foucault would have it, this is "power that lets itself be invaded by the pleasure it is pursuing; and opposite it, power asserting itself in the pleasure of showing off, scandalizing, or resisting. Capture and seduction, confrontation and mutual reinforcement; parents and children, adults and adolescents, educators and students, doctors and patients." And for Walker, this list would include the slave mistress and her conscripted lover. Liberation is not in the form of the plantation rebellion or the runaway slave in search of the Underground Railroad. Instead, it is the naughty tongue of a slave mistress tickling the barrel of a kneeling soldier's rifle, or the chicken drumstick, willfully abandoned in favor of his tender sexual advances. Did Walker's suggested forms of bodily sovereignty exist in spite of slavery? Or were they more so the case under the confines of slavery? Although Walker seems to leave very little to the imagination, the spaces she does leave blank are reserved for questions such as these. With historical accuracy effectively suspended, her cutouts, for all their clarity, in the end become a Rorschach test whose highly subjective readings are consciously overdetermined. In avoiding Walker's conclusions, however, it begs to be asked, where does our imagination go? Does it lapse into a moralizing tone? Or does it allow for more complex human relations to emerge, relationships which for better or worse either hurt, haunt, or simply hover over us today, whether these specters be relationships between Blacks and whites or simply our relationship to the stereotypes Walker employs?

Walker does not control these specters as much as she wields them. Violently humanized through acts involving the grotesque, Walker's characters are violently racialized through her use of stereotypes. Her stereotypes, however, exceed the immediate pain associated with demeaning images of African Americans. Her images encompass the obverse, the fear that one's actions will correlate to a stereotype. Under these circumstances, the onus is to prove what one is not rather than what one is. While the stereotypes a group creates of itself fall under the category of parody, the dilemma arises when a group, because of preexisting imagery, is unable to parody itself before others. Filled with a shameless humor, the early careers of Richard Pryor, Redd Foxx, and Rudy Ray Moore, for example, involve African Americans parodying themselves to themselves through the exploitation of stereotypes. Walker likewise embraces, even exaggerates stereotypes. But Foxx, Pryor, and Moore's exploitation of stereotypes was at the service of humor, while Walker's work moves toward anger as her attempts to violently humanize stereotypes only leads to the creation of even more questionable stereotypes. Walker's recasting of stock Black antebellum characters is an exchange of one stereotype for another as the sexual sovereignty of her mammies, sambos, pickaninnies, and slave mistresses is eclipsed by the myth's surrounding Black sexuality, myths which contemporary reality has only further confounded. For proof, one need only refer to the Anita Hill/Clarence Thomas hearings, the confessionals of Magic Johnson or Wilt Chamberlin, or the psychosocial, psychosexual drama of O.J. Simpson; these examples corresponding to myths of Black hypersexuality and the evils of miscegeny. Again, the fear being that one's actions fulfill rather than negate stereotypes. The result is frustration over issues of audience and representation perhaps best expressed in the following bit of dialogue between Archibald and Village, two Black characters from Jean Genet's play *The Blacks*.

ARCHIBALD: They tell us that we're grown-up children. In that case, what's left for us? The Theater! We'll play at being reflected in it, and we'll see ourselves—big black narcissists—slowly disappearing into its waters.

VILLAGE: I don't want to disappear.

ARCHIBALD: You're no exception! Nothing will remain of you but the foam of your rage. Since they merge us with an image and drown us in it, let the image set their teeth on edge!

Walker's work is relentless. It ekes out much of its poetry through its excessiveness. Since her stereotype's quest for liberation through pleasure has been foiled by yet another layer of myths, Walker has had to proceed to taboos such as animality. This seems logical if not inevitable given the workings of her imagination. Legally classified as property and categorized as a species less than human, Blacks fell prey to a whole series of myths as to their animal nature. Work horses, raging bulls, and sexual bucks, Blacks, as the myth would have it, like animals had no choice but to obey their instincts. In the silhouette chosen for the invitation, Walker has juxtaposed animality with high culture. The dancer is oblivious to the snarling rodents which populate her dress. The maintenance of a Degas-like grace indicates that the events transpiring around her lower half are not foreign to her. Perhaps they are somehow a part of who she is, in which case these animals are meant to signify our lower selves, our animal selves, vestiges of which are to be found in our hairy parts. The raging animals on the young girl's dress can then be read as a substitute for the untamed hair between our legs as opposed to the sculpted hair on our heads. Poised between sex and civilization, between an aggressive animal act and an elegant refinement of manners, Walker's young dancer and her pet pals represent the height and depth of humanity.

Animal Nature/Human Nature, Life/Death, Pleasure/Pain. Walker, however, unlike Bruce Nauman, is concerned with the cruel aspects of human nature set within an historical context as the anachronistic character of her medium suggests. Skiagraphy, Découpure, Shadowgraphy, Papyrography, Scissorgraphy, and Black Shade, these are some of the names that black paper portraiture has had throughout its life from the mid-seventeenth century to the end of the nineteenth century. Although he did not invent black paper portraiture, the name and indeed the word *silhouette* were taken from Étienne de Silhouette (1709–1767), Louis XV's miserly minister of finance who apparently practiced the art. The word was brought to England and popularized by the most famous practitioner of cut black paper portraiture, Auguste Edouart (1789–1861). Edouart's career represents the height of the genre's popularity, which was between 1770 and 1850. Although it was destined to become a poor man's portraiture, silhouettes gained their dignity by having been used to capture the aristocracy and the haute bourgeoisie. Mechanized, however, within the first decade of the nineteenth century, silhouette portraiture lost most of its prestige shortly thereafter. Not only was photography a mere four decades away, but silhouette portraiture had been deemed a craft rather than an art form, securing for it a place at carnivals and in classrooms devoted to the training of "good ladies."

To say that Walker has exploited the irony inherent in the medium is an understatement. With respect to the dates that cut black paper portraiture was practiced, the form certainly reinforces the content. Slavery was practiced in the United States from 1619 until the end of the Civil War in 1865. Walker's genuine historical affinity, however, is with the slave narrative, an autobiographical genre unique to the slaves of North America. Although there are estimated to be only a hundred or so full-length book accounts by former slaves, according to scholar Marion Wilson Starling, all in all, some 6,000 slaves recorded their tales through interviews, essays, and books. The invitations Walker has designed for her exhibitions, including the one for this show, were done after a combination of typographical designs for posters announcing eighteenth- and nineteenth-century spectacles as well as the designs for the title pages of slave narratives. In this instance, Walker has aimed her wit directly at the audience. By extending this invitation under the assumption that you are indeed one of "our Negro Brethren," Walker, with all the playful antagonism of Fats Waller, is asking "Is you is, or is you ain't." Perhaps less subtle is the blurring of her own name with that of W. E. B. Du Bois and Madame C. J. Walker, an early entrepreneur in the Black beauty industry and inventor of the hot comb. Maybe the issue is not whether some imaginations are more active than others but what some imaginations are willing to wield and therefore yield. Needless to say, in Walker's mind, a Harlequin Romance becomes a deadly weapon. As Lou Rawls put it, "A mind is a terrible thing to waste." In Walker's case, however, he would probably have cut it short to "A mind is a terrible thing." The mind can be a terrible thing, a frightening thing, only because it is a powerful thing; a thing, as Walker proves, capable of breaking the shackles of history.

Discomfort

Early planning involved unusually candid conversations with project partners and their communities. Determined to be accountable to challenges raised in those discussions, the *Toward Common Cause* team often reckoned with discomfort, which became a necessary tool for individual and institutional transformation.

Change Is Always the Project

Jill Sterrett

Toward Common Cause happened because the John D. and Catherine T. MacArthur Foundation believed that anniversaries should do more than simply jog the memory. To mark forty years of the MacArthur Fellows Program, the foundation posed a question: How does art deal with the pressing issues of a community? Abigail Winograd shaped this question into an exhibition that put Chicago residents and their neighborhoods at its very center. I arrived at the University of Chicago's Smart Museum of Art in 2018 just in time to share the journey of turning the city into a free-of-charge gallery in nineteen venues and public spaces. After spending the bulk of my career on the West Coast short-circuiting industry norms in pursuit of better ways to serve artists and our publics, I moved to the South Side of Chicago to delve into the role of museums in contemporary society. To MacArthur's query on art's agency, I brought my own: How can museums mean more to more people?[1] *Toward Common Cause* was the exhibition I had been looking for. It was an invitation to probe both questions.

Planning for *Toward Common Cause* at the Smart launched in 2019, two years before the anticipated start of the yearlong, citywide exhibition. It began with a proposition about art's value in people's lives from a conference room in Chicago's Loop. On that day, we sat with potential partners from ten organizations across the city. The open invitation to participate was guided by a compass document: we wanted to lower the barriers of access to art; to explore the value of collaboration as a form of social and political capital; to go beyond the transactional to build true partnerships, even between organizations with different histories, purposes, sizes, and resources; to resist known outcomes, trusting that process would reveal unexpected and valuable opportunities. In short, we hoped to see new forms of individual and collective impact emerge. The endeavor had purpose, but how it would unfold was not fully understood. MacArthur and all the early organizers expected to test the ideas in the compass document and resisted seeing it simply as a rousing aspirational anthem (as might have happened typically). This allowed the making of *Toward Common Cause* to be fluid. When it opened in 2021, there were nineteen partners in total. Nine had been present at the 2019 launch meeting. In the end, the exhibition animated afterschool programs, libraries, art centers, museums, and noncommercial experimental galleries; it greeted Chicagoans at bus stops, on the facades of housing communities, and via broadcast radio. It is fair to say that it was made by artists, community members, and a host of culture workers down the street from a museum as much as it was made from within (see the inside front/back cover).

DF: We nurture skills of all kinds so kids can lead with their own voice. Having a voice is a human right. People bring knowledge, culture. We share the wish to be good citizens. We have this in an org like Centro, but we need partnerships. This is where partnership needs to work. To nurture relationships between. Invite everyone to be part of the change.

By 2020, *Toward Common Cause* had landed in the maelstrom of social, racial, economic, and biological world events where discomfort and even peril were the inescapable conditions of daily life. We made this art exhibition from the tumult within.[2] What was at first bumbling became improv and then a kind of jazz. By necessity, we shifted from something that was authored by and in the museum proper to a more cooperative, interdependent, extradisciplinary network of people and all their ways of being. Our meetings with partners—now mostly online—became more frequent, and small talk about personal and institutional wellbeing became indivisible from the work. Seemingly immutable museum standards were scrutinized. Cross-country courier travel and climate-controlled transit vehicles were, as needed, supplanted by Zoom consultations and U-Haul trucks. We had to let go of mastery and control in the processes of exhibition-making. In operating differently, we realized we were also rehearsing attitudes for a new kind of museum—attitudes where service to communities is direct, where partnerships are reciprocal, where goals are actions rather than aspirations. We marked (and interrogated) inherited systemic controls underpinning present-day norms that get in the way of these attitudes. Sharing that awareness here keeps us alert. Being alert empowers our next moves.

AB: After Carrie Mae Weems's show was installed, she asked us to take a moment to reflect on the space and to think about the history of the images surrounding us. It was powerful and meaningful. After the show closed, she sent a thank-you letter to the install team with a Black Panther Flag. Badass.

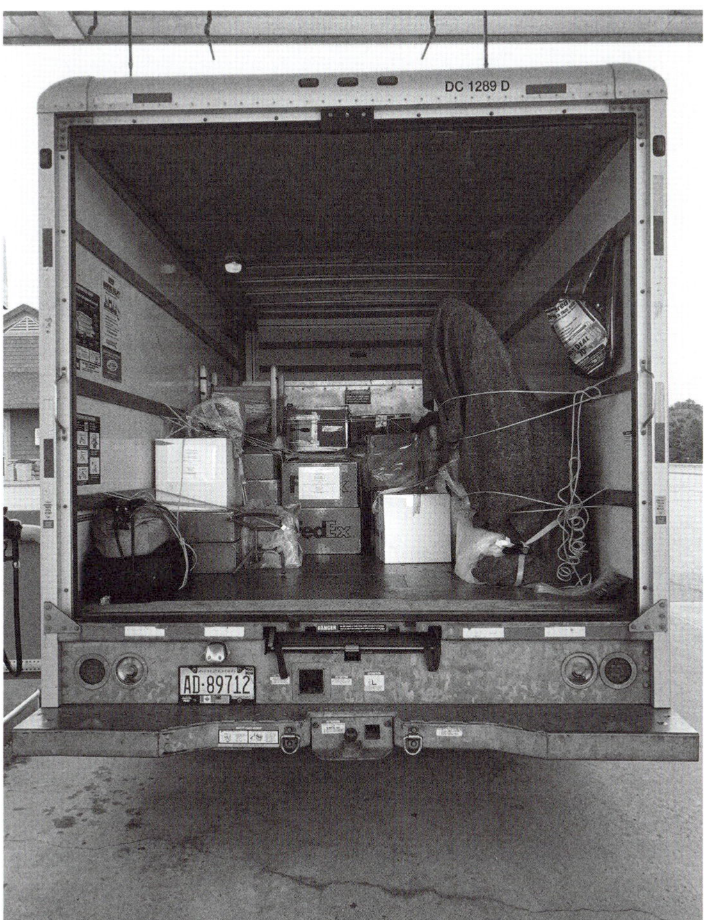

Toward Common Cause team members and studio assistants work together to transport artworks from Carrie Mae Weems's *A Land of Broken Dreams* for installation at the Reva and David Logan Center for the Arts. Photo: Jill Sterrett

Reva and David Logan Center for the Arts
The University of Chicago
915 E. 60th St.
Chicago, IL 60637

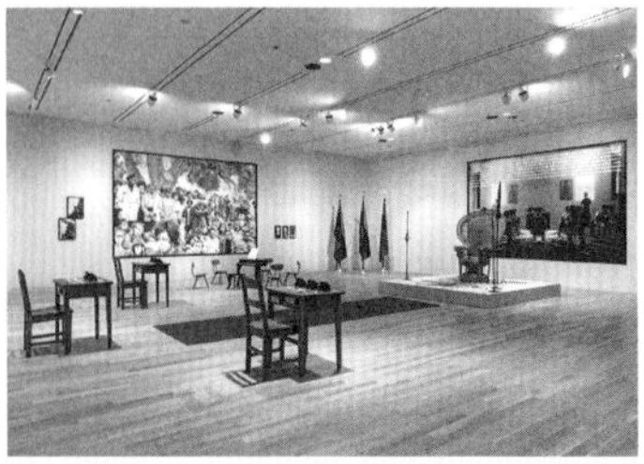

Located at the southwestern edge of the University of Chicago campus, the Reva and David Logan Center for the Arts was constructed in 2012 to serve as the dedicated space for the departments of visual arts, music, and theater. Prior to its construction, artists' studios and practice spaces were spread around the campus and often hidden away in basements of other departments. The layout of the Logan Center was designed with the hope of integrating public spaces with artistic working areas. Moreover, the center has aimed to connect the arts and humanities on campus with the neighboring off-campus communities south of the Midway.

Organized for *Toward Common Cause*, the Family Arts Crawl linked exhibitions at three participating venues—the DuSable Black History Museum, the Logan Center, and the Smart Museum—realizing those aspirations to welcome communities underserved by the cultural establishment. Held on a weekend in September, the creative trek offered family-friendly activities such as bookmaking at each of the venues in conjunction with *Toward Common Cause* exhibits, as well as indoor tours and free outdoor activities.

The Logan Center Gallery presents contemporary arts programming by both emerging and established artists. It serves as a platform for newly

(continued on opposite page)

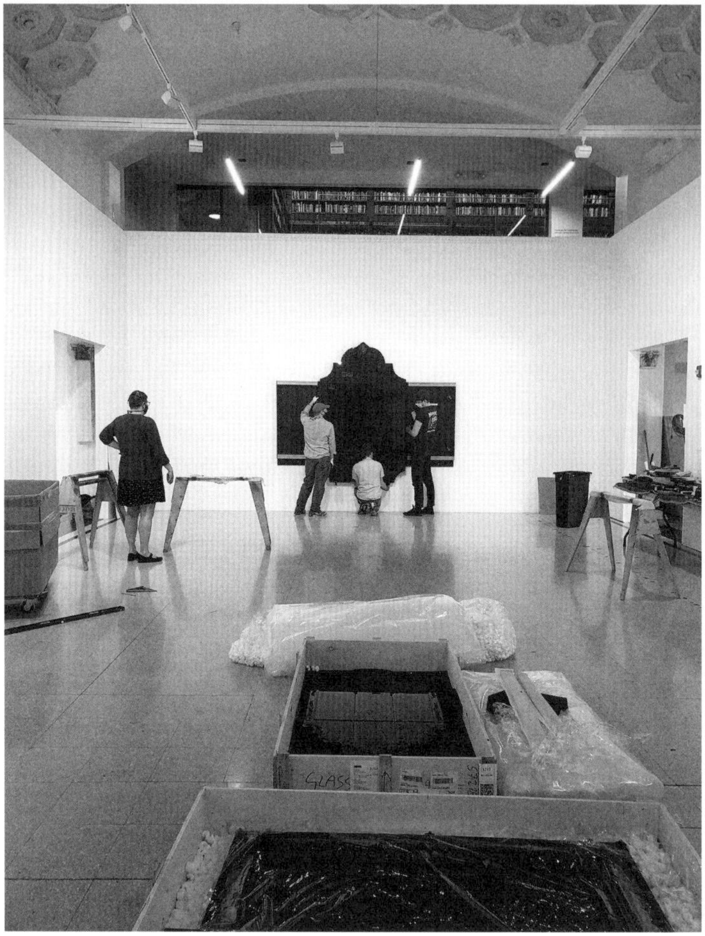

Installation team from the Smart hanging Fred Wilson's *Act V. Scene II—Exeunt Omnes* at the Stony Island Arts Bank. Photo: Jill Sterrett

On a pre-vaccine morning in the spring of 2020, I connected with Emmanuel Pratt, executive director of Sweet Water Foundation, in the Thought Barn at SWF, discussing the ways in which the pandemic was acting as a portal between one world and the next.[3] At Sweet Water, from COVID despair came renewed purpose to act. Pratt had a new outlook on growth while recording often-neglected truths to hold institutions accountable and to prevent reverting to harmful normalcies of the past. He and his team were actively creating. Sweet Water's farm became an essential business in its Englewood neighborhood. The success of its weekly outdoor market was not measured by production-per-acre but rather by how it was becoming a place to feel, touch, and eat food from the garden, and a place to go. During the pandemic, SWF instituted six-foot social distancing across its five-acre commonwealth. Today, it is a site for a mixed method of education that combines art, architecture, aquaponics, carpentry, and urban planning and a place where embracing the memory of its past is at one with constructing a present with, for, and about the people living in the neighborhood (p. 180).

Just two miles away, as interim director of the Smart Museum, I too saw the pandemic as a portal to potential. I was using the *Toward Common Cause* compass document to test new ways to make a public exhibition. The most immediate priority, though, was reshaping the work of the staff to keep everyone employed (in a moment when layoffs were rampant) while securing health benefits for our frontline colleagues who had previously been without them. Delivering on these two urgencies and making *Toward Common Cause* with unfaltering colleagues at the Smart Museum were the most consequential achievements of my tenure there.

None of this happened without discomfort. The very particular discomfort presently shaking museums and the cultural sector is an indispensable stage of industry-busting reckoning that looks variously like pain, worry, embarrassment, anxiety, or malaise. This condition sits at the very heart of the problem for this sector that purports to help people—all kinds of different people—make meaning in their lives. When UNESCO was formed in the aftermath of World War II, it sought to promote peace through international cooperation in education, arts, science, and culture. Those foundational precepts remain the bedrock of many cultural organizations today. In 1949, the twenty founding members of UNESCO implored all nations possessing art treasures to preserve them for a "universal" humankind. Today, that grand gesture sounds uncomfortably heroic and political.

Despite past pledges of global stewardship, possessing and preserving art treasures for the good of humankind has not developed into an unequivocally positive turn. The *Museums Are Not Neutral* initiative asserts more than mere skepticism about impartiality. Founded in 2017 by La Tanya S. Autry and Mike Murawski, it outs the longstanding cultural and political structures of power upon which museums operate. The web platform *Archival Decolonist [-o-]*, managed by Nathan "mudyi" Sentance, a Wiradjuri museum educator from Darkinjung Country in Australia, rebalances the biases and interpretations that come from the fact that, all too often, First Nations histories and knowledge systems have been documented through non-Indigenous peoples' interpretations and language translations without credit to the communities from which the knowledge came.[4] "It is time to stop narrating loss-less pasts from the global North" is how sociologist Fernando Domínguez Rubio put it in 2022.[5] For conservator Brian Castriota, it is about unfixing the conventions of traditional museums, "othering" historical norms precisely for the opening it creates to reckon with them and do things differently.[6]

Hull-House Visitor Response: Within the last year, Newfields, the chief art museum of Indianapolis, came under fire for an internal memo which stated a goal of the museum was to maintain a "white art audience." It doesn't get much more blunt than that. Museums, even if they are physically accessible, continue to propagate a historically white, wealthy canon of "legitimate" artwork.

Toward Common Cause happened in this microcosm of trauma, outrage, and awakening where no museum was immune to self-reflection. Across the globe, the levels of passion vented in museums through public protests, staff petitions, and union organizing were an indication of just how much people cared. What were they caring about? At the University of Chicago, students implored us—the leaders of their campus art museum—to make a gathering space for present-day critique. They demanded a larger sphere for discomfort where they could negotiate the entire spectrum of the mood. They wanted to position art in the debates of the day (and vice versa), all in pursuit of

commissioned works and research-focused projects, often involving the participation and support of visual arts faculty members. Additionally, the gallery hosts the BFA and MFA thesis exhibitions each spring. The Logan Center's commitment to exhibitions about process made it a logical space to feature the work of artist, advocate, and mentor Carrie Mae Weems in *A Land of Broken Dreams* (Scenes #27, #37).

For *Toward Common Cause*, Weems created a classroom within a classroom about the history of the Chicago chapter of the Black Panthers and its early education programs. The interactive installation was set up as a kind of study center, with View-Master stereoscopes and reading material strewn about on midcentury modern furniture; a peacock chair on a lecture platform, echoing the iconic image of Huey Newton seated on a "throne" placed among other photos and evocative objects on the walls; and photo murals featuring revolutionary leaders and landmark events in the civil rights struggles of the 1960s. Logan Center staff member Alyssa Brubaker recalled that the installation resonated deeply with the South Side Woodlawn neighborhood.

Photo: Robert Chase Heishman

a better world. Rather than accepting the museum's perceived sacred ground of neutrality, they were seeking toleration for disagreement.

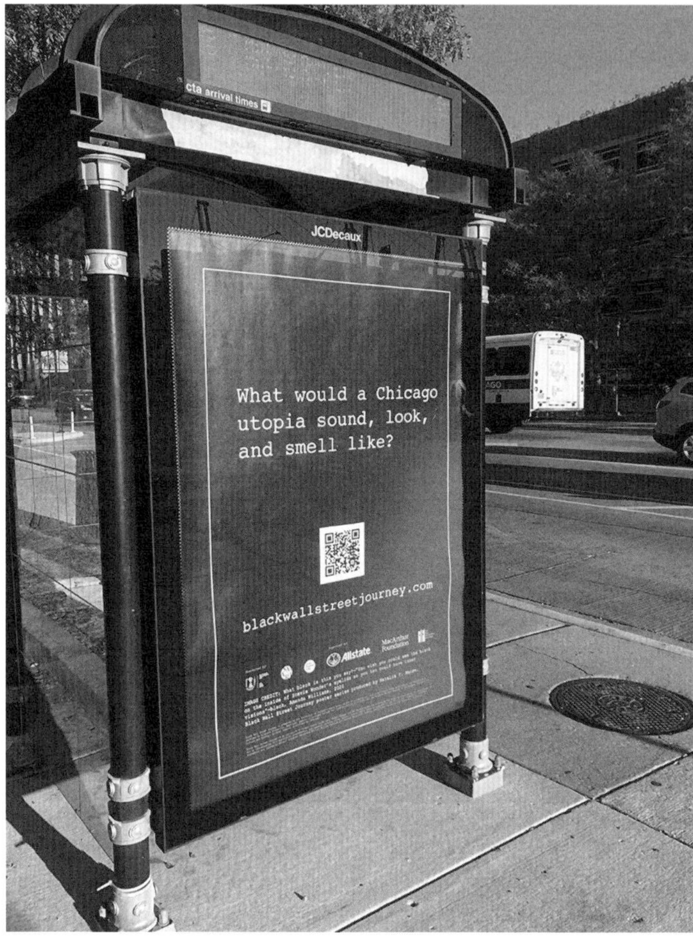

Bus-stop signage for Rick Lowe's *Black Wall Street Journey* made in collaboration with Natalie Moore and Amanda Williams. Photo: Smart Museum

Political neutrality got tricky at an institutional level in *Toward Common Cause* when Rick Lowe invited journalist Natalie Moore to produce the *Black Wall Street Journey* poster series. Working in collaboration with artist Amanda Williams, Moore sourced published information about the economic health of African American communities in Chicago for the posters that would be installed in bus shelters across the city. The advertising firm JCDecaux agreed to support the installation. When the design for twenty posters was delivered, only six were determined to be compliant with the advertising content policy of the company, which does "not allow advertising that expresses or advocates an opinion, position or viewpoint on matters of public debate about economic, political, moral, religious or social issues." Certain facts were too uncomfortable to be effective advertising. Navigating different industry norms between advertising and art, individuals could not overcome the complexity (and ultimately the paralysis) that arises when their institutions attempted to reconcile their various concerns about

Neubauer Collegium for
Culture and Society
The University of Chicago
5701 S. Woodlawn Ave.
Chicago, IL 60637

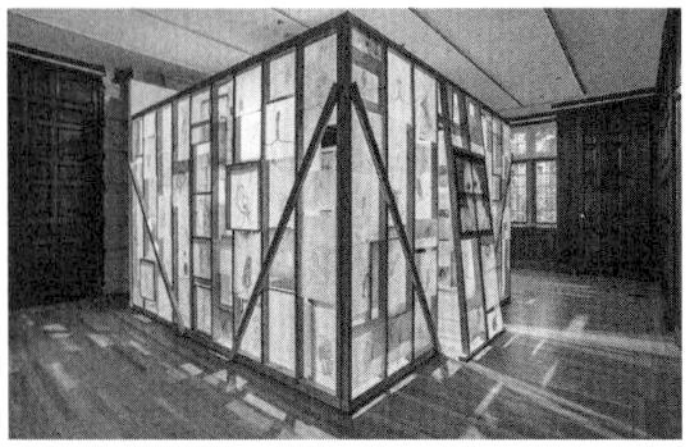

The Neubauer Collegium is committed to cooperative, cross-disciplinary inquiry and to finding new forms of thinking to address the complex challenges of our world. Located at the heart of the University of Chicago campus, in a building that was originally home to the Meadville Unitarian Seminary, the Collegium's research collaborations unfold through a visiting fellows program, art exhibitions, and public events. Statistics alone cannot sum up the Collegium's impact, but they are an indicator of its ambition and reach. Since its establishment in 2015, the Collegium has supported the work of 85 visiting fellows from 21 countries; mounted 25 exhibitions; and conducted 120 collaborative research projects. For instance, MacArthur Fellow Rick Lowe has been hosted by the Collegium since January 2019, partnering with Abigail Winograd and scholars at the university to realize *Black Wall Street Journey*.

The Collegium recognized in *Toward Common Cause* a shared ethos. They were the first partner to commit, and the only partner to articulate this spiritual synergy by inserting a preamble in the otherwise transactional terms of an exhibition partnership agreement.

The Collegium's aim to create new communities of inquiry aligns well with the Smart's mission to open

(continued on opposite page)

risk. In the end, only one poster appeared in bus shelters. All twenty were on display at the Smart (Scenes #22) along with Moore's prepared statement (p. 190).

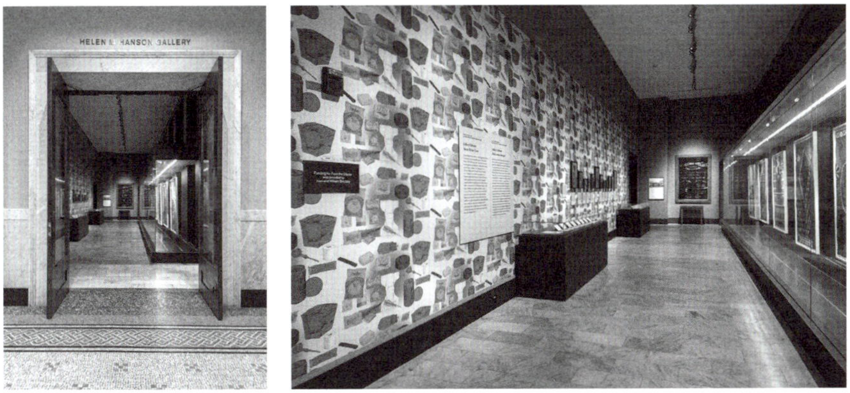

Installation view of Jeffrey Gibson's *Sweet Bitter Love* at the Newberry. Photo: Nathan Keay

PL: Shockingly palpable is the pain experienced from the legacies of these histories in the classroom, where I witness students actively grieving the absence of their countries' objects.

For several decades, museums have faced accountability to Native people on issues of possession and representation and have responded—reluctantly at first, and then with growing resolve—by repatriating works of questionable provenance, removing culturally sensitive works from view, or by rethinking interpretive wall labels and panels. Not until recently, however, has the field confronted institutional culpability for inflicted human trauma. In *Toward Common Cause*, artist Jeffrey Gibson, Tsalagihi (Cherokee) and a member of the Mississippi Band of Chahta (Choctaw), engaged with works from Chicago's Field Museum and Newberry Library. Within an intimate gallery just inside the front door of the Newberry, Gibson's *Sweet Bitter Love* laid bare some of the ways in which works by and about Native American people have customarily entered cultural collections (Scenes #34).

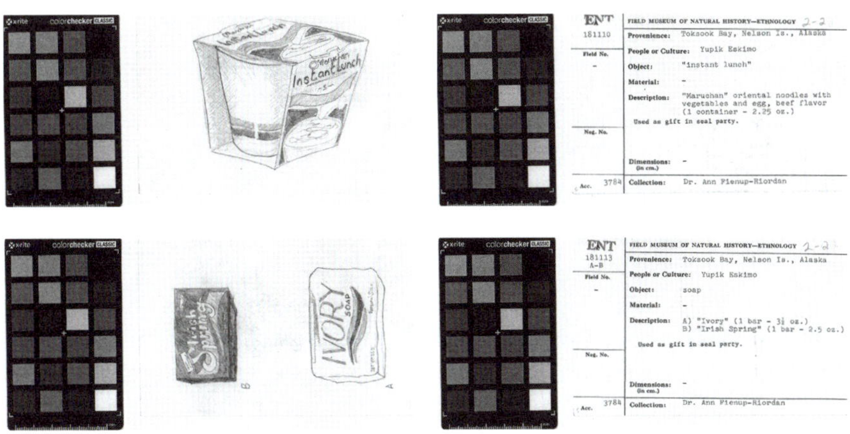

Drawings from Field Museum inventory cards: *"Maruchan" oriental noodles with vegetables and egg, beef flavor (1 container—2.25 oz.)* and *A) "Ivory" (I bar—3 1/2 oz.) B) "Irish Spring" (1 bar—2.5 oz.)*. Courtesy of Jeffrey Gibson

Gibson recalled working at the Field in the 1990s while enrolled at the School of the Art Institute. Following the passage of the 1990 Native American Graves Protection and Repa-

the world through art and ideas. Both institutions focus on the intersections of ideas and artistic practice, the Smart with its center of gravity in the visual arts, and the Collegium rooted firmly in scholarly research. The partnership between the Collegium and Smart on this specific exhibition builds on an already deep relationship between institutions. The Collegium and Smart Museum deliberately paired respective exhibitions featuring Wolf Vostell and the Fluxus Movement in 2017 ("Fantastic Architecture: Vostell, Fluxus, and the Built Environment"); the Collegium hosted artist Samson Young as visiting fellow at the Collegium as he researched the "Silver Moon or Golden Star, Which Will You Buy of Me?" exhibition for the Smart (2019). The Ida Applebroog exhibition is an opportunity to expand the relationship between institutions to include the MacArthur Foundation, sponsor of Toward Common Cause: Art, Social Change, and the MacArthur Fellows Program at 40.

Ida Applebroog's *Monalisa* opened in October 2021 in the Neubauer's art gallery (Scenes #12). It was fitting that the first project partner to commit would also stage the capstone exhibition for the yearlong *Toward Common Cause* endeavor. Constructed of 160 self-portraits of the artist's vagina, Appelbroog's series of radically feminine drawings on semi-translucent vellum formed the windows and the walls of a human-scale structure. Situated within the austere wood paneling and stone carving of the Neubauer Gallery, *Monalisa* was a gynecological retreat for philosophical introspection. The unmistakable vestiges of what had once been a men's smoking lounge in the Meadville Unitarian Seminary was a provocative backdrop for Appelbroog's work.

Photo: Robert Chase Heishman

triation Act (NAGPRA), he assisted with tribal consultations when delegations came to review their own cultural patrimony in the museum's collections. Gibson remembered a particular visit involving objects acquired from a ceremonial exchange in the Yup'ik community on Alaska's Nelson Island. To celebrate a young boy's first kill, his mother, grandmother, and sister had offered gifts. The gifts were everyday essentials—diapers, Doritos, snuff, ramen, toilet paper, and candy—items not usually thought of as collectible. Nonetheless, they were treated as acquisitions by the Field Museum. In that process, the everyday items were catalogued and bagged. No longer gifts, they became specimens seen through a Western anthropological lens. Following standard protocol, inventory cards were created for each item at the time. Hand-drawn pencil sketches completed as part of the registration process were intended as impersonal comparative reference records, more data than art. In the show, the catalogue cards were set against Gibson's wallpaper of outsized, electric-neon depictions of the gifts, the backdrop overwhelming and reanimating the institutional catalogue cards to illustrate what normalizing can do to demoralize objects through protocols of collecting and keeping.

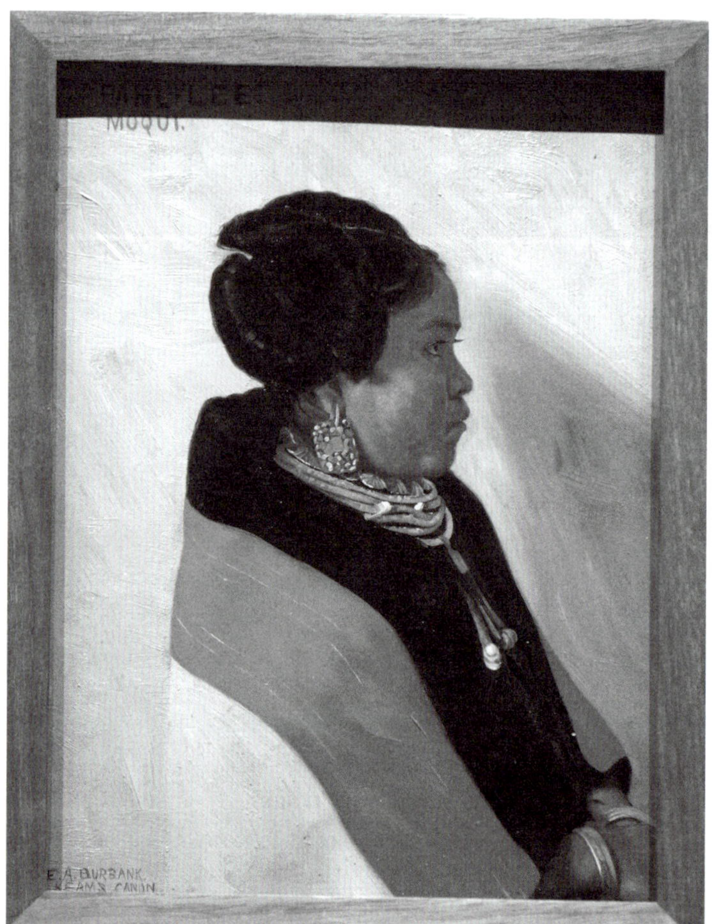

E. A. Burbank's 1898 portrait *Pahl-lee, Keams Canyon, Arizona*.
Photo: Anne Ryan

PD: Jeffrey Gibson produced a beautiful wallpaper that covered a wall from floor to ceiling. So many people ventured into the gallery, drawn by the dynamism of his work—they'd never seen the collections used in this way before or the space giving off that kind of energy.

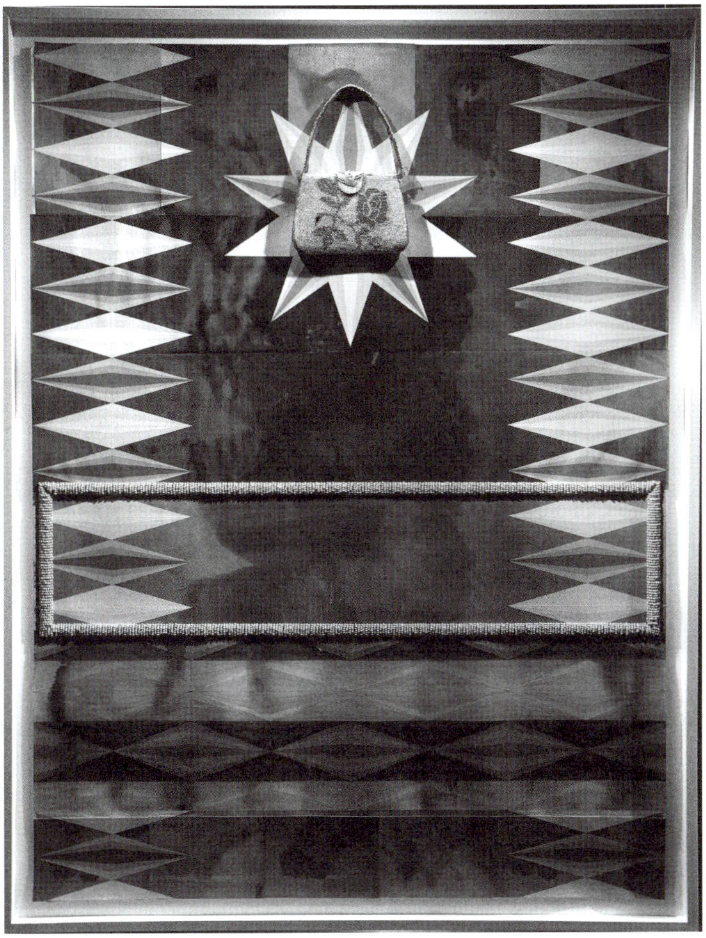

Jeffrey Gibson's *Pahl Lee*, a response to Burbank's painted portrait.
Photo: Anne Ryan

Gibson also contested the nineteenth-century portraits of Indigenous individuals painted by Elbridge Ayer (E. A.) Burbank in the Newberry's collection. Take, for example, the portrait of Pahl Lee. First, Gibson photographically enlarged Burbank's likeness of this young Hopi woman. Then he rendered Burbank's painting nearly invisible, leaving only slightly discernible vestiges through glittering layers of paint and beading. The work testifies to the endurance of Indigenous peoples and culture. More than challenging myths about their disappearance, Gibson reclaims their appearance in an act of redress.

LF: Getting *un*comfortable is not something museum leaders do well. Change is hard to navigate for those in the "in perpetuity" business. For me, it starts with personal self-reflection and new notions of accountability to the communities of which we're a part.

Every day, each of us is tasked with tuning and then retuning the ideologies, principles, and values we breathe. This is easier said than done. In moments of letting go, the process of restructuring one's mind to be in the world in a new way can feel confusing and uncomfortable because it is impossible to casually slough off inherited modes of thinking. These modes of thinking have histories, they come from somewhere.[7] They are learned from families, friends, communities, and institutions. They have emerged through trial and error. Moreover, modes of thinking derive from policies and laws that govern how we operate. In museums, these are mission and values statements and the ethical codes and bylaws of operation that regulate the work.

The Newberry
60 W. Walton St.
Chicago, IL 60610

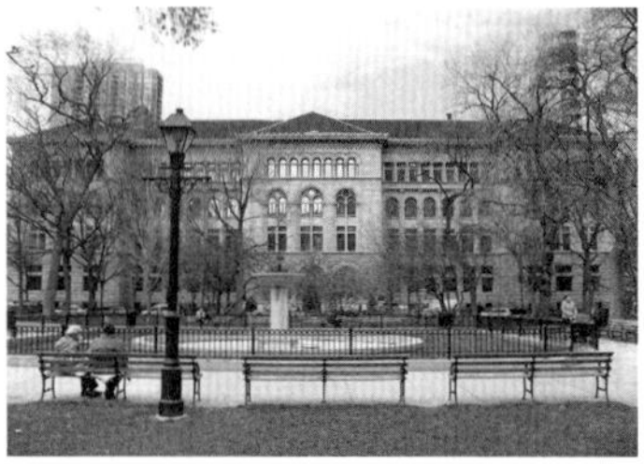

The Newberry Library was established in 1887 following a provision in the will of businessman Walter L. Newberry to support the creation of a free, public library. In 1911, the Newberry received a gift of over 17,000 items pertaining to Native American and Indigenous peoples from collector and trustee Edward E. Ayer. Several paintings from Ayer's collection, commissioned by Ayer and painted by his nephew E. A. Burbank, were the focus of Jeffrey Gibson's *Sweet Bitter Love* (Scenes #34). Gibson's exhibition reflected on how Native Americans have been brought into and represented within cultural institutions. A member of the Mississippi Band of Choctaw Indians and of Cherokee descent, Gibson responded to Burbank's nineteenth-century portraits with a set of paintings on paper presented against the backdrop of a site-specific wallpaper that incorporated drawings from a set of Field Museum catalogue cards recording a 1990 accession of gifts given during a Yup'ik ceremony. Gibson's paintings and wallpaper refuted ethnographic symbolism with shimmering layers of painted beadwork. Whereas the cards project an institutional perspective upon the gifts that they aim to document, Gibson's installation questioned our expectations about what qualifies as a cultural relic and how we collect and preserve them.

(continued on opposite page)

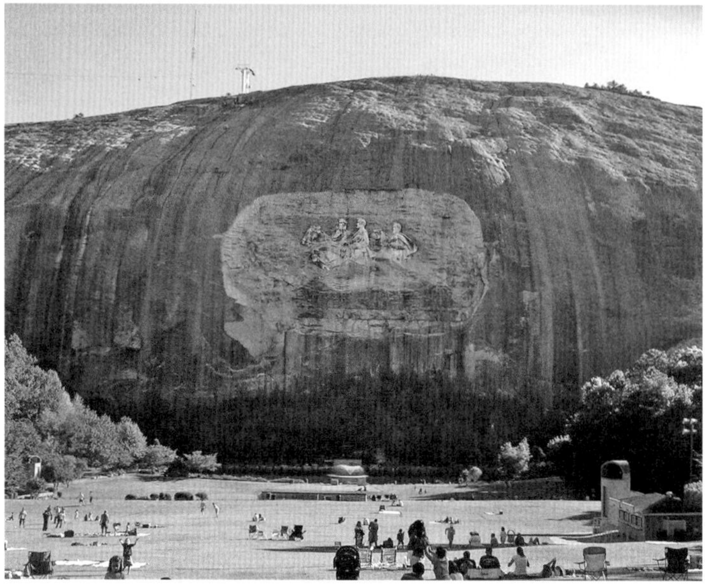

Stone Mountain Park, Georgia. Photo: Wikimedia Commons

Changing one's views is hard work. Sometimes one's perspective is jolted by seeing something for the first time that was, frankly, in plain sight all along. In her 2019 poem "Personal History," Adrienne Su remembers noticing a Confederate monument in Georgia at Stone Mountain Park that stood as backdrop through her entire childhood. Seeing it anew after the 2017 tragedy in Charlottesville, Su describes a kind of noticing that she characterized as the "shock of delayed comprehension."[8] Other times, one's viewpoint changes because the world has become truly different. 2022 was a nomadic year for me. I resided in five different cities and crisscrossed the United States twice in my car. All the while, the FM dial on the car radio was a live feed of discord on the cause and effect of environmental calamity: fires in Northern California, extreme heat in the Southwest, torrential water in the Southeast, and drought across the plains. So, when I just cannot unknow something, what will I do?

As a worker in this business of objects—in museums, libraries, and archives—I wonder how we will tend to one another and the planet with the same care we have traditionally reserved for valuable objects. As a conservator, when I see the world outside the walls of the museum burning, it leads me to double down on efforts to modulate museum climate settings—the habitually inflexible, energy-consumptive temperature and relative humidity settings that public institutions uphold for their material collections. Making this book three years after *Toward Common Cause* occurred is another example. Producing it after the fact makes it a record of impact. There's something for everyone to do from their station.

For artist Kerry James Marshall, this means continuing to make public art, something he has done for a very long time. He did more than put an artwork in a building when in 2020 he created *Untitled (Circulation)* for a West Side community center that, since 1961, has been addressing the trials of poverty by helping families support their children to become self-sustaining adults and future leaders. The organization's decision to rename itself in 2021—from Better Boys Foundation to Building Brighter Futures Center for the Arts—was inspired by Marshall's gift of *Untitled (Circulation)*. His installation drew on photographs he had taken for forty years at the Bud Billiken Parade. A South Side tradition dating back to 1929, the parade takes its name from its mascot Bud Billiken, guardian of children and a symbol of good fortune. In *Untitled (Circulation)*, Marshall's parade images are interspersed with vintage educational illustrations from disciplines such as astronomy, biology, and chemistry in a kind of film strip of human experience and learning that wraps the second-floor windows of the garden courtyard. At the opening, he said he made the work as a contemplative respite where meaning unfolds for kids over time (Scenes #9, #38; p. 140).

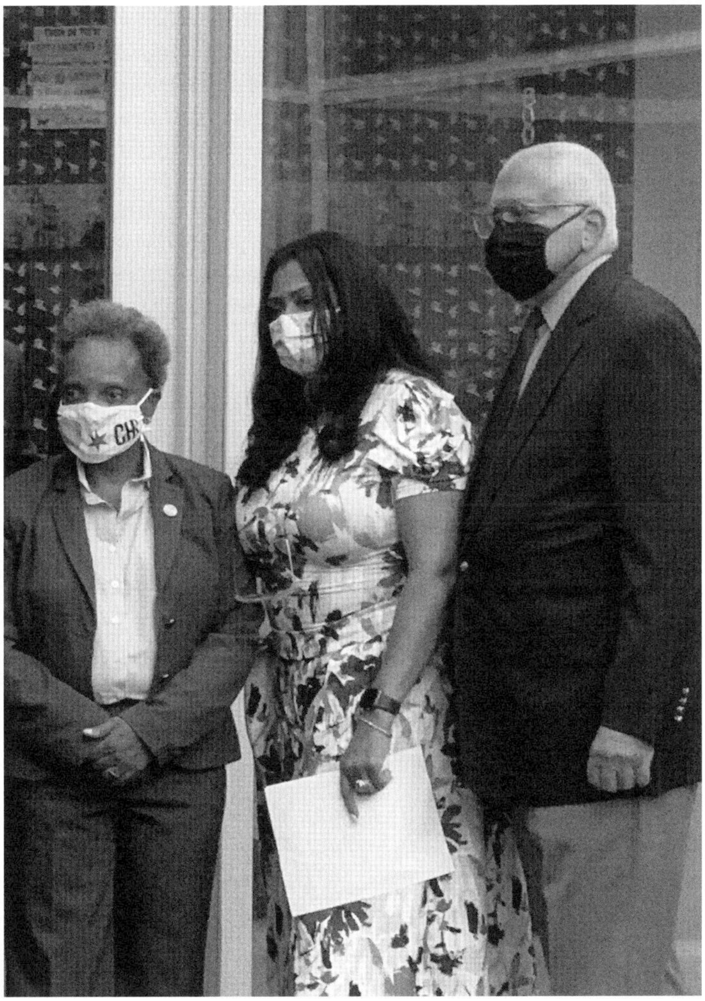

Then-mayor Lori Lightfoot, with Pamela Blackman (BBF CEO) and Troy Ratliff (BBF board member), at the opening. Photo: Jill Sterrett

When Mayor Lori Lightfoot thanked the artist that evening, she hoped aloud that Marshall's artwork would be treasured in the neighborhood. Lightfoot was talking about the kind of value that is measured over time in units of impact-per-person. I couldn't help but recall Jane Addams, social reformer and Nobel

The artist's relationship to Chicago substantially informed his project. He received his BFA from the School of the Art Institute in 1995 and worked at the Field Museum while he was a student. His job was to prepare for and assist tribal delegations coming to the Field to visit their cultural patrimony. These visits began following the passage of the Native American Graves Protection and Repatriation Act (NAGPRA) in 1990. *Sweet Bitter Love* was an opportunity for Gibson to revisit that experience, one that was painful but constitutive of his understanding of museums and their relationship to Native American culture and communities.

Photo: Wikimedia Commons

Peace Prize recipient. Just five miles from where BBF Center for the Arts stands today, Addams's Hull House social settlement opened its doors in 1889. Art was so central to life at the social settlement that a plaque in the Hull-House Museum memorializes the art gallery as the very first building constructed for the settlement (p. 96). Art's value is commonly summed by its purchase price. Its value in community might be expressed through statistics like aggregated populations served. But when the value of art is appraised by its effect on an individual being, do we know how to measure that?

Today, numbers have a special authority to resolve debates and explain how the world works. William Deringer dates the outsized influence of "facts and figures" in England to the overthrow of King James II by William of Orange in 1688.[9] Having wrested power from the monarchy, members of Parliament had to win the minds of people in public discussion. Numerical data and quantitative arguments became a sturdy platform for debate. Curiously, the methodology that numbers provided to frame one's case was more critical than the veracity of the figures. Fast forward to the present, where counting and measuring are all around us. More than a tool for debate, numbers have come to define collective and individual human welfare. Indicators underpin the gross national product, unemployment rates, and election strategies. Algorithms evaluate the success of schools, teachers, and students; they help you eat and sleep better.

Numbers also define museum achievement. Key performance indicators such as attendance, the number of objects acquired, member satisfaction, retail sales, staff diversity, and endowment growth are but a handful of metrics used to gauge success. Moreover, the museum exhibit is molded by a host of operational practicalities such as revenue sources, available square footage, access to objects, and cost of entry, all of which become stealth filters that shape a given show. Statistics track the average visitor's dwell time per artwork and how many seconds they spend reading a wall label. In the end, this package—the exhibition—can be so variously altered in planning that the process resembles the game Telephone, where a message transmogrifies as it is whispered from one person to another around a table.

Suspending some of these standard evaluation metrics to explore the attitudes outlined in the show's compass document was one of the MacArthur Foundation's gifts to *Toward Common Cause*. There was no need to count heads or collect admission, because lowering barriers of entry to art was a guiding value of the show. As my colleague Don Meyer described, *Toward Common Cause* was an experiment in philanthropy (p. 86). There was latitude for outcomes to take many different forms. Quick ROI deliverables were tabled for social and operational impacts that could unfold over time across the entire city. As I see it, the MacArthur Foundation was doing what it does: placing a bet on a challenge—in this case, a better museum—and granting us the room to pursue it creatively with our venue partners and MacArthur Fellows.

LF: How can philanthropy and museums forge a new compact based in discomfort and learning rather than growth, expansion, and measures of material success? Can we move from this moment that feels like we're *facing* the headwinds of change to recognizing that the winds of change *can be at our back and propelling us forward*?

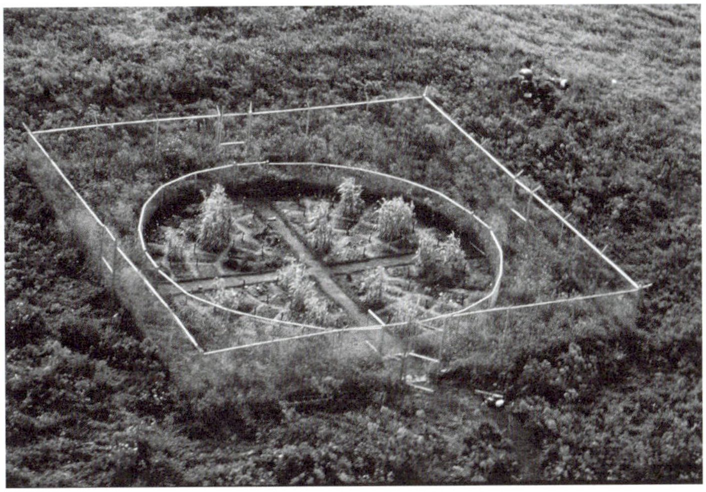

Mel Chin's *Revival Field*, an ongoing ecological project begun in 1991 in collaboration with Dr. Rufus Chaney, USDA senior research agronomist. Courtesy of the artist

JJ: As the MacArthur Fellowship is presented to those who are working creatively and pushing the boundaries of science and other disciplines, traditional metrics, such as number of publications and citations, may not be adequate measures of contribution. Novel collaborations and mentorship are examples of unmeasured contributions, and those working in cross-disciplinary ways often struggle when their field is siloed.

Artist Mel Chin taps into the special authority of the quantitative in people's lives to draw attention to qualitative experiences of living that are overlooked. His audacious, multidecade, multidisciplinary practice has placed art in improbable places, outside the confines of the museum proper, as if to remind us of its reach. Consider *Revival Field*, which began in 1991 at a Superfund site outside of St. Paul, Minnesota. The proposition: could a flowering weed that extracts heavy metals from the soil compete with other, more costly and invasive forms of remediation? Thus began Chin's three-decade collaboration with agronomist Dr. Rufus Chaney and thlaspi (commonly known as pennycress), an herb with the ability to hyperaccumulate heavy metals from the soil. More than simply testing a method for transforming a toxic landfill, Chin rethinks who is—or what constitutes—a collaborator, raising vital questions about the very nature of cooperation between all living things.

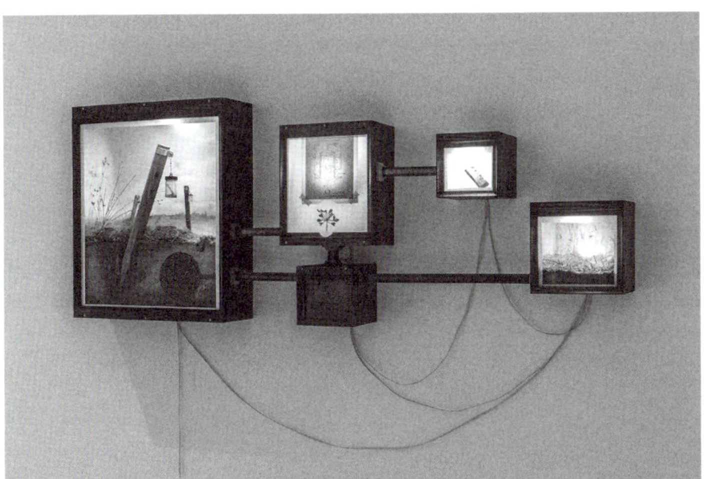

Mel Chin's *Revival Field* Diorama at the Smart Museum of Art. Photo: Nathan Keay

For *Toward Common Cause*, Chin brought his long-running *Fundred Dollar Bill Project* to Chicago. Conceived in the aftermath of Hurricane Katrina in 2005, Fundreds draws attention to the plague of lead poisoning impacting children in communities across the United States. The project symbolically monetizes the value of a child's imagination through hand-drawn works of art that take form as $100 bills. Created in towns across the country for the last seventeen years, Chin has collected Fundreds in his biodiesel armored truck and delivered the palletized loot—Fundred capital—to a reserve at the Brooklyn Museum. Occasionally, loot has been couriered to the US Capitol, where its physical presence fuels the work of community activists and members of Congress pushing legislation on lead-safe housing.

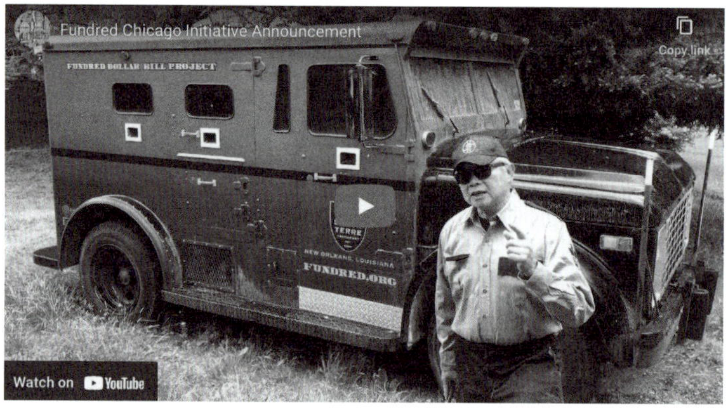

Mel Chin in front of his biodiesel truck. Screenshot from the *Chicago Fundred Initiative: A Bill for IL*, an educational video produced by the Smart. Courtesy of the Smart Museum

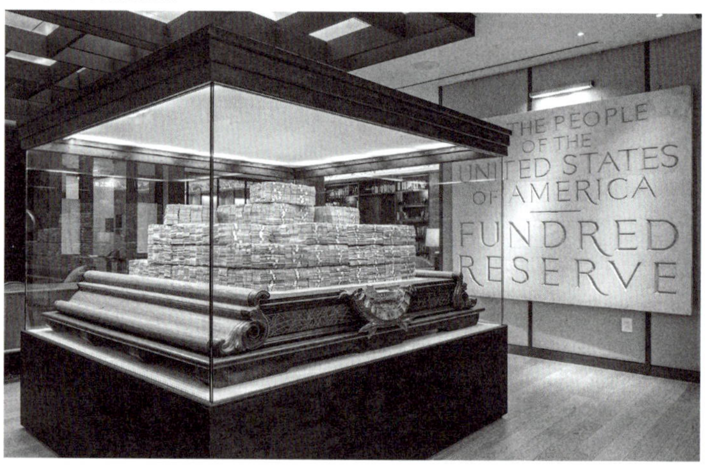

Mel Chin's *Artists of the Fundred Project* installed at the Hotel Eaton, Washington, D.C. Photo: Benjamin C. Tankersley

Chin supposes a world where hand-drawn cash—a metaphor for human imagination—represents value equal to legal tender. It is a world in which systems of human wealth include more humans, and the planet, too. Richard Powers, Pulitzer Prize–winning author of two environmental fables, *The Overstory* and *Bewilderment*, puts it this way: "the shift is about moving our conception of success from one that is dominated by numerical measures of competition to one that begins to

JW: The show seamlessly connected to our readings for the UChicago core curriculum. Mel Chin's *A Bill for IL* allowed us to exercise our newly gained theoretical knowledge after reading W.J.T. Mitchell's *Metapictures*. The curation helped the artworks resonate with both a larger Chicago audience and our specific college community.

Public Media Institute
3219 S. Morgan St.
Chicago, IL 60608

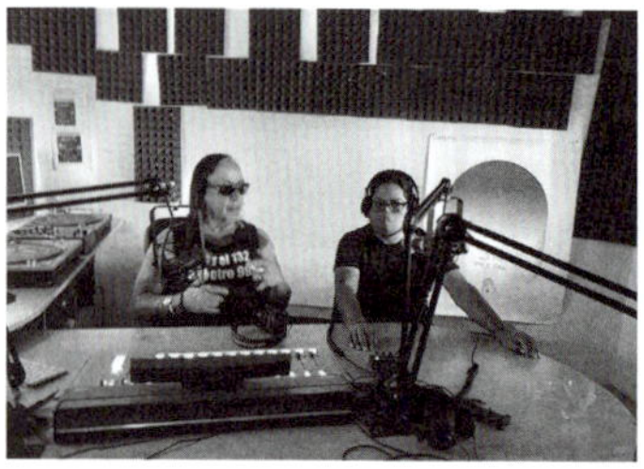

Public Media Institute is a nonprofit, community-based arts and culture organization headquartered in the neighborhood of Bridgeport. Its mission is to create, incubate, and sustain innovative cultural programming through the production of socially engaged exhibitions, media, festivals, and community spaces. Among *Toward Common Cause*'s institutional partners, PMI stands out as one of the most progressive. Rooted in the politics and culture journal *Lumpen Times*, which was cofounded in 1991 by Ed Marszewski and a large community of artists, PMI has a rich history of sponsoring projects that fall outside of conventional support structures. Its broadcasting initiatives, Lumpen Radio and Lumpen.TV, transmit free, lively, community-generated content to Chicagoland.

Determined to burst the museum and university bubble, *Toward Common Cause* in partnership with PMI extended project artwork onto the airways with the broadcast of Guillermo Gómez-Peña's *Mex Files*. Like Njideka Akunyili Crosby's murals at the Riperton Apartments, the *Mex Files* created a space for serendipitous encounters, something one might happen upon during a morning commute. PMI patiently accommodated Gómez-Peña's schedule when he had to return to Mexico City, connecting him to a local radio station there. And through its new retail concept, the Buddy store in

(continued on opposite page)

acknowledge just how important cooperation among people and the earth is."[10] In museums, we must endeavor to understand how to balance already-robust metrics for success with new kinds of qualitative measures for wellbeing to better grasp what our existing museum practices do well and where they fall short in this equilibrium with the planet, people, and their places. One of those measures will surely involve reciprocal forms of interdependence. When meaning is a thing that one does for oneself and by oneself, it can leave you feeling, in Powers's words, "a bit unsponsored and adrift beyond the accident of human experience." Art is one of the ways people are grounded in their own identity but also in the shared experiences of others.

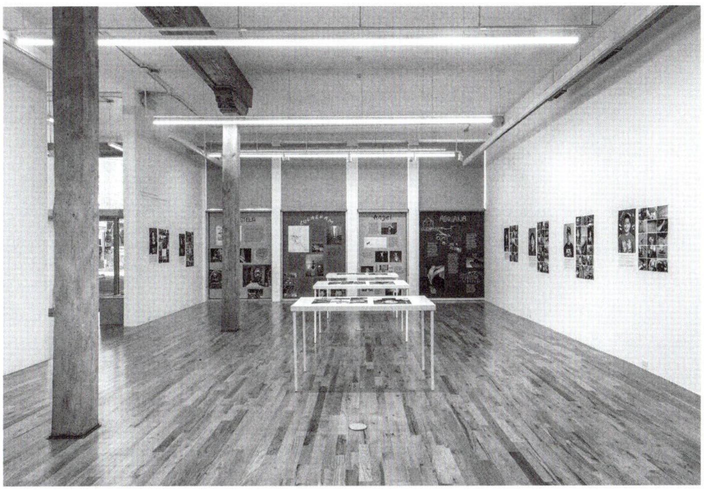

Installation view of works made by Wendy Ewald and students from Centro Romero for *Daily Life and Dreams in the Pandemic* at Weinberg/Newton Gallery. Photo: Evan Jenkins

NYT: [Students found] the common cause of the show's title in events that galvanized millions. Marestela Martinez, 13, took a picture of a mural depicting George Floyd. "I wrote that George Floyd's daughter is going to grow up and look at her father's last moments."

In the summer of 2021, you could not miss the vibrant, oversized portraits of young photographers from Centro Romero on the windows of Weinberg/Newton Gallery (Scenes #19). For nearly forty years, Centro—located on Chicago's Northwest Side—has been helping immigrant and refugee communities achieve self-reliance. For *Toward Common Cause*, artist Wendy Ewald collaborated with fifteen Centro youth for a year. With camera in hand, each student portrayed themselves through biographical stories and photographs of the world around them. Weinberg/Newton hosted their show. On a muggy summer afternoon during the installation, three gentlemen arrived to install the vinyl portraits on the exterior windows. They paused first to take in the photographic assemblies hanging in the gallery. The stories of these young people recalled their own experiences of coming to the US—experiences that, all too often, are not shared intergenerationally. When, days later, the gentlemen returned for the official opening, they came with their own children because it felt like an opportunity for conversation that is not always so easy to find.

We tend to mark and remember world-altering events at the instant when norms break—the fall of the Berlin Wall, the partition of India and Pakistan, the end of apartheid in South Africa.

the Chicago Cultural Center, which supports the work of local artists, PMI distributed Mel Chin's Fundreds.

The partnership with PMI proved crucial amid the restrictions on live events imposed by the pandemic, when providing accessibility required flexible thinking. Michael Christiano and the Public Practice team at the Smart arranged with PMI managing director Nick Wylie to live-stream various *Toward Common Cause* virtual programs and events. One of these was a panel discussion in collaboration with the US Water Alliance's *Imagine a Day Without Water*, held at the opening of *well·ness* in the Thought Barn at Sweet Water Foundation.

Operating within a truly collective institutional model, PMI makes decisions based not on money but value. Co-Prosperity Sphere, PMI's brick-and-mortar gallery space, develops its exhibition programs through group consensus, without the typical singular curatorial vision, and supported by a volunteer council of local art advisors. Almost unheard of in any organization (and certainly not in the cultural sector), all of PMI's employees are paid the same salary, no matter their position. With its ethics of democratic participation, its commitment to nurture historically marginalized communities, and its dedication to expanding access, PMI was an ideal partner in *Toward Common Cause*'s mission to break boundaries in exhibition-making.

Photo: Courtesy of Public Media Institute

This often fails to account for the long periods of incubation—the transitional push and pull of gestation—that precede these dramatic moments. In *The Quiet Before*, Gal Beckerman describes these periods of incubation as "distinct process[es] with certain conditions: a tight space, lots of heat, passionate whispering, and a degree of freedom to argue and work toward a common, focused aim."[11] Beckerman makes the case for rehearsals—for rehearsing new attitudes together and out loud. French economist Thomas Piketty tracks incontrovertible evidence from the last two centuries substantiating trends toward greater equality within most regions of the world.[12] Conceding a long road to egalitarianism still ahead, he focuses not so much on the quiet before but rather on the vital aftermath of a crisis. According to Piketty, crises are the essential spark for the processes of change in established institutions. The hard work, though, of supplanting the status quo with a workable alternative? That requires inherently contentious debate and experimentation, accepting various points of view, and compromise. Lasting and constructive social adaptation calls for multiple synchronous and interconnected frameworks of discussion and elaboration. It is here first—with individuals in tight spaces and lots of heat—that organizations reform and recast themselves.

This may be where art's superpower lies. Take, for example, Guillermo Gómez-Peña, performance artist and artistic director of La Pocha Nostra, a living, interdisciplinary, intergenerational, shape-shifting troupe for artists of various ethnic backgrounds and gender complexities. For more than twenty-five years, La Pocha has collaborated across the borders that divide people—gender, geography, ethnicity, language—in a kind of citizen diplomacy that connects them through performance. For *Toward Common Cause*, Gómez-Peña cast his gaze on the museum itself, imagining the potential of a place, borders dismantled, that could unlearn inherited practices to become open to more people. On January 27, 2021, *Toward Common Cause* was launched over the community airwaves of Lumpen Radio from Chicago's South Side neighborhood of Bridgeport with Gómez-Peña's "Open Letter to the Museums of the Future" (p. 34). From the depths of a pandemic still awaiting vaccines, Gómez-Peña did three things. He framed the stakes for the museum in this moment of crisis. He and La Pocha lit up the radio waves (breaking Lumpen Radio broadcast records), making art and cultural expression an instrument to imagine a better world. Finally, he extended an invitation to be changed and to get on with discussing, deliberating, and rehearsing new ideas and attitudes for culture work.

ET: What is the museum of the future?

FC: It's open 24 hours, to provide shelter, care, and enjoyment. There's action/inaction, but also a bit of cacophony and drama.

JG: Get a neighborhood to pool money together and purchase a home or lot and turn it into a soft museum.

SB: Also maybe one that knows when it is time to dismantle itself and cease to exist?!!

We live perpetually in some state of the quiet before a world-altering episode or its vital aftermath. Change is the condition, and it is always the project. How can museums become a force of imagination and strength for people adapting to their own rapidly changing worlds? From the experience of *Toward Common Cause* came a few suggestions. Rehearse new ideas every day. Grow toleration for disagreement. Foster coalitions where both contention and compromise are good things. Shift from competitive conceptions of success to interdependence and cooperation between people and the earth. Telling more multifaceted stories requires listening to outside communities and then looking inward to act in response. Including a fuller variety of voices, expanding the bounds of where they are heard, and confronting entrenched inequities in staffing and in collections and programs are indispensable to institutional course correction today. Walk down the street and notice how art has been dealing with pressing issues in communities all along.

This essay channels conversations with hundreds of people with whom it has been my pleasure to work. To you, a most sincere thank you. To those who will carry the torch from here, gratitude as well!

1 The question of how to make art mean more to more people guided my work at the San Francisco Museum of Modern Art from 1990 to 2018, and it continues to resonate for me years on. For me, it is a reminder that I am the accumulation of all the experiences I have had, and it's never clear when and how those influences will manifest in the present.

2 Jon Mooallem coined this phrase in a book of essays that celebrate fumbling and imperfection as life conditions. Jon Mooallem, *Serious Face: Essays* (New York: Random House, 2022).

3 Arundhati Roy, the Booker Prize–winning author, wrote an op-ed in the *Financial Times* about the opportunities pandemics have afforded humans throughout time to break with the past and imagine the world anew. Arundhati Roy, "The Pandemic Is a Portal," *Financial Times*, April 3, 2020.

4 https://www.archivaldecolonist.org.

5 Fernando Domínguez Rubio spoke at a 2022 Tate conference, Reshaping the Collectible: Learning through Change, September 14–16, 2022.

6 Brian Castriota, "Object Trouble: Constructing and Performing Artwork Identity in the Museum," *ArtMatters: International Journal for Technical Art History*, Special Edition #1 (2021): 12.

7 See Sam Wineburg, *Historical Thinking and Other Unnatural Acts: Charting the Future of Teaching the Past* (Philadelphia: Temple University Press, 2001).

8 Su used the phrase "shock of delayed comprehension" in a discussion of her poem; Elizabeth Alexander, president of the Andrew W. Mellon Foundation, borrowed Su's phrase for the title of one of her meditations on the humanity of Black American youth in *The Trayvon Generation* (New York: Grand Central Publishing, 2022), 27.

9 I heard William Deringer speak at the Neubauer Collegium for Culture and Society in 2021 where he described the special authority that numbers hold in our world. It can be directly applied in museums today. William Deringer, *Calculated Values: Finance, Politics, and the Quantitative Age* (Cambridge, Mass.: Harvard University Press, 2018).

10 Richard Powers and Ezra Klein discussed how we go about changing the way we see each other and the world; *The Ezra Klein Show*, September 28, 2021, https://www.nytimes.com/2021/09/28/podcasts/transcript-ezra-klein-interviews-richard-powers.html.

11 Gal Beckerman, *The Quiet Before: On the Unexpected Origins of Radical Ideas* (New York: Crown, 2022), 3–4.

12 Thomas Piketty, *A Brief History of Equality* (Cambridge, Mass.: Belknap Press, 2022).

Alaka Wali (AWali) in conversation with Susan Chun (SC) and Jill Sterrett (JS)

CHANGE INSIDE COMES FROM PRESSURE OUTSIDE

Dr. Alaka Wali's background in applied and urban anthropology has been the foundation of her work at Chicago's Field Museum as a curator in the Anthropology Department and founding director of the Center for Cultural Understanding and Change. A decades-long advocate for change within her home institution and for the field writ large, Wali was an important early interlocuter for *Toward Common Cause*. Though the Field Museum was not, ultimately, a project venue, Wali's practice was an important model and inspiration as the exhibition developed; in its aftermath, we were interested in continuing the conversations that had begun in 2018, when Wali was in the process of renovating and reinstalling the exhibition *Native Truths: Our Voices, Our Stories*, a project, long in the making, to reimagine and reinstall the Native North America Hall at the Field.

JS Alaka, you've worked at the Field for quite some time. Tell us what brought you there.

AWali I came to the Field Museum twenty-seven years ago with no background in museum work. This probably worked to my benefit because I was not bound by learned knowledge and preset ideas of what change would look like. In fact, I was hired because I did not have that background. This is an important part of the story.

It was the Field's centennial in 1993, and they were confronting the fact that the sheer size and scope of the collections would not amount to a case for relevance. There was an appetite for change. For example, some staff were advocating for programs in environmental conservation. It was a radical pivot from curatorial work focused on object research. I was hired in 1994 to direct this new Center for Cultural Understanding and Change because of, I believe, my background in applied anthropology and urban anthropology.

There was an appetite for navigating change but no firm idea of how to do it. I was granted the latitude to try things as long as I could raise funds to support them. Museum gallery spaces were off limits, but I could reach out to Chicago communities and build relationships with organizations outside of the Field.

JS So you were establishing the Center for Cultural Understanding and Change at the Field Museum, but it was intended to operate outside its walls?

AWali Right. There was interest in cultural diversity and how we can all live together. In fact, a phrase coined by the Field's then-president Sandy Boyd was "Living Together," which became the title of the first exhibition I curated. I'm very obliged to him. Individuals really do matter in institutions; they make a difference. If I hadn't had the background in anthropology and the desire to do work that was more engaged with communities, I don't think any of what you see now today at the Field Museum would be there.

SC When they hired you, was there already a constituency of community members or groups of advisors who were interested in the Center for Cultural Understanding?

AWali No. We created that wholesale. We had to reach out. I had a wonderful colleague, Jackie Carter Gray, who was tasked by Boyd with working on diversity. Boyd put the two of us together, and we started building these relationships with community organizations for the exhibition *Living Together: Common Concerns, Different Responses*. We intentionally built relationships with small cultural centers and museums like the American Indian Center, the Polish Museum, the Lithuanian Museum. Eventually, that outreach became the basis for the Chicago Cultural Alliance. Our intention was to work with community organizations by offering the research expertise of the museum staff as anthropologists for the cultural side.

SC What kind of reception did you get? How did people feel about the Field?

AWali I assumed reception would be hostile because the Field had not previously done a lot of outreach. But the response was quite the opposite. For the most part, cultural centers and other community organizations were glad when we reached out. They wanted the museum to acknowledge and work with them and saw the benefit of working with the Field. This has remained true up to and including our current work in the *Native Truths* exhibit. Of course, there were some people who didn't want anything to do with us, but for the most part there has been an openness and generosity.

One still has to build the trust and show commitment. In the beginning, we started by raising money that we redistributed. Some of our early partners were small centers without physical spaces. We were asking them to participate in programs, and to do so they needed resources. This can cause conflict with institutional development teams because it is difficult for them to understand or accept us raising money to give away.

SC Let's talk about co-creation. It's one thing for a big institution to bring organizations along while taking ownership of the partnership—and it's another thing entirely to make the effort to genuinely co-create, to believe that a better world is made through collaboration.

AWali I didn't learn that immediately. It took me a while to learn what collaboration means. I had done participatory action research, but building relationships, listening, and letting both parties participate is a process, and not a simple one.

JS In these early days, were there particular collaborations or moments when you thought, "Aha, maybe there's something here?"

AWali Well, external and internal partners were key to making change happen. A charismatic and visionary and dynamic woman at the Field, Debra Moskovits, was doing this work in environmental conservation. Initially, we did not interact much, we were all so busy trying to raise the necessary funds for our ad hoc centers—mine, the Center for Cultural Understanding and Change, and hers, Environment and Conservation Programs. But around the year 2000, she overheard me talking about what we call asset-based community development (a sustainable collaboration model that relies on values and builds on the strengths of collaborating organizations). It resonated with her, and we started working together in the Calumet region along the southern shore of Lake Michigan and, later, on a large successful grant for research in the Amazon.

The support of foundations cannot be overstated. Debby and I realized that our centers complemented one another. She needed and wanted social science to be part of environmental conservation work. The focus of my center began to shift toward environmental conservation through community engagement in both Chicago and the Amazon. Eventually we became one center, the Keller Science Action Center, which Debby was able to get endowed. This was a huge change for the Field.

SC And you've got "action" in the title.

AWali Yes! There was some hostility on the part of the research faculty and the administration about a center dedicated to outreach and to community work and environmental conservation.

JS You were exploring what museums can do with community groups a good twenty years ago, and the question remains as relevant today.

AWali Change *has* happened. But the work of building relationships with communities, that is an ongoing process.

SC Alaka, when was funding for the Keller Science Action Center solidified?

AWali Around 2013.

SC So more than fifteen years after you started? You were patient! Who are its constituencies? Which communities do you point to, when you describe the center's activities and its programs, its work, its research, and its practice?

AWali The center has a solid network of community groups in Chicago doing work on environmental issues, concerns around nature, access to nature. In the Amazon, we have a very strong group of collaborating nongovernmental organizations (NGOs) that have remained longtime partners of the Field Museum.

JS Do you see the Field Museum as a host for the center, or has it been integrated into the work of the museum?

AWali That is a really good question. I think once we had the endowment, it became "of the institution." The Keller Science Action Center is now integrated into the science and education division, which is where the research, collections, and educational departments are housed.

SC And at some point, you became curator of the Native North America collection?

AWali I took over curation of that collection in 2010. I offered to take on the curatorship of that collection because nobody else was going to do it. I didn't have a background in scholarship or research in Native North America, but I had certainly worked with Indigenous communities and I had worked with the American Indian Center. So I figured what the hell.

SC And you took your asset-based community development strategy and applied it within?

AWali Exactly. Up to that point, I had only minimally engaged collections. I was nominally curator of South American Ethnology at the time, but I had not built a collection. I had not contributed to the collection *per se* because I did not want to be part of a colonial project that was acquiring material culture from Indigenous communities.

At the time, I was working in the Peruvian Amazon with the Shipibo people. And another wonderful colleague—she's a volunteer—said, "Why don't we make a collection of Shipibo material culture?" And so that's how I started really thinking about what one would collect and how one would work with communities in the same engaged way that would translate into making a collection that was not based in an extractive practice.

My central questions were: What is the use of these things? What's the purpose? How can they be put to use in terms of social change? Take, for example, the Malvina Hoffman Collection, which is part of the North America collection at the Field.

It consists of a series of bronze sculptures made by Hoffman, who was a student of Rodin. Made in the 1930s for an exhibit called *The Races of Mankind*, they were deinstalled in 1968 because they were not scientifically accurate or politically correct (in the best sense of the term). And yet, they were still beautiful sculptures by a talented female artist. I asked to take care of them. But what do you do with these sculptures that are very problematic? We made an exhibition, *Looking at Ourselves: Rethinking the Sculptures of Malvina Hoffman*. We were able to use the sculptures to tell a very different story about race and racism. That process helped me think about how I could repurpose and work with problematic collections.

JS I like that problematic works were redirected toward problematic issues within the museum. Are there other examples?

AWali Yes. There was a small 500-square-foot gallery right outside the old Native North America Hall. I started to use that space to co-curate exhibitions with Native American artists, after I had co-curated an experimental exhibition with Maria Pinto, a Chicago-based artist and fashion designer.

SC So you co-curated these exhibitions and it was understood, by the museum, how you were going to go about doing that?

AWali Yes, and it was not usual.

The first exhibits I co-curated with Native American artists were with Bunky Echo-Hawk, Rhonda Holy Bear, and Chris Pappan. It shook stuff up in both the collections and exhibitions areas because Field staff were not used to working with living artists. The curators and preparators understood themselves to be working with historical objects, things that were thought of as dead.

The question was, who gets to tell the story? Typically, the curator tells the story and the artist is the guest. Living artists bringing in their own work was really a transformative moment because they wanted control of how their work—as well as the pieces that they selected from our collection—would be shown and discussed. I wanted that as well. I wanted them to juxtapose their work with pieces from the collection and tell their stories in their own voice.

SC Indeed, this is a really specific way of framing your work, "I co-curated these shows with the artists." It's more typical to say "work with artists" or to invite artists to select works from the collection. You're describing a different kind of partnership. Were these difficult discussions internally?

AWali Yeah, that's a good question. To some degree, I had earned agency to work that way. Debby and I were raising money, we were getting results, and I was not asking for a lot of space. There was resistance, but it was hard for the institution to say, "Don't do this."

Coming back to the earlier question, we were actually able to change a lot, and eventually colleagues moved into positions that allowed them to build staff and embed this kind of work. Now there are cultural anthropologists in the Action Center, and change has happened at the Field Museum. You can see it in the Native North America Hall.

You cannot ignore material resources. I had raised grants from the Ford Foundation, the Rockefeller Foundation, the MacArthur Foundation. Our work was being validated by external sources. It was also fostered by Native American people like the artist Jeffrey Gibson, who worked at the Field Museum in the 1990s. Indigenous people worked as interns or on staff. They were looking at these collections, advocating for change and increased access. They had an impact on the collection staff, who realized, "We can't keep doing things as we have done."

SC Thank you for sharing that. You provide a rationale for offering agency to makers that we sometimes lack when we think about doing this kind of co-creation work.

JS Your points are a timely reminder that transformation hinges on these issues of control. How did working with artists bring something new to the Field Museum? What was it that they could position in a different way?

AWali It's just learning to work in a very different way, navigating that, and coming to terms with it. That this is not going to follow the same old processes in which curators and exhibition developers write all the labels.

Works are still collected by curators, and then they develop the story. Putting another person into the process changes the dynamic. Time becomes a significant issue. Everything is governed by the exhibition date and working backwards from it. Traditional timelines include object selection, conservation, mounting, etcetera. It is impossible to expect people to respect or hold to those timelines.

SC Involving a maker, a creator, in the telling of the story of a work is good. Let's talk about the complicated territory of cultural context as it is offered up in galleries—the way that one person, one maker, one artist sees the story can be very different from the way the next one does. So how do you navigate those shoals? What kind of insight do you have as an anthropologist to help us to understand what an institution can bring to help the audience?

AWali Well, the way we approached it was not, "Okay, artists, you do whatever you want." We still have to pay attention to context. You have to think about the context of the museum itself. In this case, as a museum of so-called natural history or anthropology, we're not aiming to showcase art in the way that an art museum does.

SC You bring expertise in your community of visitors and need to consider what they need as well.

AWali Right. There needs to be a foundation of trust that allows for open dialogue back and forth with the maker, with the creator, with the storyteller. We had to establish that trust with our storytellers. It was easier when there was only one artist. We had a lot of trust. But when we began dealing with whole galleries where 150 people were involved, it took much more time.

There's one display in *Native Truths* of a headdress from the Blackfoot women's Stand-Up Headdress Society. It took two years of dialogue to create that display. It was definitely worth spending time with six women who were our storytellers for it. But it took more than simply asking, what do you want to say? It was about how do we work with you? How can we, together, craft this story that you want to tell?

SC Will you tell the stand-up headdress story?

AWali My colleague Dr. Eli Suzukovich (Little Shell Tribe of Chippewa Cree) worked with members of the Blackfoot community, going through the Field collections to identify an object for the display. He saw the headdress in the collection and immediately recognized that it was special. He knew some of the women in the Stand-Up Headdress Society, one of whom was Rosalyn LaPier, who is herself an anthropologist and professor. He started building a relationship with members of this Stand-Up Headdress Society. When we first started talking with them, they were very skeptical about showing it because we did not know if it was a ceremonial object, who had owned it, or how it got to the museum. These questions had to be investigated and answered. Members of the society were wary of us. They asked, why should they help us? They wanted to know how we were going to reciprocate. We said, what do you want? They wanted to be able to tell the story of their society and their own people. We agreed to help them publish a book about the Stand-Up Headdress Society.

After lots of discussion, questions remained about whether to display the headdress or not. There were doubts. Eli went to Montana to attend ceremonies and powwows to get to know the women better. Time was running short, and the headdress needed conservation. She was fragile, the headdress.

This gets back to that question of trust. Why should they trust us? We had formed a Native Advisory Board, and it made a big difference but, still, dealing with us has its risks.

When the decision was made, another member of the society, who is an expert and makes these headdresses, came to the museum with her husband and her apprentice and her apprentice's husband. The four of them spent a week with our conservator and our team. They took the headdress apart. That was when I knew transformation had happened in the ranks of collections care and management. That was the sign that there was no going back to some old way of doing things. *That* was collaboration. Trusting the expert and allowing her to take every feather off the headdress. She made a new band. We had so much fun and it is so beautiful.

JS — What a tribute to the journey of this work, Alaka. Reflect, if you will, on influencing an institution.

AWali — I like to think that I helped to create a space that allowed others to do this work and feel good about doing it. There are enough of us now to transform from within.

SC — Alaka, your practice of inclusion must inevitably also include hearing from people who feel left out.

AWali — There's some of that.

SC — Where does it tend to come from? Is there any way of characterizing it? The Field has such a broad remit, and everybody thinks it's theirs. Everybody thinks the Field should be for them.

AWali — It should be.

SC — It should be, but it means that everybody should be knocking at your door, too.

AWali — They should. Not at my door anymore, but at the door of the Field Museum. I really think if communities don't knock, nothing's going to change. There has to be that outside pressure on museums or institutions. Think about the case of the Mimbres pottery at the Art Institute. That exhibit was all set to open, and the community knocked and said, "No way are you going to do this, this is outrageous." The exhibit was canceled. If that hadn't happened, it would have been a tragedy. We have to be cognizant and recognize that change inside comes when there's pressure from outside. I was able to bring that pressure—

to leverage the community voice to make change happen. Take, for example, the Native North America Hall. If there hadn't been Native North America voices saying, "Field Museum, this hall that's been unchanged for fifty years is outrageous," change on the inside wouldn't have happened.

SC It's a delicate balance between an administration that's just reacting and one that says, well, okay, let's fix things.

AWali More and more institutions are seeing the handwriting on the wall. Especially after the summer of 2020 and the murder of George Floyd. Institutions, museums, and universities have to take inclusion seriously. They are vulnerable. Foundation funding has changed: it's hard to get a grant if you don't show that you have some skin in the game with your community. That's good, and it's still going to take time.

JS So tell us about your center today. It has grown into something. How is it viewed today by your colleagues and the leadership of the Field Museum?

AWali I think it's been accepted and is now understood as a positive force of action for the Field Museum. The fact that it's endowed gives it independence. Even though it's integrated into the institution, it's the one center in the science and education division that has its own endowment, which gives us cachet. There's no other museum of natural history or anthropology that's working in urban settings like we are at the Field Museum. Many other museums have started this collaborative work around Native American holdings, but I think at the scale that we've done it, the commitment we've made to communities, we are at the forefront.

SC and JS Congratulations, and thank you, Alaka.

Sweet Water Foundation
5749 S. Perry Ave.
Chicago, IL 60621

1

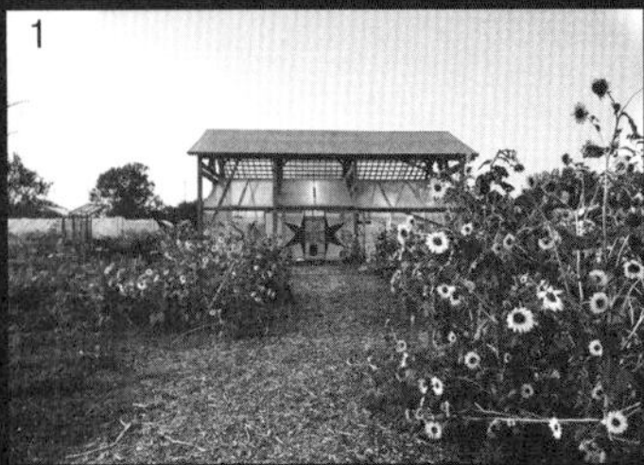

Where South Perry Avenue meets West 57th Street on Chicago's South Side there is a farm and a garden, a Think-Do House, a [Re]Construction House, and a Civic Arts Church. This is Sweet Water Foundation (SWF). Here, children and their families, volunteers, Urban Ecology Apprentices and Fellows, and Humans-in-Residence meet to learn, to work together, to be with one another.

Sweet Water's circadian cycle begins each morning at 9am sharp. Don't be late. In the spring, there are seedlings to plant. In the summer, there are crops to water, weed, and harvest. There is always furniture to build, food to prepare, compost to turn, a market to tend, and a building to reconstruct. Speak up, ask questions, engage. Learn the how and why of your work, and bend your methods toward sustainability and justice. Artist, architect, urban designer, urban farmer, and advocate of aquaponics Emmanuel Pratt is Sweet Water's inspirational wellspring, and he refers to this model of neighborhood regeneration as urban acupuncture—a natural process of healing that roots in local potential, the perpetual process of becoming, looking back to look forward, and care for generations to come. I was one of a cohort of Smart Museum staffers who went weekly to put my hands in the dirt, paint a hallway, or set the table for a meal.

It was curator of public practice Michael Christiano who forged the Smart Museum's partnership with Pratt, setting the stage for Sweet Water's participation in *Toward Common Cause*. And it was the shared interests, concerns, and convictions of Pratt, Mel Chin, and Iñigo Manglano-Ovalle that made the match between them natural. The two objects that were created with and for Sweet Water—Manglano-Ovalle's *Hydrant, 41°47′ 22.662″ N–87°37′38.364″ W* (2021) and Chin's *Safehouse Temple Door* (2021)—are not so much "on view" as they are activated by what Sweet Water Foundation does.

2

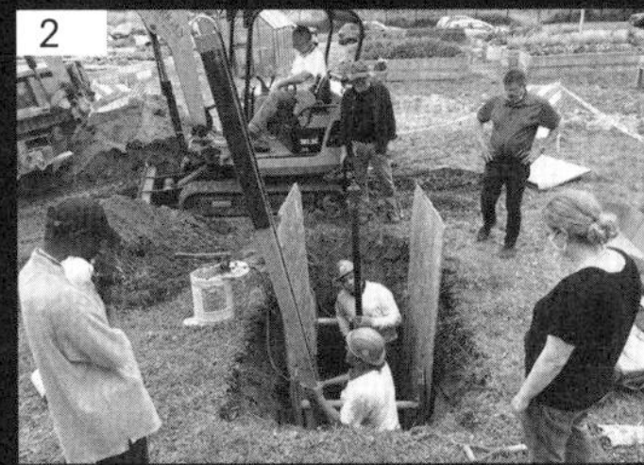

3

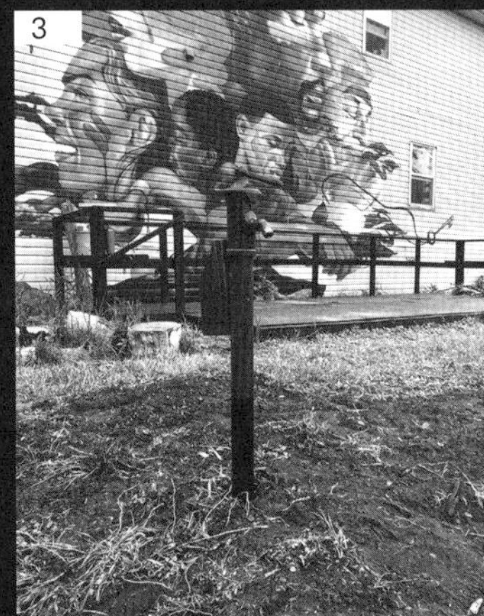

Based in Evanston, Illinois, Manglano-Ovalle started working at Sweet Water in 2020 while helping to winterize the Thought Barn. Throughout his career, his wide-ranging artistic practice has delved into the human-made consequences of the modern world. He is very good at expressing complex things simply, opting to make art that, in his own words, speaks instead of tells. *Hydrant*, part of Manglano-Ovalle's *Well* series, is a functional sculpture that delivers water to its surrounding garden beds at SWF, and growing vegetables and fruit is one way people complete the work. It is a manual pump installed by the artists at Kerrigan Brothers Plumbing and painted in Pan-African colors by the Core SWF team (Scenes #32). *Hydrant* qualifies as art because the water, manually drawn from the ground, remains perpetually free as a gift. In a neighborhood where access to clean water has not been a reliable asset, Manglano-Ovalle's move provokes questions about value and how and where it is assigned.

4

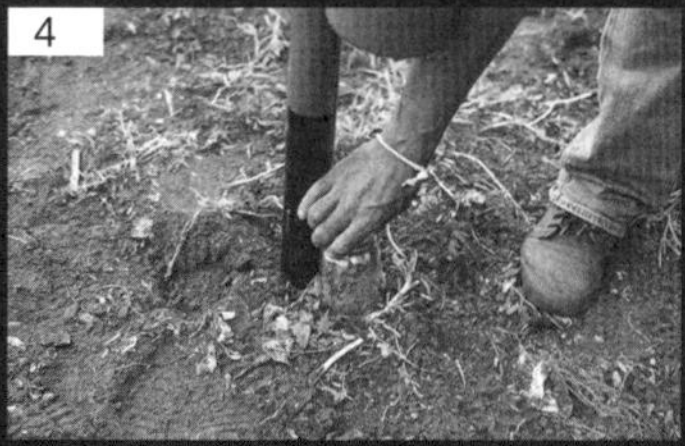

During the 2021 run of *Toward Common Cause*, *Hydrant* was also manifest on the other side of Washington Park, in a companion stainless-steel reservoir and pump that supplied SWF H_2O at a water table in the lobby of the Smart Museum of Art on the campus of the University of Chicago (Scenes #26). Operating this sleek pump manually allowed visitors to pause and to wonder why it was there, then to connect, in their minds, the water to its source in Englewood and consider the history of the university and its relationship to that place. For Manglano-Ovalle, this is another way visitors complete the work.

Mel Chin's collaboration/journey with Sweet Water began in the Thought Barn on a wintry afternoon in February 2020. Chin had traveled from his studio in North Carolina to bring Fundreds to Chicago as part of *Toward Common Cause*. Conceived in the aftermath of Hurricane Katrina, the Fundreds project injects the might of imagination into actions designed to eradicate lead in water across the nation. Since 2008, nearly 500,000 hand-drawn $100 bills have been created in schools and community organizations to express how much we value the futures of young people. Fundred dollar bills are deposited in the growing Fundred Reserve at the Brooklyn Museum in service of federal legislation for clean water and social change (p. 168). That February afternoon, Chin and Pratt talked about the abandoned church located just a block from where they sat. The church was abandoned after people were forced out by redlining and prejudice, job loss and hunger. Mike Reynolds, Sweet Water's master builder and resident wise man, put it this way: "Now we're gonna give this building a new life. It won't be traditional religion that will be brought back, but a message of hope ... of something new arising." Today the Civic Arts Church is a place to share food, to gather, make art, sing, perform, and dance. That wintry afternoon, Chin and Pratt imagined a safehouse door symbolizing the value within. Today, Chin's *Safehouse Temple Door* is a vault door at the entrance to the Civic Arts Church, a door that the community chooses to keep open always (Scenes #39).

5

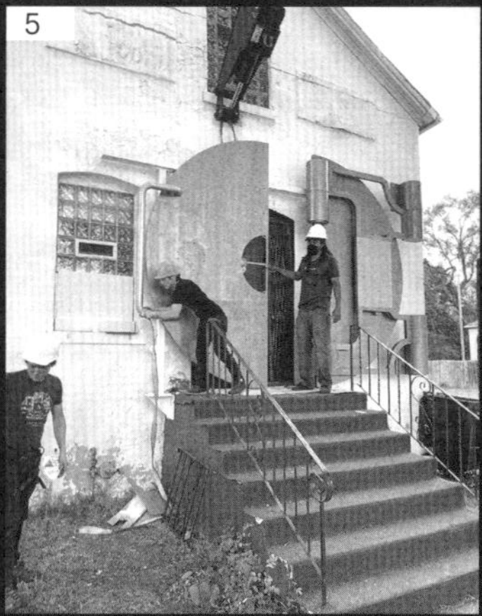

The works of Chin and Manglano-Ovalle at Sweet Water Foundation are lasting legacies of *Toward Common Cause*. The Sweet Water community is the owner and steward in the very same way it cares for the land, the food, and the wellbeing of people in the neighborhood. They are all sustainable community assets.

Sweet Water Foundation is a place where things get done. There is purpose without compromise. Impatience without apology. Rigor without pause. Join in or get out of the way.

— Jill Sterrett

1 The Thought Barn and Community Farm at Sweet Water Foundation. Photo: Abigail Winograd

2 Digging Iñigo Manglano-Ovalle's *Hydrant, 41°47'22.662" N—87°37'38.364" W*. Photo: Michael Christiano

3 The finished well installed at SWF. Photo: Michael Christiano

4 Jarred earth from the digging of *Hydrant, 41°47'22.662" N—87°37'38.364" W*. Photo: Iñigo Manglano-Ovalle

5 Installing Mel Chin's *Safehouse Temple Door*. Photo: Michael Christiano

Toward Common Cause opened a conversation about rethinking art's value beyond market determinations, attendance, and traditional critical reception, and focused instead on the less tangible: serendipitous encounters, personal interactions, the sense of agency prompted by recognition of one's community on the walls of a museum.

The following is a collection of press reviews, interviews, and excerpts from exhibition programming.

Although press coverage was wide and largely positive, it was constrained by pandemic-related travel restrictions. Not all venues simultaneously hosted the associated exhibitions, which further hindered out-of-town visitors. Notably, and despite the warm national coverage, the real homerun for *Toward Common Cause* was through local press coverage and regular weekly rundown updates from publications such as *Newcity Art*, the *Chicago Tribune*, the *Chicago Sun*, *Chicago Magazine*, and various University of Chicago campus outlets.

Reviewers were not the only outsider voices commenting on the exhibition. This section concludes with excerpts from exhibition materials produced by the *Black Wall Street Journey* team.

HOW ESSENTIAL IS ART? 29 MACARTHUR "GENIUSES" ANSWER THAT QUESTION IN *TOWARD COMMON CAUSE*

Lori Waxman
Chicago Tribune, September 27, 2021

"Why are artists and performers not considered essential workers?"

The powerhouse performance artist Guillermo Gómez-Peña posed this question during one of his pandemic radio broadcasts, and it begets more. What is truly essential? Clean air to breathe, land on which to live and move and find food, water for the hydration of all living things—this we know, even if our laws and actions have not often enough made good on their provision. But what about culture? Do we believe culture to be something so necessary a resource that it deserves universal protection and promotion?

The philanthropic foundations that give away millions of dollars per year to art institutions large and small, to scholars in the field, and to individual artists certainly believe so. None perhaps quite so boldly as the Chicago-based John D. and Catherine T. MacArthur Foundation, which since 1981 has been endowing its fellows with enormous no-strings-attached cash awards. Current "genius grant" recipients, as they're colloquially known, receive $625,000 [now $800,000] over the course of five years, and they've included some of the most consequential artists of recent times, including Gómez-Peña, Mark Bradford, An-My Lê, Julie Mehretu, Alfredo Jaar, Wendy Ewald and Rick Lowe.

Forty years seems long enough to warrant a celebration and a taking stock, and the MacArthur is doing just that. *Toward Common Cause: Art, Social Change and the MacArthur Fellows Program at 40*, which began last spring and will continue into the new year, is a citywide mega-show that offers an invigorating overview of old and new work by 29 grantees in a range of locations and formats whose diversity befits the artists' individual contributions to the initiative's central inquiry: What is universally important enough to hold in common—and what's art got to do with it?

Art's got everything to do with it, or at least something to say about it. Depending where in Chicago you live and where you visit, you'll encounter a different set of answers, or more likely questions. The greatest array can be found on the South Side, which makes practical sense—the Smart Museum of Art in Hyde Park is the organizing institution and the hub from which curator Abigail Winograd has been working on the project for nearly four years.

But it also makes meaningful sense,

because the South Side is the part of Chicago most affected by a dearth of essential resources, by private and public disinvestment, redlining and environmental pollution, all of it grounded in systemic racism. Hence the handful of new permanent or long-term installations sited in this part of town: on the facade of the Minnie Riperton Apartments, a public housing complex in Fuller Park, will soon hang gorgeous banners by Njideka Akunyili Crosby, blown-up versions of her ornately collaged canvases depicting Nigerian-American home interiors. At the Sweet Water Foundation in Washington Park-Englewood, Iñigo Manglano-Ovalle has built a highly functional take on minimalist sculpture: an elegant hydrant to deliver free and potable water for the organization's farm plots. And at BBF Family Services in Lawndale, a radiant courtyard frieze by Kerry James Marshall, interspersing his own photographs of the annual Bud Billiken Day Parade, an epic Black pride event ongoing since 1929 on the South Side, with gold-and-black images from biology, astronomy and other disciplines, is nearly complete.

Those wanting a sampler would do well to visit one or all three of the group shows on display at the Smart Museum, Hyde Park Art Center and Stony Island Arts Bank. Not all 29 of the MacArthur Fellows have work in these spaces, but most do, and the thematically grouped presentations can help viewers get a sense of the larger issues of environmental and social justice, human rights, identity and representation that are at stake.

Highlights at the Smart include an immersive room of Toba Khedoori's sensitively mute paintings of home, emptiness and destruction, and Fazal Sheikh's investigation into the near-abstract beauty of the Four Corners region, through aerial and close-up photography, a consideration of its extractive industries, indigenous collaboration and seismological sound recordings.

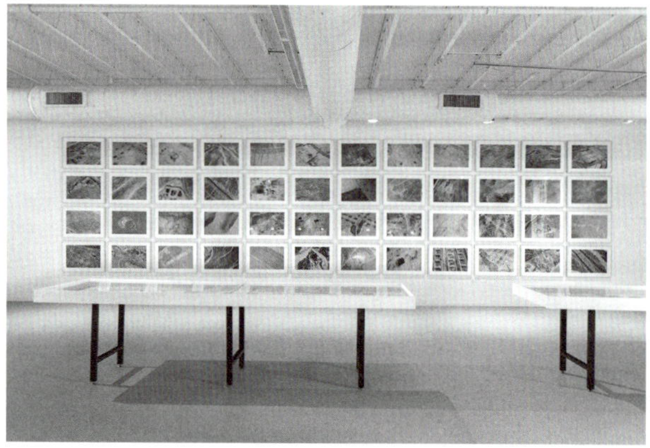

Installation of photographs from Fazal Sheikh's series *Desert Bloom* at Hyde Park Art Center. Photo: Nathan Keay

At HPAC, LaToya Ruby Frazier's fierce, heart-rending video *Flint Is Family* pairs her photographs with a narrative by Shea Cobb, a lifelong resident preparing to leave her home and extended family in order to protect her daughter from the city's water crisis.

In the main room of the Arts Bank, Fred Wilson's cluster of ornate black glass mirrors—inspired by historical Venetian paintings in which the Black figures are little known—symphonically reflects a room of dazzling artworks by Black figures of great renown: Marshall, David Hammons, Whitfield Lovell and Kara Walker.

Most outstanding of all are an awesome array of solo exhibitions and projects at venues all across town. A few are yet to come, and some—like Jeffrey Gibson's fantastical remixing of Native American portraiture at the Newberry Library on the Near North Side and Dawoud Bey's classic, tender portraits of South Side youths at Arts + Public Life in Washington Park—have already closed. A half-dozen are up at the South Side Community Art Center just through the end of September. But most of these shows are open through mid to late fall, including Gómez-Peña's thrilling takeover of the Jane Addams Hull-House Museum; Walker's horrifying mural of antebellum caricatures gracefully arranged in the DuSable Museum's magnificent Roundhouse; Amalia Mesa-Bains's glittering and homey ofrenda to her maternal family, the Cornejos, in recognition of their substantial civic contributions, part of the National Museum of Mexican Art's annual Day of the Dead celebration; and, at the Logan Center, Carrie Mae Weems's devoted re-imagining of a Black Panther Party space for the education of young people, as inspiring as it is dispiriting, because their demands of 1966 remain largely unmet.

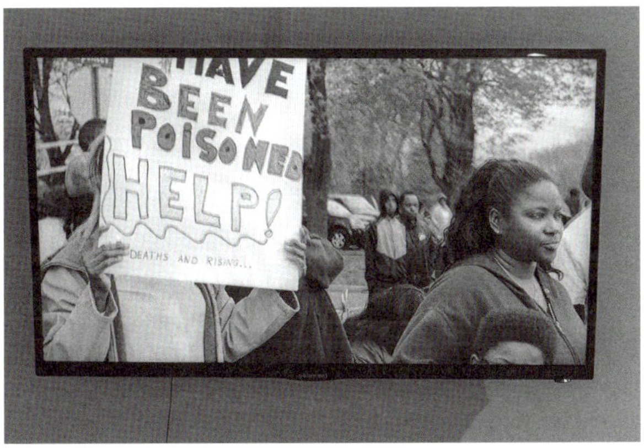

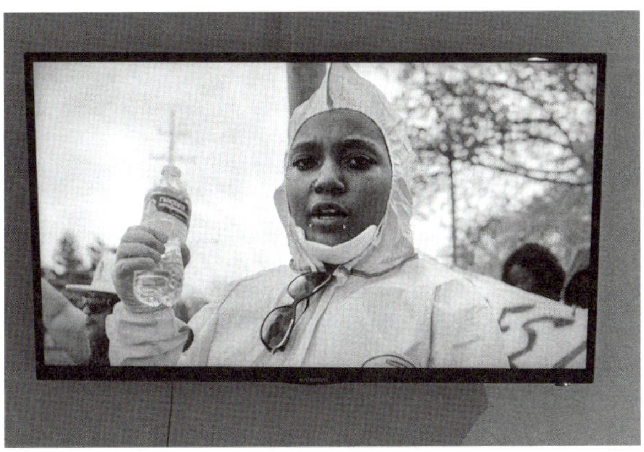

LaToya Ruby Frazier's *Flint Is Family* at Hyde Park Art Center. Photo: Nathan Keay

The most summative of the Panther's wishes was for "land, bread, housing, education, clothing, justice and peace." No art can truly meet those essential needs, but the artworks in *Toward Common Cause* employ every tactic, angle and tool to force us all to consider how we might. What could be more essential?

RESTORATIVE ACTS: A REVIEW OF *TOWARD COMMON CAUSE* AT SWEET WATER FOUNDATION (EXCERPT)

Alex Priest
Newcity Art, September 17, 2021

At the intersection of Englewood and Washington Park on Chicago's South Side, the multiblock campus of Sweet Water Foundation is a laboratory for ecologically and economically regenerative projects. Since its founding in 2014 by Emmanuel Pratt, SWF has used a blend of urban agriculture, art and education to transform spaces and buildings into sustainable community assets.

SWF is one of thirty-five partner organizations for *Toward Common Cause*, an exhibition featuring new and recontextualized work by twenty-nine visual artists who have been named MacArthur Fellows since 1981. *Toward Common Cause* aspires to "explore the extent to which certain resources—air, land, water and even culture—can be held in common; raising questions about inclusion, exclusion, ownership and rights of access." Pratt is a 2019 MacArthur Fellow and although not an official exhibiting artist, SWF is the platform for interventions by Mel Chin and Iñigo Manglano-Ovalle.

SWF as both site and project takes the curatorial statement from *Toward Common Cause* and adds layers for considering context and value in public and common causes. SWF takes multiple viewpoints from community stakeholders into consideration when adding to SWF's development. *Toward Common Cause* is no different. Even with Pratt's MacArthur Foundation affiliation, Manglano-Ovalle and Chin's installations went through a community-input process of approval before installation. The projects at SWF are, intentionally, not standalone installations in a white-cube gallery space.

Walking onto SWF's campus, there is an immediate sense of this process. I was greeted by SWF staff, volunteers and community members as I approached the Think-Do House. I could smell the nearby community garden, hear the sounds of machinery from the woodshop, see folks building new objects from recycled materials and feel collective energy vibrating out to the neighborhood. I sat in the shade ruminating on SWF's *We the Publics* manifesto and proposition to "restore democracy and truth in the republic" propped up against a garden shed. Upon meeting Pratt, I was invited into the House for a bite from the garden before heading back outside to see the work on view for *Toward Common Cause*.

Painted in green, black and red (the colors of the Pan-African flag) Manglano-Ovalle's *Hydrant, 41°47′22.662″ N—87°37′38.364″ W*, is nearly camouflaged in the yard and garden in its pedestrian functionality. That is the point. Through a complicated set of bureaucratic gymnastics, the hydrant taps into the public water source running below SWF. The water from *Hydrant* is used for the garden, which is open and available to everyone, and as an artistic gesture. The work is both simple and open-ended, pragmatic and sculptural; accessing the water from *Hydrant* is as much a public performance as a necessity.

This hydrant is given a particular context at SWF, which expands Manglano-Ovalle's artistic practice of addressing "humanity's relationship to the climate, especially its effect on water." I was reminded by Pratt how water at 57th Street and Perry Avenue holds memories associated with redlining—water is infrastructure controlled by the federal, state and city governments and clean water and water access is one of the many environmental injustices caused by these policies. But, importantly, water is also a source of life. The duality of *Hydrant* is amplified at SWF.

On the tour, Pratt grabbed a piece of kale from the garden adjacent to *Hydrant* and crushed it. The water from the kale dripped from his hand, metaphorically and literally expressing the multiplicity of water as a municipal and nourishing resource. The spigot and the kale speak to what Pratt refers to as "food apartheids." ("Food desert" is an incorrect metaphor because "deserts" are incredibly complex ecosystems full of life; "apartheids" are forms of systematic oppression.) Everything about *Hydrant* is interconnected with SWF's larger project, from the permits SWF needed to access the water, to the leaf of kale grown with the water from *Hydrant*, to the eventual consumer who is nourished by the kale. *Hydrant* merges metaphor and historic and contemporary realities. It is remarkable that a steel pipe at SWF can hold such symbolism.

Down the block on Lafayette Avenue, Mel Chin's newly commissioned *Safehouse Temple Door* is installed on SWF's soon-to-reopen Civic Arts Church. Atop seven stairs, Chin's artwork is a gargantuan ten-foot diameter functioning bank-vault door. The circular steel door serves as the front door to the former liturgical space. Two concrete pillars in the same Pan-African flag colors as *Hydrant* are erected at street level as an open gate, and viewers are required to pass through them to see *Safehouse Temple Door*. On our tour, Pratt opened the door like a banker opening a vault. Along this metaphor, Chin's door provokes questions of value and importantly who is determining value. *Safehouse Temple Door* also serves as one of multiple activation points for the *Chicago Fundred Initiative: A Bill for IL*, a collaborative action focused on lead contamination in water, soil and housing.

The context for *Safehouse Temple Door* on the former Black church is also far from a blank canvas. During the tour, I learned how the church was once a vibrant space for gathering during the Great Migration while, later, urban renewal ripped apart the neighborhood. The Civic Arts Church and Chin's workable vault door address these overlapping narratives through a community-centric architectural intervention. The two projects, the church and the vault door, in tandem assuage fetishizing art's role in neighborhood development in favor of granular human-scaled change. Like the rest of SWF's projects, there is a reminder that brokering with the local is important because, as Pratt reminds, "real people live here." As such, Chin's work at the Civic Arts Bank is as much about respecting people and neighborhood as an antidote to erasure and environmental justice.

SWF presents the restorative acts and practices of being present to the everyday life of the public. The same goes for Manglano-Ovalle and Chin's work in *Toward Common Cause*. Yet, most of the work on view is virtually invisible; it is in the relationship and conversations taking place because of the artworks. SWF and Pratt are doing this work so *Toward Common Cause* has context, value and relevance. Pratt's final remark, "We are in a perpetual act of becoming," is a resonant treatise for SWF and *Toward Common Cause*. The art of co-creating a "direct response to the everyday chaos of economic hardships, violence, perpetual poverty, and systemic racism that pervades our communities" is what is truly on view at SWF through Pratt, Manglano-Ovalle and Chin's interventions. This work at SWF needs to be experienced in real life and in real time to fully grasp its impact.

MURALS HIT A HIGH NOTE ON THIS CHA BUILDING (EXCERPT)

Edward Robert McClellan
Chicago Magazine, August 8, 2022

The Minnie Julia Riperton Apartments—yes, named after *that* Minnie Riperton, the "Lovin' You" singer who trilled notes higher than a wood thrush playing a pennywhistle, the mother of *Saturday Night Live*'s Maya Rudolph—are drab even by the utilitarian standards of the Chicago Housing Authority. Opened in 1969, and representative of that decade's bland, brutal public architecture, the building is a 14-story hinged box of brown brick and gray concrete stained by half a century of Midwestern winters. But look up—upupupup—crane your neck, squint against the sun, and see, hanging from two blank facades, a pair of murals depicting African-American family life. They were painted by Njideka Akunyili Crosby, a MacArthur Genius Grant–winning artist originally from Nigeria, and chosen by the residents, making the Minnie Riperton Apartments the only CHA building that doubles as an outdoor art gallery. It's become a point of pride for the people living there.

"They wanted to put out something that the general public notices these buildings were here," said Jerrold Herman, 66, who has resided at the senior building for a decade. "You could see it, but there wasn't any reason to notice it. Then there's you coming home to a plain place versus you coming home to a place with a mural. That's where you stay. It's an extra incentive to look up. If you look up, your head is high and your shoulders are back and all's right with the world."

The general public may not have noticed the Minnie Riperton Apartments because the building is at 43rd Street and Princeton Avenue, in Fuller Park, one of the city's smallest, littlest-known neighborhoods. Fuller Park is just a few blocks wide, squeezed between the Dan Ryan Expressway and the Chicago & Western Indiana Railroad tracks. (The neighborhood is named for Chicago's own Chief Justice Melville Fuller, whose Supreme Court issued *Plessy v. Ferguson*, the decision which allowed states to maintain "separate but equal" facilities for Blacks and whites. A bust of the judge stands in the courtyard of the Fuller Park fieldhouse.)

The Minnie Riperton Apartments are, however, visible from the Dan Ryan. That's one reason they were chosen to display the murals, which were hung high enough to be seen by highway traffic. The murals are part of the Smart Museum of Art's project, *Toward Common Cause: Art, Social Change, and the MacArthur Fellows Program at 40*, which has placed art by 29 Genius Grant winners around Chicago. The Smart Museum collaborated with the CHA Teen Program to find the right artwork for the Minnie Riperton Apartments. A group of young people who live in public housing selected 16 paintings by Crosby and set up posters in the building's hallways, so residents could choose the pair they liked best. *Home: Say It Loud* is a mural of a living room overlaid with family photos. *I Still Face You* depicts a family sitting around a table on a balcony. Loving these murals is easy, because they're beautiful.

The murals, said 18-year-old Milan Jackson, debunk "the theory of what buildings on the South Side mean and represent to the residents there. It shows the culture that the building has. It also represents unity."

RICK LOWE TALKS ABOUT *BLACK WALL STREET JOURNEY* AND BLACK ECONOMIC PROSPERITY

Excerpted from conversations at the Neubauer Collegium on October 21, 2021 (with John Rogers Jr.; moderated by Valerie Van Meter) and January 18, 2023 (with Dieter Roelstraete, Derek Neal, Adam Green, and Kate Cagney) in conjunction with Lowe's citywide public art project *Black Wall Street Journey*

Rick Lowe:
The Black Wall Street Journey is a platform that tries to reshape the narrative around the economic plight of African Americans. I was inspired by my involvement with the 1921 Tulsa Massacre centennial. Not only was the massacre a destructive event, it was also part amazing creativity and imagination. They rebuilt their neighborhood in the face of terror. This became an opportunity

to imagine what it would look like in the twenty-first century in the city of Chicago.

Valerie Van Meter:
What metrics or green shoots would we look for? Are there different measures of success we should be focusing on? When I was with the Chicago Federal Reserve Bank in 2008, we would listen anxiously to directors' reports waiting for news of green shoots. What does success look like in Chicago's Black economy?

Rick Lowe:
I've never heard that term, "green shoots," but I'm looking for those. *Black Wall Street Journey* was a response to the preponderance of information about the challenges Black communities face in this country, about how they lagged behind economically. That's what the data says. Yet that information doesn't reflect the reality I see. There are windows that I can look into and I see so much hope and prosperity. There's real, positive stuff happening. How does that become part of the narrative? How do we talk about the possibilities, economic sustainability, and the flourishing of Black communities? How can we see between these two different, sometimes conflicting narratives?

There is numerical data, but there's also perceptual information. If we look only at the end results, we've missed so much that happens in between, and the process has the potential to tell a different story. It may not be the end result, but it gives us additional insight. My job as an artist is to tell a story. That is my work. I'm trying to find a narrative that can inspire. That's the whole point, right? I want to be able to inspire people beyond what they might perceive as actually possible, and that's a big, big part of what I do.

Working with data scientists and sociologists over the last couple of years, I found, though, that I needed to know more about how data is collected and how it is actually used. I wanted to know more about how surveys are built, what questions scientists ask, because maybe they aren't asking the right questions. If I ask the other questions, we might see a fuller picture. We might see Black communities in their fullness and tell a story of possibility rather than a story of disappointments or lack.

One of the things that I found is that there's so little information about the more hopeful sides of African American economics. That's either because there's just no interest in it or that nobody's thought that it was worthy speaking about or researching. Maybe the way of gathering that information is just too complex. We need a more nuanced understanding of how Black communities work. We need to understand what people need. I can tell you from thirty years of doing community-based work that it takes years to understand those dynamics. I also know that it is incredibly important to understand and share those stories because it gives people hope. It tells a student in high school on 68th Street in Chicago that there is a future for them that is full of possibility.

One interesting study was shared productively by two sources in the same month—*The Economist* and *Jet* magazine. I expect *The Economist* to deal with more technical information. *Jet*, on the other hand . . . is an important source of information about the Black community *for* the Black community. They write about Black culture, Black life. There's value in disseminating information in both those formats. How do we do that? Can we find ways to use the artwork, *Black Wall Street Journey*, to do just that. Can we produce and use data to alter the overall perception of Black possibilities in economics?

WALL LABEL FROM THE SMART MUSEUM INSTALLATION
Natalie Moore

Black Wall Street Journey poster series, 2020–21
15 inkjet prints on paper, series of 20
Produced by Natalie Moore in collaboration with Amanda Williams

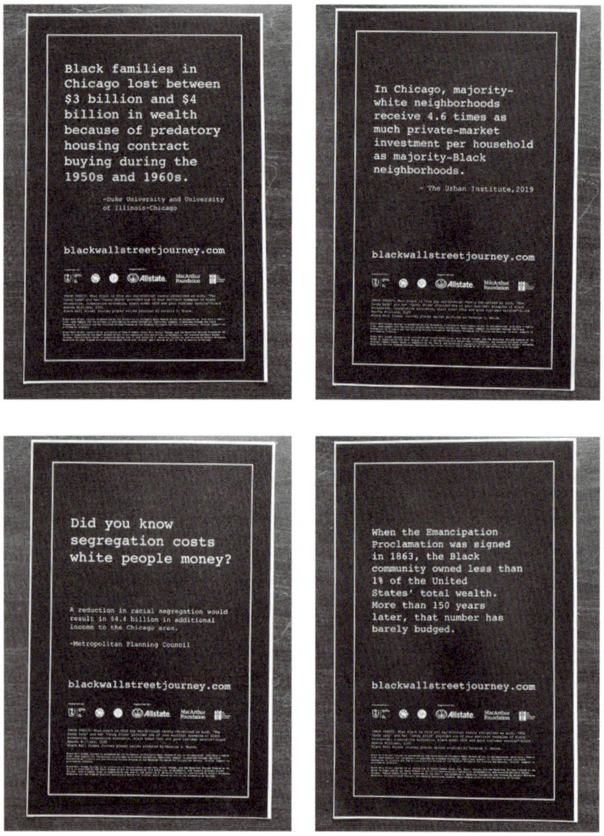

Photos: Jill Sterrett

Do these posters offend you? Apparently, for some they do.

The goal of *Black Wall Street Journey* (*BWSJ*) is to be a source of information of the economic health of African American communities in Chicago, specifically, and the nation as a whole. The multinational advertising corporation JCDecaux agreed to support the *BWSJ* through the placement of posters on Chicago bus shelters across the city. We delivered twenty posters, most of which are on display here. But upon review, the company rejected all but six posters arguing that they violated the company's advertising content policies. The policy states, *JCDecaux will not allow advertising that expresses or advocates an opinion, position or viewpoint on matters of public debate about economic, political, moral, religious or social issues*. As a journalist, my reporting is rooted in facts, accuracy and truth-telling. There are indisputable facts about the median income, wealth, and home values of Black Americans. That leads to the truth about a wide racial wealth gap in Chicago and the US. As we dream up a utopia and imagine Black prosperity, we must ask "very pointed" questions and present hard truths. JCDecaux's decision to curtail the display of the posters on the city's South, West and North Sides is disappointing. But it follows a trend. A year into a so-called racial reckoning, we are witnessing backlash from an array of institutions and political players.

The truth remains.

The following quotes are pulled from posters produced by Natalie Moore in collaboration with the artist Amanda Williams that were included in *Black Wall Street Journey* (Scenes #22; p. 160).

"What is economic freedom?"

"In Chicago, majority-white neighborhoods receive 4.6 times as much private-market investment per household as majority-black neighborhoods."
—The Urban Institute, 2019

"Black families in Chicago lost between $3 billion and $4 billion in wealth because of predatory housing contract buying during the 1950s and 1960s.
—Duke University and University of Illinois–Chicago

"Did you know segregation costs white people money?"
"A reduction in racial segregation would result in $4.4 billion in additional income to the Chicago area."
—Metropolitan Planning Council

"What would a Chicago utopia sound, look, and smell like?"

"When the Emancipation Proclamation was signed in 1863, the Black community owned less than 1% of the United States' total wealth. More than 150 years later, that number has barely budged."

Afterword: How Next?
Jill Sterrett

Toward Common Cause was built on the belief that museums will be enriched by loosening their grip—ceding control to a fuller variety of voices beyond their walls, and then looking inward to act in response. It acknowledged individuals' differences and trusted artists to create spaces across the city of Chicago where people gather to connect and make meaning in their lives.

We began with an initial proposition about art's agency that, while prescient, sounded a bit bookish when the pandemic arrived two years later. By 2020, we needed something more direct from art. Resilience was what we sought, but not the kind of stamina that motors through challenge by force of will. We were looking for the kind of resilience that is about recovering from misfortune and adjusting to change. In the spring of 2020, author Arundhati Roy composed the image of a path, a "portal, a gateway from one world to the next," where each of us must decide what we carry on our backs.[1] A year later, author Louise Erdrich composed another image of resilience in her novel *The Sentence*. It is a story that takes place over the course of a year when the pandemic wreaked havoc on the world and George Floyd's murder roiled a nation. The past haunts the "essential" workers of a small bookstore in Minneapolis again and again through the spirit of a departed customer who will not leave the premises. Erdrich's invitation to reckon—for the spirit, the bookstore workers, and us all—is an open door and a simple command: "Go."[2]

COVID stay-at-home orders shrank the perimeter of peoples' daily lives. Public gatherings vaporized. It was a humbling and chilling time for a cultural sector wholly reliant on social exchange. One-third of museums were at risk.[3] Business models, staffing structures, revenue streams, and impact measures were shaky and exposed. Did we have access to the everyday building essentials—plywood, plexiglass, and paint—that make exhibitions possible? And if so, would procuring them bust the budget? Open letters landed explosively in newspaper editorials and industry journals demanding amends for the racial, biological, and economic inequities of the industry. We were forced to rework *Toward Common Cause* many times in response to a host of new concerns. Amid this uncertainty, there was fear. There was hardship. There was protest. Were our partners and their loved ones well? Would their livelihoods remain viable?

I miss the collective urgency of that time even as I recall how the pressure—often unrelenting—to take a public position left little room to respond to the complexity at hand. Missteps were rampant. Finding the courage to act relied on making peace with blundering. In 2020, I started having coffee over Zoom with Marlies Carruth, director of the MacArthur Fellows Program. One day, while brainstorming how to take *Toward Common Cause* virtual, an option that we pursued briefly, an idea energized us. What if no one knew who was behind *Toward Common Cause*, if the participating organizations and funders were unnamed? There was something revitalizing about "unbranding" the inherited habits of physical art spaces; it lifted the weight of reputational risk, opening up options to try things. It freed us to get on with the work rather than talking about it. Throughout, the artists in *Toward Common Cause* were sources of imaginative play, go-to problem-solvers in this new realm of possible. When we received the all-clear for safe gathering in 2021, we could not unknow what we had learned when we planned a virtualized exhibition unencumbered by tradition, reputation, and expectation. We cannot unknow it now.

Trust remains a big deal. It has been called the "messy and vulnerable" issue at the root of how things are done in the industry.[4] What does this actually mean? It means confronting past mistakes. It means acknowledging personal and institutional blind spots on the inside while embracing knowledge from outside. Systems of trust root fundamentally in questions of how. They are more about mechanisms than motives. When how is recast as accountability to one another, partnerships no longer rely on the negotiated transactional features of a deal but rather on good relations and mutual service.[5]

Let go of the pretenses to the universal that have governed the modern museum for hundreds of years. Liberating ourselves from the notion of a universal mankind is about unmooring universal truths that stem from everywhere and nowhere all at the same time. What if we could accept, instead, that each of us embodies "partial, locatable knowledge" along with immense and untapped potential to sustain webs of interconnection?[6]

Show up in the present with a long view. The present is the temporal space of our actions. Prioritize audiences and circumstances of today. Build something big out of the accumulation of small, sequential things. Advocate for the time it takes to make real change, including aligned funding models where there is a sustained flow of resources.

Play is paramount (so is verve and evaluation). Resist the habits of the procedural to create space for the possibilities of what could yet be. Make room for thinking and rethinking, vision and revision, unknowing things that just yesterday seemed valid. Play, experiment, pause, reflect, play again.

For me, the most enduring takeaway from *Toward Common Cause* became decentering both art and museums to explore the conditions under which cooperation, among people and other living and nonliving things, happens. I have always had trouble compartmentalizing culture work because the efforts I admire most are connected to life's essentials—food, water, air, and shelter. The imperative to cooperate intensifies with each day. Heat waves shatter temperature records around the world. Political division, sown through tools of mistrust, continues to stymie even the most basic forms of cooperation required for people to galvanize around our collective well-being. Put simply, no industry can take refuge from these realities anymore. Four years ago, I thought we were at the forward edge of something big for museums. Now I concede, with some dismay but also resolve, that the road will be long. And yet, we carry on. Our methods morph, ironically, like a virus.

Since *Toward Common Cause*, Abigail Winograd and I have stayed the course in distinct ways. Abby has partnered with artist Jeffrey Gibson as one of the commissioners of his presentation at the United States Pavilion at the 2024 Venice Biennale. Gibson will present the first solo exhibition of an Indigenous artist since the Biennale was established in 1895. My tack has been different. After spending a good part of 2022 working on this book in California (with thanks to The Getty), I moved to Madison, Wisconsin, to work on a new history center that will open at the foot of the State Capitol in 2027. Taking on questions of history—how we know what we know and who decides?—from one of today's epicenters of American polarization was an opportunity that was impossible to pass up.

The making of this book has been a meditation on the lessons of *Toward Common Cause*. I hope it stands as one enduring record from two tumultuous years—2020–21—when there was a hue and cry for change in museums and the world. Even more, I hope that recalling that collective charge to do better redoubles resolve now.

Scan the endpapers of this book to see the hundreds of individuals who brought their vast array of skills and their lived experience and knowledge to realize *Toward Common Cause* and this companion volume. Perhaps what *Toward Common Cause* did best was to invite people and institutions across the city of Chicago to grapple with uncertainty, urgency, experimentation, reciprocity, complexity, discomfort, and value; to address them; to think differently along the way; to look and listen for impact; to be honest about what works; to be equally honest about what's left unresolved and alert to emergent rumblings. And next? From those rumblings we can begin to formulate new questions to integrate into a new, unfolding realm of possible. Most importantly, we must resist falling back to before.

1 Arundhati Roy, "The Pandemic Is a Portal," *Financial Times*, April 3, 2020.

2 Louise Erdrich, *The Sentence* (New York: HarperCollins, 2021), 374.

3 "National Snapshot of COVID-19 Impact on United States Museums," American Alliance of Museums, April 2021, https://www.aam-us.org/wp-content/uploads/2021/05/2021_Third-Snapshot-Survey-on-the-Impacts-of-COVID19-on-the-Museum-Field.pdf.

4 "The Messy and Vulnerable Truth about Trust and Museums," American Alliance of Museums blog, April 21, 2023, https://www.aam-us.org/2023/04/21/the-messy-and-vulnerable-truth-about-trust-and-museums/.

5 Max Liboiron, *Pollution Is Colonialism* (Durham, N.C.: Duke University Press, 2021).

6 Donna Haraway, "Situated Knowledges: The Science Question in Feminism and the Privilege of Partial Perspective," *Feminist Studies* 14, no. 3 (1988): 575–99.

CHECKLIST OF THE EXHIBITION

Njideka Akunyili Crosby (Nigerian-American, b. 1983) at Chicago Housing Authority, Minnie Julia Riperton Apartments

I Still Face You, 2021
Vinyl banner reproduction of the 2015 artwork
Banner dimensions: 28 ft. 4 in. × 36 ft. 6 in.
Courtesy of the artist, Victoria Miro, and David Zwirner
Scenes #14 and p. 72

Home: Say It Loud, 2021
Vinyl banner reproduction of the 2017 artwork
Banner dimensions: 35 ft. 2 in. × 34 ft. 10 in.
Courtesy of the artist, Victoria Miro, and David Zwirner
p. 72

Njideka Akunyili Crosby (Nigerian-American, b. 1983) at the National Public Housing Museum

Mother and Child, 2021
Vinyl banner reproduction of the 2016 artwork
Banner dimensions: 19 ft. 3 in. × 25 ft.
Courtesy of the artist, Victoria Miro, and David Zwirner
Cover jacket images, p. 72

The Beautyful Ones, Series #9, 2021
Vinyl banner reproduction of the 2018 artwork
25 × 25 ft.
Courtesy of the artist, Victoria Miro, and David Zwirner
Scenes #8 and pp. 72, 73

Ida Applebroog (American, b. 1929) at the Neubauer Collegium for Culture and Society, The University of Chicago

Monalisa, 2009
Gampi, Mylar, ink, pigment, oil, watercolor, and wood
110 × 144 × 146 1/2 in.
Courtesy of the artist and Hauser & Wirth
Scenes #12 and p. 160

Dawoud Bey (American, b. 1953) in collaboration with Dan Collison and Elizabeth Meister at the Stony Island Arts Bank

Julia, University of Chicago Laboratory Schools, 2003 (from *The Chicago Project*)
Chromogenic print and audio recording
50 × 40 in.
Commission, The David and Alfred Smart Museum of Art, The University of Chicago

Steven, Kenwood Academy High School, 2003 (from *The Chicago Project*)
Chromogenic print and audio recording
40 × 50 in.
Commission, The David and Alfred Smart Museum of Art, The University of Chicago
Scenes #35 and p. 58

Theresa, South Shore High School, 2003 (from *The Chicago Project*)
Chromogenic print and audio recording
40 × 50 in.
Commission, The David and Alfred Smart Museum of Art, The University of Chicago
p. 58

Dawoud Bey (American, b. 1953) at Washington Park Arts Incubator, an initiative of Arts + Public Life, The University of Chicago

Carlos, 2001
Chromogenic print
20 × 16 in.
Collection of DePaul Art Museum, gift of Dr. Bruce Johnson
p. 118

Karina, 2001
Chromogenic print
20 × 16 in.
Collection of DePaul Art Museum, gift of Dr. Bruce Johnson

Kenneth, 2001
Chromogenic print
20 × 16 in.
Collection of DePaul Art Museum, gift of Dr. Bruce Johnson

Lisette, 2001
Chromogenic print
20 × 16 in.
Collection of DePaul Art Museum, gift of Dr. Bruce Johnson

Michael, 2001
Chromogenic print
20 × 16 in.
Collection of DePaul Art Museum, gift of Dr. Bruce Johnson

Muhammad, 2001
Chromogenic print
20 × 16 in.
Collection of DePaul Art Museum, gift of Dr. Bruce Johnson

Sharmaine, Vincente, Joseph, Andre, and Charlie, 1993
Internal dye diffusion transfer print
Three prints, each 26 1/2 × 22 in.
Courtesy of the Museum of Contemporary Photography at Columbia College Chicago
p. 118

Mark Bradford (American, b. 1961) at The David and Alfred Smart Museum of Art, The University of Chicago

Dancing in the Street, 2019
Video, exhibition copy
Running time 2:50
Courtesy of the artist and Hauser & Wirth
Scenes #3

Tulsa Gottdamn, 2021
Mixed media on canvas
84 × 108 × 2 in.
Courtesy of the artist and Hauser & Wirth
Scenes #18 and p. 61

Mel Chin (American, b. 1951) at Hyde Park Art Center

Philadelphia Footed Fundred Minting Table, 2010
Cherry wood, pewter, drawing utensils, banker lamps, and artist-designed signage
Installation size variable (table: 31 1/2 × 330 × 25 1/2 in.)
Courtesy of the artist
Scenes #13

Mel Chin (American, b. 1951) at The David and Alfred Smart Museum of Art, The University of Chicago

Bird Is the Word: North Carolina Variation, 2019
Webster's Third International Dictionary, beeswax, and cherry wood
10 × 9 × 6 in.
Private collection

Revival Field Diorama, 2019
Artifacts, original stake, plants, soil, paint, paper, plaster, glass, tape, and lighting fixtures
75 × 78 1/4 × 8 1/2 in.
Courtesy of the artist
p. 167

Fundred Project, 2010–ongoing
Hand-drawn Fundred, plastic pen, and guitar case
Courtesy of the artist
p. 61

Mel Chin (American, b. 1951) at Sweet Water Foundation

Safehouse Temple Door, part of the *Chicago Fundred Initiative: A Bill for IL*, 2021
10-ft. steel bank-vault door installed on the facade of the

Civic Arts Church at Sweet Water Foundation
pp. 32, 181

Nicole Eisenman (American, b. 1965) at The David and Alfred Smart Museum of Art, The University of Chicago

The Triumph of Poverty, 2009
Oil on canvas
65 × 82 in.
Collection of Bobbi and Stephen Rosenthal, New York
Scenes #20 and p. 59

Nicole Eisenman (American, b. 1965) at the Stony Island Arts Bank

Cubist Female Innards 1, 2019
Oil on linen
30 × 28 × 1 in.
Collection of Marilyn and Larry Fields

Wendy Ewald (American, b. 1951) at Weinberg/Newton Gallery

Windows:

Exterior installation shots of portraits from *Daily Life and Dreams in the Pandemic: A Project with the Centro Romero Youth Program*, 2020–21
Scenes #19 and p. 108

Adriana, 2020–21
Vinyl window installation; *Daily Life and Dreams in the Pandemic: A Project with the Centro Romero Youth Program* (2020–21), made in collaboration with Adriana
Courtesy of the artist

Angel, 2020–21
Vinyl window installation; *Daily Life and Dreams in the Pandemic: A Project with the Centro Romero Youth Program* (2020–21), made in collaboration with Angel
Courtesy of the artist

Marestela, 2020–21
Vinyl window installation; *Daily Life and Dreams in the Pandemic: A Project with the Centro Romero Youth Program* (2020–21), made in collaboration with Marestela
Courtesy of the artist
p. 105

Zulairam, 2020–21
Vinyl window installation; *Daily Life and Dreams in the Pandemic: A Project with the Centro Romero Youth Program* (2020–21), made in collaboration with Zulairam
Courtesy of the artist

Gallery:
p. 108

Alondra, 2020–21
Installation with portrait photograph of student, compilation print of student's photographs, and student's text; *Daily Life and Dreams in the Pandemic: A Project with the Centro Romero Youth Program* (2020–21), made in collaboration with Alondra
Courtesy of the artist

Cyntia, 2020–21
Installation with portrait photograph of student, compilation print of student's photographs, and student's text; *Daily Life and Dreams in the Pandemic: A Project with the Centro Romero Youth Program* (2020–21), made in collaboration with Cyntia
Courtesy of the artist

Efren, 2020–21
Installation with portrait photograph of student, compilation print of student's photographs, and student's text; *Daily Life and Dreams in the Pandemic: A Project with the Centro Romero Youth Program* (2020–21), made in collaboration with Efren
Courtesy of the artist

Ernesto, 2020–21
Installation with portrait photograph of student, compilation print of student's photographs, and student's text; *Daily Life and Dreams in the Pandemic: A Project with the Centro Romero Youth Program* (2020–21), made in collaboration with Ernesto
Courtesy of the artist

Giselle, 2020–21
Installation with portrait photograph of student, compilation print of student's photographs, and student's text; *Daily Life and Dreams in the Pandemic: A Project with the Centro Romero Youth Program* (2020–21), made in collaboration with Giselle
Courtesy of the artist
p. 106

Irving, 2020–21
Installation with portrait photograph of student, compilation print of student's photographs, and student's text; *Daily Life and Dreams in the Pandemic: A Project with the Centro Romero Youth Program* (2020–21), made in collaboration with Irving
Courtesy of the artist

Itzel, 2020–21
Installation with portrait photograph of student, compilation print of student's photographs, and student's text; *Daily Life and Dreams in the Pandemic: A Project with the Centro Romero Youth Program* (2020–21), made in collaboration with Itzel
Courtesy of the artist

Jeancarlo, 2020–21
Installation with portrait photograph of student, compilation print of student's photographs, and student's text; *Daily Life and Dreams in the Pandemic: A Project with the Centro Romero Youth Program* (2020–21), made in collaboration with Jeancarlo
Courtesy of the artist

Kevin, 2020–21
Installation with portrait photograph of student, compilation print of student's photographs, and student's text; *Daily Life and Dreams in the Pandemic: A Project with the Centro Romero Youth Program* (2020–21), made in collaboration with Kevin
Courtesy of the artist
p. 106

Installation shot of a selection of photographs from *The Devil Is Leaving His Cave: Photographs by Children from Chiapas*, 1991
p. 108

A boy is dressed like a girl, 1991, from *The Devil Is Leaving His Cave: Photographs by Children from Chiapas* (1991), made in collaboration with Sebastián Gómez Hernández
Gelatin silver print
19 1/2 × 23 in.
Wendy Ewald Collection

A boy is playing-pretending he's a clown, 1991, from *The Devil Is Leaving His Cave: Photographs by Children from Chiapas* (1991), made in collaboration with Dolores Gómez Hernández
Gelatin silver print
14 3/4 × 17 1/2 in.
Wendy Ewald Collection

A boy was crushed by a barrel, 1991, from *The Devil Is Leaving His Cave: Photographs by Children from Chiapas* (1991), made in collaboration with Reymundo Gómez Hernández

Gelatin silver print
12 3/8 × 14 in.
Wendy Ewald Collection

A jaguar is eating chicken, 1991, from *The Devil Is Leaving His Cave: Photographs by Children from Chiapas* (1991), made in collaboration with Salvador Gómez Jiménez
Gelatin silver print
14 3/4 × 17 1/2 in.
Wendy Ewald Collection

All my brothers and sisters, 1991, from *The Devil Is Leaving His Cave: Photographs by Children from Chiapas* (1991), made in collaboration with Reymundo Gómez Hernández
Gelatin silver print
14 3/4 × 17 1/2 in.
Wendy Ewald Collection

A man killing his enemy, 1991, from *The Devil Is Leaving His Cave: Photographs by Children from Chiapas* (1991), made in collaboration with Christian Alberto López Medina
Gelatin silver print
14 3/4 × 17 1/2 in.
Wendy Ewald Collection

Death, 1991, from *The Devil Is Leaving His Cave: Photographs by Children from Chiapas* (1991), made in collaboration with Teresa López
Gelatin silver print
19 1/2 × 23 5/8 in.
Wendy Ewald Collection

Firewood fell on top of my little brother Pedro, 1991, from *The Devil Is Leaving His Cave: Photographs by Children from Chiapas* (1991), made in collaboration with Sebastián Gómez Hernández
Gelatin silver print
12 3/8 × 14 in.
Wendy Ewald Collection

Here is my cousin, Miry, with the skulls and fruit for the Day of the Dead, 1991, from *The Devil Is Leaving His Cave: Photographs by Children from Chiapas* (1991), made in collaboration with Juan Jesús Murillo
Gelatin silver print
14 3/4 × 17 1/2 in.
Wendy Ewald Collection

My dog walking in the patio, 1991, from *The Devil Is Leaving His Cave: Photographs by Children from Chiapas* (1991), made in collaboration with Teresa López
Gelatin silver print
19 5/8 × 23 3/8 × 1 3/4 in.
Courtesy of Addison Gallery of American Art, Phillips Academy, Andover, Massachusetts, gift of the artist in honor of Adam Weinberg

My father and sisters are harvesting cauliflower, 1991, from *The Devil Is Leaving His Cave: Photographs by Children from Chiapas* (1991), made in collaboration with Salvador Gómez Jiménez
Gelatin silver print
12 3/8 × 14 in.
Wendy Ewald Collection

My figure is the fig tree, 1991, from *The Devil Is Leaving His Cave: Photographs by Children from Chiapas* (1991), made in collaboration with Teresa López
Gelatin silver print
14 3/4 × 17 1/2 in.
Wendy Ewald Collection

My friends are picking flowers, 1991, from *The Devil Is Leaving His Cave: Photographs by Children from Chiapas* (1991), made in collaboration with Salvador Gómez Jiménez
Gelatin silver print
14 3/4 × 17 1/2 in.
Wendy Ewald Collection

My little sisters are standing below the orange tree, 1991, from *The Devil Is Leaving His Cave: Photographs by Children from Chiapas* (1991), made in collaboration with Javier Bautista
Gelatin silver print
19 1/2 × 23 5/8 in.
Wendy Ewald Collection

My mother is washing, 1991, from *The Devil Is Leaving His Cave: Photographs by Children from Chiapas* (1991), made in collaboration with Marcos Xilón Gómez
Gelatin silver print
14 3/4 × 17 1/2 in.
Wendy Ewald Collection

My sister carrying water, 1991 from *The Devil Is Leaving His Cave: Photographs by Children from Chiapas* (1991), made in collaboration with Luis Hernández Gómez
Gelatin silver print
19 1/2 × 23 5/8 in.
Wendy Ewald Collection

My sister is braiding her hair, 1991, from *The Devil Is Leaving His Cave: Photographs by Children from Chiapas* (1991), made in collaboration with Nicasio Peréz de la Cruz
Gelatin silver print
12 3/8 × 14 in.
Wendy Ewald Collection

My uncle and his children are thrashing the beans, 1991, from *The Devil Is Leaving His Cave: Photographs by Children from Chiapas* (1991), made in collaboration with Marcos Xilón Gómez
Gelatin silver print
12 3/8 × 14 × 1 3/4 in.
Wendy Ewald Collection

My uncle Mariano is working in the field, Mexico, 1991, from *The Devil Is Leaving His Cave: Photographs by Children from Chiapas* (1991), made in collaboration with Juan Ricardo Hernández López
Gelatin silver print
14 3/4 × 17 1/2 × 1 3/4 in.
Courtesy of Addison Gallery of American Art, Phillips Academy, Andover, Massachusetts, gift of the artist in honor of Adam Weinberg

Sebastián was punished for eight hours, 1991, from *The Devil Is Leaving His Cave: Photographs by Children from Chiapas* (1991), made in collaboration with Dominga González Castellanos
Gelatin silver print
14 3/4 × 17 1/2 in.
Wendy Ewald Collection

The devil is spying on the girls, 1991, from *The Devil Is Leaving His Cave: Photographs by Children from Chiapas* (1991), made in collaboration with Sebastián Gómez Hernández
Gelatin silver print
23 5/8 × 19 1/2 × 1 3/4 in.
Courtesy of Addison Gallery of American Art, Phillips Academy, Andover, Massachusetts, gift of the artist in honor of Adam Weinberg

The devil leaving his cave, 1991, from *The Devil Is Leaving His Cave: Photographs by Children from Chiapas* (1991), made in collaboration with Reymundo Gómez Hernández
Gelatin silver print
19 1/2 × 23 in.
Wendy Ewald Collection

The hens are piled up around an altar outside the house, 1991, from *The Devil Is Leaving His Cave: Photographs by Children from Chiapas* (1991), made in collaboration with Sebastián Gómez Hernández
Gelatin silver print
12 3/8 × 14 in.
Wendy Ewald Collection

The hens going into the kitchen, 1991, from *The Devil Is Leaving His Cave: Photographs by Children from Chiapas* (1991), made in collaboration with Vladimir Stalin Becerril Vargas
Gelatin silver print
12 3/8 × 14 × 1 3/4 in.
Wendy Ewald Collection

The phantom, 1991, from *The Devil Is Leaving His Cave: Photographs by Children from Chiapas* (1991), made in collaboration with Teresa López
Gelatin silver print
17 5/8 × 14 5/8 × 1 3/4 in.
Courtesy of Addison Gallery of American Art, Phillips Academy, Andover, Massachusetts, gift of the artist in honor of Adam Weinberg

The river monsters, 1991, from *The Devil Is Leaving His Cave: Photographs by Children from Chiapas* (1991), made in collaboration with Javier Bautista
Gelatin silver print
14 3/4 × 17 1/2 × 1 3/4 in.
Courtesy of Addison Gallery of American Art, Phillips Academy, Andover, Massachusetts, gift of the artist in honor of Adam Weinberg

The turkeys, 1991, from *The Devil Is Leaving His Cave: Photographs by Children from Chiapas* (1991), made in collaboration with Vladimir Stalin Becerril Vargas
Gelatin silver print
19 1/2 × 23 5/8 in.
Wendy Ewald Collection

The whole family is eating. These are my cousins, 1991, from *The Devil Is Leaving His Cave: Photographs by Children from Chiapas* (1991), made in collaboration with Wendy López Medina
Gelatin silver print
19 1/2 × 23 5/8 in.
Wendy Ewald Collection

Wolfman and his enemy, 1991, from *The Devil Is Leaving His Cave: Photographs by Children from Chiapas* (1991), made in collaboration with Javier Bautista
Gelatin silver print
14 3/4 × 17 1/2 in.
Wendy Ewald Collection

Untitled, 1992, made in collaboration with Tom McDonough
Two VHS (English and Spanish versions) converted to digital files
p. 108

LaToya Ruby Frazier (American, b. 1982) at The David and Alfred Smart Museum of Art, The University of Chicago

Edgar Thomson Plant and The Bottom, 2013, Edition 3 of 5
Archival pigment print
42 1/4 × 63 1/8 in.
Courtesy of the artist and Gladstone Gallery
Scenes #2

The Bunn Family Home on Ninth Street, 2013, Edition 3 of 5
Archival pigment print
42 1/4 × 63 1/8 in.
Courtesy of the artist and Gladstone Gallery
p. 57

United States Steel Clairton Coke Works, C.I.T.E. and Monongahela River, 2013, Edition 1 of 5
Archival pigment print
42 1/4 × 63 1/8 in.
Courtesy of the artist and Gladstone Gallery
Scenes #2 and p. 57

Washington Avenue and Monongahela River, 2013, Edition 1 of 5
Archival pigment print
42 × 63 in.
Courtesy of the artist and Gladstone Gallery

LaToya Ruby Frazier (American, b. 1982) at Hyde Park Art Center

Flint Is Family, 2016, Edition 5 of 5
Video (color, sound), digital transfer
Running time 11:50
Courtesy of the artist and Gladstone Gallery
Scenes #28 and p. 185

Jeffrey Gibson (Mississippi Band of Choctaw, Cherokee, Native American, b. 1972) at The David and Alfred Smart Museum of Art, The University of Chicago

STAND YOUR GROUND, 2019
Cotton and linen, digitally printed fabric, polyester thread, and cotton batting
87 1/2 × 68 in.
Courtesy of the artist and Kavi Gupta
Scenes #2 and p. 60

Jeffrey Gibson (Mississippi Band of Choctaw, Cherokee, Native American, b. 1972) at The Newberry
Field Museum cards
p. 161

Boneta, Comanche, 2021
Cotton rag paper, inkjet print, vintage beaded pieces (glass beads, polyester, thread), vintage papers, glass beads, urethane, and acrylic paint
60 1/2 × 44 in.
Courtesy of the artist and Kavi Gupta
Scenes #34

Chief Black Coyote, 2021
Cotton rag paper, inkjet print, vintage beaded pieces (glass beads, polyester, thread), vintage papers, glass beads, urethane, and acrylic paint
67 1/2 × 44 in.
Courtesy of the artist and Kavi Gupta
Scenes #34

Chief Pretty Eagle, 2021
Cotton rag paper, inkjet print, vintage beaded eyeglass case (glass beads, polyester, thread, suede), vintage beaded barrette (glass beads, polyester, thread), vintage papers, found pin, glass beads, glitter, urethane, and acrylic paint
60 3/8 × 44 in.
Courtesy of the artist and Kavi Gupta
Scenes #34

Christian Naiche, 2021
Cotton rag paper, inkjet print, vintage beaded pieces (glass beads, polyester, thread), vintage papers, glass beads, urethane, and acrylic paint
60 1/2 × 44 in.
Courtesy of the artist and Kavi Gupta
Scenes #34

Pahl Lee, 2021
Cotton rag paper, inkjet print, vintage beaded pieces (glass beads, polyester, thread), vintage papers, glass beads, urethane, and acrylic paint
60 1/2 × 44 in.
Courtesy of the artist and Kavi Gupta
Scenes #34 and p. 162

White Swan, 2021
Cotton rag paper, inkjet print, vintage beaded pieces (glass beads, polyester, thread), vintage papers, glass beads, urethane, and acrylic paint
60 1/2 × 44 in.
Courtesy of the artist and Kavi Gupta
Scenes #34

Acc. 3784, 2021
Digitally printed vinyl wallpaper
Dimensions variable
Courtesy of the artist
Scenes (background) p. 17, p. 161

Guillermo Gómez-Peña (Mexican, b. 1955) at Jane Addams Hull-House Museum

Mex Files: Audio Art & Strange Poetry from the US/Mexico Border, 2021–ongoing
Multilingual live radio and archival audio programs
Courtesy of the artist
p. 46

Casa Museo: A Living Museum and Archive, 2021
Site-specific installation including new and archival video and audio and objects from the artist's personal collection
Courtesy of the artist
Scenes #16 and pp. 35, 36, 37

David Hammons (American, b. 1943) at the Stony Island Arts Bank

Untitled (Kool-Aid drawing), 2003
Mixed media on paper, terrycloth, and silk
43 15/16 × 28 7/8 × 1 11/16 in.
Marilyn and Larry Fields Collection

Gary Hill (American, b. 1951) at the Stony Island Arts Bank

SELF (A-F), 2016
Acrylic, video cameras, electronics, and optics
Various sizes
Courtesy of bitforms gallery, New York
Scenes #33

Alfredo Jaar (Chilean, b. 1956) at The David and Alfred Smart Museum of Art, The University of Chicago

A Short Film on Monstrosity, 2018
Digital color film with sound
Running time 6:19
Courtesy of the artist and Galerie Lelong & Co.

Between the Heavens and Me, 2020
Digital color film with sound
Running time 11:00
Courtesy of the artist and Galerie Lelong & Co.

Muxima, 2005
Digital color film with sound
Running time 36:00
Courtesy of the artist and Galerie Lelong & Co.
p. 62

Alfredo Jaar (Chilean, b. 1956) at the School of the Art Institute of Chicago

A Logo for America, 1987
Digital color video with sound
Running time 10:25
Courtesy of Galerie Lelong & Co.
Scenes #4

Toba Khedoori (American, b. Australia, 1964) at The David and Alfred Smart Museum of Art, The University of Chicago

Untitled (Black Fireplace), 2006
Encaustic, wax, and oil paint on paper
141 × 205 in.
Courtesy of The Broad Art Foundation
Scenes #11 and p. 63

Untitled, 2020
Oil on canvas
28 × 63 3/4 in.
Courtesy of the artist and David Zwirner
p. 61

Untitled (Seats), 1996
Oil and wax on paper
127 × 300 in.
Courtesy of the Museum of Contemporary Art, Los Angeles, purchased with funds provided by Lenore S. Greenberg and Laura-Lee Woods
Scenes #11 and p. 61

An-My Lê (American, b. 1960) at the Museum of Contemporary Photography, Columbia College Chicago

Andrew Jackson Statue, Lafayette Square, President's Park, Washington DC, from *Silent General*, 2020, Edition 1 of 5
Inkjet print
40 × 56 1/2 in.
Courtesy of the artist and Marian Goodman Gallery
Scenes #36 and p. 69

Fragment I: Sugar Cane Field, November 5, Houma, Louisiana, from *Silent General*, 2016, Edition 2 of 5
Inkjet print
39 1/2 × 56 in.
Courtesy of the artist and Marian Goodman Gallery

Fragment II: High School Students on Fourth of July Celebration, New Orleans, Louisiana, from *Silent General*, 2017, Edition 5 of 5
Pigment print
40 × 56 1/2 in.
Courtesy of the artist and Marian Goodman Gallery

Fragment II: Migrant Workers Harvesting Asparagus, Mendota, California, from *Silent General*, 2019, Edition 3 of 5
Pigment print
40 × 56 1/2 in.
Courtesy of the artist and Marian Goodman Gallery
p. 68

Fragment II: Restoration of J.M.W. Turner's Port Ruysdael, Yale Center for British Art, New Haven, Connecticut, from *Silent General*, 2018, Edition 2 of 5
Pigment print
40 × 56 1/2 in.
Courtesy of the artist and Marian Goodman Gallery
p. 55

Fragment IV: Citrus Tree, Fowler, California, from *Silent General*, 2019, Edition 5 of 5
Pigment print
40 × 56 1/2 in.
Courtesy of the artist and Marian Goodman Gallery
p. 68

Fragment VI: General Robert E. Lee and P.G.T. Beauregard Monuments, Homeland Security Storage, New Orleans, Louisiana, from *Silent General*, 2017, Edition 5 of 5
Pigment print
55 3/4 × 39 1/4 in.
Courtesy of the artist and Marian Goodman Gallery
Scenes #36 and pp. 54, 69

Fragment VII: Land Scars from the Trans-Pecos Pipeline, Marfa, Texas, from *Silent General*, 2019, Edition 2 of 5
Pigment print
40 × 56 1/2 in.

Fragment VIII: US Customs and Border Protection Officer, Presidio-Ojinaga International Bridge, Presidio, Texas, from *Silent General*, 2019, Edition 2 of 5
Pigment print
40 × 56 1/2 in.
Courtesy of the artist and Marian Goodman Gallery

Fragment VIII: Mexico Customs and Border Protection Officer, Presidio-Ojinaga International Bridge, Ojinaga, Mexico, from *Silent General*, 2019, Edition 2 of 5
Pigment print
56 7/8 × 40 3/8 in.
Courtesy of the artist and Marian Goodman Gallery

Land Scars from the Trans-Pecos Pipeline, Marfa, Texas, from *Silent General*, 2019, Edition 2 of 5
Pigment print
56 7/8 × 40 3/8 × 1 1/2 in.
Courtesy of the artist and Marian Goodman Gallery

St. John's Episcopal Church, Lafayette Square, Washington D.C., from *Silent General*, 2020, Edition 1 of 5
Inkjet print
40 × 56 1/2 in.
Courtesy of the artist and Marian Goodman Gallery

Whitfield Lovell (American, b. 1959) at the Stony Island Arts Bank

Missoura, 2001
Charcoal on wood and found objects
108 × 124 × 45 in.
Private collection, Chicago
Scenes #21

Spell no. 15 (Remedios), 2021
Conté crayon on paper with attached found object (wood disk)
66 1/2 × 47 3/4 × 4 3/4 in.
Courtesy of the artist and DC Moore Gallery
Scenes #6

Spell no. 18 (L'âme est ouverte), 2021
Conté crayon on paper with attached found object (a slice of amethyst)
66 1/2 × 47 3/4 × 5 3/4 in.
Courtesy of the artist and DC Moore Gallery
Scenes #6

Whitfield Lovell (American, b. 1959) at the South Side Community Art Center

After an Afternoon, 2008
Radios with sound
59 × 72 × 11 in.
Courtesy of the artist and DC Moore Gallery

Spell no. 12 (Black Maybe), 2021
Conté crayon on paper with attached found object (rope)
66 1/2 × 47 3/4 × 13 3/4 in.
Courtesy of the artist and DC Moore Gallery

Spell no. 13 (Esperanza), 2021
Conté crayon on paper with attached found object (white dove)
66 1/2 × 47 3/4 × 8 3/4 in.
Courtesy of the artist and DC Moore Gallery

Spell no. 14 (Assegai: Spear of My Nation), 2021
Conté crayon on paper with attached found objects (flags)
66 1/2 × 47 3/4 × 9 3/4 in.
Courtesy of the artist and DC Moore Gallery

Spell no. 16 (I Am Here Because There Is You), 2021
Conté crayon on paper with attached found object (aluminum tray)
66 1/2 × 47 3/4 × 6 1/4 in.
Courtesy of the artist and DC Moore Gallery

Spell no. 17 (Richesse Noir), 2021
Conté crayon on paper with attached found objects (wood bowl with alabaster fruit)
66 1/2 × 47 3/4 × 9 3/4 in.
Courtesy of the artist and DC Moore Gallery
Scenes #17

Spell no. 19 (A Thousand Years of You), 2021
Conté crayon on paper with attached found object (book: E. B. Reuter's *The American Race Problem*)
66 1/2 × 47 3/4 × 11 3/4 in.
Courtesy of the artist and DC Moore Gallery

Rick Lowe (American, b. 1961), at The David and Alfred Smart Museum of Art, The University of Chicago, the School of the Art Institute of Chicago, and Urban Juncture Foundation

Black Wall Street Journey, 2021
24-hour Black wealth video stream, *Black Wall Street Journey* library and journal installed alongside a collaborative poster project by artist Amanda Williams and journalist Natalie Moore
Scenes #22 and pp. 114, 142, 160, 190

Rick Lowe (American, b. 1961) at Urban Juncture Foundation

Series of posters, public murals by Dorian Sylvain, a *CHOP IT UP* conversation series about the Black economy, and a program in collaboration with the Smart Museum of Art and Chicago Housing Authority's 2021 summer teen program.
pp. 125, 126, 127, 142

Iñigo Manglano-Ovalle (American, b. Spain, 1961) at The David and Alfred Smart Museum of Art, The University of Chicago
Water Table, 41°47'36.993" N—87°36'0.726" W, from the series *Well*, 2021
Water, reclaimed ash table and benches, stainless-steel reservoir, hand pump, and glasses
Courtesy of the artist and Rhona Hoffman Gallery
Single bench on loan from Rául Niño and Molly Zolnay
Scenes #26 and p. 65

Slashed Gallons of Water, 2016, 2021
Found image, digital print on paper
28 × 22 in.
Courtesy of the artist and Rhona Hoffman Gallery
Scenes #26 and p. 65

Iñigo Manglano-Ovalle (American, b. Spain, 1961) at Sweet Water Foundation

Hydrant, 41°47'22.662" N—87°37'38.364" W, 2021
Water with steel and brass components
Exposed elements: 36 × 24 × 6 in.
Courtesy of the artist
Scenes #32 and pp. 180, 181

Kerry James Marshall (American, b. 1955) at BBF Building Brighter Futures

Untitled (Circulation), 2021
Site-specific installation of photographs (taken 1998–99) printed on gold adhesive vinyl
Dimensions variable
Courtesy of the artist
Scenes #9, #38, and pp. 140, 141

Kerry James Marshall (American, b. 1955) at the Stony Island Arts Bank

Heirlooms and Accessories, 2002
Inkjet prints on paper in wood frames with rhinestones
Three, each 51 × 46 in.
The Smart Museum of Art, Purchase, Smart Family Fund Foundation for Contemporary Art, and Paul and Miriam Kirkley Fund for Acquisitions

Julie Mehretu (American, b. Ethiopia, 1970) at The David and Alfred Smart Museum of Art, The University of Chicago

Landscape Allegories, 2004, Edition 1 of 7 APs
Suite of seven copperplate etchings, with engraving, drypoint, sugar-bite, and aquatint
Each 19 × 21 3/4 in.
Courtesy of the artist and Marian Goodman Gallery
p. 56

Amalia Mesa-Bains (American, b. 1943) at the National Museum of Mexican Art

Circle of Ancestors, 2020–21
Family photos, seven mirrored enhanced and painted chairs, ash, paper flowers, and electric candles
Chairs (each): 38 × 18 × 21 in.
From the collection of Richard L. Bains
Scenes #29

Circle of Ancestors, 2020–21
Folding book
Book (closed): 16 × 11 1/2 in.; shelf: 96 × 24 in.
From the collection of Richard L. Bains

Amalia Mesa-Bains (American, b. 1943) at Weinberg/Newton Gallery

Carlos Cortéz with César Chávez, 2021, from *Dos Mundos: Mexican Chicago* (2020–21)
Light box
24 × 36 × 1 in.
From the collection of Richard L. Bains
p. 108

Carlos Tortolero, 2021, from *Dos Mundos: Mexican Chicago* (2020–21)
Light box
24 × 36 × 1 in.
From the collection of Richard L. Bains
p. 108

Culture, 2021, from *Dos Mundos: Mexican Chicago* (2020–21)
Shadow box
30 × 40 × 6 in.
From the collection of Richard L. Bains

Juana Guzman, 2021, from *Dos Mundos: Mexican Chicago* (2020–21)
Light box
24 × 36 × 1 in.
From the collection of Richard L. Bains
p. 108

Labor, 2021, from *Dos Mundos: Mexican Chicago* (2020–21), Edition 1 of 2
Giclée print
25 3/4 × 31 7/8 in.
From the collection of Richard L. Bains
Scenes #31

Labor, 2021, from *Dos Mundos: Mexican Chicago* (2020–21)
Shadow box
30 × 40 × 6 in.
From the collection of Richard L. Bains

Leadership, 2021, from *Dos Mundos: Mexican Chicago* (2020–21), Edition 1 of 2
Giclée print
25 3/4 × 31 7/8 in.
From the collection of Richard L. Bains
Scenes #31

Mexican Chicago, 2021, from *Dos Mundos: Mexican Chicago* (2020–21)
Illustrated book
Open in accordion formation: 15 × 96 in.
From the collection of Richard L. Bains
Scenes #31 and p. 108

Military, 2021, 1 of 2, from *Dos Mundos: Mexican Chicago* (2020–21)
Giclée print
25 3/4 × 31 7/8 in.
From the collection of Richard L. Bains
Scenes #31

Religion, 2021, from *Dos Mundos: Mexican Chicago* (2020–21)
Shadow box
30 × 40 × 6 in.
From the collection of Richard L. Bains
Scenes #31

Sandra Cisneros, 2021, from *Dos Mundos: Mexican Chicago* (2020–21)
Light box
24 × 36 × 1 in.
From the collection of Richard L. Bains
p. 108

Sports, 2021, from *Dos Mundos: Mexican Chicago* (2020–21), Edition 1 of 2
Giclée print
25 3/4 × 31 7/8 in.
From the collection of Richard L. Bains
Scenes #31

Trevor Paglen (American, b. 1974) at the Stony Island Arts Bank

They Took the Faces from the Accused and the Dead..., 2019, Edition 3 of 5
Set of 14 pigment prints
Each 11 1/2 × 13 1/2 in.
Courtesy of the artist, Altman Siegel, San Francisco and Pace Gallery
p. 93

Fazal Sheikh (American, b. 1965) at The David and Alfred Smart Museum of Art, The University of Chicago

Methane gas emissions, San Juan County, Utah, 2017–21
FLIR infrared camera video
Running time 10:38
Courtesy of the artist

In Place (Four Corners region, Utah, Arizona, New Mexico, and Colorado), 2017–21
Installation: 66 archival pigment prints printed on Innova Natural Cotton Rag 315 gm, an offering (basket with landscape fragments) from Jonah Yellowman, and seismological sound recordings of butte readings by Jeff Moore
Each print 43 11/16 × 31 3/8 in.
Courtesy of the artist
Scenes #5 and p. 60

Mexican Hat Uranium Mill Tailings Repository, Mexican Hat, Utah, 2018
Disposal cell containing 1.3 million tons of toxic waste and uranium tailings, mill, buildings, and a schoolhouse constructed from contaminated material
Archival pigment print
38 × 52 1/2 in.
Courtesy of the artist

Fazal Sheikh (American, b. 1965) at Hyde Park Art Center

Al-'Araqib, from *The Conflict Shoreline* (2010–15), printed 2021
Archival pigment print
30 3/16 × 45 1/4 in.
Courtesy of Yale University Art Gallery, purchased with a gift from Jane P. Watkins, M.P.H. 1979

Al-'Araqib, from *The Conflict Shoreline* (2010–15)
Videos of the demolitions, produced by the villagers of Al-'Araqib and by members of its extended community
Running time 14:05
Courtesy of the artist

Desert Bloom, 2011
48 archival pigment prints
Each 21 7/16 × 29 1/4 in.
Courtesy of Yale University Art Gallery, purchased with a gift from Jane P. Watkins, M.P.H. 1979
p. 184

Nuri Al-Uqbi, Al-'Araqib, from *The Conflict Shoreline* (2010–15), 2011, printed 2021
Archival pigment print
23 5/8 × 21 5/8 in.
Courtesy of the artist

Sheikh Sayach, Al-'Araqib, from *The Conflict Shoreline* (2010–15), 2011, printed 2021
Archival pigment print
23 5/8 × 21 5/8 in.
Courtesy of Yale University Art Gallery, purchased with a gift from Jane P. Watkins, M.P.H. 1979

Scroll from *The Conflict Shoreline*, 2016
Archival pigment print

23 3/8 × 117 1/8 in.
Courtesy of the artist

Scroll from *The Conflict Shoreline*, 2016
Archival pigment print
23 1/4 × 117 1/8 in.
Courtesy of the artist

Shahzia Sikander (Pakistani American, b. 1969) at the Museum of Contemporary Photography, Columbia College Chicago

Flared, 2020
Ink and gouache on paper
98 × 51 in.
Courtesy of the artist and Sean Kelly, New York
Scenes #10 and pp. 69, 70

In Flight 1–2, 2017
Ink and gouache on paper
Two prints, each 14 × 11 in.
Courtesy of the artist and Sean Kelly, New York

Kinship, 2019–20
Ink and gouache on paper
60 × 96 in.
The Alex & Patricia Farman-Farmaian Collection, New York
p. 68

Of Masks and Bull 1–2, 2017
Ink and gouache on paper
Two prints, each 14 × 11 in.
Courtesy of the artist and Sean Kelly, New York

Oil and Poppies, 2019–20
Ink and gouache on paper
98 × 51 in.
Courtesy of the artist and Sean Kelly, New York
Scenes #10 and pp. 69, 70

Promiscuous Intimacies, 2020
Patinated bronze
42 × 24 × 18 in.
Courtesy of the artist and Sean Kelly, New York
Scenes #10 and p. 69

Rapture, 2017
Ink and gouache on prepared paper
15 × 11 1/2 in.
Courtesy of the artist and Sean Kelly, New York

Reckoning, 2020
HD video animation with sound; music by Du Yun and animation by Patrick O'Rourke
Running time 4:16
Courtesy of the artist and Sean Kelly, New York

Kara Walker (American, b. 1969) at the DuSable Black History Museum and Education Center
Presenting Negro Scenes Drawn Upon My Passage Through the South and Reconfigured for the Benefit of Enlightened Audiences Wherever Such May Be Found, By Myself, Missus K.E.B. Walker, Colored, 1997
Paper
Installation size variable
Collection Museum of Contemporary Art Chicago, gift of Susan and Lewis Manilow, 1999
Scenes #7, #23, and pp. 90, 91, 92

Kara Walker (American, b. 1969) at the Stony Island Arts Bank

Freedom: A Fable, 1997, for the *Peter Norton Christmas Project*
Pop-up silhouette book
9 5/16 × 8 5/16 in.
Gift of the Peter Norton Family
Scenes #21

Carrie Mae Weems (American, b. 1953) at the Reva and David Logan Center for the Arts, The University of Chicago

A Land of Broken Dreams, 2021
Photography, video, news media sampling, and ephemera
Courtesy of the artist
Scenes #27, #37, and pp. 97, 158

Carrie Mae Weems (American, b. 1953) at the Stony Island Arts Bank

Untitled (Black Love), 1992
Gelatin silver prints
Three, each 28 1/2 × 28 1/2 in.
Gift of the Estate of Lester and Betty Guttman

Deborah Willis (American, b. 1948) at the Stony Island Arts Bank

The Clothesline 1: Women's work never praised never done (Votes for Women with beauty shop and Adella Hunt Logan), 2020
Archival print on Epson Ultra Premium Luster
16 × 24 in.
Courtesy of the artist and Kalia Brooks Studio
Scenes #15 and p. 94

The Clothesline 2: Women's work never praised never done (Angelina Weld Grimke and Ida B. Wells), 2020
Archival print on Epson Ultra Premium Luster
16 × 24 in.
Courtesy of the artist and Kalia Brooks Studio
p. 94

The Clothesline 3: Women's work never praised never done (portraits of Nannie Helen Burroughs, Harriet Forten Purvis), 2020
Archival print on Epson Ultra Premium Luster
16 × 24 in.
Courtesy of the artist and Kalia Brooks Studio
p. 94

The Clothesline 4: Women's work never praised never done (Frances Ellen Watkins Harper, the dress, Mary Church Terrell), 2020
Archival print on Epson Ultra Premium Luster
16 × 24 in.
Courtesy of the artist and Kalia Brooks Studio
p. 94

The Clothesline 5: Women's work never praised never done (Nannie Helen Burroughs and first vote photo by Ernest Withers), 2020
Archival print on Epson Ultra Premium Luster
16 × 24 in.
Courtesy of the artist and Kalia Brooks Studio
p. 94

Fred Wilson (American, b. 1954) at the Stony Island Arts Bank

Act V. Scene II—Exeunt Omnes, 2014, Edition 2 of 6
Murano glass and wood
87 × 128 × 8 3/8 in.
Courtesy of the artist and Pace Gallery
Scenes #6 and p. 158

Xu Bing (Chinese, b. 1955) at The David and Alfred Smart Museum of Art, The University of Chicago

Forest Project: Children's Drawings, 2013
35 mixed-media drawings
Each 12 13/16 × 16 1/4 in.
Courtesy of the artist
Scenes #25 and p. 61

Forest Project: The Blue and Green Wonderland, 2014
Nepalese paper
38 9/16 × 292 15/16 in.
Courtesy of the artist
Scenes #25

ARTISTS IN THE EXHIBITION

These artist biographies are drawn from texts produced for the *Toward Common Cause* website by Laura Steward and University of Chicago graduate students: Ella Anderson, Katherine Beavis, Joyce Chung, Jad Dahshan, Benjamin Diego, Alexandra Drexelius, Nathan Cairn Goldthwaite, Jialu Guo, Jennifer Harris, Katerina Korola, Simone Levine, Zahra Nasser, Marie-Capucine Pineau-Valencienne, Zsofi Valyi-Nagy, and Christine Zappella.

Njideka Akunyili Crosby's pictures present viewers with familiar scenes of everyday life, colored by private moments of her own and representations of her diasporic identity. Born in the Nigerian city of Enugu, she moved to Lagos at age thirteen and immigrated to the United States at sixteen. Her strikingly layered images feature photocopied transfers of family photographs, Nigerian newspapers and magazines, acrylic paint, charcoal, and colored pencil.

While distinctly complex, Akunyili Crosby's human subjects typically engage in quiet activities; some sit pensively at the dinner table, while others tenderly caress one another, as in intimate depictions of the artist and her husband. Her works open windows—both literal and figurative—to disparate spaces, worlds, and time periods, drawing a formal parallel to the complexities of straddling two complicated places, a native home and an adopted home, while resisting stultifying labels. Njideka Akunyili Crosby was named a MacArthur Fellow in 2017 as a Painter.

The career of Ida Applebroog, a self-proclaimed "image scavenger" and prolific drawer, spanned five decades and numerous media, from artist's books to sculpture to puppets to video and installation. Her work is mostly figurative, with characters that are cartoonish, androgynous, and often grotesque. Images interplay with text, sometimes boldly stenciled, sometimes scrawled in cursive.

For Applebroog, remaking did not mean rehashing. It was an opportunity not only to resuscitate old figures but to update them, to give them voices that speak to new audiences, including who she herself had become. As art historian Jo Applin has argued, by remaking her images, Appelbroog refused to "let them settle as evidence of a feminism or self-past." Instead, her remade drawings present "evidence of practice, of a practicing body." Weaving together the past and the present, she collapsed the distinction between the two. Ida Applebroog was named a MacArthur Fellow in 1998 as a Painter.

For Dawoud Bey, portraiture is a process through which artist and subject meet in the middle. Each portrait begins with Bey gaining consent from someone to serve as his sitter. From there, Bey takes the time to become familiar with them by engaging in conversation and building trust, so that his camera can do more than record an artificial impression. He then works to render the subtleties of his sitter's gestures, posture, and expression, all within the rectangular space of a photograph.

Over several decades, Bey has photographed the youth of Chicago's South Side. As with his adult subjects, he works dialogically with his young sitters, whether photographing them in the studio, on the sidewalk, or in the classroom. Deepening these relationships, the artist led community workshops in which he distributed cameras to young people and taught them both basic photography skills and how to direct a critical lens on mass media. Dawoud Bey was named a MacArthur Fellow in 2017 as a Photographer and Educator.

Mark Bradford is known as an abstract painter, though paint plays a minor role in his works. Instead, Bradford builds up layers of paper and other materials that he has collected from everyday life, creating thick surfaces that he then burrows into, sanding sections out, or blasting them off with a pressure washer.

Bradford's earliest works were made of end papers from his mother's beauty salon in South Central Los Angeles. The social meaning of these papers, which are essential to the work of a hairdresser, connects two worlds, those of the salon and avant-garde painting. Similarly, other works use masses of merchant posters Bradford finds pasted up around his neighborhood. These signs, advertising payday lenders, bail bondsmen, and the purchase of "ugly houses," carry significations of a neighborhood in crisis and appeals for justice into his densely constructed pieces. Mark Bradford was named a MacArthur Fellow in 2009 as a Mixed Media Artist.

It is difficult to find an overriding theme or medium that binds Mel Chin's many projects over his forty-year career. Chin describes this evolutionary quality as a "catalytic concept" that "allows something to form after you're no longer there." He credits the conceptual art of the 1960s and '70s with privileging the idea of a work over its form, and humorously describes himself as a "recovering conceptual artist." Chin is viewed as a pioneer of socially engaged art confronting serious issues.

Chin's projects are lively entities, in constant states of transformation, that challenge traditional museum practice. "Each project," he writes, "is based on an arc that eventually must lead to transformation. . . . Museums that show this work can't just show the evidence; they have to join the action." Chin's *Chicago Fundred Project: A Bill for IL* advocates for regulation of lead contamination, which has generated a public health crisis in cities from New Orleans to Flint to Chicago. Mel Chin was named a MacArthur Fellow in 2019 as an Artist.

Nicole Eisenman's work has expanded the critical and expressive capacity of the Western figurative tradition through works that foreground the desires and anxieties of our culture at large. Her paintings, drawings, prints, and, more recently, monumental sculptures manage to balance her specific individuality with universal concerns like loneliness, gluttony, power, sexual desire, and bloodlust.

Eisenman is a self-described storyteller, and allegory and pastiche have long been critical elements of her practice. In *The Triumph of Poverty*, a bedraggled crew of people trudge across the surface of the painting, accompanied by a man in a top hat and tuxedo who is literally ass-backward. A second group of people, lifted directly from Pieter Bruegel's 1568 painting *The Blind Leading the Blind*, parallels their progress in miniature along the bottom edge. Nicole Eisenman was named a MacArthur Fellow in 2015 as a Painter.

Wendy Ewald is an artist defined by collaboration. Over a fifty-year career, she has distributed cameras to children and adults, teaching photography skills and asking them to photograph their lives—the quotidian and extraordinary. There is a documentary quality to the work that might be classified as anthropological, were it not for the fact that Ewald is more interested in the perspective of those being studied than those doing the studying. Drawn to places of conflict, she shifts the focus from events to people, from her early work in Appalachia to South Africa, Mexico, England, Israel, and the West Bank.

In series like those presented in *Toward Common Cause*, Ewald delves into childhood play and fantasies. Refocusing the lens of "art" through children's eyes allows the truth to become clearer, avoiding news-media tropes of regions where life is difficult. Wendy Ewald was named a MacArthur Fellow in 1992 as a Photographer.

LaToya Ruby Frazier is known for her collaborative storytelling with the people who appear in her photographs, videos, and texts. Frazier grew up in the postindustrial wreckage of America, in Braddock, Pennsylvania. The work that first brought her acclaim, *The Notion of Family*, features Frazier herself, three generations of Frazier women, and her hometown. Braddock, a majority-Black city, is near ruin as a result of official negligence, deindustrialization, and environmental degradation.

Frazier's work has expanded beyond the bounds of her hometown to other working-class cities, and continues to build on the conceptual legacy of documentary photographers. It directly calls out the racism that drives a wealth of ills, including healthcare inequality, poverty, and environmental toxicity. Often her photographs are presented with texts written in the words of the subject depicted, sometimes with health statistics or other damning records. LaToya Ruby Frazier was named a MacArthur Fellow in 2015 as a Photographer and Video Artist.

Jeffrey Gibson, an artist of Choctaw and Cherokee descent, incorporates elements of Native American traditions with a modernist visual vocabulary. His mixed-media approach draws upon his early and extensive studies in painting. Now expanded, his practice encompasses sculpture and installation on a monumental scale. Wall-mounted works, bolstered by material supports spanning canvas, panels, and quilts, contain layers of painted text and vivid ornament and beadwork; the patterns recall traditional handiwork as well as mass-produced motifs used in wallpapers and textiles.

Gibson challenges authorship by lifting text from fiction, theory, and song lyrics and inserting them into new contexts. Phrases such as "ALL I'M ASKIN' IS FOR A LITTLE RESPECT" and "I LOVE IT WHEN YOU CALL ME NAMES" are painted in barely legible graphic fonts over dense geometric backgrounds. The artist's use of abstraction and obfuscation mirrors the severance of text from its source. Emphasizing the displacement of text, he articulates a violent mechanism by which cultural objects can be coopted and stolen by people and systems in power. Jeffrey Gibson was named a MacArthur Fellow in 2019 as a Visual Artist.

Guillermo Gómez-Peña's experimental "ethno-techno art" meditates on the hybrid identities that form within and move across borderlands such as that between the US and Mexico. The riveting, collaborative performances he orchestrates can take the form of anything between a Spanglish spoken-word recital and a guerrilla television act. Everything from cultural fetish items and racist memorabilia to robotic arms and myriad costumes are featured in the artist's anticolonial critique of US empire and its racial politics.

In 1993, the artist founded the transdisciplinary performance art troupe La Pocha Nostra with Roberto Sifuentes and Nola Mariano. With an ever-fluid cast of members hailing from different generations, ethnic backgrounds, and gender complexities, the group works across photography, video, installation, and performance to tear down the walls between the practice and theory of art, as well as between artist and spectator. Guillermo Gómez-Peña was named a MacArthur Fellow in 1991 as a Writer and Interdisciplinary Artist.

David Hammons's conceptual practice conjures the act of recycling. There is no excess in his work. To the contrary, his materials—grease, dung, hair, bones, and empty bottles—already account for the excesses of human activity. The resulting visual permutations are marked by their bareness, their thrift, and their simplicity. Indisposed to adopt any singular style, his performances, sculptures, installations, and ephemeral outdoor interventions never feel heavy-handed.

Hammons moved to Los Angeles in 1963 to study art. While he would later move to New York City, the outsider attitude of the L.A. art scene would continue to inform his career. In the politicized context that was marked by the race riots and demonstrations of the '60s, Hammons work was often labeled as protest art. Yet this characterization fails to capture the heterogeneity of his offensive strategies, which are self-effacing at every turn. David Hammons was named a MacArthur Fellow in 1991 as a Sculptor and Installation Artist.

Since 1970, Gary Hill has evolved into a cross-disciplinary artist working from a *core principle*. Often with strong conceptual aspects, the artist has maintained high variability and unpredictability over five decades. Proceeding with one or more principles at a time (e.g., the *physicality* of the medium and of languaging and imaging; *liminality* or the intense space between contraries and extremes of appearance), he constructs works that embody multiple planes simultaneously—physical, personal, ontological, social, political—without reification of any one of them. Result: a singular event of reflexive speaking that marries mind and machine beyond any notion of reference as such—no stable signifier or signified, yet intense engagement at personal, emotional, and intellectual levels. Later works in computer animation—e.g., *Liminal Objects* (1995–), *Frustrum* (2006), *Isolation Tank* (2010–11)—challenge one's sense of "object" and mind-body boundaries and the very basis of our "reality." Major projective installations—*Tall Ships* (1992), *HanD HearD* (1995–96), *Viewer* (1996), *Wall Piece* (2000), *Up Against Down* (2008), *None of the Above* (2022)—raise these issues of physicality, objectivity, polyvalent signification, and language itself to a further human dimension—a principle of torsional engagement both within one's own mind and body and up against the surface and face of the other. Gary Hill was named a MacArthur Fellow in 1998.

Alfredo Jaar is a witness to unspeakable tragedies. He creates contexts that compel people to look at things they would rather look away from—genocide, mass starvation, industrial brutality—and to feel empathy, rather than shock or revulsion. In his best-known body of work, *The Rwanda Project, 1994–2000*, Jaar demanded that the Western world pay attention to the Rwandan genocide and its aftermath. In 1994, he traveled to Rwanda and neighboring countries to witness the genocide and took thousands of photographs that he deemed too horrific to exhibit. Instead, he sought a balance between creating a spectacle and presenting information, between ethics and aesthetics.

Jaar's 1997 work *The Silence of Nduwayezu* consists of a pile of one million slides that, viewed through a magnifying glass, all feature a tightly cropped image of the eyes of one boy. This five-year-old Tutsi child, whom Jaar met at a refugee camp, had witnessed the brutal murder of his parents and was so traumatized he had not spoken for weeks. Jaar captured the enormity of the tragedy in one person's experience, magnified a million times. Alfredo Jaar was named a MacArthur Fellow in 2000 as a Photographer.

Toba Khedoori became known in the 1990s for the meticulous draftsmanship of her large-scale paintings on waxed paper, which feature perspectival renderings of objects and architectural fragments hovering in vast expanses of blank space. The spare world of Khedoori's paintings is populated by familiar objects that structure our reality. Doors, hallways, windows, rows of seats, a chain-link fence—her repertoire evinces a particular affinity for elements of the built environment that mediate both access and exclusion.

Treated with Khedoori's singular combination of intricate detail and resolute abstraction, these objects appear shorn of context and devoid of human figures, at once familiar and anonymous, reticent and inviting. But if human presence has been evacuated from the space of representation, it paradoxically reemerges on its surface. Subtly luminous, the waxed paper reveals a host of small marks—dust, stains, and other bits of debris, traces of brushstrokes—a prompt to consider the artist at work. Toba Khedoori was named a MacArthur Fellow in 2002 as a Painter.

An-My Lê, who left Vietnam with her family in 1975, began making landscape photography in 1994 after returning to the country for the first time. "I wanted to show Vietnam in a way I had not seen it shown before," she reflected, "not devastated, not victimized, not romanticized. I felt I could do that best through my exploration of the landscape." In Lê's most well-known series, *Small Wars*, she worked with Vietnam War reenactors in the forests of North Carolina and Virginia. In photographing a reconstruction of war rather than war itself, she gave the genre a new twist—pointing deliberately to the fact that a photograph is always a mediation of reality and mining this slipperiness as a space of possibility.

Since 2015, Lê has used her large-format camera to cast a critical eye on the current political landscape of the American South, from the legacy of the Civil War and Confederate monuments to the US-Mexico border and its terrain and inhabitants. An-My Lê was named a MacArthur Fellow in 2012 as a Photographer.

Whitfield Lovell's work challenges us to remember a past obscured by history. The Black men and women in his drawings, rendered from antique photographs selected from family albums and flea market bins, are gone and largely forgotten. But Lovell conjures their memory into the present, reproducing their portraits on walls, reclaimed wood panels, or yellowed paper in the spectral monochrome of Conté crayon.

Lovell's art responds to the loss of personal history. In his recent *Kin* series, he imagines his anonymous subjects as forgotten ancestors. In these and other works, the artist creates a space for himself—in history as part of an imagined family, in the archive as a collector of vernacular photographs and untold stories, and in art history as the history painter of a systematically forgotten past. Whitfield Lovell was named a MacArthur Fellow in 2007 as a Painter and Installation Artist.

Rick Lowe proposes solutions to real-world problems in ways that draw attention to the problems he is trying to solve. His works function like a band-aid—simultaneously helping to heal wounds while drawing attention to them, working practically and symbolically. His best-known work is Project Row Houses, which began in 1993 in Houston's Third Ward neighborhood with twenty-two derelict "shotgun" houses and now encompasses five city blocks. Its mission: not only to preserve these houses, whose architectural style is associated with Black neighborhoods in the South, but to create new social structures to lift up the creative potential of local people.

Social sculpture for Lowe means approaching society itself as a work of art, endeavoring to mold society as a sculptor might mold clay. For this reason, he foregrounds the participation of others in all his projects, designing them as platforms to amplify the creativity of people who have been systematically undermined in their communities. He is currently a professor of interdisciplinary practice at the University of Houston. Rick Lowe was named a MacArthur Fellow in 2014 as a Public Artist.

Iñigo Manglano-Ovalle's works "speak but don't tell." They have an underlying politics, but never reveal his position. Unlike many of the artists included in *Toward Common Cause*, he does not issue direct calls to action. Instead, his works investigate and reveal the conceptual scaffolding, be it ideological, aesthetic, or philosophical, that underpins our individual experiences of the world. His use of all sorts of media—sound, sculpture, performance, video, and more—defies categorization. What the projects all share, despite their great variety of forms, is a sustained interest in how complex natural and human-made systems constantly reshape the modern world.

For more than two decades, Manglano-Ovalle has used meteorological and geological phenomena as metaphors for addressing social, cultural, and political climates. Climate itself, and specifically water in all its forms—as vapor in clouds, solid in icebergs, and even as liquid in a simple glass—often is the substance (material) by which he engages the complexities of migration economies, resource access, and social justice. Iñigo Manglano-Ovalle was named a MacArthur Fellow in 2001.

Born in Birmingham, Alabama, Kerry James Marshall absorbed history from a young age. The civil rights era defined his childhood; after moving with his family to Los Angeles, he witnessed the Watts riots at just nine years old. It was early on, too, that Marshall knew he wanted to be an artist. He read widely about art history, educating himself on European painters, such as Goya and Ingres, and the American giants of midcentury abstraction. Though Marshall wanted to make work on the same level as these white male artists, he did not want to adapt their ways.

In the 1980s, Marshall began to paint figures that were—quite literally—as black as night. He recalled moments of Black history, from the Dutch colonization of South Africa to Black athletes' leather-gloved salute during the 1968 Summer Olympics. He lifted settings from canonical paintings—Turner's slave ship, Impressionist picnic spots. Converging in Marshall's canvases, these symbols create tension between each other and the two-dimensional plane they cohabitate. Kerry James Marshall was named a MacArthur Fellow in 1997 as a Painter.

Born in Addis Ababa, Ethiopia, Julie Mehretu is a world-renowned painter who lives and works in New York City. Her practice in painting, drawing, and printmaking engages us in a dynamic visual articulation of contemporary experience, a depiction of social behavior and the psychogeography of space, by exploring palimpsests of history, from geological time to a modern-day phenomenology of the social.

Mehretu's work is informed by a multitude of sources, including politics, literature, and music. Her most recent paintings have incorporated images from broadcast media that depict conflict, injustice, and social unrest. These graphic images act as intellectual and compositional points of departure; ultimately occluded on the canvas, they remain as phantom presences in her highly abstracted, gestural works. Mehretu's practice asserts the role of art to provoke thought and reflection, and to express the contemporary condition of the individual and society. Julie Mehretu was named a MacArthur Fellow in 2005 as a Painter.

The multimedia installations of Amalia Mesa-Bains meld art, science, and history to tell intricate stories. Building from her own Mexican heritage, her work contemplates the meanings of multiculturalism as well as demographic shifts in the United States. Mesa-Bains, who holds a PhD in clinical psychology, says her clinical work has pushed her to investigate the psychological effects of colonial artifacts, including objects of scientific racism and "cabinets of curiosities" such as those commonly showcased at World's Fairs.

Mesa-Bains has become known for her site-specific installations and ofrendas, temporary altars constructed for the Day of the Dead. When invited to show her work in a museum, she often utilizes objects in the permanent collection to construct a specific narrative, separating them from their institutionalized meanings. Her installations explore colonial histories and femininity within the Mexican community, augmenting stories her mother and grandmother told. She is the co-author (with bell hooks) of *Homegrown: Culturally Engaged Criticism*. Amalia Mesa-Bains was named a MacArthur Fellow in 1992 as an Artist and Cultural Critic.

In December 2018, artist Trevor Paglen launched a small satellite into space with the aim of deploying a diamond-shaped balloon that would orbit the Earth. The highly reflective inflatable sculpture would appear in the night sky to the human eye as a bright artificial star. Due to a government shutdown, the artwork was never deployed, but Paglen's research-driven practice reveals much more than the perils of bureaucracy. Despite the failure to fully launch, *Orbital Reflector*, Paglen's first space-art endeavor, well describes his enduring insights around the power of a simple change in perspective. Drawing upon formal study of geography in graduate school, Paglen is well versed in looking at the natural world. Photography remains a primary tool to decipher and unearth relationships between technology and the environment. Working in the tradition of landscape portraiture, his photographs often illuminate the barely visible unnatural networks and systems that exist just beneath the surface: behind a mountain is a military base, below the seabed is a fiber-optic cable, and between a star and the edge of a cloud is a classified satellite. Trevor Paglen was named a MacArthur Fellow in 2017 as an Artist and Geographer.

Fazal Sheikh seeks to restore face, voice, and agency to the world's displaced peoples. His work is often visually stunning, but beneath its aesthetic qualities lies a deeper purpose of aiding refugees around the world in their ongoing struggle to secure the basic needs of human sustenance.

Sheikh primarily works through the medium of photography, which lends itself to the realism that he needs to communicate narratives of the displaced. His photographs are often portraits that humanize their subjects, giving names and faces to refugee groups that sometimes number in the millions. Sheikh's recent work features "portraiture" of natural and human-altered landscapes. These landscapes can be pockmarked by both forces of nature and human hands, their surfaces tensile enough to record political, cultural, and personal history and yet fluid enough, alive enough, to wash these histories away with time, healing, adaptation, and change. Fazal Sheikh was named a MacArthur Fellow in 2005 as a Photographer.

Walk into the South Asian galleries at a Western museum or leaf through a survey book on Persian art—you will find artworks isolated against white gallery walls, images cropped from pages aged hundreds of years, sculptures extracted from temples and set against jet-black voids. For Pakistani American artist Shahzia Sikander, seeing centuries-old artworks ripped from their original contexts and elevated to artificial pristineness opens the questions of "What is tradition?" and "Who gets to decide what is traditional?"

Invoking historic visual languages and spanning media as disparate as mosaic and digital animation, Sikander's work contemplates these questions in a distinctively contemporary artistic practice. In her miniature paintings, figures cast off their frozen poses and flat profile views, and are animated with emotions like despair and desire. They take on narratives such as ancient wars, colonialism's aftermath, and the rise of transnational corporations. Shahzia Sikander was named a MacArthur Fellow in 2006 as a Painter.

Kara Walker works with shadows. Black silhouettes depicting antebellum America pop against a never-ending white. But there is something unnerving about these scenes, and a second glance will reveal the figures are staged in violent acts. Walker's work treads the line between history and myth. With her distinct style, she transforms what we thought was familiar into uniquely uncanny shapes.

Walker has dedicated her career to exploring themes of race, gender, and violence in society in a wide array of artistic media. She is not bound by material. Working across the spectrum, she has used paper, sculpture, painting, and installation. Amid these changing forms one thing becomes clear: Walker's true medium is history. Whether through paper, allegorical sculpture, or musically accompanied installation, her work pulls from styles and stories ingrained in our cultural memory. In harnessing history, she casts shadows on our present, her work confronting viewers with the silhouette of our past. Kara Walker was named a MacArthur Fellow in 1997 as an Installation Artist.

Throughout her career, Carrie Mae Weems has created art that explodes damaging stereotypes and belief systems that have preserved the class, race, and gender status quo. She employs a variety of media, including photography, video, sound, text, and textiles, which she often arranges in site-specific installations such as *Heave*. Produced in response to the unleashing of white supremacist rhetoric and actions in the wake of Trump's election in 2016, *Heave* suggests that dismantling "the changing same" (the artist's words), in which oppressed people remain oppressed, requires collective action and solidarity.

Weems's practice embraces activism within and outside the art world. She has organized public art projects and convened critical discussions on the politics of cultural institutions. Her voice has opened pathways to multicultural inclusion, challenging curatorial discourse and practice, and her art has reinvigorated narrative forms such as social documentary and oral history. Carrie Mae Weems was named a MacArthur Fellow in 2013 as a Photographer and Video Artist.

As a scholar, archivist, author, curator, and artist, Deborah Willis has discovered, researched, and shared the work of thousands of Black photographers throughout the United States from the 1840s to the present. Her work as a scholar has made visible the lives of ordinary Black Americans that were absent or obscured from the record, and her work as a photographer has expanded this practice. An undergraduate paper became the foundation for her first book, *Black Photographers 1840 to 1940: An Illustrated Bio-Bibliography* (1985), followed by *Black Photographers Bear Witness: 100 Years of Social Protest* (1989).

Willis makes photographs that explore the same themes she investigates in her scholarship, but with a particular emphasis on femininity, beauty, and love. Her ongoing project *Went Looking for Beauty: Refashioning Self* includes both intimate images of garments from her friends' closets and "Street Views," in which she documents gloriously dressed people on the street, often in Harlem. Deborah Willis was named a MacArthur Fellow in 2000 as a Historian of Photography and a Photographer.

Fred Wilson is a conceptual artist primarily working in installation and sculpture. Central to his practice is the representation of race within the context of colonization, slavery, and abolition through the use of satire and irony. His exploration into museum collections and the institutional language of display has led him to question the biases and limitations of interpretation of artworks. By reframing objects and cultural symbols, Wilson not only challenges the relationship between museums and their collections, but also exposes the socially constructed nature of display itself.

In his groundbreaking exhibition *Mining the Museum*, held at the Maryland Historical Society in 1992, Wilson excavated objects forgotten or long banished from view in the museum's archive and presented them with his own models of categorization and visual language such as new wall labels, sounds, lighting, and nontraditional pairings of objects. For instance, a silver tea set was paired with slave shackles in a vitrine. The installation demonstrated that the prosperity signaled by the one could not have been attained without the other. Fred Wilson was named a MacArthur Fellow in 1999 as an Installation Artist.

Xu Bing, among the most prominent Chinese artists on the global stage, finds shared meaning across traditional art forms. Expanding the parameters of contemporary Chinese art while centering shared human values, Xu invites people from every background to the same platform for reflection and discussion.

Forest Project is based in a social program that moves funds from developed countries to Kenya for replanting forests. The artist teaches Kenyan children to draw, and their drawings are sold on the internet; in other words, painted trees on paper will be transformed into real trees planted in the fields of Kenya. Like many of Xu's works, *Forest Project* is an experiment involving art, education, and capital to link industrialized human society with the natural environment. He uses the internet to connect different spheres, then lets the resources flow between them. Xu values the notion of common property, long undermined, and this social consciousness, together with the profound visual texture of his works, ground his inclusive aesthetics. Xu Bing was named a MacArthur Fellow in 1999 as a Printmaker and Calligrapher.

ARTISTS CONSIDER THE MUSEUM OF THE FUTURE

We invited a few artists who participated in *Toward Common Cause* to share their thoughts in response to Guillermo Gómez-Peña's "Open Letter to the Museums of the Future" (p. 34), specifically about what such a proposal might entail. The responses that follow are deeply abstract, underscoring the shared recognition of the challenge involved in envisioning a museum of the future. Perhaps this suggests that a literal approach may not be the immediate next step on the long journey ahead that institutions and art professionals must navigate.

Iñigo Manglano-Ovalle

An attempt to say something that actually
    holds water:

To point out the obvious—the already known
That which is in our bodies
    which we embody and imbibe
That which is below and above us
    below and above the ground
That surrounds us and in us
That fills and occupies every cell
    of every living thing and being
That holds up what we call structure
    skin and flesh
Without which collapse is certain
    for beyond thirst is desiccation
    death by want or absence
Today's drought is tomorrow's flood
    in it we sink or swim
For a fleeting moment we hold it
It is ours before it passes through us
    to replenish a common reservoir
    to be shared or withheld

Reminder to self:
    To make a cooper's bucket you must first cut
    down a tree.

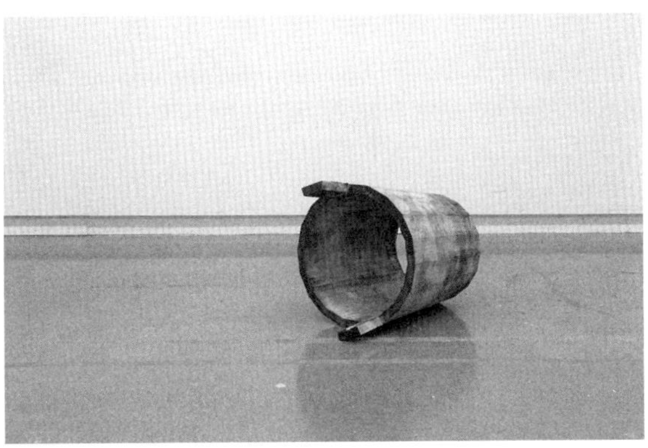

A Question of Worlds
Mel Chin

A world rich and corpulent, subject to spoilage and rot, emerges from the gutter. Normally hidden, it establishes control by dishing out small portions of fat and protein to nurture the illusion of freedom or choice, but actually it's fueling division or stasis. A floaty inconsequential moon remains in its gravity. A renegade particle breaks off from this moon and enters the mediated climate of a polarized world. Possibilities of what this infection could spawn are loosely depicted. Could it be a new moon of chaos, one neutered and ineffective, or one with an activated viable atmosphere, motivated to spit out its moxie to wrestle once more in the desperate climate of the real world?

The artist's contribution continues with the drawing on the following spread.

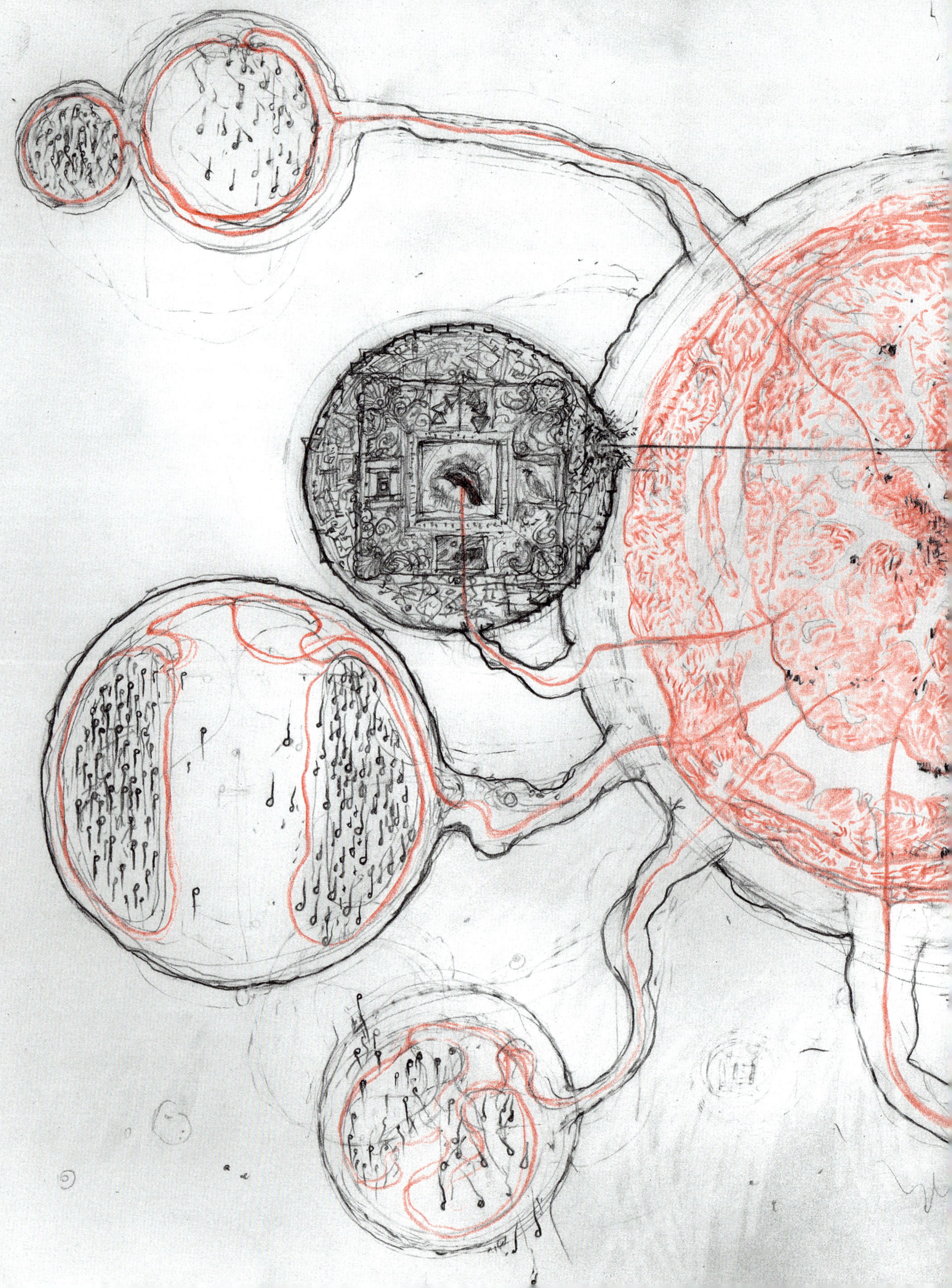

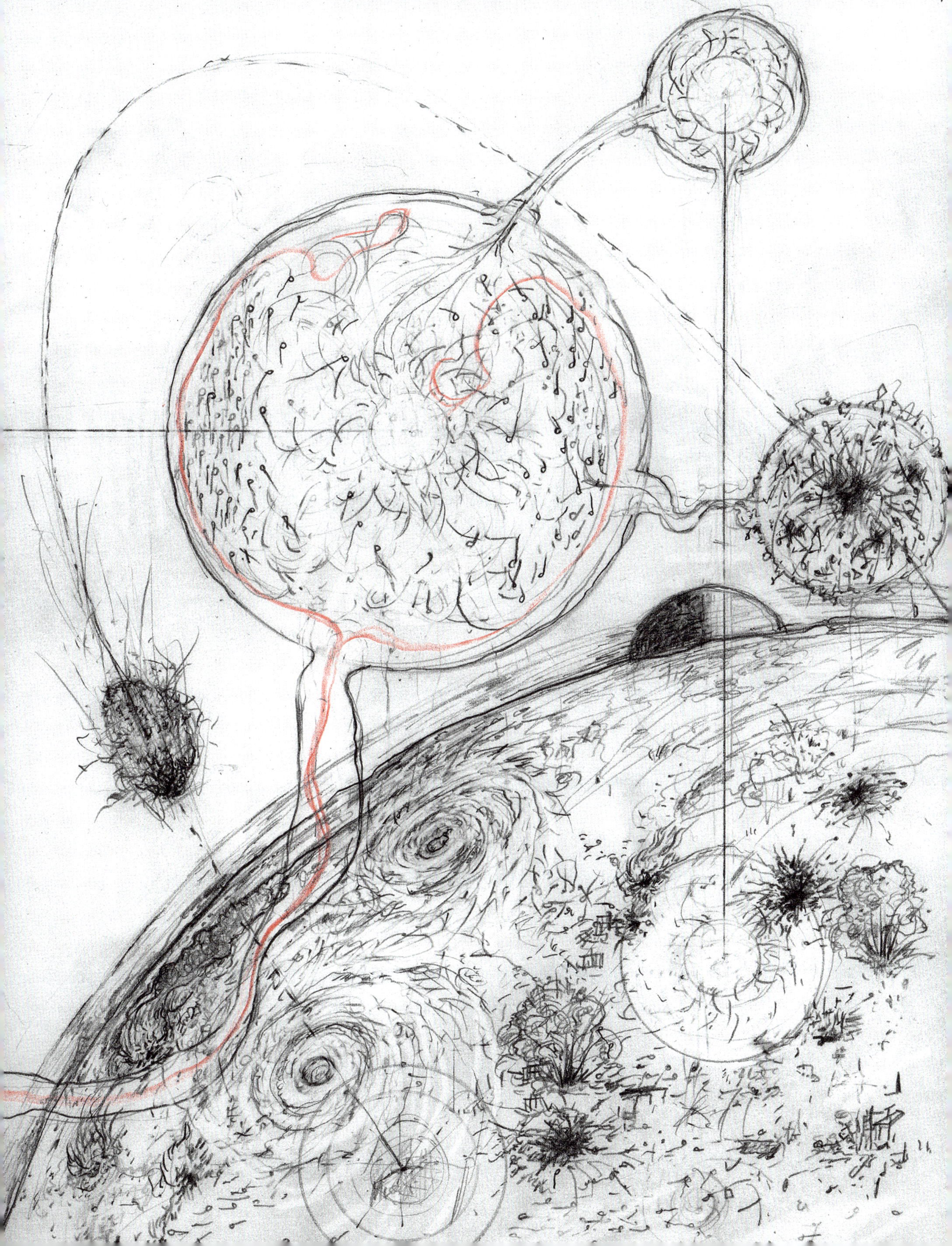

EXHIBITION DOCUMENTATION: CHICAGO DEMOGRAPHICS AND CULTURAL OFFERINGS

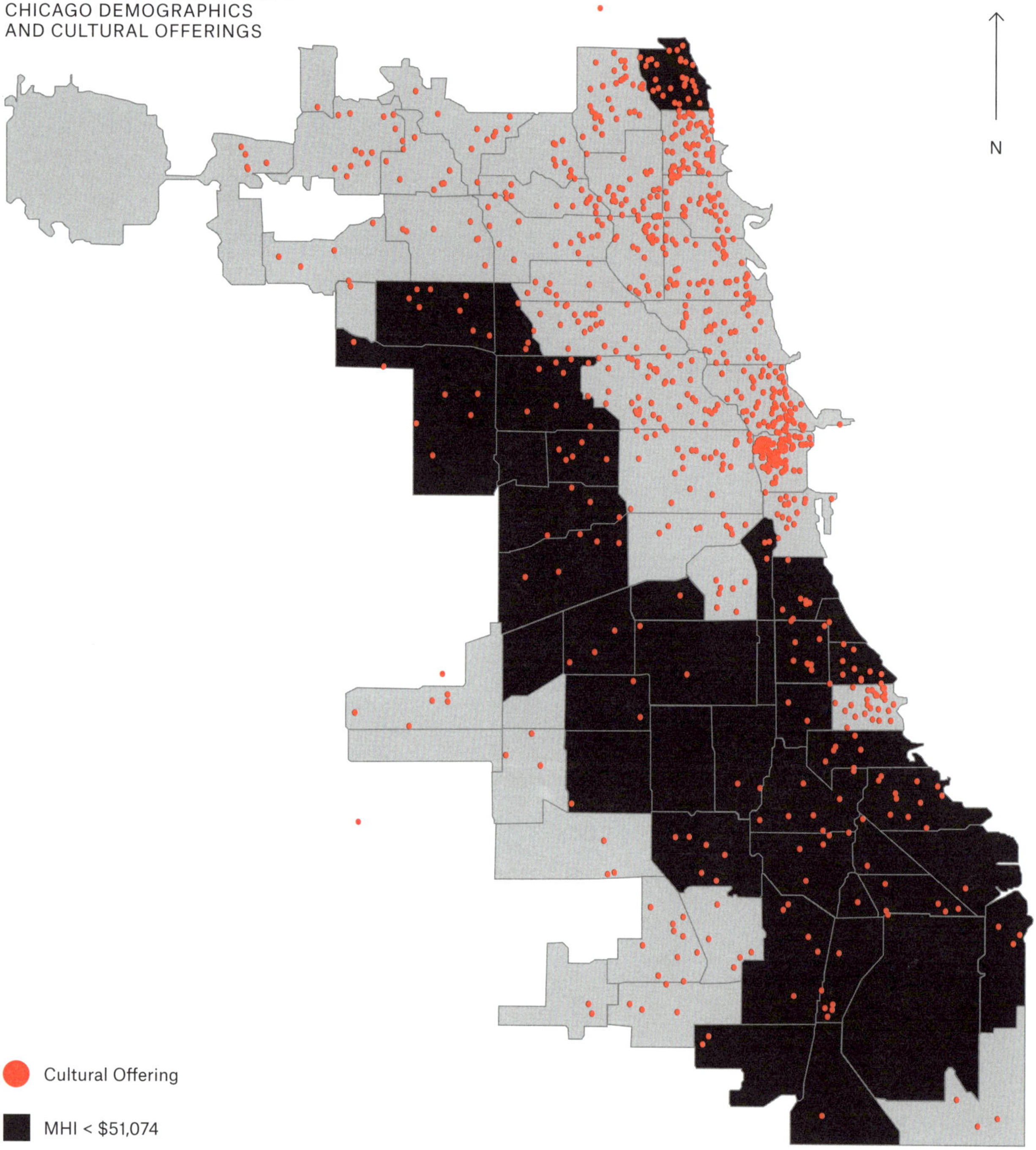

In 2019, the MacArthur Foundation's Chicago Commitment team revised its approach to grantmaking in support of arts and cultural organizations through its "Culture, Equity, and the Arts" initiative. "Heat maps" created by the Field Foundation in 2017 revealed that resources made available by MacArthur at that time were made disproportionately to arts and cultural organizations located in higher-income communities. This finding was a call to action, and MacArthur adopted a new participatory grantmaking process, centered on feedback from community stakeholders, to address this discrepancy in cultural resources. As planning for *Toward Common Cause* commenced in earnest, the Field Foundation's maps were top of mind, and there were concerted efforts throughout the planning process to identify and work with venues in community areas outside those with the densest cultural infrastructure. This proved challenging, however, as infrastructure is needed to host exhibitions, programs, and performances—especially when presenting the work of highly acclaimed artists with international careers. The map here shows the geographic distribution within the city of Chicago of cultural offerings (in red) relative to community areas with median household incomes of less than $51,074 (in black).

EXHIBITION DOCUMENTATION: SCHEDULE

The following dates illustrate the exhibition schedule as it occurred. *Toward Common Cause* was not bound by the rigid schedule of a single institution's program calendar. There was no singular opening date, and events and educational outreach programs extended up to a year before and after the opening celebration held at the Smart Museum on July 17, 2021.

DATE	EVENT
July 2017	The first formal memo generated by the MacArthur Fellows Program presenting the idea of an exhibition of artwork by MacArthur Fellows to celebrate the program's 40th anniversary is issued.
March 2018	Abigail Winograd and the MacArthur Fellows Program team meet in person.
May 2018	Invitations to participate are issued to the first group of artists and venues.
June 2018	The initial proposed checklist and themes are approved.
July 2018	Abigail Winograd is formally confirmed as exhibition curator.
March 26, 2020	Governor Pritzker issues Public Health Order No. 2020–3, instructing residents to stay at home and closing many public indoor and outdoor spaces.
May 2020	Loan forms are sent
July 24, 2020	Public Health Order No. 2020–9, Phase IV, allows for the cautious reopening of Chicago's businesses while maintaining certain closures of public spaces.
October 2020	The first *Toward Common Cause*–associated public program takes place at Pueblo Unido Gallery, Centro Romero.
November 12, 2020	In response to a spike in COVID infections and hospitalizations, Mayor Lightfoot issues a stay-at-home advisory; it is extended in January 2021.
December 2020	The Smart Museum's working checklist is finalized.
March 2021	The majority of partner agreements and loan agreements are signed (almost a year after the original deadline).
June 2021	Installation of *Toward Common Cause* commences at the Smart Museum.
October 2020–October 2021	Venues hold opening events for their presentations, including a public opening reception at Centro Romero.
March 2022	The deinstallation of Njideka Akunyili Crosby's banners at the National Museum of Public Housing marks the final exhibition work to be removed. As of the publication of this volume, works by Kerry James Marshall, Mel Chin, and Iñigo Manglano-Ovalle remain in place in the locations selected for their *Toward Common Cause* presentation.
April 2022	A proposal for an accompanying publication, including a table of contents, budget, and timeline, is submitted to and approved by the MacArthur Foundation.
May 11, 2023	The Illinois state of emergency related to COVID ends.
April 2024	*Art in Pursuit of Common Cause* is published.

EXHIBITION DOCUMENTATION: BUDGET

In this publication, we have made an attempt to be open and transparent about the processes of exhibition-making, its challenges and outcomes. We had always planned to publish the budget for *Toward Common Cause*: we were curious to compare our budget—for a show occurring during a global pandemic and involving dozens of partner organizations—with budgets for more straightforward shows. However, we have discovered that, particularly in recent years, budgets for museum exhibitions are rarely straightforward and almost never publicly discussed. The growth of curatorial and exhibition studies programs means that shelves of books have been written in the past thirty years about the politics and ethics of exhibition planning, institutional practice, and philanthropy. Yet not a single one of those volumes offers practical guidance on developing budgets or the ethical implications of budget decisions.

In fairness, exhibition budgets are complicated documents. They obscure a myriad of expenses and investments, including organizational overhead and the investment of time spent writing grants and fundraising. Efforts to attribute income to an exhibition—from ticket sales, merchandise, and new or renewal memberships—can be equally difficult. Most importantly, budget numbers do not accurately capture the enormous amounts of unpaid or undercompensated labor and expertise required to make exhibitions happen.

The graphic represents an overview of our exhibition and catalogue spending, broken into major categories. As with much of *Toward Common Cause*, the pandemic's effect on our work is evident. For example, the UofC moratorium on nonessential travel meant that our budget does not accurately reflect the amount typically spent on travel for curators, artists, or couriers. In the period immediately following the COVID lockdowns, there was little taste for a gala opening, and thus no expenses reflected for Development.

These figures—approximately $1.9 million for the exhibition and an additional $220,000 for the publication—reflect expenses only. Because the exhibition was free to the public at all venues, and the catalogue was not produced during the run of the show, no income was recorded for ticket sales or merchandise.

12.95%
The staffing figure does not capture staffing at partner venues or their contributions to production or programming.

2.85%
More than half of the adult programming budget was for workshops and participatory artist projects.

1.43%
The K-12 programming budget was spent principally on the multiyear teen program.

.23%
PR and paid advertising expenses were lower than might be expected though unpaid advertising and strong press coverage ensured local awareness of the exhibition.

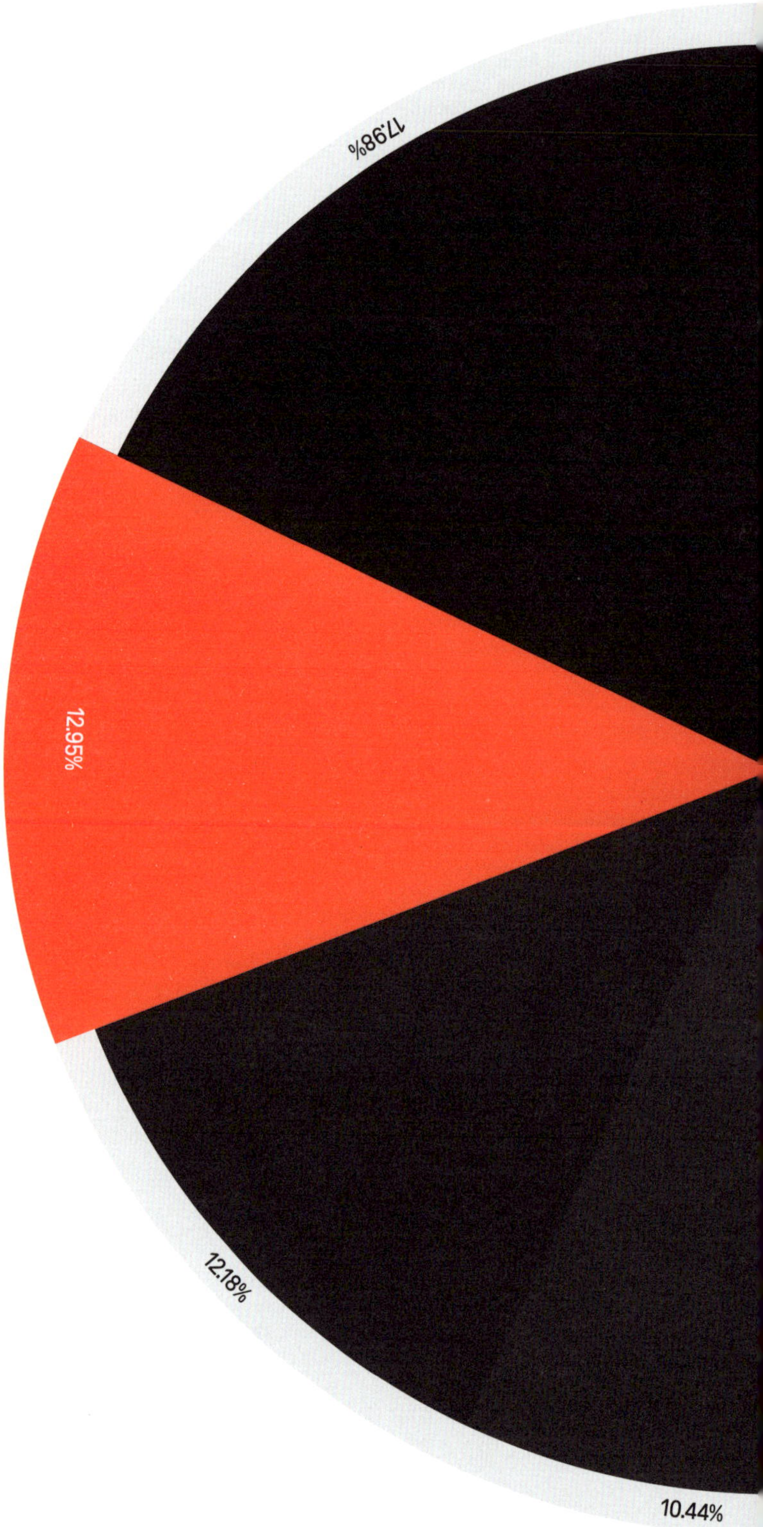

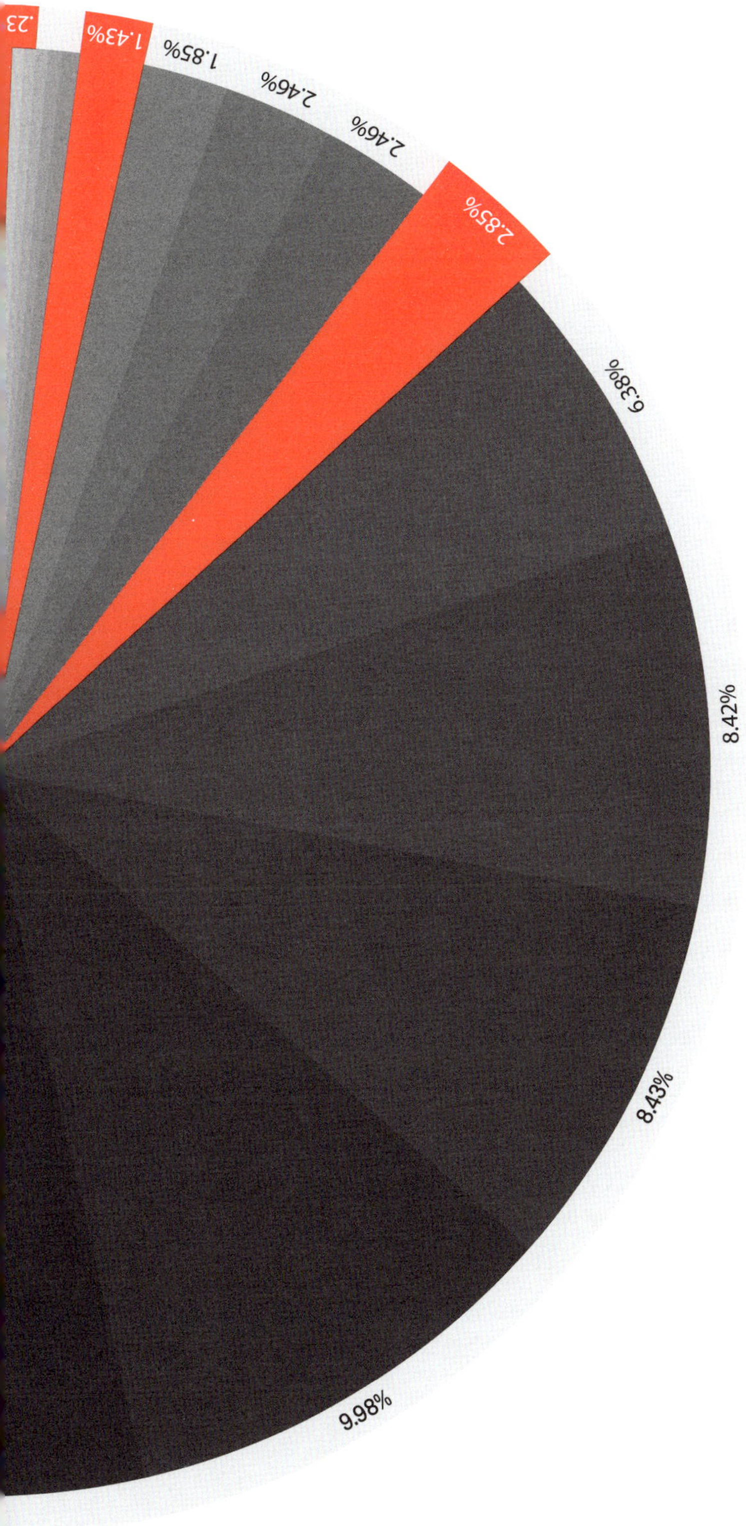

%	EXPENSES	USD
17.98%	Exhibition production, including construction and demo, furniture, AV, lighting	$379,437
12.95%	Staffing	$273,413
12.18%	Shipping, crating, storage, courier travel	$256,993
10.44%	Exhibition publication	$220,325
9.98%	Commissions, artist fees	$210,675
8.43%	Conservation, matting, production	$177,879
8.42%	Overhead contribution	$177,706
6.38%	Program planning	$134,606
2.85%	Adult programming	$60,134
2.46%	Web design and development	$52,017
2.46%	Graphic design	$51,907
1.85%	Graphics production	$39,896
1.43%	K-12 programming	$30,076
0.39%	Author fees	$8,250
0.30%	Collateral production, including map and guide	$6,391
0.28%	Research	$5,875
0.26%	Photography and videography	$5,574
0.26%	Copyediting	$5,504
0.23%	PR and advertising	$4,892
0.18%	Supplies and miscellaneous	$3,699
0.14%	Loan fees	$2,959
0.13%	Graphics installation	$2,636
100%	TOTAL	$2,110,844

CONTRIBUTORS TO THE CATALOGUE

Jane Addams co-founded Hull House, a settlement house providing social services to members of its Chicago community, in 1889 ("At the Intersection of Daily Life and Imagination There Is an Art Studio: A Conversation across Time between Jane Addams and Staff at Pueblo Unido Gallery," p. 98).

Marlies Carruth is Director of the MacArthur Fellows Program ("Introduction," p. 10).

Mel Chin is a MacArthur Fellow whose work was included in *Toward Common Cause* ("A Question of Worlds," p. 211).

Michael Christiano is currently Director of Visual Arts & Museum at the Colorado Springs Fine Arts Center at Colorado College. He was previously Deputy Director and Curator of Public Practice at the Smart Museum of Art at the University of Chicago, and in this capacity served as one of the *Toward Common Cause* project leads ("Be Water," p. 112).

Peter Fitzpatrick is a Special Advisor for Community Engagement in the Office of the Provost, Columbia College, and Co-Director of Pueblo Unido at Centro Romero ("At the Intersection of Daily Life and Imagination There Is an Art Studio: A Conversation across Time between Jane Addams and Staff at Pueblo Unido Gallery," p. 98).

Jeffrey Gibson is a MacArthur Fellow whose work was included in *Toward Common Cause* ("We Have to Insist," p. 130).

Guillermo Gómez-Peña is a MacArthur Fellow whose work was included in *Toward Common Cause* ("An Open Letter to the Museums of the Future," p. 34).

An-My Lê is a MacArthur Fellow whose work was included in *Toward Common Cause* ("Much Unseen Is Also Here," p. 66).

Iñigo Manglano-Ovalle is a MacArthur Fellow whose work was included in *Toward Common Cause* (p. 211).

Amalia Mesa-Bains is a MacArthur Fellow whose work was included in *Toward Common Cause* ("We Have to Insist," p. 130).

Don Meyer is Senior Program Officer for the MacArthur Fellows Program ("Beyond What We Know: Philanthropy, Experimentation, and the Support of Creativity," p. 86).

Veronica Nabor is the Teen Leadership Coordinator for the Centro Romero Youth Program ("At the Intersection of Daily Life and Imagination There Is an Art Studio: A Conversation across Time between Jane Addams and Staff at Pueblo Unido Gallery," p. 98).

Dorian H. Nash is the Director of Learning and Cultural Workforce Development at the National Public Housing Museum, formerly Manager of Public Programs at the Smart Museum of Art at the University of Chicago ("Be Water," p. 112).

Jason Pallas is a Visual Arts Teacher at the University of Chicago Lab School and was previously Associate Director of Public Practice at the Smart Museum of Art at the University of Chicago ("Be Water," p. 112).

Tommy Rock is currently a Postdoctoral Research Associate and Presidential Postdoctoral Research Fellow at Princeton University. His research focuses on environmental hazards related to uranium mining and oil and gas exploration in the Navajo Nation ("Ways to Walk in Beauty," p. 75).

Susana Salgado is the Director of the Youth Program at Centro Romero ("At the Intersection of Daily Life and Imagination There Is an Art Studio: A Conversation across Time between Jane Addams and Staff at Pueblo Unido Gallery," p. 98).

Fazal Sheikh is a MacArthur Fellow whose work was included in *Toward Common Cause* ("Ways to Walk in Beauty," p. 75).

Shahzia Sikander is a MacArthur Fellow whose work was included in *Toward Common Cause* ("Much Unseen Is Also Here," p. 66).

Jill Sterrett (volume co-editor) is currently Director of Collections at the Wisconsin Historical Society. For *Toward Common Cause*, she served as one of the project leads as Interim Director of the Smart Museum of Art at the University of Chicago ("Change Is Always the Project," p. 156; "Afterword: How Next?," p. 192).

Alaka Wali is Curator of North American Anthropology at the Field Museum. She was the founding director of the Field's Center for Cultural Understanding and Change ("Change Inside Comes from Pressure Outside," p. 172).

Hamza Walker is currently director of LAXART. He was previously Curator and Director of Education at the Renaissance Society at the University of Chicago ("Presenting Negro Scenes Drawn Upon My Passage Through the South and Reconfigured for the Benefit of Enlightened Audiences Wherever Such May Be Found, By Myself, Missus K.E.B. Walker, Colored," p. 146).

Carrie Mae Weems is a MacArthur Fellow whose work was included in *Toward Common Cause* ("We Have to Insist," p. 130).

Abigail Winograd (volume co-editor) is Commissioner and Curator of the US Pavilion for the 60th Venice Biennale, Co-Director and Chief Curator of the Pueblo Unido Gallery, and an independent curator. She was MacArthur Fellows Program 40th Anniversary Exhibition Curator; during the planning and implementation of *Toward Common Cause*, she worked from the Smart Museum of Art at the University of Chicago ("All Flourishing Is Mutual," p. 50).

Jonah Yellowman is a Diné elder and spiritual advisor ("Ways to Walk in Beauty," p. 75).

For artists whose work was included in Toward Common Cause, *additional biographical information can be found under Artists in the Exhibition.*

PUBLICATION ADVISORY COMMITTEE

Tiff Beatty, Program Director of Arts, Culture, and Public Policy at the National Museum of Public Housing

Zachary Cahill, Director of Programs and Fellowship at The Richard and Mary L. Gray Center for Arts and Inquiry, The University of Chicago

Mel Chin, MacArthur Fellow and *Toward Common Cause* artist

Michael Christiano, Director of Visual Arts & Museum at the Colorado Springs Fine Arts Center at Colorado College, former Deputy Director and Curator of Public Practice at the Smart Museum of Art, The University of Chicago

Lori Fogarty, Director and CEO of the Oakland Museum of California

Iñigo Manglano-Ovalle, MacArthur Fellow and *Toward Common Cause* artist

Don Meyer, Senior Program Officer, MacArthur Fellows Program, The John D. and Catherine T. MacArthur Foundation

Dieter Roelstraete, Curator at the Neubauer Collegium for Culture and Society, The University of Chicago

Peter Samis, former Associate Curator of Interpretive Media at SFMOMA

Jennifer Scott, former Director and Chief Curator at the Jane Addams Hull-House Museum

Jacqueline Stewart, Professor in the Department of Cinema and Media Studies and Director of Arts + Public Life, The University of Chicago

J. Gibran Villalobos, National Engagement Manager for the National Museum of the American Latino Act, Institute of Museum and Library Services

Deborah Willis, MacArthur Fellow and *Toward Common Cause* artist

For artists whose work was included in Toward Common Cause, *additional biographical information can be found under Artists in the Exhibition.*

ACKNOWLEDGMENTS

The process of exhibition and bookmaking is inherently collaborative. There are too many people to properly list, but we have made an honest effort to name all of our contributors, collaborators, confidants, and co-conspirators in the endpapers of this book.

We do want to thank the MacArthur Foundation for its willingness to experiment with us. Beyond their financial contributions, they gave us the latitude to try new things and allowed us to dream up schemes that challenged established operating procedures. They were unfailingly committed to allowing us to execute our vision. We are grateful for their confidence and glad of their partnership.

— Abigail Winograd and
Jill Sterrett

This volume documents the exhibition *Toward Common Cause: Art, Social Change, and the MacArthur Fellows Program at 40*, a multisite exhibition organized by The David and Alfred Smart Museum of Art, The University of Chicago, and curated by Abigail Winograd. The exhibition, which was supported by The John D. and Catherine T. MacArthur Foundation, ran throughout 2021 into early 2022.

Exhibition venues included: Washington Park Arts Incubator, an initiative of Arts + Public Life, The University of Chicago; BBF Building Brighter Futures Center for the Arts; Centro Romero; Chicago Housing Authority, Minnie Julia Riperton Apartments; DuSable Black History Museum and Education Center; Hyde Park Art Center; Jane Addams Hull-House Museum; Museum of Contemporary Photography, Columbia College Chicago; National Museum of Mexican Art; National Public Housing Museum; Neubauer Collegium for Culture and Society, The University of Chicago; The Newberry; Public Media Institute; Reva and David Logan Center for the Arts, The University of Chicago; School of the Art Institute of Chicago; The David and Alfred Smart Museum of Art, The University of Chicago; South Side Community Art Center; Stony Island Arts Bank; Sweet Water Foundation; Urban Juncture Foundation; Weinberg/Newton Gallery.

The publication has been supported by
The John D. and Catherine T. MacArthur Foundation.

Publication Team
Susan Chun, Publication Director
Maggie Jensen, Managing Editor
Philomenia Mariani, Editor

Design by
Dylan Fracareta, I-C-C-P

Prepress by
Professional Graphics, Rockford, IL

Printed in Belgium by
die Keure

Published by
The Richard and Mary L. Gray Center for Arts and Inquiry, The University of Chicago
Zachary Cahill, Director of Programs and Fellowship

Distributed by
DelMonico Books • D.A.P.
Mary DelMonico, Publisher

Library of Congress Control Number:
A Library of Congress Control Number is on file and available upon request.

ISBN 978-1-63681-129-1

Contributors to the catalogue have been compensated according to current W.A.G.E. guidelines.

Wherever possible, photo credits appear with images; additional credits follow.

Scenes from *Toward Common Cause: Exhibition photography*: Spencer Bibbs (1, 30); Amber Marie Green (27); Robert Chase Heishman (12, 37); Evan Jenkins (19); Nathan Keay (2, 5, 6, 7, 9, 10, 11, 13, 14, 16, 17, 22, 25, 28, 29, 31, 34, 35, 36, 38); Iñigo Manglano-Ovalle (32); Jonathan Loïc Rogers (8); Leslie Schwartz (26); Jill Sterrett (23, 39); Michael Tropea (18, 20); Abigail Winograd (24); Nancy Wong (21, 33) Artworks: Courtesy of Mark Bradford and Hauser & Wirth (3); Courtesy of Alfredo Jaar and Galerie Lelong & Co., New York (4); Courtesy of Deborah Willis (15)

We have made every effort to contact rightsholders, to obtain all necessary permissions to publish image and text materials, and to provide accurate credit information. Please contact the publishers with any corrections.